SEX, POWER AND TRAVEL

Ten Years of *Arena*

Edited by Dylan Jones

First published in Great Britain in 1996 by
Virgin Books
an imprint of Virgin Publishing Ltd
332 Ladbroke Grove
LONDON W10 5AH

A catalogue record for this book is available from the British
Library.

ISBN 0 7535 0013 2

Typeset by TW Typesetting, Plymouth, Devon

Printed and bound in Great Britain by
Mackays of Chatham PLC, Lordswood, Chatham, Kent

Contents

Acknowledgements   vi
List of Contributors   vii

Introduction   x
Dylan Jones
Baptism for a Heavyweight   1
Mike Tyson by James Truman
Art is Money   6
The New Power Brokers by Gordon Burn
An Everyday Story of a Suburban Sex Kitten   14
Mandy Smith by Gordon Burn
What's So New About the New Man?   19
Three Decades of Advertising to Men by Jon Savage
The Big Olive   24
Milan by Tony Parsons
Double-Breasted Suit, Collar & Tie   34
Tom Wolfe by Gordon Burn
The PoMo Dance   38
Post Modernism by Tom Baker
Where's the Beef?   40
The Penis by Julie Burchill
All Mouth and Trousers   44
The Professional Cockney by Stuart Cosgrove
The Smirk   50
The Eighties' Wink by Steve Beard & Jim McClellan
Take Me to the Bridge   53
A Weekend with David, Michael & Florence
by Kathryn Flett   56
New Frontiersman
The Wild West Man by Ian Penman
Will of Irony   66
The Tribulations of Ironic Existence by Dylan Jones
The Tattooed Jungle   69
The Decline of the Working Class by Tony Parsons

Man Out of Time 75
P. J. Proby by Dylan Jones

The Curse of the Pub-Human 86
Why the British Public House Must Die by Geoff Deane

The Real Thing 89
The Greatest Football Match by Neil Lyndon

Punchlines 93
A Day in Front of the Amstrad by Geoff Deane

The Euroman Cometh 96
The New Breed of Internationalist by Rob Ryan

The Last American Class Act 104
Paul Newman by Nick Kent

The Race to Offend 117
The Ultimate New York T-Shirt by Alix Sharkey

Essex, Innit? 119
A Native's Guide to Cortina Country by Mick Bunnage

Tie Me Up, Tie Me Down! 124
New York's Favourite Dominatrix by Rob Ryan

The Taming of the Superbrat 130
John McEnroe by Kathryn Flett

Less Than Zero 132
What Men Know About Cunnilingus by Jessamy Calkin

Auto-Erotica 135
Women & Cars by Jim McClellan

Havens of Comfort, Pavilions of Splendour 140
The Best Hotels in the World by Jon Futrell

Male Order 147
The Ideal Man by Jessica Berens & Jessamy Calkin

Muscle Building 150
The Penis Expander by David Bowker

Here Comes the New Lad! 154
The Unreconstructed Man by Sean O'Hagan

The Mad Bastard Capital of Australia 158
Kalgoorlie by Douglas Kennedy

All Boys Together 167
The Myth of Male Bonding by Peter Howarth

Kiss Kiss! Bang Bang! 171
Robert Bly & the Men's Movement by Mark Cooper

In the Presence of Royalty 178
Prince by Simon Mills

Rare Proofs 180
The *Arena* Literary Parody by Tony Parsons,
Steve Beard, Marek Kohn, & Dylan Jones

Fields of Dreams   191
Baseball's Spring Training by Robert Elms

Porn Again   196
What Women Want From Erotica by Jessica Berens

Dressed to Frill
Why are Rock Stars So Badly Dressed?   200
by Mark Edwards

Male Rape   206
The Love Which . . . by Marek Kohn

Dino!   214
Dean Martin by Kevin Jackson

Single File   221
The Bachelor Decoded by Neil Spencer

This Gun's for Ire   226
The Legend of the Colt .45 by Rob Ryan

The Man Who Came in From the Cool   230
Donald Fagen by Barney Hoskyns

It's a Man's, Man's, Man's, Man's World   235
Heroes by Alan Moore

Gender Benders   238
Why Women Shouldn't Drink by Tony Parsons

Equal Measure   242
Why Women *Should* Drink by Suzanne Moore

**Thirty-Nine Minutes and Ten Seconds
with Marty**   244
Martin Scorsese by Rob Ryan

One for the Road   251
Route 66 by Dylan Jones

Playboy of the Western World   255
Hugh Hefner by David Ritz

Top Management   263
The Breast by Imogen Edwards-Jones

My Angel is a Centrefold   265
Anna Nicole Smith by Ian Katz

The Frog on the Tyne   275
David Ginola by Simon Kelner

The Right Stuff   282
Michael Portillo by William Shaw

The New Lass   295
Girls Will Be Boys by Ed Barrett

How Italian Are You?   299
The Arena Quiz by David Quantick

Acknowledgements

As well as thanking all the contributors included in this collection, I would also like to thank David Bailey, Lindsay Baker, Richard Benson, Phil Bicker, Robert Black, Peter Blake, Marissa Bourke, Debra Bourne, David Bowie, Michael Bracewell, Dick Bradsell, David Bradshaw, Neville Brody, Karen Brown, Louisa Buck, Russell Bulgin, Anna Chapman, Sam Chick, Louise Chunn, Tim Clark, Alexander Cockburn, Russell Cronin, Kevin Davies, Adrian Deevoy, Robin Derrick, Lynn Doughty, Paul Du Noyer, Sandra-Jane England, Ekow Eshun, David Eyre, Lizzie Fairrie, Anthony Fawcett, Jeffrey Ferry, Matt Fiveash, Richard Ford, Stephen Fry, Tamara Fulton, Charles Gant, William Gilchrist, Albert Goldman, Carole Harris, Sheila Hayman, Ashley Heath, Dave Hill, Alan Jackson, Tony Kaye, David Keeps, Sean Langan, Mark Lebon, Carol Leggett, William Leith, Kimberley Leston, Christian Logan, Julie Logan, Ian MacDonald, Don Macpherson, David Mamet, Natasha Marsh, Mark Mattock, Crystal McClory, Gillian McVey, Jamie Morgan, Regine Moylett, Paul Murphy, Tim Nicholson, Adair Nye, Susana Paz, Mal Peachey, Tony Peake, Christian Penhallurick, Norm Peterson, Ray Petri, Jacqui Pinto, Derrick Procope, Paul Rambali, Jay Rayner, Simon Reynolds, Cynthia Rose, David Rosen, Judy Rumbold, Fiona Russell-Powell, Kevin Sampson, Robert Sandall, Charles Shaar Murray, Jo-Anne Smith, Giles Smith, Paul Smith, Rod Sopp, Martin Spence, Colin Spencer, Simon Staines, Deyan Sudjic, Anna Swallow, John Sweeney, Pat Sweeney, Ian Swift, Chris Taggart, Steve Taylor, Karl Templer, David Toop, Grant Turner, William Ward, Albert Watson, Norman Watson, Elizabeth Watson, Jim White, Lesley White, John Williams, Richard Williams, Kate Withers, Kelly Worts, Ian Wright and everyone who has worked for *Arena* over the last ten years. Also, a very special thank you to Nick Logan, without whom etc . . .

Contributors

Ed Barrett is commissioning editor of *Arena*

Steve Beard is giving birth to *Voodoo Ray*

Jessica Berens is the author of *Queen Of The Witches*

David Bowker is a freelance journalist

Mick Bunnage writes for *Loaded*

Julie Burchill is the author of *Girls On Film*, *Love It Or Shove It* and *Ambition*

Gordon Burn has written *Somebody's Husband Somebody's Son*, *Pocket Money*, *Alma Cogan* and *Fullalove*

Jessamy Calkin is senior editor of British *GQ*

Mark Cooper is a series producer for the BBC

Stuart Cosgrove is controller of arts and entertainment at Channel 4

Geoff Deane is a television scriptwriter

Mark Edwards writes on media and the arts for *Arena* and the *Sunday Times*

Imogen Edwards-Jones is *Arena*'s Carnal Knowledge columnist and author of *The Taming of Eagles*

Robert Elms is a journalist and broadcaster

Kathryn Flett is associate editor of the *Observer Life Magazine* and former editor of *Arena*

Jon Futrell writes for *Arena*, the *Observer* and the *Sunday Times*

Peter Howarth is editor of *Arena*

Barney Hoskyns mans *Mojo*'s US bureau

Kevin Jackson is a contributing editor of *Arena*

Ian Katz is the *Guardian*'s New York correspondent

Simon Kelner is the editor of *Night & Day*

Douglas Kennedy is the author of *Beyond the Pyramids: Travels in Egypt* and *In God's Country: Travels in the Bible Belt*

Nick Kent is the author of *The Dark Stuff*

Marek Kohn writes for the *Independent On Sunday*

Neil Lyndon writes for the *Sunday Telegraph*

Jim McClellan writes on cyber issues for the *Observer*

Simon Mills is a contributing editor of *Arena*

Alan Moore is the author of *Watchmen*, *V For Vendetta* and *Halo Jones*

Suzanne Moore wrote *Looking For Trouble*

Sean O'Hagan has written for the *Guardian* and the *Times*

Tony Parsons is a contributing editor of *Arena* and a columnist for the *Daily Mirror*. He is also the author of *Despatches From the Front Line of Popular Culture*

Ian Penman writes for the *Guardian* and the *Wire*

David Quantick writes for *Arena*, *Q* and the *Independent*

David Ritz is the author of *Divided Soul*, *Rhythm and the Blues*, *Family Blood* and *Passion Flowers*

Rob Ryan is a contributing editor of *Arena* and deputy travel editor of the *Sunday Times*. He is the author of *Stay Healthy Abroad*

Jon Savage has written *Time Travel*, *England's Dreaming*, and edited *The Faber Book of Pop*

Alix Sharkey files a weekly column for the *Independent*

William Shaw writes for *Arena* and *Details*

Neil Spencer is a columnist for the *Observer*

James Truman is editorial director of Conde Nast, USA

Tom Baker died in 1988

For Pat, Tom, Ray & Kimberley

Introduction

Some things you just can't anticipate. When, in the summer of 1991, we commissioned Douglas Kennedy to travel to Kalgoorlie, in the middle of the Australian outback – The Dead Heart – we had no idea that the resulting piece would prove to be so incendiary. Kennedy profiled a town only just on the threshold of the twentieth century, a gimcrack outpost notable largely for its mining, fighting, drinking and whoring; a place which seemed as though it was populated by nineteenth-century frontiersmen – broad-backed, red-necked men whose gratification and sense of worth was defined simply by gold, beer and women (and not always in that order). A one-horse town still enveloped in a distinctly Wild West ethos, in Kennedy's hands Kalgoorlie displayed all the modern Hogarthian characteristics of Ocker hell.

'I stopped by the oldest hotel in town, The Exchange, for a beer. The saloon doors flapped behind me as I entered, and I was carefully eyed up by a dozen or so customers perched on bar stools and already engaged in the business of drowning a few brain cells before lunch. There was a pair of off-duty miners – beefy gents with faded tattoos and biceps that appeared to have been bred on steroids – engaged in an analytical discussion about the personality deficiencies of their pit foreman.

' "The bloke's a complete fuckwit," one of them said.

' "Too right," said his mate. "And he's also got a head on him like a robber's dog."

'There was also a pair of burnt-out housewives – dyed blonde hair; faces that were elaborate bas-reliefs on premature age lines, and dripping pancake make-up; cigarettes between their teeth: "Told Geoff I simply wasn't going to take it any more. Told him I was going to piss off back to Perth and leave him here holding the bloody baby."

' "How'd he take the news?"

' "Split my lip, the bastard." '

The July issue of the magazine had only been on sale in Australia for a few days before we were inundated with faxes from various residents of Kalgoorlie, most of them offering to fly all the way to London to punch our collective lights out. Then, a few weeks later, we were sent a copy of the town's local paper, the *Kalgoorlie Miner*, with a cover line proclaiming: 'UK Magazine Tags Us As No-Hopers'. They had taken offence at Kennedy's description of Kalgoorlie as 'the mad bastard capital of Australia' as well as 'the wanker capital of the world' and, not content with devoting the cover and 2,000 words to the subject, printed our address, telephone and fax numbers in case any residents felt the need to share their own sentiments with us. Consequently we spent the next two weeks trying to avoid any phone calls of an Antipodean nature. We're not exactly sure how many copies we were selling in Kalgoorlie at the time, but we sold out that month.

It certainly wasn't our intention to incite the wrath of the citizens of a small Australian settlement, but over the last decade we seem to have managed, quite inadvertently, to insult or inflame everyone we've come into contact with. OK, maybe not everyone, but there are a lot of people out there who seem to have been enraged – one way or another – by some of the things we have published. In passing, there was Tony Parsons' explosive 'Tattooed Jungle', a magazine article which became many more newspaper articles (some of which were even written by Tony), a television programme, even a series – a veritable cottage industry. Or should that be council house? Parsons is used to being vilified, but this, along with pieces such as 'Pretty Ethnics' and 'Why Women Shouldn't Drink' made him, and us, broad targets for the PC brigade.

We kept a check on male sexuality, though; it was part of our mandate. When Sean O'Hagan invented the New Lad in *Arena* in 1991, it not only spawned a hundred editorials, so-called zeitgeist-defining radio and TV programmes, it was also partly responsible for the birth of such media monsters as *Loaded* and *Men Behaving Badly*. We charted the rise of the New Lad, invited ourselves to the funeral of the New Man, pondered the New Lass, and fell under the spell of Robert Bly. The essentials were discussed, obviously: fellatio, cunnilingus, anal sex, masturbation and circumcision were all debated long before such topics became an immutable component of every men's magazine which came in our wake. Using columnists such as Kimberley Leston, Jessamy Calkin, Kathryn Flett, Jessica Berens and Imogen Edwards-Jones, sex was discussed as frankly and as openly as possible, though it's a sad indictment of the men's magazine market that the best writers on the subject are still women (who rarely feel the need to lie, exaggerate or envelop their copy with self-consciousness).

When writing about women, some of our writers tend to get their own back. Geoff Deane, for instance, so infuriated an ex-editor of *Elle* with one of his missives that she was prompted to write to us: 'Everything [he] knows about women could be written on the end of his penis,' she said, thoughtfully. And who were we to argue?

Before *Arena* was launched in 1986, there were no men's magazines in Britain. There were genre-specific titles (fishing, motoring, etc.), there was the style press, and there was pornography, but there was no general interest magazine which covered fashion, food, film and literature as well as sport, women, cars and the modern malaise. Since the demise of *Town* in the sixties, the general interest men's magazine had become, if not the holy grail of British publishing, then at least the Bermuda Triangle. No one could try it and survive. Until we proved them wrong.

Because we were the first, we had the run of the toy shop, commissioning anyone within earshot to go out into the big bad, matt-black, post-feminist world and bring back stories on everything from the Colt .45 and nouvelle cuisine to skin care regimes and sartorial promiscuity; from the Foreign Legion and Mike Tyson to mountain biking and Robert Bly; from the perfect martini to the perfect blow job, the fastest cars to the fastest women, the strongest beer to the strongest chorizo. We sent journalists to Hollywood and Romania, to Milan and Leningrad, New York and Beijing. On one occasion we even tried sending someone to the moon, though the nearest they got was Peckham.

'Ten years ago magazines for men were grimy products stacked on the newsagent's top shelf, safe from prurient little fingers,' wrote Stephen Fry a little while ago. 'Personally, I'm a sucker for all this . . . If I actually met the Ideal Man who brought the grooming accessories, wore the Hamnett and Paul Smith suits and aviator sunglasses, drank the Manhattan, saw all the Wim Wenders movies and lived in the granite and chrome flat – I'd clock him one on his be-moussed pate. But we men have spent long enough mocking women for their magazines, now it's our turn to be mocked.'

Typically, it wasn't the moisturisers or the flat-fronted trousers which stirred our souls, nor the eight-button polo shirts or the modernist bachelor pads. No, the greatest satisfaction has usually come from the features: What Makes Michael Portillo Tick? The Myth of Male Bonding. The Post Modern Dance. The Smirk.

Irony. The Curse of the Pub-Human. The Problems with Essex. Auto-Erotica. Male Rape. What Women Really Want From Pornography. Heroes. Sissies. Italians. Route 66. Cyberspace. And beyond . . .

Over the last ten years *Arena* has published dozens of award-winning features (as well as beautifully choreographed photographs and layouts), though some of our finest moments have been on the letters page. The magazine has always attracted a huge amount of mail – letters, postcards, faxes (and once even a bomb) sent by those diligent souls who feel strongly enough to put pen to paper (or whatever it is they do with their computers these days). Most magazines tend to run letters which contain nothing but praise; *Arena*, however, has always had a policy of taking the rough with the smooth, while many topics have continued on the letters pages long after the rest of the magazine has forgotten about them. One particular article by Ian MacDonald, concerning some arcane aspect of Soviet history, was debated in Despatches for nearly a year. The letters deserve an anthology of their own, but in consolation I'll leave you in the hands of John Ferguson, from Dublin, who sent the following for publication in *Arena* 36. Sod.

ARENA: THE MOVIE

FADE IN
Ext: Day. Open on a once smart Docklands lair, now a crumbling Portakabin. A faded 'For Sale' sign creaks in the wind.
Int: Day. The walls are white, the floor, varnished; the decor is a mishmash of matt black items of unfathomable use, furniture for aliens and fifties American tat.
ARENA Man: *He's not the gay blade he used to be; his belly sags (can't afford health club subs) over faded trews (Armani, spring '88) into which is tucked a Rupert Bear pyjama top. No longer a confident bark, his voice has lapsed into a peevish suburban whine, honed by a crippling mortgage, a stagnant market in dubious creative talent and an ill-considered and noisome child (who, incidentally, only ever stops wailing in order to vomit).*
Love, have you seen my new brocade Oliver Sweeney house shoes? Read about them in ARENA; luvverly, as they say, jubberly. A snip at £125 . . .
ARENA Widow: *AW is a long-suffering, Mother Theresa-like figure; she has never been forgiven for not being Oriental.* They make you look like a nancy boy, dear.

AM: But I'm a shoe man, you always call me your 'shoe man' when we . . . *you know* . . . of a Saturday (*flapping his arms*) with our inflatables and your G-thingummy . . .

AW: When we fuck, dear, and that's 'new man' (*muttering*) as in I wouldn't mind one. I wish you'd get batteries for that hearing aid.

AM: Morrissey never had batteries . . . in the olden days . . . (*defiantly*) didn't need 'em . . . (*musing wistfully now, a tear dislodging a tinted contact lens*) National Health glasses, flowers in his bum pocket . . .

AW: Read your magazine, dear.

AM: Ooh look, here's an article on how to tie your shoelaces. Jolly dee . . . I'll try that . . . (*fumbles on floor with a pair of deck shoes*) . . . Hmm, not as easy as it looks . . . aagh.

AW: Oh lord, get up . . . and wipe your nose, it's running again. Look, leave the shoes where they are.

AM: Perhaps you're right, mum's the word . . . Be safer if I check for testicular cancer, follow the nice pictures in my mag . . . have a bit of a rummage . . . (*he flips through ARENA while thus occupied*). Oooer, look what Brando's been saying – 'Here I am, a balding, middle-aged failure. I feel (fnuh! fnuh) a fraud when I act. I've tried (Ooo-er!) everything – fuc . . . *you know*-ing, drinking, work. None of them means anything.' Ooh, sounds a bit peeky, doesn't he. Gippy tummy, I expect, chakra's out of sorts. Should get that seen to.

AW: He said that in 1963, dear, it's a retrospective.

AM: It looks like an interview.

AW: It's supposed to. Why don't you read the lovely Robert Elms piece. You like him, don't you, dear.

AM: Oh yes, old Elmsy, fashion ger-oo, mates with that Sadie, fine set of tonsils in her day, go on my . . . hur hur, you know . . . son. Remember his nov *The Crack*? What was that line? . . . really made us stop and think. 'Here is a towel for your tears, dry your eyes for now we are friends.' Something like that. (*Scanning page*) Hmm, doesn't seem to like Yanks much, old Elmsy. Claims they're loud.

AW: I expect we'd all raise our voices if we came from the same country as the Grand Canyon, the deserts, the Rockies, the Sierra Nevadas, Elvis, the Blues, New Orleans, New York and San Francisco instead of a nationwide suburb punctuated with urban knots of grot and bad temper. Besides, Elmsy's hardly a shrinking violet, is he dear?

AM: Ooh, sounds as if Marlon's not the only one with gippy tummy. (*Returns to mag, nodding and sucking his teeth, indicating bemusement*) Brill, here's an article on footie boots . . .

FADE OUT

Baptism for a Heavyweight

Mike Tyson by James Truman
December 1986

S O HERE IS MIKE TYSON: 20 years old and built like a truck, with a shock absorber for a neck and arms like diesel pistons; unbeaten in 27 fights, a professional for less than two years, and an 8½-to-1 favourite to become the youngest-ever world heavyweight champion in Las Vegas on November 22. The obstacle, which is called Trevor Berbick, is given so little chance that, leading up to the fight, the only attractive action in Vegas was betting on the number of rounds he'll survive. It's almost unheard of for a challenger to go into a title fight with odds like these. But then, as they say in the trade, Mike Tyson is the hottest piece of property since Hiroshima.

But then again, they're forever saying things like that in the trade. The language of boxing is all about extremes; it swings between hyperbole and cynicism so easily that it admits no middle ground, because the hyperbole is usually cynical and the cynicism is always rampant.

What's been interesting about Mike Tyson over the past 12 months is the degree to which he's enjoyed one without suffering the other. He has yet to face a world-class opponent and his swift ascendancy has been, if not exactly stage-managed, certainly well-marketed. And yet no one, not even the most enthusiastic of pessimists, has chosen to doubt him. So what is this breach of procedure? Why should Tyson, alone among men and prizefighters, be immune to charges of being a worthless bum?

The obvious reason is that he is a genuinely exciting boxer. A two-handed puncher of unmistakeably bad intention, he fights like a speeded-up Rocky Marciano, a more dependable and fluid George Foreman. That is, he can do more than merely bash people. Though he hasn't yet had to call upon it, he does show some rudimentary defence: a well-concealed chin, good lateral movement and an ability to anticipate and absorb punches. Which is to say that while he won't ever be mistaken for Muhammad Ali, he knows several things that would come as news to poor Frank Bruno.

But aside from this, Tyson has timing on his side. The heavyweight division, the traditional flagship of pro boxing, currently has so many proven bums on its books that it becomes pointless to conjecture on the unproven. Over the past three years there have been no less than seven different heavyweight champions.

Part of the blame for this lies with the WBC, the WBA and the IBF, boxing's three governing bodies, which have all elected to name their own champions rather than acknowledge the others'. The rest of the blame lies with the fighters, who have been too incompetent either to unify the title or hold on to their part of it. Larry Holmes, the one major talent, might have done so; instead he fought a light-heavyweight last year, lost his title, and now appears too old to ever regain it.

His popular rival and expected successor, Gerry Cooney, fell apart after losing to Holmes in 1982 and has only made feeble stabs at a comeback. Tyrell Biggs, winner of the gold at the 1984 Olympics, showed early promise as a professional, and then disappeared into a drug clinic. Another two up-and-comers murdered people and look to be pursuing their careers in jail. Michael Dokes, a recent WBA champion, was busted in October for dealing cocaine. And then there are the fat men. One-time contenders like Greg Page, James Broad and Tony Tubbs are now so overweight that they can't fight more than five rounds without running out of gas. (Tim Witherspoon, the WBC champ, is munching promisingly in reserve.)

So it may be that Mike Tyson is already king of the heavyweights. In absence of the real thing, the boxing press in America has been having a field-day with paper fights, predicting how he'll wipe out the competition. Tyson himself says that he never thinks beyond the next opponent, but at the same time his handlers talk about his limitless capacity to win, given his continued interest. They use the word interest a lot, and it's a very polite euphemism for the murderous discipline a fighter must subject himself to in order to stay on top.

Unlike other athletes, boxers spend most of their career in seclusion; they prepare for months eventually to face a stranger who is not an enemy in a violent confrontation which will publicly and unambiguously display the strength of their will, the limits of their courage. The kind of psychological pressure this imposes is something few fighters talk about. Tyson, who talks about most things in sentences of one word or less, becomes unusually expansive on the subject.

'What it is is fear, and it's something you have to learn to live with,' he says in his quiet, unexpectedly soft voice. 'Fear is like fire, if you control it, it keeps you warm, if you don't it'll burn the house down. Sometimes it's so great that it intimidates you, and you can no longer perform the way you want to perform. Then you realise fear's your best friend. It's like a snap, a little snap of light I get when I fight. I love that feeling. It makes me feel secure and confident, it suddenly makes everything explosive. It's like: "Here it comes again. Here's my buddy today".'

Though it turns out that Tyson isn't the author of this philosophy, he has adopted it as his own. Its author is a boxing manager/trainer called Cus D'Amato, who rescued Tyson from reform school seven years ago, adopted him as his son, and changed his life. At that point it wasn't going so well. The youngest of three children, Tyson grew up in a poor, crime-infested area of Brooklyn, New York. Apparently a gentle, shy boy who played with his sister and kept a coop of pigeons (he always was a contender), he kept out of trouble until the age of 11, when his family moved to an even tougher neighbourhood. At first, he says, he put up with being bullied by the older boys, but the day one of them tried to steal a pigeon he exploded and 'kicked the living crap out of him'.

Having discovered he was good at fighting – he was already huge – he turned to mugging and robbery ('I did it for fun') and within a year had landed himself in reform school. It was here, under the tutorship of one of the guards, that he learned the basic boxing skills. Just before he was due to be released on parole, the guard took him to meet D'Amato, whose gym in Catskill, upstate New York, had become a refuge for more than a few wayward city kids. Something of an anomaly in boxing – he was once called the only honest man in the business – D'Amato had been training and fathering young prospects for years; since the early Fifties, in fact, when he had discovered Floyd Patterson in a home for emotionally disturbed boys and steered him to the heavyweight title.

The sight of Mike Tyson jangled some memory bells. After watching him spar for a few rounds he took him aside and told him he could become the youngest heavyweight champion in history (Floyd Patterson, the current record-holder, won it at 21). He wasn't so sure, but accepted D'Amato's offer of his home and boxing expertise. In addition to sharpening his ring work, he went to work on his head, implanting his belief that victories are won by the mind more than the body, and instilling his own neatly-homilised philosophies on fear and courage and discipline.

3

'Cus always wanted to push you, find out what made you work. Then afterwards he would put on a little more pressure to find out what would make you break. He said it built character. At the beginning it used to drive me insane. I felt like choking him. I'd ask why he didn't just spank me instead.'

In 1981, the year D'Amato became his legal guardian, Tyson began to box competitively as an amateur. His only two losses were to Henry Tillman, and the second of them – by a highly disputed decision – meant that it was Tillman rather than Tyson who went to Los Angeles to compete for (and win) the Olympic Gold. It also meant that when Tyson turned pro, at the beginning of last year, he started out as a complete unknown.

Nevertheless, his ascendancy was extraordinarily swift. To keep him sharp, D'Amato had him fighting bouts every three weeks or so, and by the end of his first pro year he had won 15 in a row, all by knockout and 11 by first-round knockout. In a division plagued by inactivity, he was the only news. To make sure it was broadcast, his New York management company went to town, compiling cassettes of his knockouts and sending them to sports writers across the country, hustling him on to magazine covers and pitching exclusive TV contracts to the networks and cable companies.

So within a year, D'Amato's first prediction already looked like an inside possibility. But another of his predictions, that he might not be around to witness the fruition of the first, had already come true. He died last November, at the age of 77.

Tyson still lives in Catskill, in the same elegant wooden-frame house where he first learned about boxing. It only takes a brief walk up the town's main street to realise this is his home. Many of the shop windows have his pictures and write-ups pasted up to see; the waitress at the local restaurant will tell you what he likes to eat; the driver of a local cab will tell you how much he tips ('tell you the truth, I think he's a little tight-fisted').

This all turns out to be useful information, because Tyson has disappeared. He hasn't shown up for training in three days, and though a few vague excuses are offered, it's fairly clear that no one knows where he is.

His trainer, an excitable man by the name of Kevin Rooney who is also a D'Amato protege, delivers himself of some insults, asks not to be quoted, and tells me about Trevor Berbick instead.

'I'll tell you about Berbick. I've watched him closely. He's a little crazy, a little off. I don't mean that in a bad way, I don't think he'd

4

ever kill anybody, but when you're a little crazy you take chances, do awkward things, and that's why this may be a tough fight. But Mike's been so active lately that he's turning into a warhorse, and he's also extremely fast and powerful. This guy's tough – and a little crazy – but how much he'll be able to take before his will's broken is debatable. If Mike goes right out and puts it on the guy, the chances are it'll be over in one round. Otherwise, I see a knockout in one of the later rounds. Unless he loses, the son of a bitch.'

Two days later, Tyson reappears. It turns out he had been to visit a girlfriend and decided to stay. Relations between he and Rooney are more than a little strained; they keep disappearing into a back room, and coming out each time looking progressively more strained.

Meanwhile, groups of local townspeople are milling in and out of the gym, taking pictures, asking for autographs and producing odd little gifts. They've probably seen him every day for the past seven years, but they're approaching him like he had just landed. He makes a brief attempt at graciousness and then swiftly walks out.

'Boxing is just my life and people make this really big thing out of it,' he had said on another occasion. It doesn't take a genius to realise that the interest his handlers are afraid he'll lose is not so much his interest in boxing as in the big thing that goes with it – the celebrity that Muhammad Ali thrived on and that few of his successors have known how to deal with.

Later that afternoon, back at his house, it's the same thing. The phone is ringing off the hook. A TV crew is positioned on the front lawn, waiting to shoot some film of Mike walking through the autumn foliage. A local artist, who seems to have dedicated her life to painting large oil portraits of Mike Tyson and Cus D'Amato, is unloading a selection of them from her car, in case the TV people want to film them.

And Tyson, meanwhile, is up in his pigeon coop, waiting for everyone to go home. But they don't. The TV crew need an interview, and can't leave without it. Since they're from the company which is sponsoring his fight with Berbick, from which he'll emerge a million dollars richer, he doesn't have much choice.

After a few preliminary questions, the interviewer asks him what word would best characterise his quest for the championship.

'Destiny. No matter what happens the job has to be done. Providing I don't get injured or killed, the job has to be done. Cus told me that it was my destiny.'

'How are you mentally dealing with the possibility of becoming the next champion?'

'Sometimes the pressure is overbearing, but I chose this business and now I have to deal with it. But I'm always going to walk the streets without bodyguards. I don't take success that seriously.'

'Have you had to keep things inside since Cus died?'

'I always kept things to myself, even when Cus was around. I prefer to keep things to myself.'

'How did Cus prepare you for all of this?'

'I remember when I was 13, 14, I complained a lot that no one liked me, that no one really knew me, and that girls didn't like me. And he always used to react in the same way. He told me: "One day I'm going to have to buy you a bat to keep all the girls off. One day you're going to wish you didn't know so many people." And he was right.'

Copyright © James Truman, 1986

Art is Money

The New Power Brokers by Gordon Burn
December 1986

L ONDON, MID-AUTUMN. The sun streams through the windows of the Waddington Gallery on the corner of Cork Street where a lunch party is in progress to celebrate the new show of work by the British sculptor Anthony Caro, and the beginning of a new season. Wine is poured, tit-bits are offered, the cocktail chatter ebbs and flows and a young woman – attractive, blonde, wearing multi-coloured designer glasses – approaches the owner of one of the smaller Cork Street galleries, who has already reached the coffee stage.

'Which one,' she asks him only semi-confidentially, removing her glasses and raking her hair, 'which one is Sarah Kent?' Sarah Kent is the art critic of *Time Out* and, as it happens, isn't there. 'I want to ask her to come and review my show.'

'Who was that?' Bernard Jacobson is asked casually, once the young woman, wine glass in one hand, Filofax in the other, has drifted away. 'Oh,' he says, declining a chocolate-dipped cherry, 'that was Richard Branson's sister.'

'What's the greatest price you've paid in your career?' an interviewer recently enquired of the American writer Richard Ford, to which Ford replied: 'Writers don't have "careers". Advertising executives do.' This, it is becoming increasingly clear, would be regarded as a quaint, rather old-fashioned notion by battalions of young artists on both sides of the Atlantic, who have stripped the Warhol dictum that 'making money is art and working is art and good business is the best art' of any irony and taken it as the text, framed and hung in 'lofts' from Stepney to SoHo, by which to conduct their professional lives.

'Being good in business,' Andy reiterated at dictation-speed, 'is the most fascinating kind of art . . . I like money on the wall. Say you were going to buy a $200,000 painting. I think you should take that money, tie it up, and hang it on the wall. Then when someone visited you the first thing they would see is the money on the wall.'

Whatever her work is like, Richard Branson's sister is obviously an artist totally at one with the modern world. Fill that Filofax! Collect those contacts! Get up! Get out! Get On! 'It's a modern phenomenon,' as one of the pre-eminent London 'gallerists', Nigel Greenwood, glumly confirms, 'and it's yuppiedom.' Crates of Becks beer, compliments of the manufacturer, have replaced rotgut and white Rioja at both the smartest and the most 'streetcredible' private views.

If yuppiedom has a spiritual home on Cork Street it is at Number 9, the location of the Nicola Jacobs Gallery. Prompted in the taste department, in the first instance, by her friends the clothes designers Georgina Godley and Scott Crolla, and guaranteed financial backing by her father, owner of the British School of Motoring, Nicola was in the vanguard of the latest trend (or 'tendency', as the art magazines prefer to call it).

Full-page ads in *Harpers And Queen* and *Interiors* trumpeted the arrival on the scene of both Nicola herself in her power suits, and her showplace for burgeoning talent. 'Have you ever bought an original painting? It says an awful lot more about you than any furnishings ever will,' Nicola cooed from behind a bowl of 'Hockney-esque' tulips. 'You too can attend a private view! It's a very nice way to spend an evening.' A new age had dawned.

Once again Andy appears to have been the inspiration here. 'If a guy has, say, a few thousand dollars to spend on a painting, he doesn't wander along the street till he sees something lying around that "amuses" him. He wants to buy something that's going to go up and up in value, and the only way that can happen is with a good gallery,' Andy has counselled in another standard text, *Popism: The Warhol 60s*. 'It's a matter of marketing ... you need a good gallery so the "ruling class" will notice you and spread enough confidence in your future so collectors will buy you, whether for five hundred dollars or fifty thousand. No matter how good you are, if you're not promoted right, you won't be one of those remembered names.'

Not surprisingly, Nicola had dozens of young hopefuls trying to batter the doors down before the first customer (oops 'client') had been admitted to her new premises. 'You get them for a reasonable price,' as she disarmingly confessed to her potential punters, 'and hope they take off.'

Some, of course, find it easier to get a foot in the door than others. Some, like the young Iranian-born painter, Hercules Fisherman, keep on knocking and don't get in. A former student of the 'cheeky chappie' Eighties art star, brought to you courtesy of Beck's beer, Bruce McLean, Fisherman has to settle for wall-space in West End media haunts like L'Escargot and Moscow's, or end-of-the-line galleries in Bethnal Green. Others have the door thrown open in welcome before they have even alighted from their *deux-chevaux*.

After the Anthony Caro lunch at Waddington's, Bernard Jacobson wandered back across Cork Street to his own gallery which was showing the first one-person show by a young Slade-trained artist, Celia Paul. Paul's work had been enthusiastically received by *Time Out*'s Sarah Kent: 'Paul's women are not the flirtatious flibbertigibbets of male fantasy,' she noted with approval, 'nor the virgins, whores, harridans and madonnas of the masculine codex, but a more substantial breed of forceful beings, by comparison with whom her men seem vulnerable and neurotic.'

What Kent neglected to mention was the artist's relationship to Lucien Freud, whose paintings her own resemble to the point of parody, or the fact that the central painting in the show had been purchased – oh hallelujah! – by Charles and Doris Saatchi, currently the biggest collectors of contemporary art in Europe, probably the world (and, incidentally, two of Bernard Jacobson's oldest friends).

The Saatchis' standing as power-brokers on the international art scene, which their purchasing power has conferred on them, has become legendary in recent years. They started buying art in bulk in the mid-Seventies, and among the first to benefit from their patronage was the bulky American artist Julian Schnabel – 'the art equivalent of Bruce Springsteen', as he has been dubbed by Peter Blake, with whom Schnabel shares a London dealer, Leslie Waddington.

'There's that same unhealthy nationalism,' Blake says. 'That almost fascistic chauvinism. They've both been far too successful on the basis of far too little talent. It's a contrived thing. The American art market needed a new star to sell in the late-Seventies, a new "movement", and Schnabel happened along almost by chance. The Saatchis virtually bought out one of the first shows – something like ten out of the 12 pictures – and these were later shown at the Tate, which sets a false market.

'Schnabel, in the meantime, started to believe his own hype. He has become more and more arrogant, and less and less pleasant. You could learn to live with the unpleasantness and the lack of modesty, though, if he had a bit more talent.'

The inflation of the reputation of Julian Schnabel has been more thoroughly documented than the rise to prominence of any other painter in the post-War, certainly the post-Jackson Pollock, period. Julian was 'larger-than-life'; 'good-value'; a 'personality'; an up and at 'em, knock 'em in the aisles, verbals merchant. He was the perfect package for a late-20th century, getting and spending, commodity-culture. The ultimate chat-show fodder.

See Julian with his beautiful wife relaxing in the grounds of their fabulous Long Island mansion! See the Schnabels at home in Manhattan with their Florence Knoll table and their Max Beckmans, in the pages of *House And Garden*! See Julian's beautiful wife modelling her own-designed Ava Gardner-style evening dresses and Stephen Sprouse graffiti suit in the sweet-smelling pages of *Vogue*! 'Young, attractive, active,' the captions burble. 'The time, easily, is theirs.'

Hardly surprising, then, that Schnabel, yuppie-supreme, should have become a role model for the 'baby-boomers' – the salad-and-spritzer, Nikes-with-everything, the great Polo-wearing masses who have migrated to New York in their hundreds of thousands in the 1980s to make, deal in and purchase art. Art, Tom Wolfe has written, is the new religion; 'Art today – not religion – is the religion of the educated classes.'

* * *

In 1950, there were only about 50 modern artists living in New York, who depended mostly on each other for support, and less than 20 galleries. Even as late as 1961, only about 21 artists of the older generation, according to the art critic Thomas Hess, were making what could be called 'a living' in a city which had become the capital of contemporary art. 'From the start,' Suzi Gablik points out in her book *Has Modernism Failed?*, 'the mystique of modern art has always been that it is not generally popular, or even comprehended, except by an elite few.'

Marcel Duchamp, asked once how many people *really* liked avant-garde art, replied: 'Oh, maybe ten in New York and one or two in New Jersey'. That was in 1945. Forty years later, there is a two-billion-dollar-a-year art market in New York alone, 14,000 artists with gallery affiliations and 100,000 more shuffling for position. The education system in America turns out as many graduate artists every two years as there were *people* in 15th-century Florence. In the Seventies, they all (including Julian Schnabel) grew up wanting to be Andy Warhol ('compulsively addicted to glamour, openly aligned with the competition for money, status and power,' in the words of Suzi Gablik). In the Eighties, they all grow up wanting to be Julian Schnabel.

'Not enough can be said of the importance of developing an entire image for the artists I represent,' Mary Boone, Schnabel's dealer and the woman credited with orchestrating his career, told *Life* magazine. 'Placing the painter in certain shows, getting the right attention from the right art magazines, throwing the right parties at the right clubs. It's all so very important.'

It is comments like this that have led the art critic Robert Hughes to describe the art world now as looking 'more like the fashion industry than its former self . . . the market pressure for accessible, undemanding, lavishly emotional art is now extreme . . . the new audience for art is insecure, uninformed, grasping, easily led . . . the new collectors (are) prepared to buy anything that sounds "hot" . . .

'They are rich. Sometimes, the degree of their success and wealth is puzzling to them, and there is something a little expiatory about the way in which they buy. Most of the time they buy what other people buy. They move in great schools, like bluefish, all identical . . . If one wants Schnabel, they all want Schnabel; if one buys a Keith Haring, two hundred Keith Harings will be sold . . . Many of them seem to believe, quite sincerely, that Western art began with Andy Warhol. The others only behave as though it did.'

Julian Schnabel, in other words, had found his public. And, by a careful monitoring of the Schnabel flight-pattern, the young practitioners of 'the vandalism aesthetic', such as the graffittists Haring and Jean Michel Basquiat, came to see the future. 'I wouldn't be surprised if I died like a boxer, really broke,' Basquiat has said, 'but somehow I doubt it.'

'Success and security now play such a central role in the American imagination that even artists have learned to strive along an imposed scale of careerist values, mapping out their lives like military strategists,' Suzi Gablik writes. 'The vanguard concept has been traded in for good marketing strategy, and has become a big, booming juggernaut.'

It seems somehow inevitable that the new 'hot' artist in America, the 'neo-abstractionist' sculptor, Jeff Koons, should have spent the last six years supporting himself as a salesman on Wall Street, selling commodities and mutual funds. And that his most impassioned supporter, the writer Jeffrey Deitch ('I am probably the only person who ever went to the Harvard Business School to study art criticism') serves as art advisor to Citibank, the largest bank in the world.

The surest sign that the neo-expressionism of Schnabel and his European counterparts has peaked and that we're now entering the age of 'geometric abstraction' and 'post minimalism', is the way the British critical establishment, previously highly resistant to the Schnabel brand of attention-grabbing and bombast, have, on the basis of the mini-retrospective of his work which has just closed at the Whitechapel Gallery in London, started to take him to their bosom.

The Saatchis, significantly, have already turned their attention to Jeff Koons and his contemporaries, who are consequently about to enjoy their hour in the sun. The Saatchis on this occasion, however, almost missed the boat. An enterprising American family, the Schwartzes – mother, father and son – got there before them, and Charles and Doris have had a lot of catching up to do.

'A bandwagon starts and in today's artworld the bandwagon gets rolling quickly and is immediately international and influential in every corner of the artworld,' Deitch, Koons' promoter, told the magazine *Artscribe* in April. 'The first groups of buyers are always very adventurous . . . But soon the momentum starts and it gets in the air that this is the next hot thing and a different sort of audience starts getting in on the act; people who want to buy cheap before the really big money comes in . . . In New York we have a situation where (the museums and established commercial galleries) are simply not there when the new art is there and the artists, who aren't willing to wait, open up the businesses themselves.'

London's most notorious example of this particular brand of private enterprise are the self-styled 'Grey Organisation', a kind of Sham 69 or Dallas Boys for the 1980s, given to mouthing self-serving drivel like 'We've embraced success but we've also by-passed all the boring institutions like art school; we want to make money, fast' and throwing paint (only once, and very tentatively) at the gallery windows in Cork Street.

All this proved, apart from a depressing lack of imagination (a distinct drawback in a trio intent on hyping themselves as 'the most energetic "now" painters around') was that they'd heard the story about the failed 'radical' Armenian painter who walked into the Museum of Modern Art in New York, whipped out an aerosol can and wrote KILL LIES ALL in red letters across the surface of Picasso's 'Guernica'. Five years later Tony Shafrazi, through the medium of his own SoHo gallery, was selling graffiti to New Yorkers. 'My feelings tell me,' Shafrazi told a reporter, 'that what is taking place now is a renaissance akin to that of the early twentieth century.'

'America is a great, wonderful, capitalist country,' a spokesman for the Grey Organisation assured a journalist from one of the colour supplements a few weeks ago. 'It's the only place on earth where young artists like us are treated with the respect we deserve. New York appreciates us. We've got an exhibition at the Civilian Warfare Gallery called "Alive and Awake". Next stop Germany, Japan. Yeah, Britain's finished.'

To her credit, the journalist wasn't fooled. 'In these days of creeping trivia, when hype has become an end in itself,' she concluded, 'the Grey Organisation epitomise the artistic nonentities who fill the space round advertisements for Levis jeans, pop records and Panasonic portable stereo equipment. Looking great in "the pics" is the singular skill of this trio of poseurs.'

Earlier this year, exactly a quarter-of-a-century after he first exhibited in public, Charles and Doris Saatchi acquired their first painting by the British artist Patrick Caulfield.

Caulfield paints on average nine or ten pictures a year, and his output is decreasing as he grows older. The conditions of maximum exposure – of Eighties-style 'supply-side aesthetics' – demand two paintings a week. Caulfield has consistently refused to push himself forward, or to look, behave or otherwise announce himself as an 'Artist'. There is no trace in his accent of the relatively humble beginnings which he is reluctant to talk about, but only because he considers that line of biographical narrative 'too corny'.

Although regarded as a member of the 'second wave' of British pop artists at the beginning of the 1960s, which included David Hockney, Peter Phillips and Allen Jones, Caulfield has never really belonged to any group movement. Typically, when his immediate contemporaries were painting comic-strips, toothpaste tubes and other ad-mass imagery, he was painting Islamic daggers and Turkish pottery, Greek ruins, necklaces, ponies.

The surface of Caulfield's mature paintings isn't scabbed and studded with antlers, or overlaid on rawhide or linoleum. The surface is clear and clean; the imagery anonymous and uninflected – pipes, bottles, unremarkable domestic, restaurant and office interiors; the style deliberately bland, detached, impersonal; the intention – the antithesis of the art of bluster and self-assertion, of tedious and noisy 'self-expression' – to record and celebrate the monotonous and the ordinary and, in the process, release their mystery: 'the shock of the familiar'. He is Pinter or Beckett – one of his few heroes – rather than Tennessee Williams or Albee.

Marco Livingston, in his catalogue essay to the 1981 retrospective exhibition of Patrick Caulfield's work at the Tate, said that it took him six months to get Caulfield to talk about the paintings. Caulfield has no public-relations person, not even a discreet one, beavering away on his behalf, quietly and behind the scenes. He has betrayed no wish to be touched by, let alone stay drenched in, what Robert Hughes has called 'the glittering spray of promotional culture'. It is no part of his ambition to belong to the tough little world where (Hughes again) 'the machinery of fashion, gossip, image-bending, and narcissistic chic taps out its agile pizzicato'.

He lives modestly, sees his friends regularly, drinks, watches, walks the streets unmolested and goes on adding to a body of work that is rigorous, independent, imaginative and truthful, and guaranteed to make him one of those remembered names. 'Six days a week Caulfield travels to his working studio overlooking the rooftops of Soho, stares at a blank canvas, worries, goes down to the pub for a drink and then another, doodles in a notebook, does a bit more worrying, and goes home convinced of his utter sterility,' the *Observer* noted recently.

Although he has nothing against them, Caulfield doesn't touch designer beers. The odd Guinness, maybe; but mainly Scotch with just a splash of water.

Copyright © Gordon Burn, 1986

An Everyday Story of a Suburban Sex Kitten

Mandy Smith by Gordon Burn

March 1987

T HIS IS HOW IT WORKS THESE DAYS: her manager gets on the blower in the car in which they are travelling and alerts the gorillas on the door at the Hippodrome that they are on their way. And the gorillas – that is, the chief gorilla, the one with the most neck spilling over his collar – gets on *his* blower and alerts the snappers standing guard outside the Lime-light, the Caprice and Langan's Brasserie that live meat – London's *livest* on this strangely balmy late autumn evening – is on the hoof and heading Leicester Square-way.

'MANDY AT S'FLLW,' the message dancing across the little quartz windows of the lensmen's radio-pagers says, and it is enough. All they need. They are up – vroom, vroom! – and away. By the time Mandy has sipped a few sips of lime-and-Per-rier, pushed a few leafs of oak-leaf salad around her plate and is ready for dancing, the gang's all there. 'Mand! Mand! ... Over-here, Mandy! ... Bit more of that, Mandy! ... Great Mandy! ... Fab'louse Mand!' they give it to her over the disco throb, dragging their space-boots and equipment bags over the ululating disco tiles, as Mandy licks her pale lips and tosses her long hair, twitches her hips, hugs herself to herself and rolls her big, black, keep-off-come-hither eyes.

Mandy's manager, meanwhile, denim shirt slashed to the waist and a skin problem lurking under his Marbella tan, is fully occu-pied fending off 'Page-Three girls' and 'glamour' models, and the other pieces of jailbait and night-time flotsam who are intent on crashing Mandy's scene. Mandy would never do 'Page-Three'. Would never, in other words, bare her bazoomas for the mass-market dailies, *The Star* and *The Sun*, whose circulations are exponentially related to their morning 'nipple-count'.

'Others have launched their careers that way. But if Mandy did it,' her manager says, 'it would be pure pornography. It would be selling her breasts.' Mandy would be elevated a little bit above. Maurice Boland knew that much the minute this whole Mandy thing smacked him between the eyes.

From the roots of his blond-streaked hair to the tips of his Spanish-heeled boots, by way of his bared brown belly, Maurice Boland is unreconstructed playboy. A drummer with the Irish 'beat' group, the King Bees in the early Sixties, Maurice moved on to found Dublin's hottest night-spot, Sachs's, named after Mr Brigitte Bardot number-three, Gunther Sachs. And that's Maurice for you, right there. Gunther and 'BB'. Beautiful People. For two decades, they fuelled Maurice's fantasies and peopled his dreams.

Christmas in St Moritz for the opening of the Cresta Run and New Year's Day in Gstaad; February on Mustique and summers in St Tropez; astightasthis with Prince Rainier, Prince Aly Khan, Porfirio Rosa; choppers, custom cruisers, Rollers. That's what Gunther and BB had. And that's what Maurice saw marching into Cuba, the club he owned in Marbella, the night Mandy Smith walked through the door two summers ago.

'Would you be lookin' at that gorgeous girl. That's a gorgeous girl. That's another Bardot,' Maurice told himself and, later that night, his wife. What he couldn't know – what nobody knew outside the closed circle in which she moved – was that Mandy was sitting on a story with the potential to make headlines as big as any BB ever made in her 'sex-kitten' heyday.

'The media are very easy to manipulate, especially in England. If you give them a tag, they'll just go for anything,' Mick Jagger once said, commenting on how easy it was for the Rolling Stones' then manager, Andrew Oldham, to get 'Would you let your sister go with a Rolling Stone?' stories into the scandal sheets. Jagger called the British press 'pathetically amusing, but it's efficient at spreading news, wow, you can't beat it. You don't have to do a thing. When you get the ball rolling, they do it all for you.'

ROCK STAR'S CHILD LOVER AGED 13: Scandal of Rolling Stone. WORLD EXCLUSIVE: Scandal of rock superstar who shared lovenest with gymslip sweetheart – MY SCHOOLDAYS AS STONE'S CHILD BRIDE. JAIL THIS WORM WYMAN FOR LOVING MANDY, 13. MP SLAMS STONE – 'a sick pervert'. EXCLUSIVE: The story that shocked Britain . . . every mum and dad of a teenage girl must read it. POLICE HUNT DIARIES OF BILL'S CHILD LOVER. I'M SCARED MY MANDY GREW UP TOO FAST: She's still a baby ... with teddy bears and rag dolls.

These were the headlines that flashed in front of Maurice Boland's eyes the minute that Mandy, now a house-guest in Marbella, told him about her secret past as Bill Wyman's prepubescent lover. How they became inky reality is a murky area. Boland's version is that Mandy spilled the beans to a friend who happened to be a freelance journalist and also happened to be staying with him in Spain at the time (and has since suffered a heart attack fretting over the way 'his' story was wheedled out of him and hijacked by a team of hacks from the *News Of The World*). Mandy herself is more candid: she was going to be 16 on July 17, 1986, and as soon as she was, that was it then: the world was her oyster.

Boland was clever enough to register from the beginning that there was more to the product, as he put it, than a scandal. There would be recording contracts, he promised, videos, modelling assignments, a book. He was controlling the hottest property – it was to become his chief selling-line in the marketing of Mandy – since (yes) Brigitte Bardot. ('She's very Bardot,' Maurice enthuses. 'Very, very, very Bardot. She doesn't like animals being killed and she would like to get behind no-cruelty cosmetics *if* the price is right.')

'They all say,' Boland says, 'whoever they are, "Maurice, this girl is very special. This is a very special human being". And she *is* special, that little monkey. Specialness at sixteen. Having Mandy means you don't have to get into anything tacky. We've got her very big contracts within the City. We're very, very, *very* careful what work we do.'

The main thrust of his strategy since the story broke in early August had been to haul Mandy out of the mire of tabloid scuzz and scandal and take her bang-down-the-middle, mums-and-dads mainstream. This meant saying 'no' to £50,000 from the *News Of The World* for more dirt on her relationship with Wyman, Boland claims, and 'yes' to £3,500 from the more up-market *Mail On Sunday* for an article which raved about the 'sensational natural beauty' of 'a deeply thoughtful girl'. Brutus jeans were next in the ring with £10,000 for a 50-minute photo-call, and a London 'hair design studio' reputedly paid her £5,000 to appear in a white wedding dress at a nightclub. ('Just magic,' Maurice remembers. 'I was in tears.')

All of this was small beer, however, compared to what Mandy

could expect to earn as a 'personality' model-cum-recording art-iste. 'I don't know if she can sing, but does it matter?' her manager had asked in the early days of their career. 'Who can?' But now, ten weeks down the road he had changed his tune. 'She's just re-corded a huge great big ballad,' he said. ' "Behind All This I Am A Woman". When she got to that line she filled up. She broke down in the booth. We all looked at each other and said, "Yes, she is an artist". It was that moving, we're leaving it in.'

'Yer what?' Mandy said when she was asked about this milestone in her recording career some days later. 'Whaddja mean?' Her first single was going to have been a remake of the death-of-a-biker tear-jerker, 'Terry', but this had been shelved in favour of an orig-inal song. Was this because of royalty considerations, Mandy was asked, and immediately replied no, because royalties revert to the artist after 20 years and 'Terry' was more than 20 years old.

'Terry' reached number-four in the British charts in December, 1964, six years before Mandy was born. Brian Jones had been dead for a year-and-thirteen days on July 17, 1970, and Bill Wy-man, the oldest and always least glamorous of the Stones, was already 34. Wyman was 47 when he spotted Mandy dancing with her 15-year-old sister at the British Rock and Pop Awards at the Lyceum in London 1983 and sent the video-maker Julien Temple over to ask them to join his table.

Mandy noticed that the waitresses, all of them well advanced in years, seemed to be making much of the old rocker, but neither his name nor the name of the group he had been part of for almost quarter-of-a-century meant a great deal to a girl of 13. The follow-ing day there was a message when she got home from the Holy Family of Enfield, her convent school, in drab and suburban far north London. And, encouraged by her mother, this resulted in dinner at Tramp. Tramp would become Bill and Mandy's favourite haunt in London because of the quality-control which let Prince Andrew, among others, in, but kept the paparazzi and other rub-ber-neckers on the pavement outside.

Mandy's definition of a good time during her years with Wyman was simple: no photographers. They would arrive at parties and premieres separately or, learning that the snappers were out in force, not at all, which led to rows. Wyman took her out of her Catholic school when she was 14 and installed her in a private school more convenient for his apartment in King's Road in Chelsea, where she spent many nights kicking her heels, waiting for him to come home.

He would never allow her her own bank account, which meant that she was dependent on him for everything. 'Sometimes he even asks me the price of things like butter, or the roast for the weekend,' Wyman's first wife told 16 magazine in 1966. 'Right off, he can tell you the difference between the price of steak per pound in England and in America.'

'He's not stingy,' Mandy said. 'Well, *slightly*. After the first few months I had to put it to him; If you want me to go to these places with you and look nice, I have to wear the right clothes. I just wasn't, like, a girl who had nothing when I met him. But it made me want these things more.'

According to the papers, she 'frequently mingled with megastars like Rod Stewart and David Bowie and dined with Elton John and Mick Jagger'. She encountered Jerry Hall on only one occasion. 'I met her once. Just briefly. Say no more. She *looks* very pleasant.'

Bill Wyman – 'the quiet Stone' – always had a reputation for preferring to be upstairs watching *Fantasia* on the video or tapping Stones data into his computer than downstairs where his wife wanted to be, in Keith's suite at the Plaza, partying with the rest of the Stones. On Mandy's evidence, he hasn't grown any wilder as he's piled on the years.

'I always think of him as being just like his parents. I think of him as being Bill Perks, which is his real name. The ordinary guy. Like, he can go on stage and be really hyped up and just come off and watch TV or play cards. So okay, he was a big rock star – he is a big star – but he's an old man. He's 50 this month [it was October] and he's not looking forward to it. He always said he's going to hide away.'

Theirs doesn't appear to have been either a storybook romance or a grand passion. It appears to have been a case of world-weary Humbert Humbert-ism on the one hand and of not looking a gift-horse in the mouth on the other. Ask any of the principals about the moral dimension and they end up talking, in one way or another, about the economics.

'I'm out earning a crust for my family. And I'm totally happy in my work. I love it, love it, love it,' the manager says. 'Mandy and myself are like as one person. I can feel it. This enormous wave. I can feel the whole thing there. It's totally creative. Every day creating for Mandy. There's not one teenager in England who wouldn't like to be a Mandy Smith.'

'She turned down so many things in her life,' Mandy says of her mother, Patsy. 'My mum – she says, when these chances come along, you don't let them go that easy. I wasn't too keen on him in the beginning, but my mum, she said, He's got a choice of any woman he wants in the world, and he's picked you. But' – she half-closes and heavily hoods her eyes in the way that gets photographers crooning, 'Oh wicked, wicked Mandy. Mmm, I like it. Like that. Reeelly wicked, Mandy!' – 'who's to say I'm not just a good Catholic girl?'

Fittingly, perhaps, Mandy's new boyfriend is an accountant. A long-haired Scottish fiscal whizz. Presently unemployed, he's looking to Mandy to provide the opening he needs into one of the fun industries, music-biz, greater show-biz or Leisure. Mandy's ambition, of course, is to become an actress, although she's never been star-struck, she says.

'I met just so many great people. Film stars, actors, singers, royalty. But famous people, basically they're just human beings. They *are*. Like with Bill. I was always fairly laid back. Never all over him. I was so laid back people knew I wasn't just a silly young girl out for what I could get. I always acted older than my age.'

Copyright © Gordon Burn, 1987

What's So New About the New Man?
Three Decades of Advertising to Men by Jon Savage
March 1988

THE CAMERA PANS INSIDE a warehouse, funky but expensive: in these days of crammed two-bedroom flats, space is at a premium and an open plan, ex-industrial environment is highly desirable – hence its heavily featured appearance in Euro MTV and 'Streets Of Fire'. Time for some significant moments. We see a scantily-dressed young man – very good looking but *not gay*.

His gestures are carefully, deliberately clumsy: he is hunting for his breakfast. There's no woman around to get it for him: as he grimaces at the cat, the only other occupant of this space, he reaches for . . . his reliable flexible friend. He slips on some clothes

(American Classics) and saunters to the cashpoint through a post-industrial, post-vandalism street scene: the final long shot shows him at the window of his wharf with his cat, gloriously alone. It's Sunday.

Our Wapping wonder, reading the newspaper that is produced just down the road, is a glaring example of the way in which advertising and marketers are attempting to get to grips with the young male market. He's glaring because he's not quite right: you end up by remembering the tableau, not the product, and by suspecting that the ad is not so much targeting the requisite market as displaying an internal adland ideal.

Yet he's nearly there: the image of the softer, almost 'feminised' male who does the shopping and dares to consume has become an adland staple – often called 'The New Man'. This creature does have some counterpart in reality: current advertising uses sophisticated social research to fuel its flights into fantasy. But it's important to remember that, despite its formal innovation, advertising is not concerned with creating new social trends but in reflecting existing conditions at a safe distance and in a palatable manner. It is by nature conservative, although not as conservative as its clients.

It is axiomatic that advertising exists in order to sell things. These days, the sort of products usually being sold are not necessary but convenient or highly specific, tied in not with need but with *lifestyle*. A late Sixties term from the time when increased consumer spending really began to bite, 'lifestyle' has become a UK advertising reality since the early Eighties, tied in with new market research techniques like group discussions.

The key idea, often called 'market segmentation', is to do with specific targeting. 'It's recognising that many people are sufficiently well-off and trained as consumers,' says Peter York of market planners SRU. 'Many products now have what is called Added Value. It says *I* will buy this because it has something for *me*.' This idea – that you are what you buy – is of paramount importance: current in America since the early Seventies, it has spread to the UK only in the past few years.

The greater sophistication of market research and advertising techniques has gone hand in hand with the search for new markets. In this, the young/young middle-aged male market has been one of the last great unknowns. The history of teenage marketing originated in the immediate post-war period with successful campaigns and products aimed at young women. The young male market has been notoriously difficult.

Indeed, the whole business of selling things to men has been fraught with difficulty. There is not only the problem of getting men to spend money on themselves – not thought until recently to be a masculine activity – and training them as consumers, but the problems of targeting and representation. 'Advertisers have been looking to grab that sector for a long time,' says Lucy Purdy of RBL (Research Bureau Ltd). 'They know that the fashionable young man is out there, but they don't know how to address him. You can't address all men; there has been no one image specific to all men.'

There's no problem with advertising cars, car-phones, petrol and that sort of executive stuff. From the famous 'National' ads of the late Fifties on, all you have needed to display are the right social cues of the time: status, power, speed, beautiful women or whatever. Similarly, advertising cigarettes and drinks has been straightforward, complicated only by the guidelines about cigarettes and the current lager wars. These are things that men do. It's when you get on to sex roles, narcissism, and personal growth – the staples of the new male consumption –that the problems start.

It's all right when a man says, 'Look at what I have accumulated.' Far more difficult when a man says, 'Look at me!' The mere act of display is problematic and potentially alienating to the male viewer. As Andy Medhurst writes in _Ten-8_: 'To put a body on display is usually to render it passive, to make it available for the bearer of the gaze, but that runs the risk of conflicting with our ideologies of "masculinity", of "feminising" the body in question.'

Within the terms of UK advertising in the Fifties, representation was hardly an issue. In contrast to the detail already to be found in America, British ads were very primitive, simply displaying the product or relying on an assumed knowledge of traditional class codes. It was very much A Gentleman's Wardrobe: ads for shirts would display an image of Regent Street behind the product and everybody would know what this meant. A static class structure was matched by a static view of consumption: you bought things to last.

Images of men were generic – often conveyed by an idealised drawing – and if there was any detail, it was to do with the war: there was little inherent sex or glamour in being a man. As the American model of consumption – a high turnover operation with a design aesthetic as a key selling point – came over to Britain from the mid-Fifties on, advertising to men slowly changed (although not as quickly as advertising to women). It began to take on the American hallmarks of travel, power, money and sex appeal.

The central idea here was cool. There was no one unifying image for the mass male market in the Fifties: most people didn't think like that and if they did, the male icons were either too weedy (Dirk Bogarde), too tweedy (film stars like Kenneth More), or too rough (Elvis and the consequent rock'n'roll stars). James Dean hadn't yet made the transition to youth cultural archetype. A sequence of extremely successful films translated youth-oriented mod styles and ideologies into an acceptable, older masculine image. Starting with *Dr No* (1962), the Sean Connery James Bond films mixed in American ad values – travel, money, power and sex – with a new style of technology consumption, and an age-old patriotism.

This new cool became an instant adland hit: it marked an increasing democratisation of consumption by apparently eradicating old class boundaries. A big mid-Sixties fantasy that had originated in the teenage market was the idea of classlessness: the new leisure wear would be modelled by carefully rough looking models to signify a *déclassé* butchness. Just in case, these ads added an adoring female or two for the sake of clarity – as they continue to today, if ironically.

Such Sixties ads reflect a confidence in a unity of taste that had disappeared by the end of the decade, as advertising unwillingly mirrored the social and gender changes of the period. Ads from the early Seventies reflect a deep social fragmentation rather than a market segmentation: main themes reflect a post-hippie idea of 'escape' mixed in with a bit of ethnicity and you see the beginnings of nostalgia creeping in to the most basic adverts. Interiors that in the Sixties had been sharp and modern were now countrified and muted: the man was still pictured with woman and children – recognising his perceived economic dominance. *He* paid for the G-Plan, even if he didn't actually choose it.

Advertising is most effective when there is a consensus of taste and values which can be translated into a visual or verbal shorthand; the Seventies crisis of representation, which reflected a wider crisis of values, resulted at the end of the decade in an absence of all but the most basic male images. Just as in the Fifties, ads often displayed nothing but the product, or else, like Brut or Denim, they were butch in the most crass way possible.

Several factors have contributed to the considerable change that has occurred in male ad imagery. As Lucy Purdy explains: 'There is the change in men's lifestyles and the change in the way in which advertisers now target their advertising, both of which date from the early Eighties. There is now a much more sophisticated planning approach within agencies: people employed as researchers have a much more sophisticated methodological tool – the group discussion – and they are much more involved creatively in ads than before. There is much more understanding about how consumers behave and feel.'

Purdy's research with Mantrack, a report produced by RBL since 1985 'as a targeting tool for clients who sell products or services to men', has turned up influential findings about changes in men's lifestyles: 'It is fair to say that traditional male/female roles *have* changed a little. Men are more likely to be on their own, are more likely to buy products that appeal to themselves. There is also a range of domestic tasks, like shopping, which it is socially acceptable for men to do.' A good example of the domesticised male is to be found in the current Ross convenience food ad.

This research has coincided with, and fuelled, a more concerted attack on the problematic male market. The advertisers' task has been made easier both by the return to a social consensus (of the well-off) under the Conservatives – epitomised by the media term 'Yuppie' that came in here after 1985 – and the massive input of fresh male imagery provided by the Style Press.

It is now possible to conceive of a consensus, shorthand male image in a way that was not possible even five years ago: you can see these images – short-haired, polo-necked, be-501'ed, derived straight from Soho 1985 – all over current lager ads. These images from Style Culture, first disseminated through the pages of magazines such as *i-D* and *The Face*, are an acceptable solution to the problems of male representation.

The image is up-to-date yet aspirant, recognisably male yet admitting a certain vulnerability, still able to be interested, obsessed even, with clothes, male toiletries and new gadgets. They are an index of how the concerns of Style Culture have helped to fuel a new type of consumption and have codified a fresh marketplace: the 19–45-year-old male.

But how *new* is our New Man? Beneath the compulsively attractive surface, the same old angst gnaws. There is still the same old problem involved in putting the male body on display, now exacerbated by renewed social sanctions on homosexuality. Despite the fact that the gay milieu informs male representation at every level, it is now doubly necessary to disavow this. One solution is the use of women as props. But, even ironicised, this does not accord with social or commercial expectations: men are being asked to consume in areas that are traditionally 'female'.

'You can't assume that the New Man is a feminist man,' says

Lucy Purdy, 'he's just more narcissistic.' The dominant New Man advert is remarkable indeed for its *absence* of women: women are either a threat (at their most extreme, personifying the AIDS virus in *Fatal Attraction*) or simply irrelevant to the new, self-enclosed world of male pleasure and vanity. Far from marking a real change in gender roles, the New Man is yet another example of masculinity's privileged status in our society – the same old wolf in designer clothing.

Copyright © Jon Savage, 1988

The Big Olive
Milan by Tony Parsons
May 1988

T OURISTS SKIP MILANO. It is first thing on a bleak Monday morning in the Eurolounge at Heathrow, and nobody here is going to Northern Italy to see the sights. Just to underline this impression of high powered, international commerce ready to get out there and generate some serious lire, Ian Rush walks into the Eurolounge just as the flight to Milano is starting to board.

'Hi, Ian!!'

'Hi.'

His skin has a sickly, poor boy pallor, the complexion of someone who had a fishfinger childhood, and he has a sad, hangdog expression that only lightens up when he sees a friendly face. Then he seems shy and touched. He has the brightest eyes I have ever seen, huge moist blue searchlights, and these beautiful Bambi peepers shine from his unhealthy face like jewels floating in a sea of suet, reflections of the sporting genius of his soul.

It is the morning after the fifth-round cup match between Liverpool and Everton and Rush is flying economy with his wife of six months on a British Airways Boeing 757 to Milan. From there he will be whisked off to nearby Turin, home of Gianni Agnelli, the owner of Fiat, Juventus and Ian Rush.

Rush has not had an easy time in Italy – his lack of goals and Italian taking their toll – and he does not look happy to be going to work now.

As our plane passes over the black Alps and their sun-dappled, snowy peaks, Rush starts to pick a scab on his right ear, just above the lobe. By the time we are on the ground and in the coach taking us to the terminal, the melancholy striker's ear is pouring with blood. He dabs at the wound unhappily with a piece of caramel-coloured kitchen towel.

He is met inside the terminal and whisked quickly through customs, a man who never dreamed that becoming a lire billionaire could be this hard.

Milano sprawls at the foot of the mountains, shrouded in Alpine mists and the pale sunshine of Lombardy. 'It is prosaic and winterish,' Henry James wrote of the city, 'as if it were on the wrong side of the Alps.'

The Milanesi would like that – they like to boast about their big-cocked work ethic, and they love to compare their city to New York. 'For Italians,' says the writer Gregorio Magnani, adapting Sinatra, 'if you can make it there, you can make it anywhere.'

Tired of southern sloth, thousands come to the city to work (though they head for the nearby lakes and mountains at the weekend). This is the town where they never hold their carnival on a working day. The town where the traditional '_Buon Giorno_' (good day) is often replaced by '_Buon Lavoro_' – do good work. Captains of service industries bolt a small, black, potent cup of coffee standing up in a bar and tell you, with paranoid relish, what southerners say about the Milanesi. Things like, 'Why should we work when we have the slaves of Milano?' and 'Roma eats while Milano works'. You have not experienced just how virulent a north-south divide can be until you have heard an Italian talk about his country's two nations.

Terroni is what northerners call southerners, and it is an epithet guaranteed to start a fist fight in any bar south of Florence, loaded as _terroni_ is with all the fear and loathing and atavistic dread of a term like _nigger_. 'Oh, _terroni_ is bad,' someone told me. '_Terroni_ is very bad . . .'

But though the Milanesi are far from being lazy Latins pinching bottoms and loafing amid the sun, sea and pasta, and though they are always telling you that their country has two borders – the Alps and the Mediterranean – and that they are on the wrong side of both of them, Milano is a totally Italian city. This is, after all, the home of the glamorous _Made In Italy_ label and Milano, as she is, could exist in no other country. Under that misty, industrious surface there lurks a peculiarly Italian passion. You feel it out at

Linate airport when the baggage handlers stage another wildcat strike and all the foreign businessmen have to waddle down the windy runway with their own suitcases. And you feel it in the heart of the city when a soldier on leave asks you for directions and then, realising that you are a foreigner and do not speak Italian, he laughs and *hugs* you.

But most of all Milano feels Italian at night, especially when it is after one and, in a striking display of civil anarchy, all the traffic lights are switched to amber. That is when some charming slave of Milan will tell you that everything in this town is business, and all anyone thinks about in his office is *moda, moda, moda* (fashion) and – yes – he has to be in the offices tomorrow morning but first you *have* to see this Brazilian bar or transvestite club or Hollywood (pronounced 'Ollywood), and as he comes up to another amber light, he guns the motor and slams his foot to the ground.

Definitely Italian.

Some graffiti di Milano: 'Timberland are best'.

Now, whatever way you look at it, that sure beats 'Gooners Run Tottenham Yids', and it says a lot about the city. The *paninari* (sandwich boys) posing with spotty machismo in Italy & Italy (imagine McDonald's with cold quarter pounders and cod gold Roman columns) are obsessed with America and *moda*. But even at their dumbest – and all these ageing *paninari* think that enough nights in a Burghy bar will turn them into Tom Cruise – the Milanesi have a certain grace. 'Timberland Are Best'. You almost expect them to round it off with 'Discuss'.

Actually, fashion fans, I can exclusively reveal that the sandwich boys are moving away from their Republican flyboy look and getting into a mode of *moda* that is derived from our own fair land. Downtown in Milano, near where the *pans* roam Wendy and Burghy, Quick and Italy & Italy, there is currently a proliferation of shops selling what can only be described as green wellie chic; hunting, shooting and fishing clothes, which run the gamut from heavy mock-Church's brogues to the most chinless, tweediest togs imaginable. This is all symptomatic of the way young Milanesi – unlike, say, the young people of Paris – fail to cherish and love their own culture as much as it deserves. They will grow out of it of course – the million lire suits at Giorgio's store on Via San Andrea are always only a block or two away.

Milan is a city built in a series of concentric circles which echo the borders of the city walls down through the centuries. You buy a metro ticket for 700 lire (35 pence) from a newstand creaking under the weight of publications that are mostly concerned with AC Milan, clothes, hard core porn and horoscopes – football, fashion, fucking and the future, the great loves of the Milanesi – and then it is a clean, fast ride to the town's geographic and historic heart, the fabulous Duomo.

The Duomo – which means simply cathedral – is one wild church, the third largest in the world, a statistic that does nothing to convey the insane grandeur of the place. This Gothic extravaganza, the biggest on the planet, juts into the cool blue city sky like some mad eruption of faith – a massive white marble temple exploding with a forest of well over one hundred thin marble spires, another hundred leering giant gargoyles and a bewildering array of thousands of statues. Begun in 1387 and finished some 500 years later, the cathedral's construction has inspired an old Milanesi saying '*Lungo come la fabrica del Duomo*', which means something is taking as long as the building of the Duomo.

Poets through the ages have struggled to convey the mad, heroic beauty of the Duomo. 'It is the most princely creation that mankind has ever taken from thought to deed,' said Mark Twain, while even the normally po-faced Henrik Ibsen was moved to write, 'Whoever designed that work ought to create a new planet and launch it into space.' Emilio de Marchi was suitably moist-eyed and Italian about the Gothic marvel. 'It's our Duomo,' he said. 'It's the church of our families, it's home, it's huge, it's all marble, it's beautiful, ornate, splendid, it's one of a kind.'

It is also a church that is still used, very much in working order. In the cool shadows inside, among the massive white columns and the infinite stained glass windows, Milanesi businessmen in their lunch hour kneel before the Madonna and child, make the signs of the cross and clasp their hands in prayer. One of them – wrapped up against February in a deep camel hair coat, squat and heavy bearded, like a company man Martin Scorsese – catches my eye. He looks like the archetypal hard nosed, go-getting Milano corporate cowboy. The sight of him – with his head bowed, his lips muttering in supplication, not worried if he gets the knees of his million lire suit messed up – is strangely moving. After long minutes lost in prayer he eventually rises and checks his watch. Five past two. Time to get back to the office.

Maybe he had time for a slug of *espresso* standing up in some bar before he got back to his desk. This is a city that is fuelled by ambition and coffee beans, and within sight of the Madonnina di

Milano, the beautiful golden statue that crowns the Duomo's glory, there are literally hundreds of bars serving the need of coffee society.

Milan is the home of the 60-second coffee shot. *Cappuccino* – which is known by its pet name of *cappuccio*, or *cappucci* in the plural – is only drunk at breakfast. '*Spruzzo di cioccalato?*' means, do you want cocoa powder sprinkled on your *cappuccio*, to which you must reply with an excited, '*Si, si! Grazie mille, signorina!*' After your breakfast – which will consist of *cappuccio*, a *brioche* and a *panini* containing ham, cheese and something unexpected – I always had a fried aubergine you would die for – drinking the frothy stuff is not really on, though the Milanesi are far too sweet and cool to make a big deal out of it if you insist. Instead there is an infinite variety of coffees to bolt at the bar or linger over at a table (though the Milanesi are not that big on lingering). Take it *lascio* (straight and strong) or have a *caffe doppo* (double espresso). Have a *caffe ristretto* (extra strong), a *caffe fredo* (cold), *caffe fiordipanna* (with ice cream), or a *caffe corretto* (with cognac or grappa). You can take it in so many ways, but in the end there is only one way to take it. Going to the office, coming home from work, diving into a bar for two minutes on your way from A to B – drinking coffee is not a sedentary occupation – there is only *espresso*, knocked back standing up at the bar. Taken habitually, quickly, needed more than wanted. Small cups, smaller measure. Get it down, get out of there, get on with your life. *Buon Lavoro, amico*.

Money is on the streets and in the air. Memories of Italia as the hungry exhausted nation it was immediately after World War Two can be confined to the history books next to images of a bombed-out and broke Germany.

This is Italy after *Il Surpassimento* – literally 'the surpassing' – meaning that the country's standard of living has now overtaken that of both France and the UK. Milan is the slick engine of Italy's economic recovery. When the city made the cover of *Time* last summer the magazine reported a staggering increase in Italy's growth rate from 0.5% in 1983 to 3.5% a year later, settling down to a still impressive 2.7% 18 months ago.

Unlike the UK, Italy has built up its service economy while keeping its traditional manufacturing industries very much intact. So Milan is the centre of the fashion, marketing, telecommunications and advertising (there are 680 agencies in the city) industries, while also finding room just down the motorway for steelworks, car plants and a huge chemical manufacturer, Montedison, a company with 70,000 employees that is quoted on the New York stock exchange.

'The city gives birth to more businesses than babies,' says Socialist mayor Paolo Pilliterri.

You've come a long way, *bambini*.

Milano is where you see the best looking people in the world trying to look the richest. They are pretty convincing, especially down in the Quadrilatero D'Oro, Golden Rectangle, the central area bordered by the wide, lush Via Montenapoleone (known as Montenapo – the Milanesi are big on affectionate abbreviations) on the west side and the narrow opulence of Via Del Spiga on the east. These two streets – the Rodeo Drive and South Molton Street of Italia respectively – are formed into the Quadrilatero D'Oro by Via Manzoni on the north side and Corso Venezia on the south side. In this small, rich area, which would be easily swallowed by Soho, you will find the greatest concentration of label power in the world. This is where Stendhal's dictum that 'Milan is a wealthy republic dedicated to art and pleasure' really stands up and crows.

Montenapo has jewels from Misani and Faraone and a couple of Gucci's. There are furriers here – the women of Milano love their furs to a degree that would be morally and financially unthinkable in London; sable and mink with enough zeros on the price tag to make you go crosseyed. Corso Venezia is for silver, china, crystal and gold, while Ettore Sottsass Jnr's Memphis outfit is on Via Manzoni. On Via Del Spiga, that rich man's alley, there is Ferre, Fendi, Lancetti and Versace. The men with their names on the labels are here too – Gianni Versace lives on the nearby Via Gesu, and Giorgio Armani, whose four shops are all in the neighbourhood, resides very comfortably on the Golden Rectangle's adjacent Borgonuovo.

This is the place where the look you see all over this town reaches its most perfect expression. It is the monied, high gloss look of the women of Milan, the lovely Milanesa, where the fashion plates melt to flesh, and blood and looks and lire walk hand in glove. The Milanesa share a concept of beauty. They all want to look this way and in the Quadrilatero D'Oro they do it to perfection.

The Milanesa look is mostly legs and fur – a boxed mass of some ritzy animal skin and taut, pencil thin legs in shiny dark tights click-click-clicking on high Fuck Me heels. They have expensively tailored black hair framing the faces of knowing angels and their brown eyes are often hidden behind shades. What they look like of course are *models*. Not the models you see flying into moda mecca at the airport or the models – sulky, skinny, droopy girls – checking into the Hotel Diana or the models out at Porta Genova. No, the Milanesa are a classic glossy fantasy made pampered flesh. The models the women of Milano look like are the ones in the magazines.

The real thing head out to Porta Genova where Fabrizio Ferri and Flavio Lucchini have their sprawling Super Studio, the largest complex of photographic and TV studios on the planet. This is the true, glossy heart of the fashion industry. Under a sky that is filled with a network of black tram lines like giant spider webs, tall thin girls from across the planet cross a small bridge with their portfolios in large, flat leather cases, their 'book', that touching begging bowl of beauty.

An infinite procession of heart thumping beauties – and more than a few ugly ducklings, the models who are 'different' or 'unusual' – cross that bridge in search of work. There are shy French ones, ballsy Americans, overpainted English roses – the more fly models come to castings clean-faced, that is, without make up – and they all head out to the endless acres of light and space at Super Studio where there is always more work and the smell of fresh emulsion paint in the air.

Fabrizio Ferri, who is a photographer as well as co-owner of Super Studio (the other owner, Flavio Lucchini, is a publisher of *moda* titles like *Donna* and *Mondo L'Uomo* – between them these guys have got it sewn up) flicks through a young designer's portfolio, quickly skipping over *The Face* cover of Isabella Rossellini. Fabrizio is looking at the book with his wife and Isabella is an old flame.

Sometimes in Milano you feel you are being suffocated by the fashion industry – *It's only frocks!* you want to scream. But out at Super Studio, in the belly of the *moda* beast, you realise that it is always much more than that. Out in this self-contained world there are 20 studio options, some of them interlocking, it is like a massive pre-war movie set, bustling with people and props, action and money. The sickly sweet smell of paint and cosmetics are everywhere, and there are rooms the size of warehouses full of shoes and clothes and people pulling at them, high black rooms blazing at one end with a blinding artificial light in which a man is fanatically polishing a tiny spot on a brand new car, and – in this industry where beauty is a raw material, where looks are a commodity, a talent, a skill – every minute more flesh for fantasy arrives.

'Like a meat rack,' someone observed, but the girls arriving in twos – models always run in pairs – for calls at Super Studio seemed to me to be far too human, too vulnerable, too painfully diffident to be mistaken for sides of beef. Anyone looking for a meat rack in Milano has to go to the Cimitero Monumentale after dark.

The Cimitero Monumentale is the massive, neo-Gothic burying ground of the bourgeoisie of Lombardy and along its high, imposing walls is the traditional hunting ground of the prostitutes of Milan. But the whores who ply their trade along the perimeters of this giant graveyard are transvestites, many of them in the middle of the long, painful, plenty-lire process of changing their sex.

On the Via Censio, what looks roughly like a girl is disgorged from a big white van. The _Mafioso_ are in everything here and a low-ranking wise guy sits quietly in a nearby parked car as the tart – a crossover between the genders – totters across the street. She is wearing an unbuttoned fur coat, high heels and a heroin glaze. Beyond her there are close to three miles of whores along the walls of the graveyard and a slow wagon train of kerb-crawling Fiats.

Most of the tarts are dressed, despite the temperature hovering around the freezing mark, in only the regulation fur and heels. I take my companion's word for the fact that most of them have tits _and_ a cock. I never quite understood the sexuality of the men in this city. The best looking women in the world – the Milanesa not the models – are in this town and yet all the sex for sale is by these sleazy 'tranny' mutants. Maybe Milano men, some of them anyway, like the best of both worlds, someone suggested, while another companion predicted that, with its deadly combination of homosexuality, smack and rubber free sex, Milano is ripe for an AIDS epidemic to match the one in the city to which it likes to compare itself.

Slipping away from the tranny run, we drop into a bar for a late drink. It is in the early hours now, there are only a few people in the joint but Milano still does it right. The vodka comes in a frozen glass, the cognac comes in a warmed glass, and a Marguerita is served with a salted rim. Still looking at the world through a grappa haze – the traditional unholy trinity of apple grappa, honey grappa and the killer pepper grappa – we race home through the amber lights.

There are more trannies on a couple of the TV shows – big ugly buggers fooling no one – selling hard-core videos with nursery school plotlines (the chance meeting *à trois* on the beach seemed to be a particular favourite) with all the stilted banality of the local car salesmen you see selling second-hand autos on local television in the States.

When I fell asleep around four, what looked like a girl was rubbing her butt with a balloon, there was still heavy trading going on in the shadows of the Cimitero Monumentale and I was finally starting to understand the desperation with which the Milanesi bolt down their early morning *espresso*.

When it is morning in Milan you ingest your *panini* and *brioche* without ever letting your fingers touch your breakfast. Everything comes tucked up in a small paper napkin that must always be kept between fingers and food. Businessmen delicately dab their lips, drink their *pronto caffe* with heaped spoonfuls of sugar and run for their train.

Milano was the home town of Mussolini's *Fascisti* – the party was founded there in 1919 – and though there is no plaque on the lamp posts where partisans strung up and then beat to pulp the bodies of Benito Mussolini and his mistress, the unlucky-in-love Clara Petacci, there is a huge, fabulous butcher's shop called La Prima – the first, the prime – at the nearby Loreto metro, where the endless sides of prime beef hanging on hooks serve as an ironic reminder of the bloody fate of both *Il Duce* and Italian Fascism. The most permanent reminder of the city's blackshirt past is the gigantic Stazione Centrale, the building designed – as is the way with dictators through the ages – to inspire awe. It is the city's major railway station and still in full working order – even if these days the winged horses the size of small office blocks on top of this Olympian ideal look a little laughable.

Italy is a country forever stumbling on the rubble of its past. All over Milan there are the bomb craters of construction work and signs boasting of the building of the town's third metro line – 'The Third Line Advances!' Except that the third line is advancing at snail's pace and has been doing so for years because the construction work keeps unearthing more priceless archaeological ruins.

Up in the misty streets of Milan the girls in fur click by on their heels and their younger brothers or sisters exchange Burghy-flavoured kisses in the middle of the Galleria. It is real teen tongue-down-your-throat passion, for one of the many fine things about the Milanesi is that they have no shame. They heavy pet in public, they

double park, treble park, sideways park, and even the haggard mas-
turbators buying their wet sex, anal sex, Ilona Staller sex, hard core
wank rags from the newstands do so with no furtiveness and stand
in the street examining their purchases with frowning interest.

Milanesi outbursts are always inventive, curses tending to in-
voke images of despair and pain. There is, _Non rompere le balle_
(don't break my balls), and that old standard, _Mi stai sul cazzo_
(you're on my prick), plus the three little pig curses – _Porca_
Madonna (pig Madonna), _Porca Dio_ (pig God) and, best of all,
Porca Misera (pig misery).

They are big on hand gestures. The undersides of the chin quickly brushed with the back of the hand (don't break my balls), the
same gesture executed slowly (a Lombardy shrug) or the forearm
quickly chopped with the side of the hand (let's go, _amico_).

In more reflective moments, the Milanesi murmur the word,
'Bo', which is not so much a word as an existential gasp, a philosophical shrug of the soul. 'Bo.' One time my taxi – yellow cabs
only here in the Big Olive – swung round the corner into a misty,
lemon coloured street that was paralysed with traffic.

'Bo,' my driver said quietly to himself, meaning we come from
dust, we return to dust, this is a brief intermission, that's the way
it is. 'Bo.'

Milan is too Italian to truly emulate the pressured, cooking atmosphere of New York, though the city does sprint at around the
same pace as dollar belt cities like St Louis, Chicago or Houston,
places where people come for days at a time to do business and get
out again, cities with a lot of visitors and a zero rating of tourists.
But for all its Lombardic work ethic, the Big Olive has a delicacy,
an easy grace about it that exists on all levels here from the garden
of the Hotel Diane where Paolo Roversi, a 16 million lire a day
fashion photographer, meets Nino Cerruti to discuss his new catalogue, all the way down to the tiny bars on Corso Garibaldi where
street sweepers and builders drop in for a mid-afternoon liqueur or
a glass of Sassela Valtellina.

And down in the Piazza La Scala, where the souvenir stalls are
selling small golden replicas of the Madonnina, La Scala ashtrays
and Ruud Gullit hats (a red and black AC Milan baseball cap and
dreadlock wig combined), you can pick up your copies of the pink
daily sportspaper, _La Gazetta Dello Sport_, and the glossy monthly,
Forza Milan! (come on/go for it/let's do it, Milan), where students
of the British game are surprised to find – among the usual action
shots, match reports and profiles – a series of photographs of star

players, the cream of world football, hard at work in their kitchens. For one of the most popular features in this AC Milan club magazine are players' recipes (Mario Bortolazis' *Quaglie Con Riso* – quail in rice – looked particularly tempting). No wonder some of our boys find it hard to settle out here.

And when you are leaving Milano, when you are on the road to the airport somewhere between the pale mountains and the hazy, lire-crazy Big Olive itself, it suddenly hits you how you are going to miss this place.

And you think of tonight, when you will be back home, and how the bridge at Porta Genova will be empty but the garden of the Hotel Diane will smell of campari and soda, and of how they will soon be heading for the pink and white neon of Le Tre Gazzelle on Corso Vittorio Emmanuele for a 60 second *espresso* hit. And of how, much later, the drums will be beating at Leoncino – 'the little lion' – the secret Brazilian club down a dark flight of stairs on Corso Garibaldi, and of the whores lining up for a couple of miles by the walls of the Cimitero Monumentale, and when you remember what it is like in the early hours hurtling towards a string of locked amber lights you think to yourself . . . *ah, Forza Milano . . . Bo.*

Copyright © Tony Parsons, 1988

Double-Breasted Suit, Collar & Tie

Tom Wolfe by Gordon Burn
July 1988

ALWAYS MAINTAINED that if anybody in an interview asked me what I wear to bed I would say double-breasted pyjamas with big lapels and frogging. Those things are so beautiful. They're what people *should* wear in bed. And I do in fact own several pairs, but they're made of such wonderful, heavy material, and all houses and rooms in America are so hot, you can't possibly wear anything like that. So my *official* answer is that's what I wear, but in fact I like nightshirts and the best ones I have are made by my mother.

In the morning I listen to the radio. I wake up to WINS, which is an all-news station, and I'll listen for barely an hour and 15 minutes. Although I go on doing it, I realise that it's a form of junky-ism. Brain-candy, like Warhol's *Interview* or watching soap-opera on television. You realise you've heard the same news item four times, and you're still listening.

Things are a little different since we've had a baby, though I must admit when I hear any crying in the night I mostly just roll over.

I get up at 8.30 and do some rather perfunctory exercises, touching my toes and that sort of thing. However I do stand on my hands. Unaided. A physical education teacher told me when I was in college that if you would stand on your hands 25 times a day, you'd remain in *top* shape up until you're 105 – at least. And he's probably right. The trick, though, is to find 25 times in a day when you can do this, and lead a normal life. Try it in New York and they'll lock you up.

But anyway the memory of this has made me do one hand-stand in the morning. The only thing is, my nightshirt comes sliding down over my head, so I have to make sure I'm out of window-range. Not that anybody would want to look in and see me up-ended.

I save my main wash of the day for last thing in the evening. I brush my teeth with Craig Martin toothpaste as it's the only one I can keep down. It doesn't do much for your teeth, but at least you don't throw up. My wife is usually up and doing something productive by this time, like taking care of the children or fixing breakfast, or maybe she's at work. She works at *Harpers* magazine.

In the morning I have my own blend of cereal. I have some Alpen muesli, some Post raisin-bran and some wheat-germ mixed up with some peaches, if they're in season, otherwise stewed apricots which my wife usually boils for me. And some Bigelow's constant comment tea. It has a little orange flavouring in it.

And then I make some feeble attempt to start some work at my desk. Right now I try to work every day, but I seem to spend the first two-thirds of the day doing a little of this and a little of that and, finally, if I get some work done, I'll do it in the evening. I keep telling myself that one day I'm going to get organised like Hemingway – 'Woke up as first light hit block by quarry' – but I somehow always end up working at night.

I lead a vertical life. We live on the top three floors of this building, and most of the morning I go up and down stairs answering the doorbell. Somebody was supposed to deliver a table today, so I kept roaring down to see if it was there. Because when they say 'sidewalk delivery' here, they mean it. They're going to leave the thing on the street.

I always look through the peep-hole, not that it makes a great deal of difference, of course, the people look so bizarre on the other side. You could hardly tell a friend if one came. You can just about make out the contours of a United Parcel delivery man.

This morning, as a matter of fact, one of the astronauts came by. Pete Conrad's one of the astronauts I wrote about in *The Right Stuff*, and he came by with his wife about eleven. If they'd been free, I would've indulged the Conrads in the great New York vice, the lunch. When I finished *The Right Stuff* I treated myself to some Lucullan lunches. The Emperor Lucullus, you know? He was quite a big trencherman.

Half the big corporations that remain in New York are here only for the lunch. You can move to Pleasantville and have a wonderful, serene atmosphere, and no place to eat except the company dining-room. It really is a big factor.

Then I wander over to the bank, cash a cheque. I think there's a little more cash being carried since the credit card companies started sending out all these really nasty letters about the interest rate going up and having to pay faster. Now we're all enjoying the novelty of spending real money.

I also end up doing a lot of window-shopping. I love to go down Park Avenue and take in the Mercedes showroom, which Frank Lloyd Wright designed. It's a forerunner of the Guggenheim. There's also a fabulous bathroom showroom up in the forties.

I can waste *days* in New York, just window-shopping. It's just marvellous. Where I grew up, in Richmond, Virginia, the biggest event was the State Fair which arrived for two weeks in September. Here, it's all year round. You have to keep your eyes open at all times.

I almost always wear a collar-and-tie, and lately a double-breasted suite, regardless of the weather. Where I grew up, all the men wore seersucker jackets with big halfmoon sweat-stains under the arm-pit. I thought they came that way. Some summers I've rented a place out of town, some I haven't. I like it here fine in Manhattan in the summertime. Nobody's here. You've got the place to yourself, and you just sweat it out.

I realised early on that clothes are one of the few honest express-ions people make about themselves. It's one of the few ways people reveal how they think of themselves and how they want to be treated. And I've bought a lot of clothes recently.

In the last few years, while I was writing the astronauts book and then the novel, I really had the idea it was evil to go out and buy things. Typewriter guilt. Whereas, in days gone by, that had been one of the ways I would break out of writer's block. Go get some clothes made. I'm now looking for someone who makes socks, which kind of seems like a last frontier.

My other cure for a block is to read Henry Miller. And the Miller I read more than anything else is _Tropic Of Cancer_. I found out that Philip Roth had done the same thing before he wrote _Portnoy's Complaint_, which actually I think is a terrific novel.

Miller in turn, of course, copied Céline, and Céline would spend four or five years making _Journey To The End Of The Night_ seem spontaneous. And that's the hardest thing in the world, I think, really. One of the most artificial and interesting and effective things in writing is to make the written word seem spontaneous. There are some Russian writers who I think are useful for that same purpose.

I do, I must say, get a lot of looks on the street that are not approving. People here don't want to be singled out for attention, and that may be wise. I have a feeling, however, that the more outrageous and unusual you look – unless you look unusually frail – the less interested muggers are going to be.

I don't think they want anything that looks unpredictable. I think they don't want the pimp look, and people who dress in a pretentious vein like myself share that quality with the pimp. The place I go to get my hats is frequented only by pimps and eccentrics.

So anyhow, after all these various fits and starts, in the evening, having accomplished nothing all day, I do the Royal Canadian Air Force exercises. As far as I know I'm the last person anywhere who does them. It's mostly hopping up and down. But the nice thing about them is that it only takes eleven minutes and you can do them anywhere.

I wish I could think of some terrific lies for you, but there it is. Not a very fascinating sort of day.

Copyright © Gordon Burn, 1988

The PoMo Dance

Post Modernism by Tom Baker

July 1988

W HAT IS POSTMODERNISM? The question is asked often enough, if not too often. Goddamn it, it's even the title of a book by Charles Jencks, who has built (or perhaps that should be designed) himself a neat career out of asking and pretending to answer it. But really, one is not even sure how one writes the bloody thing. Postmodern? Post-Modern? PoMo?

I first heard the word in 1984 at a lecture by the French thinker Jean-Francois Lyotard called 'The Postmodern Condition'. I don't remember much about it, except that it was obscure in a way that was more prosaic than seductive, and that it hung around the words 'crisis of legitimation'.

Four years later and I seem to be hearing it every day. The steady debasement of art-words into common clichés is nothing new. Surrealism, for instance, which even went to the trouble of making manifestos, saw its keyword revived as an alternative to 'wow'; 'Uh, like, y'know, it was, er, surreal, yeah.' Likewise 'postmodern' has become the smart version of 'designer' or 'style' – an all-purpose tag with built-in intellectual cred.

Still, one has to admit that it is a very useful word. You can apply it to architecture, music, clothes, painting, salad vegetables, literature, kettles, restaurants, films, mineral water; anything, in short, you don't quite know what to say about. The trouble is that, after a while, it gets difficult figuring out what Jorge Luis Borges, Talking Heads, Arugula, the Starn Twins, Jean-Paul Gaultier, Pee Wee Herman and bottles of Ramlösa water have in common.

The one thing they share is that they are all 'postmodern'. Still, that doesn't say much about *how* they do what they do, only *when* they happen to be doing it. If we want to get literal about it, then the word 'postmodern' is not only meaningless but self-contradictory, unless referring to the future. But then, for the truly 'postmodern', there is no future, only a massive past, to be sampled, plundered and appropriated until the Cruise comes home. An orgy in the library.

There is something arrogant and smug about any self-conscious use of the prefix 'post'. It carries such an implication of tired superiority. It is also incredibly depressing, since it suggests a full stop or, to borrow the vernacular of PoMo, an impasse. Maybe that's why the anniversaries seem to be multiplying of late. This year was the anniversary of 1968. Last year was the anniversary of 1967. Sometimes it feels as if we are attending the wake of history.

If describing something as 'postmodern' makes the speaker feel smart, then I suppose that is only fitting, since cleverness is what it is all about. Cleverness, self-consciousness and irony of the most earnest, unamusing kind. While a 'postmodern' play and a 'postmodern' building may seem to have plenty of differences in style, they will be sure to share one thing in common: both will be about themselves. Similarly, when you turn the page and the novelist pokes his head out of the paragraph and waves hello, you know you are reading a 'postmodern' novel. You also know that you are smart. 'Dear reader' was never like this.

Call me a sentimental fool, but one of the things I have always valued in any form of art is its ability to make me forget, however temporarily, that is a piece of art. But the 'postmodern' dance, having deconstructed the myth of the imagination, has no time for this. And here we have the problem. The problem with 'postmodernism' is that it heralds the triumph of the intellect over the imagination, of criticism over creation.

Deconstructing a myth does not kill it. At least, one hopes not; a world without myths would be a sorry place indeed. Apart from anything else, there would be nothing to deconstruct anymore. Still, since the 'postmodern' age is – or acts like – the last age, we don't need to worry about that any more. Don't tell me you didn't know we were on the Eve of Deconstruction.

As it happens, what we have done is exchange the myth of the artist (original, creative genius, that sort of thing) for the myth of the critic. There is nothing wrong with being a critic, but a critic should be a fan, and his or her views on a work of art ought to be addressed principally to other fans, not to the artist. Anything produced with critics in mind is a dead end. Besides, it ought to be axiomatic that a critic's knowledge is derived from the material s/he writes about, as Shoshana Felman (literature), Rosalind Krauss (art) and Roland Barthes (everything) have shown. Not the other way round.

The 'postmodern' boom seems to have coincided with the *amockalypsism* of the early Eighties. Perhaps it will fade with the Reagan–Gorbachev accord. Certainly people seem to be fed up with 'witty' jackets, sculptures that illustrate catalogue articles, television programmes that assume an attention span of half a minute and lists masquerading as magazine articles. But where can we go from here? What are the prospects for post-postmodernism?

Where's the Beef?

The Penis by Julie Burchill
September 1988

'Those English girls, they do love a big cock. Size queens, we call them.' – Andy Warhol to Fiona Russell Powell in The Face

T HE BODIES WHICH WOMEN are born with, from the Rokeby Venus to the Goude Grace, have always been the slaves of male taste and artistic whim. The ideal woman shouldn't have feet of clay; but it will be better for her popularity if she has breasts, hips and lips of clay – all the easier to cut down and build up with the changing trend. It has always been men who have judged and shaped the wildly contradictory ideas of beauty that women feel compelled to live up to.

Many of these image-makers are misogynist; a leader in the field, a stylist feared beyond all others, asked a girl I know, 'What's it like being a woman – walking around like an open wound?' Unfortunately, she didn't ask him how it felt walking around like an itsy-bitsy teeny-weeny cocktail sausage. It is to such men that the image of women is entrusted.

Whereas blacks who bleach their skin are seen as self-loathing traitors to their race, women who undergo medical mutilation are not perceived as in any way sick. The breast is currently the most pathologised part of the female body and has less chance than any other part of the body bar the teeth of going to the grave intact. Interestingly, one of the most unappealing words of recent years has been 'boob', denoting a breast, a mistake or an embarrassment. That a slang word for the penis might denote a mistake or an embarrassment is unthinkable (though much more accurate, some would say).

The shaving down (Dido Goldsmith) or the pumping up (Mariel Hemingway) of the breast has made men millionaires. Even more than public breast-feeding, cosmetic surgery has rendered the breast a public property, a family affair, with little left to mystery and imagination. In a riotous story of American mores, Jacqueline Stallone first found her daughter-in-law with another woman (and it wasn't the Avon Lady) when she went over to the house to help Brigitte choose her new silicone implant by way of a gesture of reconciliation. Just like picking out wallpaper.

No part of the female body escapes the schizoid scrutiny of meat à la mode. Behinds: one decade Monroe, the next Twiggy – try performing *that* miracle of deflation. Hips: from La Lollo to the Shrimp. Hair: the blonde bimbo and the brunette vamp have been played off against each other since Pickford and Bara. Even mouths can't make up their mind where to draw the line; Clara's bow or Nastassia's overbite? Surgery and silicone, lyposuction and lipstick, diet and dye; all the sleight of hand that carvery and cosmetics can manage make the modern girl.

Men, even in the meat markets of entertainment, do not face these pressures. The rules are so different that even that which is unattractive – Woody Allen's skinniness, Dustin Hoffman's dwarfism, Bruce Willis' chrome dome – are re-interpreted as 'off-beat' sexiness. Men alter perceptions to accommodate their bad features; women alter themselves. It's the difference between self-defence and suicide.

Every physical setback that can befall a man has been thoughtfully kitted out with a safety net of its own; no wonder they fly through the air with the greatest of ease. Keep taking the tabloids: WHY BALD MEN ARE SEXY, WHY UGLY MEN ARE SEXY, WHY OLD MEN ARE SEXY, WHY ROBBIE COLTRANE IS SEXY (surely the hardest one to stomach). Men are judged as the sum of their parts while women are judged as some of their parts; men are judged as an entity, and their failings alchemised into trademarks, while women are judged in cold feet and inches. Men have charisma; women have vital statistics. Considering the merciless scrutiny to which their bodies have been subjected down the centuries, it really is time that women – always too nice for their own good, especially when horizontal – took the gloves off. Or more specifically the English Glove, as the French call the condom, and had a good hard look at what's inside. Because there you will find the most vital statistic of all.

* * *

In recent years, ever since the so-called sexual revolution – a licence to print funny money if ever there was one – there has been a great deal of stress laid by would-be sexual experts on the idea that penis size is unimportant. As with most liberal sexual ideas, what makes the world a more comfortable place for men makes it a duller and more dangerous one for women – including pornography, kerb-crawling and 'no fault' divorce. The myth of all penises being equal is another one – started, I can only conclude, by a sexologist who had the misfortune to be hung like a hamster.

Technique, not size, is what matters, goes the line. But after three decades of this accepted wisdom, 98 per cent of women interviewed by author and sex researcher Shere Hite declared themselves 'disappointed' with heterosex. If all men are equal, and technique can be learned, why should this be so? The answer is that once the foreplay's over, what's left in the bed is the three of you – the boy, the girl and the beef.

The denial of the importance of size is just another brick in the wall of male ego armour, and has done absolutely nothing for the sexual enjoyment of women. On the contrary, it has given them yet another sexual failure to take the blame for – if any size will do, it must be *my* fault I don't feel anything.

Nonsense. Show me a frigid woman and I'll show you a little man. Face it; no one, given the chance, would *choose* the small model. If they're so adequate, why is the dildo industry built on twelve-inchers? Why do pop stars stuff things down their trousers rather than bind down the offending object? And why are condoms never marked Small, Medium and Large but Large, Jumbo and Super Jumbo?

How big is big? More than eight inches. More than ten can be problematic, but not half as problematic as less than seven. All men and women with the sense they were born with know this, despite 30 years of establishment bleating to the contrary. The penis is mightier than the sword of Damocles when it comes to hanging over the heads of men, threatening to puncture their sense of self with every step they take towards the bed. Their obsession, far too heavy for them to carry alone, has been pushed on to the shoulders of women, blacks and other beasts of burden since the year dot. But the myth of penis envy has no grounding in fact; I have never met a woman who contemplated the extension without a degree of horror. As a Verity Bargate heroine says when asked by her leering Freudian analyst if she has ever wanted one, 'No, because it might be small. And men seem to worry about that.'

The proof is in the cuttings on the plastic surgeon's floor; since

the first sex change in 1952 – the American GI George Jorgenson –
there have been hundreds of thousands of male to female oper-
ations. But not until 1977 was the first reverse operation performed
on a girl student from Missouri, and less than 50 have followed.

It is not women who suffer from penis envy but *men*, envying other
men's; one man's meat is another man's quarter-pounder. When
not kidding themselves that women want to be constructed like
them, they are tormenting themselves that the 'inferior' races are
hung like *Übermensch*. Racist literature – such as it is – from the
Ku Klux Klan to the British Movement, spends an unnaturally long
time brooding over the sexual desires and capacities of its *bêtes
noires*.

Clever black men have always exploited this legend. Jack Johnson, the first black heavyweight champion of the world – dying in
1946 – rode round Chicago in his Stutz Bearcat with his white girl
and white wine sipped through solid gold straws, even playing
Othello. When he said 'I can get any white woman I want,' a hundred Texans arrived in a lynch party. Rioting whites, every time
Johnson knocked out a white man or knocked up a white woman,
caused the deaths of 19 people in seven years. Johnson was unrepen-
tant; hearing talk of his 'gigantic, over-sized thing', he laughed and
wrapped yards of gauze bandages around it before parading round
the ring in the skintight trunks of the day. Loose boxer shorts as we
now know them were introduced soon afterwards.

The great white hope today is that the racists were wrong and
all men are created equal, especially from the waist down. The biggest black box office draws of today are effete or asexual –
Murphy, Prince, Jackson. Millie Jackson has a routine about how
bad black men are in bed, while Richard Pryor says, 'We can't go
all night. *I* can't. I can go for two minutes, and then I need eight
hours sleep and a bowl of Wheaties.' No wonder the white boys
love him. (White girls, however, have yet to be convinced; some
years ago a London model agency took an informal poll of its girls'
sexual tastes. Black men won by a nose. Or something.)

As surely as blacks were once slaves to whites, white men are
slaves to their genitalia. Only they will never be free. Female sex
symbols are shown in gloating biographies in a constant state of
anxiety over the size and shape of their breasts the minute they hit
26 – big deal; a good 90 per cent of men worry about the size and
shape of *their* equipment from the age of 12 till the day they die.

The tensions in this silent war of self-loathing constantly erupt.

The murder of women by men they are married to or live with is running ever higher, usually over some alleged sexual slur. The husband of a flat-chested woman can drool over Linda Lusardi eight days a week, and if she killed him for it she'd be awarded a one-way ticket to Broadmoor. But let a woman disparage a co-habiting penis, and she can be killed on the spot by its owner while *he* gets away with a suspended sentence – they call it a crime of passion when what they mean is a crime of temper tantrum. She 'taunted' him, the defence invariably say.

Pretending that all men are born equal has done nothing to quell their sexual neuroses; sex crime of all sorts, from indecent exposure to incest, is on the eternal up. So why shouldn't we at least enjoy the luxury of telling the truth? Which is that the small penis is the mourner at every wedding and the time bomb in every bed, ready at any minute to have its pin pulled and its bluff called by a cross word.

'But it's not their fault!' soft-hearted, half-witted Earth Mothers will bleat. Well no; but is it any woman's fault that she's a 32B in a culture which worships Samantha Fox? If women can take the rap for the bodies they are born with, so can men, the sensitive little blossoms. Until then, until they learn to say what they want, women are going to have to like what they get. Time to take the gloves off – and hit below the belt.

Though Miss Burchill believes this to be a fine piece of writing and the very first of its kind, she no longer believes it to be true. In fact, the smaller the better. A complete absence is particularly welcome.

Copyright © Julie Burchill, 1988

All Mouth and Trousers
The Professional Cockney by Stuart Cosgrove
September 1988

ACCORDING TO POPULAR HISTORY, a cockney is someone who is born within the sound of Bow Bells, in the few miles of East London bordered by Stepney, Mile End and Bethnal Green. But as history adjusts to everyday parlance, a cockney has become someone who drives taxis, supports Millwall, drinks down the Balls Pond Road and in the eyes of BBC producers is the veritable salt of the earth. The cockney has been severed from the lived experiences of East London and become a type: 'You know what ahm sayin'?'

Cockneys are no longer defined by their place of birth nor by the shifting fortunes of the East End. The Victorian opium dens of Whitechapel Road, the Jewish immigrants in Bethnal Green, the anti-fascist defence of Cable Street, the camaraderie of dockers' apprentices, and the community values that still linger on in the displaced new estates of Basildon, have been swamped by Derek Jameson's 'cor blimey' diplomacy and the dregs of Jim Davidson's joke-book.

The real life virtues of cockney culture have long been subsumed by the caricature and corruption of cockney manners that today passes for the real thing and which has made the professional cockney one of the boom professions of the Eighties. The extent of media coverage has allowed cockneys to assume a complex of such superiority that they – and they alone – see themselves as the chosen people. But chosen by whom? And for what?

When the cockney ceased to be a real person and became a generalised type, the floodgates opened in the East End and a new enterprise culture focused on the docklands. It had nothing to do with converting old warehouses into new art galleries and wine bars, and much more to do with converting old stereotypes into new contracts. The era of the professional cockney had arrived in earnest.

From the blitz years, when the British film industry pumped out morale-boosting scenarios of ordinary folk, to be followed later by a series of domestic crime capers set in post-war London, the fictional cockney ceased to be simply an old music hall sideshow *à la* Max Miller and became an important character in the dramatic map of urban Britain. A landmark was *The Blue Lamp* (1950), a troubled examination of post-war male youth, in which the hapless Jack Warner – the archetypal London bobby – is shot dead by a teenage Dirk Bogarde, only to be magically resurrected as the BBC's early evening copper *Dixon Of Dock Green*. 'Evening all!'

Ironically, it was miles away from the East End, in the film studios of Elstree and Ealing, that the cockney was caught in the full beam of projected fiction. At the height of a bungled and inept bank robbery a pair of demob suits would dash into The Strand and hail a passing cab, and there sitting in complete innocence would be the happy cabby, played inevitably by the late Sam Kydd,

'Where to, Guv?' his only line as he unknowingly drove the crooks around the Monopoly board of bad editing.

Inevitably, the American imperialisation of the British film industry, the advent of television, and the multiplication of media outlets has shifted the centre of cockney creativity away from Elstree and in the process opened up untold opportunities for the professional cockney.

The BBC proved an even happier meeting place for the cockney than the film studio. From Stepney's favourite son, Des O'Connor, to Hackney's omniscient bore, Dennis Norden, the BBC has always been duped by a birth certificate franked by the holy fathers of Commercial Road. Imagine their excitement the night that Fred Housego won *Mastermind*. 'You wot? A cabby with brains. Well would you Adam and Eve it?'

Television has always been Barking mad. Only the BBC, ancestral home of the likeable scrap metal merchants *Steptoe And Son* and the cockney bigot Alf Garnett, could have seriously contemplated a weekly soap-opera called *EastEnders*. Only the BBC could be gullible enough to offer a part to cut-price cockney Mike Reid, and tolerate his twice weekly stumbling through unlikely pub dramas.

The cast of *EastEnders* or at least its main *dramatis personae* provide the best contemporary evidence that the cockney exists only in the realm of the social imaginary. Dirty Den is played by Leslie Grantham, a one-time cabby who served a jail sentence for manslaughter. Leslie's life is not real in any measurable sense, but a series of postures refracted through one of the professional cockney's most common pursuits: crime and punishment.

Dirty Den – the bastard as barman – is undoubtedly a character of the Eighties, a John Courage Thatcherite living under the rays of *The Sun*. But Grantham, more of a stereotype than the one he plays, is a cockney from the 'Scrubs, a man whose early life is a confused mess of half-remembered images taken from *Dixon Of Dock Green*, the twisted mythologies of the Kray Twins, the dialogue of a scene from *The Sweeney*, and next week's episode of *The Bill*. When Dirty Den quits Albert Square for good, Grantham will undoubtedly retire to a villa overlooking Marbella where he can rest forever on a self-satisfied sun-bed, and toy with the immortal line, 'You grassed me to the filth, you dirty slag.'

Anita Dobson, Den's 'fictional' wife, who was born in Bancroft Road Hospital off the Mile End Road and educated at Stepney's Coburn School For Girls, has all the right credentials. A drama school training at RADA has given her a plummy actress's voice, so her version of the East End has by necessity become a romanticised landscape that stretches from the spirit of the blitz to her favourite pie shop on the Bethnal Green Road.

If professional cockneys are not imagining a life of crime, they are wandering minstrels of a dispersed yesterday, yearning to be a chorus in Chas and Dave's next song. Anita Dobson's book *My East End*, a haberdashery stall of personal memories and social history, takes the reader on a journey into the heart of the professional cockney, quoting from Dickens and Hazlitt *en route*. Anita dwells on the magical land of rabbit and rhyming slang, virtually crying with the pain of lost youth as she recalls Tommy Steele – the professional cockney's answer to Rick Astley – singing his unforgettable masterpiece 'What a mouth, what a mouth, what a north and south.'

In the misty eye of the professional East End melancholic there is generally a happy reflection of days spent shopping in Petticoat Lane, or a Whitechapel streetmarket. It is here amongst the traders and the hawkers that the entrepreneurial spirit of cockney mythology was supposedly born. In the underworld of war-time spivs, cheap perfume sellers and modern-day ticket touts the professional cockney comes to life. In comic incarnation he is the likeable Del Boy from *Only Fools And Horses*; in reality he is Stan Flashman touting cup final tickets or a smug casual trying to make a buck outside Hammersmith Odeon.

The instinct for profit and a mouth as big as Bournemouth are essential characteristics for entrepreneurs in an era where the old rules have been put on hold. Alan Sugar, the most successful businessman of recent years, and boss of the Amstrad personal computer corporation, celebrated his first 20 years in business in July. In a gratingly sycophantic feature in the magazine *Your Computer* his story was told in full. Hail the pearly king of floppy discs.

'Alan Michael Sugar had a humble start,' the magazine reports. 'Born in 1947, he grew up in a Clapton council flat with a father who earned pocket money boiling beetroot before dawn for a local greengrocer.'

But the days of boiling beetroot were soon to give way to even greater enterprise. After leaving school at 16 and saving £80 he set up a business selling car aerials around the street markets of East London. Now worth an estimated £400 million, the magazine enthused that Sugar's fortune had been founded on 'the rough and tumble world of the stallholder and flypitcher'.

Alan Sugar is the professional cockney *par excellence*, his style is neither the imagined criminality of the East End gangland nor the twilight romanticism of Anita Dobson's Old Kent Road. Sugar's model of excellence is more likely to be Del Boy and the lads down Leather Lane market. He once told a mesmerised audience at the City Business School that the economics of computer technology were founded in East London. 'Marketing is just a stall in Petticoat Lane,' he told the assembled. 'The owner of the stall is offering his wares. The sales pitch, albeit very rural and loud, is no different from what a high cost advertising agency might apply.'

The rise of Alan Sugar's style of hi-tech cockney corporatism in which computers and cabbies share a secret power known simply as *the knowledge* has its direct equivalent in that other masonic order: the brotherhood of style.

Had Sugar been born a few years earlier he might have sold op-art T-shirts from a stall in Carnaby Street and exploited the street-wisdom of a passing cockney waif.

The early years of the Sixties and the social mobility that lay behind mod culture provided a whole generation of young Londoners with a tailor-made career on the catwalks of everyday London. Originally restricted to a few streets in Soho and Chelsea, by the Eighties the virus of style and its main carrier, the sharp cockney kid, had spread into an epidemic of models, designers, pop writers, DJs and style-counsellors.

The whole labour exchange of the 'youth era' was an obvious haven for professional cockneys, their proximity to the source of new styles and their contempt for the other world that lay north of Watford made them the most obvious page-boys for Britain's entourage of new fashion.

The cockney as style-king, a legacy that stretches from David Bailey's early photographic career to Jonathan Ross's *Last Resort*, finds its greatest expression in Len Deighton's *The Ipcress File*, a 1962 novel which became a manifesto for mod behaviour.

The novel's central character, a recalcitrant spy who's at odds with the authorities above him, acts out the flash behaviourisms of the loafer dynasty. Played to perfection by Hollywood's favourite cockney Michael Caine when it was made into a film, the words of *The Ipcress File* read like a day in the life of the London boulevardier.

'I walked down Charlotte Street towards Soho. I was probably seeking excuses to delay; I bought two packets of Gauloises, sank a quick grappa with Mario and Franco at the Terrazza, bought a *Statesman*, some Normandy butter and garlic sausage. The girl in the delicatessen was small, dark and rather delicious. We had been flirting over the mozzarella for years.'

How many times has Jonathan Ross retraced those steps as he heads up Charlotte Street to Channel Four? Deighton's novel signals a critical departure point for Londoners: an era where the West End became the only significant theatre of style, turning the East End – the habitat of the true cockney – into a place to boast about coming from. (Remember punk? Remember when assumed cockney accents were more ubiquitous than tartan bondage strides?) Even warehouse parties, the return of the cockney repressed, were West End values shunted up Old Street when the Old Bill were sleeping.

The rise of boutiques, club culture, small circulation magazines, and what is now described as the media, provided a new space for cockney enterprise. According to procedure London invented everything, so what more natural habitat for the young cockney fledglings than the aviary of trendy London?

As old faithfuls like Anita Dobson and Alan Sugar remember their version of the East End over a cup of hot tea in the rapturous company of a passing cabbie, the style cockneys give recourse to a different set of fantasies: a trial for Chelsea, a fight down in Brighton, a night at Le Beat Route and a best mate who's now inside. Danny Baker carried the fantasy on to television, Gary Crowley took it to radio and Spandau Ballet resolved their fantasies in pop.

But as London's young elite taught the world what was cool, the image of their beloved city and its typical citizen had been annexed by a different kind of elitism. Ironically, it was a political selfishness that combined the economics of Alan Sugar's market-stall, the Victorian myths of Anita Dobson's imagination, and the uncompromising violence of one of Wimbledon's less subtle tackles. Satirised to an extreme by Harry Enfield's Loadsamoney, the cockney has become a shabby personification of greed and arrogance.

In 1988, the term cockney has been cut adrift from any real relationship to the East End. It simply exists as a patronising cypher for beliefs that are nothing to do with the multi-cultural community in Spitalfields or the changing society of Docklands, and more to do with a series of prejudices that owe more to Thatcherism than living in London.

The time has come for Londoners to take the initiative to put the professional cockney to sleep: somebody has hijacked your stereo-type. 'Know what ah mean?'

Stuart Cosgrove is a professional Jock. Some of his best friends are Londoners, as it happens.

The Smirk

The Eighties' Wink by Steve Beard & Jim McClellan
September 1988

Amongst the saving faces of the decade (Reagan's charismatic idiot grin, the New Man's rueful half smile) there's one that sticks out as very late Eighties – the smirk. Either side of the Atlantic there's an obvious icon, Bruce Willis or Jonathan Ross. Both are smartasses in smart suits presiding over tongue-in-chic exercises in postmodern TV camp, and both have a smirk continually playing across their lips, an expression which says, 'Hey listen, don't take it seriously, this is ironic'. In Willis' case it's almost terminal, a silent scream – 'Hey, this is ironic you guys' – a perma-smirk etched across his face in a perfect diagonal down which you could roll a Motown 45.

And this look fitted the whole routine perfectly; the yuppie sex comedy, the self-conscious trickery, the hip references to pop culture, from *Top Cat* to The Temptations, the fast one-liners. Holding it all together was the Willis smirk. It took a while to perfect. Early on Bruce didn't really have the juice. His suits weren't sharp enough, his hair was too long and, crucially, he had too much of a pouty grin.

That face didn't fit at all. Pouting is too 'pretty', too mute, too above it all. It belongs back with English pop stars, neurotic boy outsiders and ethnic male models. It's hands off, whereas the smirk is hands on; someone with a smirk wants to play. If a pouter opens his mouth he expects or hopes to silence the opposition with a resounding put down. Smirkers like to leave room to manoeuvre. They like banter, wind-ups, one-liners, innuendo and gossip. Conversational cut and thrust is their ideal.

It's a matter of hints, dares, nods and winks. The smirk is knowing, amused, cynical and mocking – one element in a charismatic
calculus of economic gestures, shrugs and shuffles, hip-sways and
sashays, which measure the straight line from minimum movement
to maximum force. It's a change of tack from those outrageous ex-
penditures of yesteryear, Mick Jagger's leer and Johnny Rotten's
sneer. The smirk is something rationed, the face pulled by the
fatally smooth operator, by the expert seducer. Think of Mickey
Rourke; James Dean reborn with a smirk instead of a surly pout.
His immaculate cool guy routine in *Diner* as he effortlessly explains away the pecker-in-the-popcorn joke to his unnerved date in
the cinema lobby is a textbook exercise in how to tip the wink to
the boys without batting an eye.

But smirking means more than just giving the lie to the ladies. It
hints at moral dilemmas magically resolved, secret knowledge,
mysteries. It's a sign of a compromised conscience automatically
justified, simultaneously guilty and not guilty – what German
writer Peter Sloterdijk calls 'enlightened false consciousness'.
Exactly the attitude given by Dennis Quaid in the first, cynical (and
best) half of the *The Big Easy*. He plays a bent cop whose hit-and-
run smirk is the perfect flexible response to the inroads 'frigid', 'uptight' Ellen Barkin tries to make into his conscience. He gives her
the come-on she can't resist and the come-uppance she can't forgive. Jack Nicholson has a similar effect on three of Hollywood's
leading ladies in *The Witches Of Eastwick*. Finally clocking in a
performance which uses more of his face than just his forehead, his
smirk challenges them to believe he's not the devil in disguise.

Of course a smirk doesn't work for everyone. It can keep at
bay a receding hairline – think of Willis' spiky quiff, long on attitude and short on hair. Can a bald man smirk? It's a question
Bruce must have asked himself more than once. What about a
man in a toupée? No chance. And some situations aren't cut out
for it either. Smirking at the bank manager as you try to explain
your debt crisis is not a good idea. The delinquent yuppie indulging in a spot of recreational shoplifting might flash a knowing
smirk at a customer who catches him out, but it wouldn't work
with a store detective.

It's not an exclusively male preserve. Think of Mae West, Jean
Harlow and film noir *femmes fatales* like Lauren Bacall. In the
Eighties there's Paula Yates and Jerry Hall, those brazen hustlers
who've made a little go such a long way. The great heroine is
Mandy Rice-Davies, queen of getting away with it. 'Well he would

say that, wouldn't he?' is like a rhetorical smirk – all hidden knowledge, innuendo and barefaced cheek. Her smirk had it all: sex, corruption and success. Little wonder she's been canonised in the Eighties.

For the boys there's Orson Welles. His first appearance in *The Third Man* as black marketeer and con-artist Harry Lime is like the primal scene of smirk. Exposed in a shadowy doorway by the flick of a light-switch, his smirk taxes the credulity of Joseph Cotton, who thought he was dead, and dares us not to believe that crime doesn't pay. This is the smirker as tragic genius or fallen angel, completely different from today's immaculate multi-purpose media smirkers.

Bruce Willis, Jonathan Ross, Paula Yates, Jerry Hall – they've all torn a leaf out of the Welles account book by smirking their way into a career of permanent endorsement. But there was a genuine pathos about Welles' hustlings. He was trying to raise cash for pie-in-the-sky film projects which never got off the ground, whereas the new guys on the block are just seeing how far they can string out a line of chat before they get the chop. After all what is it they're pushing? Wine cooler (Willis), lager (Ross), low-alcohol wine (Yates) – watered-down, fizzed-up, de-alcoholised alcohol. And Jerry Hall? Bovril and cheap hair dye.

The smirk here is simultaneously celebrity get-out clause and audience challenge. It says, 'I wouldn't be seen dead buying it personally but here's another pay-cheque. Can you believe it?' These are careers based more on *F for Fake* than *The Third Man*, where the smirk lets you in on the joke but keeps the punch-line to itself. After Ross mugs his way through a third series, another ad and another front cover, you begin to think he's putting you down as much as putting you on. It's enough to make anyone a little down in the mouth.

Copyright © Steve Beard & Jim McClellan, 1988

─────────────

Take Me to the Bridge

A Weekend with David, Michael & Florence
by Kathryn Flett

March 1989

IVING IN FLORENCE must be a little like being in the 1989 cast of *The Mousetrap*. All you're expected to do is remember the lines and make sure the plot continues to unfold in time-honoured tradition. For the Italians, who, after all, appreciate being appreciated for themselves, being upstaged by a city must be an unsettling experience, but they are resigned to it. Like them, the first-time visitor should just go with the flow. The city is ridiculously beautiful. You know that – you've seen *Room With A View*. But Florence could probably get away with being half as gorgeous as it is and still leave you besotted. However, nothing in Florence is done by halves.

Despite having come for a quiet regenerative weekend, on arrival all I could hear was the sound of several thousand natives, who, having clocked-off, were all in desperate search of the Florentine crack. Against my better judgment I thought I'd join them.

I discovered that in Florence you are only 20 minutes walking distance from everywhere, or at least after I had walked for 20 minutes I found myself on the Ponte Vecchio at sunset. Despite having been recently re-plastered, the Ponte Vecchio at sunset is not to be sniffed at. It's small enough to feel a bit exclusive, even when shared with 500 Americans, and the view does not let you down. Peering into the Arno from the centre of the bridge, you can still watch huge lazy fish – with typical Latin insouciance – hang around in gangs. Despite being sepia-tinted like the rest of the city, the Arno is as yet unsullied by product endorsement from multi-nationals, with not a Coke can or McDonald carton in sight. At sunset, whilst throwing up its day job as Florence's answer to Hatton Garden and turning into a cross between Camden Market and Glastonbury with Gucci, the Ponte Vecchio somehow manages to remain A Thing Of Beauty and A Joy Forever. You realise that the place has you in its grip when a trio of hairy dissolutes strumming 'Blowing In The Wind' are not an immediately offensive proposition, unlike the one I received from the maracas player.

Even investing in a fake Louis Vuitton bag from one of the pavement hustlers comes closer to patronage of the arts than a tacky rip-off. This is the moment you feel yourself losing control. My response to this light-headedness was to down a swift *espresso* and head for the nearest church, which in Florence is always very near indeed. But I wasn't after just any old Renaissance pile, so I went to Santa Croce.

From the outside Santa Croce is relatively unassuming – at least compared to the Duomo, the city's cavernous *cassata* of a cathedral – but inside it more than makes up for any shy and retiring exterior. Walking through the front door one is confronted on the right by Michelangelo's final resting place. I don't know if he specifically asked to be buried here, but if I was Michelangelo there would simply have been no alternative. Santa Croce, crammed with the tombs of god-like men, is clearly the only place in which to seriously consider languishing for all eternity. Machiavelli is further up on the right, next to Rossini and a memorial to that other local-boy-made-good, Dante. Galileo, meanwhile, has practically the whole of the left-hand side to himself, hemmed in only by the occasional breathtaking, priceless work of art by Donatello. In appreciation of all this I found myself filling the Sante Croce steeple fund coffers with thousands of lire. Meanwhile the coachload of Japanese couples who had entered with me made sure the roof was catered for well into the 22nd century. We lit votive candles like crazy. It was that kind of place.

Feeling a bit over-aestheticised, it was time to think seriously about an evening in with the minibar and several hours of Italian TV. On Channel 9 I found a game-show of stupendously soporific proportions was under way. The game consisted primarily of a foam-rubber room within the studio, through the walls of which anxious contestants were urged to squeeze, foamily, via narrow slits. I thought this said a great deal about the Latin temperament, but not half as much as what was taking place on Channel 27. As I turned on to the cable porn show, I tuned right out and dropped off, missing, in the process, the outcome of The Girl In The Diaphanous Negligee Vs. The Bunch Of Gladioli. Shame.

Almost the best thing about hotels is breakfast in bed, the others being plastic shower caps and sachets of Easi-Wipe shoeshine. It's not hard to put away cappuccino, ham, eggs, croissants, toast, rolls, cheese, marmalade, cereal and orange juice when it's delivered by sleight of hand to your door at 9am. I needed building up, I decided, for today was to be Michelangelo's-David-and-Botticelli's-Venus day.

David is housed in a singularly unimpressive locale, the graffiti-splattered but loftily titled Academia Bella Arti. The Academia people try very hard to pretend that there's much more to their Academia than David, but who are they kidding? Fra Lippi? Who needs the Good Father when you can have The Big Dish? David is *very* big and *very* dishy. He has perfect pecs, a stony *hauteur* and is much taller in the flesh than in his photographs. So his right hand is a little bigger than his left – I saw no one asking for a refund. When faced with David, carved by Michelangelo from a single block of stone and without the benefit of a model, I felt a little sympathy for the fragile Italian male ego. Fact: the best-looking man in Italy is a figment of someone's imagination.

I lingered with David awhile to better study his profile, those shoulders, and a perfectly turned calf or two. And then I got the hell out into the fresh air.

Florence is awash with honeymooners, second honeymooners, dirty-weekenders, or just couples. Like Venice, it's a place to share with The One You Love, but as I'd reluctantly had to leave him behind in The Academia, it was back to solitary pavement-pounding. I began to feel a little wistful, thwarted perhaps, emotionally destitute even. Forlorn, lonely, tragically beautiful me made for The Uffizzi with the sole intention of throwing myself into a torrid affair with the smoothest Gianni-come-lately on the block. Either that or the Arno. But after queuing for 40 minutes with a young American couple bickering in front of me, all thoughts of unbridled lust in the afternoon hinged on finding the right mozarella and tomato *panini*.

The Uffizzi is big and full of art. I missed Botticelli's Venus on the first lap but caught up with it later. It was big and arty and I was, frankly, underwhelmed. But the Caravaggios, half a dozen rooms further on, with all that peel-me-a-grape erotic lighting and lush flesh, were the business. A sandwich seemed like a good idea.

I did other things in Florence. Like cracking open the minibar champagne and swigging it straight from the bottle on my balcony while the Florentine church bells tolled for me and my gall. Things like visiting the Giardino De Boboli and finding they had shut five minutes before I arrived. Dining out, enigmatically, on my own. Forcing myself not to spend 150,000 lire on a Moschino scarf. Buying, instead, postcards of David. And then it was time to leave.

The 12 o'clock train would get me to Pisa airport in plenty of time for my flight at 2.20. Handing in my keys at reception, I was informed of the 24-hour train strike, and of the lone bus that went to Pisa (but not the airport) via Rome or Bangkok, and which wouldn't arrive until 2. I was also informed of the price of a taxi to the airport and resigned myself to the inevitable. Switching my flight to the following day, I reacted to a now-familiar lightheadedness by downing a swift *espresso* and heading for the nearest church. Thanks, God.

Copyright © Kathryn Flett, 1989

New Frontiersmen
The Wild West Man by Ian Penman
March 1989

> '*Anti-fashion! Terrific. Everybody had sworn off fashion, but somehow nobody moved to Cincinnati to work amongst the poor. Instead, everyone stayed put and imported the poor to the fashion pages.*' TOM WOLFE

ON THE COVER OF *Vanity Fair* is a loving anniversary album snap of a gnarled and plaintively retro couple from the Ol' West. PARDNERS IN STYLE: HOME ON THE RANGE WITH . . . Robert and Mrs Redford? Clint and Mrs Eastwood? Ronald and Mrs Reagan? Any of these might grace the cover of *Vanity Fair* in cowboy rags, tags and bobtails . . .

The answer is none of the above. This is the couple who would dress down the Redfords, the Reagans and the Eastwoods should they go for that particular angle. This is Ralph and Ricky Lauren, immaculately scuffed and scruffed, living lovebirds on the New Frontier. The only thing which blots the yesteryear effect is the glare from Ralph's gleaming snow-white choppers, which look like a year of any cowboy's tax returns.

Flip *Vanity Fair* over on its back and we find *the* advertisement for this sort of thing: the Marlboro man. Strange enough that this image – by now hilariously malaprop through its entry into gay iconography – is still there, bluntly unironic in the saddle. Stranger still that *Vanity Fair*, the first and last word in American urbanity, should be bookended by two caches of honcho imagery.

Or is it? What better way of signifying a sweet uncomplicated marriage than being snapped by funky Bruce Weber in prairie dress? Instead of being framed by LA pool or in NY sitting-room – where everyone knows that couples spend no time together except to bicker or batter – Ralph 'n' Ricky are arranged as if to say *this* is where *we* belong. Forget all that hi fashion empire lark, we have desert hearts; we cleave not only to one another but to the past – that's where we're coming from.

Presumably no one *needs* to be there on the ranch (the Double RL, 13,000 acres in southwestern Colorado: 'an authentic, rustic, nineteenth-century cattle ranch, no expense spared'); it's more like your Seventies British Rock Star retiring to the country for privacy (the sort of privacy you invite fashionable photographers to capture and display for all the world to see) and 'roots' – even if your actual roots are in a tenement in Hull or the Lower East Side.

To plump for the 'authentic' over the 'fake' these days is a meaningless distinction, a virtual irrelevancy, for it amounts to the same thing: a cultural decision, a choice, an advertisement for yourself. This is how Ralph 'n' Ricky come over in that garb: *authentically fake*. Along similar lines, I recall a Herb Ritts photo of Mel Gibson which did its darndest to make him look like something that had stepped out of a *Grapes Of Wrath* dustbowl; it doesn't come with info attached so you're left uncertain whether he was got up this way for a role, or whether it's all Ritts's printing and artifice. Whether it's one or the other or a mixture of both, ambiguity wins out. Really, what is it a picture of?

We're obviously on some sort of frontier, here.

The Frontier is the point, the subliminal line, where America marks and markets the confusion of its past. The Frontier is both a real historical moment and a lingering, pervasive iconography, to be dipped into to sell everything from cultural integrity to low-tar fags. Ransack US cultural forms and you will find The Frontier constantly dissimulated, lurking, metamorphosed.

The Frontier is crucial because in its essence it fuses the historical and the aesthetic: it founds American history as an imagistic lure. The Frontier is the founding terrain for all subsequent mythic routes; the many frontiersmen – trappers, traders, miners, cattlemen, farmers – gel into the essence of Independent Man.

The 'crisis of the Frontier' comes when the safety valve of free land is gone, and with it the possibility of a continuous re-creation of society. 'The end of the West' is a break for the border. The Frontier has to confront its own frontier, its own end – a boundary in which you change into something else or wither away and die; in which you learn a new language of mobility and motility. It's a shift to do with the taming of nature and the taming of the essential nature of men. The brutal nature of this man's world must be softened to fit in with a capitalistic tendering and cultivation of Mother Nature. The wandering, plundering, all-male gang represents death, or at least something that cannot reproduce itself. The outlaw leaves no legacy but myth, and must give way to legislations of every kind. Politics especially is always represented in Frontier paens as *a priori* a corruption: as an essential corruption of unwritten laws, a division of man from what makes him beat, from what he should Know and Do unprompted.

The cultivation of the Frontier involves the stripping away of European graces and foibles in the confrontation with raw nature. There is an almost literal birth of profit from dust – in this Garden of Eden money might grow on trees. What mustn't be forgotten is that to the God fearin' who settled in this Frontier world must have seemed like a literal enactment of Biblical narrative. The Bible would be the solace and framework to deal with premature death, hardship, the brutality of the moment; and the myths of the West have operated over the years in a very similar way to that of the Bible: historical facts and figures have transmuted into myth, people 'believe' in them not just as a transcendent fiction, but as a grid for moral behaviour. But if the West is a negative theology in which Might is Right (and the cowboy an avenging angel), it is just as likely to produce gun-toting delinquents out for all they can get when times give them nothing; the journey from Billy The Kid to Gary Gilmore is not very far.

Frontier America is a child that must renounce its wild wings of want to be adopted into the public Good. But only so far: the American Dream will always be that of the hick who hits the top – and who needn't change that much to do so.

The idea is that you – Howard Hughes, Elvis Presley or Ronald Reagan – triumph preciseiy through your hick attributes, your 'knack'. The nightmare side is that the world of opulence and power is not your natural realm – your past will show through, give you away, bring you down (like James Dean in *Giant*).

The world of Frontier nostalgia, it need hardly be said, is very much a boy's world. The attachment to Smalltown that can be found from Springsteen to Sam Shepard, across Dirty Realism and grungy Rockism, could be considered ever so slightly umbilical.

Needless to say, no girl ever wanted to traipse back to the small-minded town of drudge and damaged nerves. 'The only way I can end it,' said uptown girl Madonna, of the pressured life she has won for herself, 'is if I move to Boise, Idaho, and live on a farm and milk cows for the rest of my life. But I'm not going to do that. I prayed for 17 years to get out of the Midwest and I don't want to go back.'

The immigrant Jewish/Italian Big City has always been about smart talk and sophistication; about dressing up rather than down, and about the vaporous money of the idle rich which comes out of the air rather than the ground. You can't imagine Springsteen inside a suit, mixing a Martini for his doll in some penthouse. Boys eulogise the badlands where airy nothingness seeps into your poor soul; boys find something petty-Ulysses about these journeys into the dead interior. The girls know it's just about being tied to a life that's killing your spirit – they want to get out and stay out.

In the Western, 'whatever its plot line, the violence of nature and of men will be an essential part of its landscape; and it will probably reach its moral and emotional climax in a singular act of violence . . .' (_BFI Companion_). This is also what we have most disliked in America as a geopolitical force: the inability to reason and the consequent espousal of violent solutions to complex problems. Politically, the idea of the Frontier is linked with the reality of American expansionism: we imagine that the Frontier was an especially violent environment; and that this Frontier mentality has played a dominant role in shaping American institutions and national character.

Rambo is the ultimate _emusculation_ of the lost Frontier. The establishing Rambo film (_First Blood_) is about the Frontier community itself turning on the lone wolf – one of its own who strayed, in a far-flung American Frontier action. The whole series exploits the bereaved anger of Vietnam veterans, in whose figure is restated the classic Frontier-type bitterness of having been 'cheated out of' some right or legacy that had been fought for.

Rambo deserves our respect for his self-sufficiency and his sense of the Right Thing to do (echoes of Ollie North), and 'his major political battle is against that image of all governmental action – or inaction – that we disapprove of, the bureaucracy' (Robert Phillip Kolker, _A Cinema Of Loneliness_, 1988). In the last Rambo film, the evil Russian was presented as Computerman – all alienated technology – whereas Rambo is essentially a barely updated Mountain Man, knife in teeth, at home in nature while wreaking havoc through it.

A man often condemned as the most boorishly apocalyptic Frontiersman of the modern age was Sam Peckinpah, 'patron poet of the manic depressives', as Pauline Kael once called him. But Peckinpah the man, rather than myth, had a real claim on at least the Frontier angle of his mythic world. It *was* his world to begin with:

'When I was five or six years old I remember riding my horse up around the pines in Crane Valley. Her name was Nellie, and I'd only have a rope around her neck for a rein – a hand-made hackamore. It was where my grandfather, Denver Church, ran his cattle. And a couple of miles away, my Grandfather Peckinpah had built his sawmill. It was the finest time of my life. There will never be another time like that again.'

The Peckinpah family is rooted in California pioneer history: there is a Peckinpah mountain and Peckinpah mill north of San Francisco; and the prospecting town of Coarsegold in *Ride The High Country* (aka *Guns In The Afternoon*) actually existed; and there really were places with names like Hooker's Cove, Whiskey Creek, Deadman's Gulch, Dogtooth and Shuteye. When Peckinpah grew up life would have been more nineteenth than twentieth century in flavour.

In his Westerns, Peckinpah shows both sides of his lost Eden – the grotesque and the grand; that people had a communal dignity although at the edges egalitarianism was always exploited by less salubrious elements. *Ride The High Country* and *The Wild Bunch* are masterpieces of Frontier iconography – analyses of violence and violent analyses; films that expose the dying of a certain yearning, but cannot stop themselves from adding to it. The topographies of subsequent films may inhabit the modern highway, town and city, but they detail the same mental landscape: the loner who is dogged down by logic; the disappointment of living on, separated from the real code, the code of the wild.

In *The Wild Bunch* everything is staged on the crumbling, insecure, violent borderline – not just between two nations, but codes of civil law and savage retribution, old and modern. The outlaws' anachronistic code has no-place in *modern* society and the border is literally the site of this no place. The film essays a very real historical breach between times – the coming of the automobile, organised capital, automatic weaponry, etc – and the infamous choreography of violence becomes a ritual interruption which marks beginnings and ends.

America's abiding topic since the late Fifties has been the Self, and the only true freedom left might be freedom from the shackles of self-analysis. This is one reason for the eternal return of the mute, self-contained Frontiersman; his trail is still the site in the nation's unconscious, where a 'man can be free', alone with his thoughts, or just alone with his horse. In the Sixties and Seventies the car and bike were substituted for the horse, but the appeal was the same: urban man was overstimulated and oversensitised and the boundless range became the endless Road.

On this Road stumbled such mangy conglomerates as The Beats; Ken Kesey's Merry Pranksters; the hippie dudes of *Easy Rider*; the Hell's Angels; Bob Dylan's Rolling Thunder Review. These *à la mode* outlaws were on the run from a straight society which allowed for no wandering. Beats and Hippies dropped out into mountain ridge, desert and cliff-edge retreat, into the wagon-circle self-defence of the Commune.

Recently we've seen the advent of Designer Hippiedom, with the all-purpose purging paraphernalia of New Age. The very phrase seems to have something Frontier about it – the promise of a revision, a cleansing return to certain values.

Bruce Springsteen has been many monuments to many people, and retained throughout a dogged sincerity, a strong-jawed work ethic, a wild romanticism – all marks of a Frontiersman. The garrulousness of his song, the windiness and spoiled optimism, the strenuous work-out marathon of his shows says Frontier all over.

Early Springsteen is decidedly urban: it's all flashing flick knives and tail fins. But in 'Nebraska' and 'Born In The USA' he returns – as did fiction, cinema and politics in the Eighties – to the small-town heartland; the tone is wistful-prosaic, Springsteen's characters are men for whom all frontiers have crumbled.

His return coincided with the Reaganite realignment of the broken white picket fence. His pessimism is rousing: it re-invigorates even at its most despairing. It is what those who love him love him for; and what the great unmoved like myself feel uncomfortable with. In 'Born In The USA' the smalltown man was bent and bowed, his turf run down, emptied of employment and purpose and hope.

If Springsteen's smalltown is a boulevard of broken dreams, Ronald Reagan's was a cherry blossom time of family picnics and Bible readings. The point is that neither one is any more or less authentic than the other: that to which Reagan appeals in America is a reality we would be unwise to scoff at. Both Springsteen and

Reagan work as artful condensations of the vocabulary of nostalgia and lack. The appeal is to the breakdown of a frontier on which you know you can stand; which you can cultivate, better and pass on to happy, healthy children. Reagan especially appeals to the sense of moral frontiers – a frontier being something over which you pass never to return home again, with all the overtones of fall and sin and come-uppance; with the City identified as probably inferior and a distant source of sin and contamination. Reagan's frontier can be taken in an almost literal sense of the hearth and its values; of plain-speaking and common sense in man and money management. Thatcher has tried to do something similar but without the same fundamentalist charge – all problems are displaced from government responsibility back on to the Family. It's politics as *Bonanza*; if a man isn't strong enough to manage his kinfolk then maybe he just deserves all he gets . . .

Reagan's term saw lots of photo opportunity snaps of the Great Communicator roaming his ranch in backyard clothes – born to run for the USA! And we gazed upon that iconic reverse crotch shot of Springsteen's 'Born In The USA' sleeve – stars and stripes, white T-shirt, workingman's non-sexual-preference-signifying cap in the back pocket, the complete ensemble. Once Levi 501s successfully re-produced themselves every other company picked up the denim tab. In the glitzier pages both Calvin Klein and Georges Marciano's Guess? campaign shot peachy young models in every stage of ranch-hand rough and tumble. *Paninari* favourites Chipie have gone one step further with an entire range of rodeo wear for the city dweller – thick yellow rodeo gloves to furl round your scooter handles or mountainbike grips.

Think of all the different appeals to Frontier authenticity that have been stitched into denim down the ages. As Duncan Webster points out in his book *Looka Yonder* (*The Imaginary America Of Popular Culture*), no one ever sold a pair of jeans, period, without reference to some period guise: 'The Lee Rough Riders campaign of 1986 consisted of images of work frozen as history and tradition. Underneath is the slogan "The Jeans That Built America", while in the corner one sees the Lee Rough Riders patch ("Founded Kansas 1889") and this information: "Heavyweight 15 oz. denim. Original leather patch. Stonewashed finish, Copper rivets. Brass buttons. Heavy-duty fly. That's how we build the jeans that built America." '

It's all there in the constellation of unflash adjectives – authentic, original, heavyweight. As is the case with many appeals to the

Spirit of the Lost Frontier, the historical accuracy is not in doubt; Levi did, after all, launch their denim workwear for lowly cowboys and girls. Its origins are on the trail – where it would once have denoted a proud underclass; work, ceaseless work, from which the outsize denim gradually assumed a gnarled, plaintively parched character, the second skin of gnarled plaintively retro-characters.

Denim is democracy dressed down. Such is its global success as fashion esperanto (the original product of the American underclass to be taken up by the rest of us), it's become the symbol (with Coca-Cola) of America's state as the world's premier symbol market.

Sam Shepard is the Frontiersman's Harold Pinter, for whom the frontier ('the West's spiritual wasteland') is Buddhist: you trip out into the wilderness to contemplate … nothing. John Lahr: 'Shepard is dramatising the confusion of the West, neither pioneer experience nor earthly paradise.'

Shepard constructs an iconography out of the detritus, out of the cast-off and the cheap plastic emblem. In this sense he is more 'honest' than the tradition of the Marlboro/Hemingway brute; he does at least admit the possibility of failure. Shepard's New Frontiersmen characters are crippled, unpleasant, asocial – their isolation is manifestly not 'self-contained'.

Shepard and myriad Dirty Realist writers deal with what remains of life still lived on borderlines, still inhabited or haunted by Frontier melancholy or resentment. The Dirty Realist school may be vibrantly pessimistic, but they vibrate with Frontier longings all the same. The late Raymond Carver and Richard Ford had regular hunting and fishing trips together, and made a pact that should either one ever 'queer up' – like all the New York literary cissies they knew – the other would be enrolled as mercy killer.

Dallas has a certain appeal based on a craftily buried disjunction between the rolling plain and the glitzy mall. Rather than having unrelieved skyscraper glamour and intrigue, _Dallas_ exploited the idea that these people weren't civilised old money, they were upstarts – bed-hopping, deal-welching lower orders in _Vanity Fair_ schmutter. It uses one of the oldest Frontier devices in the book – endless genealogical tangles; the eternal return of illegitimate and forgotten offspring, inheritees of name and fortune. Sex in _Dallas_ may be sanitised or plain absent, but _by implication_ it carries on to the boardroom floor and into the penthouse sheets the ranch-hand's sweat, and a furry of bucking stallion flanks and snorting nostrils.

The Ewing family may be the last popular Frontier family, having hewn its good fortune from the oil-choked soil.

De Niro in *The Deer Hunter* is the repackaging of the Hemingway Frontiersman in whose figure self-sufficiency produces quasi-fascism, and Back to Nietzsche a Right nutter. Mind you, if your love life consisted of assignations in a trailer with Meryl Streep, maybe you'd go and take it out on little furry animals, too.

Somewhere close by is Hunter S. Thompson, who is now, as his latest collection *Generation of Swine* testifies, living in almost permanent self-exile in his neo-Aspen hideaway. His Woody Creek eyrie is, like the man himself, full of snow and high and twisted. He's the modern Frontiersman *par excellence* – into weaponry, bikes, the freedom of the open road and the free citizen's right to carry arms. Even ensconced in the wilderness he is cocooned by hi-tech props, a battery of guns, hi-fi equipment, motorbikes, Fax machines, 24-hour 20-channel satellite TV, etc. The sense in which he actually *lives* in the wilderness is debatable (unless it's a creative one, to judge by most of the book). He's turned himself into a totem of free craziness, of freedom as an indulgence. He's the Rambo of the deadline, a violent, spoiled child too long in the playpen. He declaims off the top of the head and everything is kept in; his previously gripping on-the-trail yarn-spinning has soured into whiskey-soaked old-timer tub-thumping. The best and worst of American literature is grounded in this idea that the speech, not text, is where it's at, where it (America, American truth) comes from and returns to. Thompson places bets by satellite but his heart seems to be turn of the century. He would seem to offer proof that any geographical-metaphysical remove is a self-perpetuating dodge: the wilderness of the self cannot be filled.

Sam Shepard: 'People want a street angel. They want a saint with a cowboy mouth.' It's ironic that Method screw-ups like James Dean and Montgomery Clift – neurotic shadows from an urban Boystown; city boys steeped in self-analysis and prescription uppers and downers; ambisexual cruisers – became such cowboy pin-ups. The iconic postures of Dean – crucified on a rifle, lounging on a porch in cowboy hat and boots – probably signal the beginning of gay appropriation of Out West imagery. And Paul Newman's cissified Billy the Kid in *The Left-Handed Gun* begins the downfall of the Western hero as a monument to certainty; throughout the Sixties and Seventies he would become ever more a locus of doubt, of doubtful heritage and delineation.

The Method was a disaster for all concerned. Urged to 'express themselves' these boys found only an emotional desert, although maybe this is why they were made for the Western: the Western landscape's mythic power is essentially one of vast _emptiness_.

It could be that even though the Western is said to be dead, it survives in various buddy-buddy guises. _Taxi Driver_, the iconic film of the Seventies, is very much _The Searchers_ updated, exploiting the fundamentally violent vocabulary of the Frontier code – the lone avenging angel, mute, simmering, cut off from women and the family, exploding through his gun.

In retrospect, many US films of the Seventies can be seen as an abreaction to the emergent power of Feminism. Rather than finding a new vocabulary to react to it, the True Men of these films stroll back into the vast silent wastes of some pseudo-Frontier.

It's long been an objection that the unrosy reality of something like Country and Western is educationally subnormal rednecks riding around with Creationist bumper stickers on their pick-ups and racist hatred in their hearts. As John Lahr says of Shepard, 'He makes myths out of a place whose spiritual impoverishment belies the Romance about it.' American pastoral is so resonant because even the earliest folk music of the US is charged with an ambiguity and indecision that is thoroughly _modern_.

But such is today's investment in leisure fantasies that a simple chord of yearning can soon be whipped up into Mexican eateries on every High St, and C&W 'theme' nights and endless highways in every advert. It becomes a 'return to authenticity' packaged with all the slick artifice our leisure industries can muster. What attracted us to begin with – the taint of 'not belonging', the tremulous chorus of loss – may become spoilt by wall-to-wall embellishment and media tie-ins. A taste for a little C&W ties you in to the roots/ World Music return to 'authenticity'.

Perhaps the lesson from such 'revivals', however suspect and paradoxical their movement, is that from a spiritual wasteland people can sculpt lasting monuments; the marginal elements can have a little sway.

The Frontier lives on across every American dream, good and bad; psychoanalyse the country and you find America ceaselessly expanding to conceal a basic want, a terminal insecurity – the longing for belonging. No other country is so obsessed with the moment of Creation, the beginning, the birth. America is criss-crossed with a palmistry of loss, resettlement, nostalgia. The only way this Frontier country can face the dangerous leap of the Future, it seems, is in violent denial or a backward glance. The day-dream of America's eternal future promise is ceaselessly sought in trajectories of escape and resettlement; America's interior is a frontier that will never heal but never again expand: such is America's wound, song and sadness, but also its endless possibility, its raw art.

Copyright © Ian Penman, 1989

Will of Irony

The Tribulations of Ironic Existence by Dylan Jones
September 1989

'THOSE WHO CAN, DO: those who can't, spoof,' said Julie Burchill recently, illustrating a problem which has become something of an epidemic: irony. It's in the music we hear on the radio, on television, it's in the shops, on our backs, in our bellies. Earlier this year New York's *Spy* magazine devoted almost an entire issue to the problem, enrolling ironists in the Eighties' register of socio-economic cults. To paraphrase the extraordinarily ironic Huey Lewis, it's no longer hip to be cool, it's cool to be ironic.

Irony is the product of post-war leisure culture, but it only started to become annoying in the early Sixties with Pop Art, when Lichtenstein's comic book parodies and Warhol's consumerist metaphors began attracting attention. America began producing thousands of consumer durables which would later turn out to be ironic. Then Pop begat Camp begat Kitsch begat Trash begat (finally) Irony.

Irony Chic is revival tours, Chevy Chase, Bill Murray, 'The Monkees' Greatest Hits' (1989 version), Paul Smith shirts (the 'classics with a twist'), illustrated socks, Bruce Willis recording Sixties R&B tunes, Vogueing, the three-volume set of TV theme tunes, 'Television's Greatest Hits', junk fetishism, books like *Roadside America*, vintage clothing, Home Maker dinner services, Goober Grape peanut butter and grape jelly (irony is often a coalition of good and bad taste), multi-coloured surfing shorts, 1950s cocktail shakers, Jean Paul Gaultier, 1960s Hawaiian shirts, madras sports jackets, lava lamps, the theme from *Thunderbirds* playing over the

end credits of _The Late Show_, _Lost In Space_, _Neighbours_, liking
Guns N' Roses, the Fifties, Sixties, Seventies, Eighties, Nineties –
anything, in fact, that makes a virtue of its archness or naffness.
And the thing that's weird about the irony boom is what's being
made now – irony TV such as _Thirtysomething_, watched with a
bitten lip while producing exasperated cries like 'How could he say
that?!' and 'Oh, look, can you believe this?' (If honest, most postmodern architects would admit that they're only ironists.)

The point about irony is the way people _knowingly_ indulge it:
watching _Saturday Night Fever_ is OK as long as you let on that
you know it's bad. But this isn't just quirky, passive consumption
by middle-aged art-students: irony chic is now being manufactured
to cater for the demand, and now thinks of itself as an art-form in
its own right. _Vanity Fair_'s James Wolcott put it another way: 'It's
the approach of postmodernists from David Letterman to David
Byrne, putting ironic quotation marks around stupid so that
'stupid" becomes smart. Kitsch is king – yesterday's obvious is today's pop sublime.' Once the domain of the cognoscenti, irony,
like sushi, is everywhere.

The way we look back always says more about the present than
it does about the past. _Absolute Beginners_ reveals more about the
ridiculous mid-Eighties obsession with Soho and the retro-con-
sumer boom than it does about 1950s London. And in our current
cultural impasse, the colonisation of the recent past – its music, its
television, its fashion and foibles – says more about us now than
it does about us then. A nation of adults that still consumes as
teenagers curls up in front of _The Phil Silvers Show_, buys Ray-Ban
sunglasses and listens to records made by 40-year-old men trying
to sound like the rebels they didn't dare be when they were in their
teens. It's frightening, this ironic world; I mean, really, who wants
to live in a world that's forever being re-recorded by Jeff Lynne
('You know, on some of that stuff, he makes Orbison/George Har-
rison/the Eurythmics/Tom Petty/Ralph Lauren sound just like The
Beatles'). There's nothing tongue-in-cheek about seeing the world
through the jaundiced eyes of the desperately ironic.

On New York's Columbus Avenue, Los Angeles's Melrose Avenue, and in London's Covent Garden, there are dozens of shops
devoted to the art of the arch: pink flamingoes, postcards par-
odying the harmony of suburban domesticity, plastic diners and
miniature fridges with even smaller magnets, Pee Wee Herman
dolls, funny wrist-watches, coffee-table books devoted to fast-food
packaging, and kitsch boxer shorts – the list is endless. Phillip

Retzky, the owner of Little Rickie, a haven for such things in Manhattan's East Village, told me he's *never* surprised at what people will buy. 'There isn't a day when someone doesn't come into the shop, look aghast, and scream "*I* remember that!" They really will buy the most extraordinary things – stuff from their childhood which they probably hated at the time. Today we're all groomed to consume, and no matter what you do, you can't avoid it, but people here consume with a sense of humour.'

Irony thrives because it keeps the consumer at a distance – it never means involvement, which is just as well, the ironists say, because there isn't much they'd want to be involved with these days, thanks.

Professional trouser-sniffer Albert Goldman once said that youth culture was really only a mother substitute, anyway, so maybe our infatuation and pillaging of our youth is an extension of this. But it's inevitable that irony won't inspire the kind of adjectives – sawtoothed, soaring, delirious, passionate, lonesome, ominous – lavished on those po-faced souls who, with craven bravery, dare to create something *original*.

In the pantheon of irony TV David Letterman is God. By becoming America's first self-deprecating chat-show host he inadvertently encouraged a posse of nascent British ironists – Jonathan Ross, Clive Anderson, Tony Slattery, Roland Rivron – all of them equipped with gaudy neckties and smirks. All have realised that the chat-show is the perfect medium of the times, the decade of the raised eyebrow. To them, being thirtysomething gives them the right to parody.

'Our customers – the 20 to 40-year-olds – have helped create irony chic,' says Phillip Retzky. 'Now, though, it's being sucked up by the media – first it's chic, then it's fashion, then it's over. It's starting to appear in Macy's for Chrissakes – you've just got to look at a Jonathan Demme movie to realise how mainstream it's all become.'

And that's the problem: irony is becoming identifiable, as are the ironists. It won't be long before irony will be fashionable, and, consequently, soon back in the bargain bins; this can only mean that it will soon be hip to appreciate (in an ironic way) things which were once considered awful, which became cute and kitsch, which then became ironic, then fashionable, and are now so completely out of favour that they have to be funny again. Confusing, isn't it? As for the ironists, now that they've become identifiable, they will surely vanish. To be ironic is to place yourself outside of reality; but once reality catches up with you, then it's time to get back to the real world.

Copyright © Dylan Jones, 1989

The Tattooed Jungle
The Decline of the Working Class by Tony Parsons
September 1989

ROTTWEILERS JUST CAN'T HELP acting on impulse. After the early summer's rampage of the killer mutts, the nation finally woke up to the fact that there are an awful lot of dangerous, dumb, ugly animals in our midst and that many of them own very large dogs. Rottweilers tore a baby from its cot, they left a five-year-old needing 21 stitches, they killed an eleven-year-old girl in Dundee. Naturally enough, the dog owners were _hurt_. Oh, Rambo loves kids. My Psycho wouldn't hurt a fly. Napalm has a heart of gold.

'Rocky bit the vet but he asked for it,' said Arthur in the _New Statesman_. ' 'Cos he stuck a syringe up his arse.'

A word you find cropping up again and again in Arthur's conversation is _respect_. Rocky is a pussycat; just treat him with respect. All the indignant owners of these misunderstood pooches – the playful Pit Bull Terrier, the kind-hearted Alsatian, the peaceable Rottweiler, the gentle Dobermann – are very big on respect. Sick and tired of being pushed and pulled by the elemental forces of the naked city – another burglary, more smashed glass on the pavement and another car radio gone – they want a little respect around here, and their combination bodyguard, burglar alarm and stiff-dick substitute will ensure they get it.

It is symptomatic of the long spiritual decline of the working class (and having this kind of dog is as working class as fishfingers and Ford Escorts) that they see owning an animal that is capable of killing a small child in a few frenzied minutes as a suitable way to win the respect of their fellow citizens. Thirty years ago the grandmothers of the Arthurs of this world would get on their knees and scrub their front doorstep clean every morning. They wanted respect. Today Arthur's dog – or one just like him – will squat blank and drooling on somebody else's doorstep and shit all over it. He only wants respect.

The working class has come a long way in recent years, all of it down-hill. They no longer look like the salt of the earth. They look like one big Manson Family. There never *used* to be all these people drinking Tennents – always those cheap and potent bruise-blue cans of Tennents – in the street at nine o'clock in the morning. Lager at dawn, that macho valium. And there never used to be all these fat tattooed slobs, dressed for the track and built for the bar, leaning out of the window of their van – those rusty white vans – and screaming with rage, 'Yew carnt! Yew farking *carnt*!' as they cut you up and mow down a Lollipop lady.

They are the reason you prefer to avoid Indian restaurants at closing time. You see them at the post office on Monday morning, at the football ground on Saturday afternoon, at every pub – those manly troughs – at any time. They belch and fart and threaten their way through life. They are the lager vomit on the Union Jack. They turn the city into a tattooed jungle. They spoil everything.

The trouble with the working class today is that they are such peasants. Something has died in them – a sense of grace, all feelings of community, their intelligence, decency and wit. Socialism is finished here because it is no longer possible to feel sentimental about the workers.

They love their country – eat shit, you Argie sheep-shaggers – but they don't care enough about the street they live on to bother binning their rubbish. My skip overfloweth. These people make the city streets look like a toilet in a Turkish prison – Rambo steamingly defecating, Little Wayne tossing away his crisp packets, dad's tattooed arms working away on his motor, dumping his derelict big end in the nearest rose bushes when it no longer functions. The way they foul the streets in the tattooed jungle is positively Elizabethan. In fact everything about these rich serfs in their velcro-welded sneakers and boulder-rubbed denim is a throwback to the bad old days, the days when being born on the wrong side of the tracks meant you would always be a dumb prole.

They are the real class traitors, betrayers of the men who fought the Second World War, those men who fought for Churchill but voted for Clement Attlee. But in the tattooed jungle they have no sense of history. The true unruly children of Thatcherism, they know their place and wallow in their peasanthood.

Two years ago I sat in front of a pack of them at Wembley when England played Holland. These well-heeled oiks were perfect emissaries of the *prole nouveau*. They were not particularly young (all over 30), they were certainly not poor (they lounged in the best seats consuming an abundance of booze, spliff and even what they called 'blow'), and yet, with their racism, their mindless desire to consume to excess, and especially with their farting, they were quintessential tattooed jungle, real radicals, the Mujahadin of yobism. One of them kept elaborately breaking wind.

'Kentucky *Fried*!' he declared every time, and the others roared.

But being born at the shabbier end of the social scale should never be enough to make you a farting philistine.

At a gallery in New York in the Fifties, a rich female collector commented admiringly on the manners of a young unknown artist called Jasper Johns. She said that Johns – born in Georgia, raised in North Carolina – must be a member of the southern aristocracy. The painter soon put her right.

'Oh no,' he said casually. 'I'm trash.'

In the tattooed jungle they are happy to advertise the fact. Say it loud: I'm plebeian and proud. All notions of social mobility or cultural aspirations are well suspect, squire. They cling to all those bogus clichés about the working class – that they have no airs and graces, that they lack pretension and are honest, loyal, humorous and hardy – all that sentimental bullshit that leads nowhere but to some poor Indian waiter being insulted on the Holloway Road or some little kid being slapped by the vegetables in Sainsbury's.

'Do as you're *bloody* told, Kylie!'

They sour everything they come into contact with – even on that sweet night of wonders when Arsenal won the league and we poured out on to the streets of Highbury and made our way to the ground, even on that night with a team that included Thomas and Rocastle, with Davis on the touchline, you could hear them chanting those white trash mantras of bile that would not be out of place at a Nuremberg rally.

'*We hate the Tottenham yids, we hate the Tottenham yids.*' You can spot them coming a mile off – in the tattooed jungle everybody turns into a fat fuck at 20. Though they deride the intellectual, they mercilessly punish their flesh and blood with an unforgiving hedonism. Mine's a large pint of biriani and a vat of something yellow. Fill Little Wayne's nose bag full of sugar, and a duty-free pack of Silk Cut for the wife.

In fact, here 'it' comes right now. Coo, wot a state, eh, John? Her bottled blonde head wreathed in cigarette smoke – you have to smoke in the tattooed jungle – she totters on her high are-you-free? heels (her concept of glamour is derived from soap operas and prostitutes), her spreading haunches squeezed into robot-mottled denim, or, when the summer comes to the city, a skimpy mini-skirt made of the finest man-made fibres. It is then that you notice her remarkable legs. They are not shaved. They are not waxed. These pins are positively *scalped*. Obviously treated with battery acid, they actually *gleam* with hairlessness and she totters on those bald white legs like some gross travesty of a 'real' woman – *get stuck into that, yew carnt*!

Call me old-fashioned, but it still shocks me when I see that some of these women are, in the fashion of merchant seaman, tattooed. They tattoo everything that moves in these parts. All the men are tattooed, some of the women and, worst of all, so are some of the faces. In 40 years' time there are going to be all these little old men with free bus passes and an eagle tattooed on their forehead.

They will be doing it to babies next. And Alsatians. One of the worst things about these people is that they always act like the disenfranchised, even when they have money. You make a mark on your body when you feel you can't make a mark on your life.

Many forces have conspired to build this unthinking, brutal tattooed jungle. The death of the grammar schools – those public schools without the sodomy – resulted in state education relinquishing its role of nurturing bright young working-class kids. And then there is the betrayal of the ordinary people by the Labour Party – it's a sobering thought that the last Labour Prime Minister was Jim Callaghan! – and its descent from the natural party of power to a bunch of secular Mullas, endlessly arguing about theological fine points while the country rots, while Thatcher and her suburban pirates run down the health service and the schools and turn this country into a land fit for selfish little shits.

But most of all it has been made a barfing reality by the very roots of our culture. To be born an Englishman – ah, what an easy conceit that builds in you, what a self-righteous nationalism, a secure xenophobia, what a *pride* in your ignorance. No other people speak so few languages. No other people – certainly not the Germans, Italians or French, and not even the multi-ethnic Americans – have an expression that is the equivalent of 'greasy foreign muck'. The noble, wisecracking savages depicted everywhere from *EastEnders* to *Boys From The Blackstuff* are exercises in nostalgia who no longer exist.

They have their videos and their turbo-charged Capris, but the British working class have lost something more valuable. Look at their faces in footage of cup finals in the Forties and Fifties. You do not have to look through pinko-tinted glasses to see how hopeful and happy and fundamentally *decent* they look, with their suits and their NHS teeth and their heartbreaking rattles. Kids used to stand on orange boxes; now you think long and hard before taking a small child with you to a match.

There was a time when I wanted – more than almost anything – to see England win the World Cup one more time before I died. Now I don't even want us to qualify for the thing. I don't want to see English football supporters in Milan and Rome and Naples and Florence next summer. I am sick of my country being embarrassed by my asshole countrymen.

There was recently a wonderful story about a colonial outpost of the tattooed jungle by Ian Jack. Writing in *Granta*, his article was called 'Gibraltar', and it started out as an investigation into the death of three IRA members at the hands of the SAS and evolved into something more. Jack is neither a Thatcher toady nor a Troops Out lefty.

'I write as a Scot,' he said, 'and one with too much of the Protestant in him ever to empathize much with the more recent traditions of Irish republicanism, as well as an ordinary level of human feeling which precludes the understanding of the average IRA bomber. But the longer I spent in Gibraltar, the more difficult it became to prop up the shaky old structure – that lingering belief in what must, for lack of a more exact phrase, be called the virtues of Britishness.'

What is so wrong with this country is that it never questions those virtues, it never doubts itself in its murderous loathing for the other. No other country in the Western world has such a slavish devotion to the concept of military glory – as an SAS officer told the enquiry in Gibraltar, his unit's initials provide a 'sexy headline' for the tabloids. Jack's story was illustrated by a stunningly ugly photograph of a young man on the beach of Gibraltar. Judging by his haircut and his demeanour, he is an off-duty serviceman. He is flamboyantly flexing his muscles and there are baroque, mawkish tattoos all down his muscular limbs. His hair is cropped and, inside his stupid Union Jack swimming trunks, he has a semi-erection. The leer on his face says that he is unbelievably pleased with himself. He brings to mind his spiritual mate – the young wife who displayed her sagging breasts to the Task Force when it was departing for the Falklands, the unknown English Rose who got her tits out for the lads.

Oh patriotic tattooed jungle, how you mock the concept of freedom, democracy and liberty when you produce this race of mindless gluttons, how profoundly depressing that the unchained spirit breeds such as you. Especially in the year when communism was finally seen globally as a bankrupt philosophy that carries the seeds of its own destruction, in this year when Mao stands revealed as a liberator of the scale of Hitler and Stalin, how wretched and sad it is that they are dying from the Black Sea to Peking for the kind of rights that we take for granted, for the freedoms that we piss all over.

'In the end you must either allow people liberty or you must shoot them,' wrote William Rees-Mogg. 'If a man claims a vote you must either give him a vote or be prepared to take his life.' The vote, Bill? I'd rather have a can of Tennents.

After the slaughter in China it was a revelation to go down to the Chinese embassy in Portland Place and witness the protest of the ordinary Chinese people of London. The quiet, angry dignity of their picket across the street from that large silent house where not a Maoist stirred was truly moving, awesome in its calm outrage, fuelled by a moral fervour that has been missing from the British for years. As far as I am concerned, they should let every last one of the four million residents of Hong Kong into England. It would definitely improve the place, for these are people who seem to aspire to something higher than the coarse delights of the tattooed jungle. In fact if you invert that old racist cliché, the one they used to trot out all the time during the Vietnam War, then it finally turns out to be true.

Life just doesn't mean as much to us as it does to them.

Copyright © Tony Parsons, 1989

Man Out of Time

P. J. Proby by Dylan Jones

December 1989

P. J. PROBY IS TEACHING ME TO SING 'SOMEWHERE', explaining how he came up with his version, the definitive version, of the *West Side Story* ballad. With a disconnected stare he's looking in my direction, singing at the top of his voice, somehow managing to wring four bruised syllables from the song's title: 'Sum-mah-way-er, Sum-mah-way-er!' He looks pleased with himself for getting this far.

'I made a bastard version of that song, mixing Billy Eckstine with Della Reese, making it a little black in the process. I could never figure out why no one could get a hit with "Somewhere" – you had the Johnny Mathis version which was very pretty, you had the Matt Monro version which was very Sinatra, but still very good ... I couldn't understand why no one had ever hit. Then I was laying in bed one night and it struck me like a shot: no one had ever hit with that song because they'd all been too good! The public doesn't like perfection, so I figured the way to get a hit with "Somewhere" was to fuck it up a little, play it down. I fucked it up and it became a monster.'

At the begining of 1965 P. J. Proby was at the height of his career. With three Top Ten hits under his belt he was the biggest male singer in Britain. A protégé of pop svengali Jack Good, he had become the most desired pop performer in the country in a matter of months. His brazen sexuality, explicit way of dressing and husky, sensual voice made him the biggest thing to hit the country since Elvis. And P. J. Proby was here in person!

On record, with his impassioned, swollen singing, he sounded like a possessed Johnny Ray, his intense ballads and raucous rock'n'roll picking up where Elvis left off. But it was his live performances which brought the myth to life, his savage yet girly sexuality causing hysteria among his pubescent female fans. ('Those girls would tear their knickers off,' he once told a journalist, 'throw them on stage, and I thought they were handkerchiefs. I'd pick one up, wipe my face with it and then realise I was bathing my face in piss.') He pounded his way through the coarse, melodramatic songs, offering his moans of despair and relief.

He was the embodiment of rock'n'roll burlesque, a singer who bridged the gap between pop and cabaret before either Tom Jones or Elvis. Here was a performer who spanned light and dark, good and bad. He performed a surreal collection of songs – a bit of rock, a bit of music hall, mixed up with more than a hint of melancholy. He was a mesmeric performer, his self-obsessive, self-destructive persona showing itself to full effect when Proby was hamming it up in the spotlight. And Proby was always good at hamming it up.

His clothes were the ultimate in daring: tight, white satin hipsters, white satin shirt and white satin Anello & Davide shoes, with little gold buckles. He had a false ponytail made by Bermans & Nathan, which he had safety-pinned into his own hair at the back. He had his suit copied in ten different colours of velvet, with matching velvet shoes, and he eventually grew his own ponytail. At some of his early personal appearances he would get his dresser to split his shirts down the seams with a razor blade, and lightly tack them together with thin thread, so that the seams would pop open at appropriate times in his set, leaving him free to walk about the stage naked from the waist up, while adoring nymphets soiled the seats below.

Proby came to Britain instead of Elvis, and to a lot of people he was as good, if not *better* than the King of rock'n'roll . . . Proby was *live*, he was here in the flesh. He personified the glory days of Sixties pop frenzy, the shining star with the dark underbelly, the complete showman, lusting after wine, women and immortality. Proby was the basis for the hero of Nik Cohn's rock'n'roll novel *I Am Still The Greatest Says Johnny Angelo*, the portrait of a doomed rock star.

But it all came to an end on January 29, 1965, at the Castle Hall, Croydon, on the first date of a nationwide tour that also featured Cilla Black. During the climax to one of his crowd-pleasers, Proby's blue velvet trousers split wide open. They split again two days later at the Ritz Cinema in Luton, and then again a few days later. That night the curtain literally came down on his career, and he was thrown off the tour to be replaced by Tom Jones.

In a fit of moral panic, what seemed like the entire British establishment came down on him like he was the embodiment of the devil himself. He was banned from performing in every major venue in Britain, and then, on February 8, was banned from any show on the old ATV television network. The BBC soon followed suit. In America, Elvis Presley was once only allowed to be filmed from the waist up; ten years later in Britain, P. J. Proby wasn't allowed to be filmed at all. Confronted with this media blackout, Proby went underground, where, for the most part, he's remained ever since.

The man who became P. J. Proby (real name James Marcus Smith) was born into a wealthy Texan family on November 6, 1938, in Houston. Mollycoddled as a young child, his parents separated when he was nine, he was made a ward of the State of Texas, and was forced into military college, where he remained until his mid-teens. On leaving, at 17, he made the first big decision of his life – to move to Hollywood. But his regimental upbringing had hardly prepared him for the debauchery and skullduggery to be found in California. 'Normal relationships just didn't exist there,' he once said, 'all you had were homosexuals passing themselves around all the directors and the girls doing the same thing.'

He soon fell in, and in no time was recording rock'n'roll under the name Jett Powers. He became a Hollywood hyphenate, recording his own songs, writing songs for other people, singing on other people's records, and acting in B-movies and TV westerns. In the early Sixties he even recorded demos for Elvis, having been befriended by him when Presley dated Proby's sister. The songs Proby ghosted turned up on the soundtracks of Presley's many movies of that period.

In 1963 Jett Powers was quietly getting on with his life when Eddie Cochran's ex-fiancée, Sharon Sheeley, introduced him to pop svengali Jack Good, and P. J. Proby was born. Good was so impressed with Proby's long hair (the only other singer to have long hair at the time was Phil May from the Pretty Things) and his 'baroque vocal talents and dark charisma', that he immediately signed him up.

Good originally wanted to cast him in a rock version of *Othello*, but instead put him on the pilot for his TV pop show, *Shindig*, before bringing him to London to appear with John, Paul, George and Ringo on the huge TV special *Around The Beatles*. Proby, a heavy drinker since 15, was habitually inebriated, and he arrived in Britain completely drunk, wearing tatty jeans, a cowboy hat and a pair of Tuesday Weld's knickers. He was met by a rented Rolls Royce and a gang of reporters who had been hounded up by Good, and for the next year P. J. Proby was to experience what it's like to be a fully fledged star – a man with an entourage, a man with money, a man with good suits and bad women, a man with an audience. But his first week in London was a nightmare, he now says, living in Earls Court with no money, riding the buses to learn the currency ('I used to watch the conductor, that was the only way I could get used to it'), but as soon as his first record hit, he was swept up into the lap of the gods.

Like many people who hit success in the Sixties, Proby's life moved at a fairly rapid pace. In the next 18 months Proby had seven Top 30 hits in Britain, starting with the uptempo 'Hold Me' (his biggest hit, it went to number three in May 1964), through 'Together', 'I Apologise', 'Let The Water Run Down' and 'That Means A Lot', to his classic, enigmatic ballads 'Maria' and 'Somewhere', the two Leonard Bernstein/Stephen Sondheim songs from *West Side Story*. But the trouser-splitting experience all but finished his career, and though he continued having the occasional hit right up to spring 1968, his time as a pop star was effectively over. Proby went from being a star to someone of whom nothing was expected.

The moral panic surrounding P. J. Proby's thighs now seems ludicrous, but at the time the Grades, the Delfonts, Mary Whitehouse, Lord Longford and every righteous theatre owner in the country were up in arms about this shocking, degenerate Texan.

Proby has persistently said the promoters ganged up on him because he blabbed to the press about the dirty deals they were involved in (scalping tickets, overcrowding venues, etc), but the fact remains it was Proby's crotch, not his mouth, that got him into trouble.

When the sexually provocative on-stage antics of 19-year-old American soul star Bobby Brown upset the police in Columbus, Georgia, earlier this year, he was fined $652 and held in custody for an hour. The next day he was pulling exactly the same stunts somewhere else; for Bobby Brown to be hounded out of the entertainment industry like Proby was he would probably have to bugger a dead pony on stage. Then again, he might even get away with that.

In February 1968 Proby declared himself bankrupt, with debts of over £80,000. He returned to America, but was lured back to Britain in 1971 by Jack Good to play Iago in his rock version of *Othello*, called *Catch My Soul*. The next 15 years are a litany of unfulfilment. But though he spent most of the time wandering the north of England in abject poverty, he did find time for the occasional live performance ('I was the first person to bring a Las Vegas-style show to northern clubs,' he says), and in 1977 took up with Good again, taking the starring role in the West End musical *Elvis*. He had a brief dalliance with the Sex Pistols, though inevitably nothing came of it; and in 1978 even recorded with the Dutch rock group Focus.

For most of this time Proby's life was a nightmare of smalltime – in the past ten years he has been a caretaker, janitor and farm hand. Disillusionment, lack of foresight and a taste for alcohol have played havoc with his life.

Rare newspaper appearances have usually been because of his wives, all six of them: in 1978 he was cleared of shooting his fourth wife, Dulcie, with an air pistol; in the mid-Eighties the tabloids went wild when they discovered he'd married a 16-year-old girl called Alison Hardy (in fact, she was only 14). Most recently, he was in the papers when he appeared on Derek Jameson's Sky TV chat-show, attempting to sing while allegedly mauling one of the programme's young assistants – 'all bullshit,' P. J. insists.

Now a fragile 50-year-old man, he lives alone, an alcoholic, in Bury, near Manchester, and supports himself through his Social Security payments, the occasional royalty cheque, and handouts from his friends at Savoy Records.

Dave Britton (43) and Mike Butterworth (slightly younger) set up Savoy Books in Manchester in the mid-Seventies, to produce new imprints of classic neglected books, re-issuing works by Henry Treece, Jack Trevor Story, Nik Cohn (the rights to *Johnny Angelo* cost them £500), Harlan Ellison and Michael Moorcock. They also experimented with new books, and later comics and children's books, often publishing what was unlikely to be published anywhere else, either on grounds of taste, morals, or popularity. They are the last of Britain's underground publishers, dedicated to 'soliciting moral outrage'. Savoy have been labelled both pornographers and neo-fascists, while others have found them seedy, odd, or just immature. There is certainly no other company like them in Britain.

When they started to sell and publish erotic material in 1980, they were raided by the police. Titles such as *The Gas*, *The Tides Of Lust* and *The Screwtape Lettuce*, as well as thousands of pounds worth of retail stock, were seized from the Savoy office and their chain of shops by police acting under personal instructions from Chief Constable James Anderton. This led in 1982 to 19 days in prison for Britton. (They were most recently raided in September this year principally because of Britton's novel, *Lord Horror*.)

In 1981, as a result of continued police harassment and the collapse of their distributors, New English Library, Savoy's book operation went into liquidation. Undaunted, Britton and Butterworth continued to publish, using different imprints and widening the scope of their activities.

Dave Britton had met P. J. Proby in 1982 – ostensibly with the idea of writing his biography, which he still intends to publish one day – and wondered if it might be possible to get him back into the studio. Proby fans both, he and Butterworth knew he hadn't made a record for 15 years.

In the course of this 15-year decline, Proby had found that people who made themselves available to him wanted one of two things: to fuck him or manage him. Britton didn't want either.

'It struck me as really sad that here was this great voice, this legendary singer, who couldn't get a deal anywhere. So we threw ourselves in at the deep end and dragged him into a studio with some musicians to do "Tainted Love". It was farcical, *Spinal Tap* wasn't in it. But it worked in an odd kind of a way, and we took it from there.'

Their strategy was to take classic songs, and warp them, debunk them, using only the limited technology available to them and Proby's voice. They chose songs which meant a lot to people, in the hope of offending as many as possible. Thus the 1985 release of 'Tainted Love' was followed by Joy Division's 'Love Will Tear Us Apart' (1986), David Bowie's 'Heroes' (1986), the Sex Pistols' 'Anarchy In The UK' (1987) and Prince's 'Sign Of The Times' earlier this year. Proby has also covered songs by Iggy Pop and Roxy Music, as well as a truly manic version of T. S. Eliot's 'The Wasteland'.

Depending on your taste, these records are either deconstructed classics or pathetic junk. But to dismiss them as junk is to miss the beauty, and the joke, of the exercise. These songs have been fed through a blender, stuck together again and then had Proby's ferociously drunken vocals laid over the top. They are seismic masterpieces of bad taste, berserk sorcery, little tainted epics.

'It's a serious business, it's serious *outrageous* art,' says Britton. 'We're not messing about. Jim's always taken songs and warped them, only we're maybe warping them a bit more – we're trying to create the aural equivalent of the Dennis Hopper character in *Blue Velvet*. We're carrying on in the great Proby tradition. He was always butchering people's songs. It's not a frivolous thing – it takes an awful lot of money to make these records, money we can't

really afford. Maybe when we've stopped doing them and Jim's under the ground, people will realise that they're quite remarkable
records, quite strange, but different.'

A lot of Proby's Savoy records are passionately horrific, great
slabs of fierce, scary pop; often, however, he sounds simply silly,
like a little boy shouting a dictionary of obscenities or an incoherent drunk singing Abba songs. 'Hardcore' is a pornographic rap
which Savoy released as a 'duet' between Proby and Madonna. A
kaleidoscope of monotony, it nevertheless created a certain
amount of controversy; they were told they would be sued by her
record company, but nothing ever came of it. The best response
came from Madonna's fan club, wanting to know where and when
it had been recorded.

A new single, a remarkably subdued version of the Phil Collins
hit 'In The Air Tonight', is his most straightforward, and, God for-
bid, sounds vaguely commercial. It will probably be the last Proby
record on Savoy, as they're quickly running out of time, money
and enthusiasm. They've found it impossible to secure a distributor
for the Proby records, and those copies which haven't been posted
to journalists are stacked in the many cardboard boxes that line
the hallway in Savoy's Manchester office. 'We've given it our best
shot,' says Britton.

Savoy have not had a great relationship with the music press,
who, it appears, either find the records distasteful, or regard them
as some kind of exploitative wind-up – Savoy as post-McLaren art
guerrillas. Britton steadfastly refutes this: 'If we weren't using him,
someone else would be. We're using him to make art. The alternative to us being here is five years of nothing. What's better? Of
course it's our perception of him, but we believe we're making
great records in the Proby tradition. Occasionally I do feel guilty
about it, because Jim hates the records – he particularly loathed
"The Passenger" (originally by Iggy Pop), he kept shouting "Fucking shit, what a load of crap, fucking awful song" – but Jim's never
been happy with any of his stuff; he hated "Hold Me" and a lot
of his other singles. Are we really doing any harm? We pay him
for his work, we're always slipping him money. Is that really so
bad? He can walk away any time he likes, he's quite free. I'm doing
this because I believe in him, because I'm trying to draw out his
talent. And yes, in my madness, I really think he could come back.'

In the past five years, Britton and Butterworth have been as good
to Proby as they can; they've supported him from time to time,
paid the odd bill here and there, and persistently tried to ween him

off the booze. 'We've tried time and time again to dry him out, but he's not interested. He's too far gone – he says he wants to die through alcohol, and he knows what he's doing so that's his right. Maybe I lack courage to really take him in hand, but I wouldn't be that presumptuous, really. It's a man's right to die how he likes.'

'. . . Haa-aarrrkah!'

P. J. Proby enters the small, cluttered Savoy office clearing phlegm from his throat.

'. . . haaaaa-aaaarrrrkaaaaah!'

He stumbles into the room in a plastic anorak, his denim dungarees disappearing into oddly immaculate cowboy boots. Apart from the boots, he looks terrible, like he's just spent the past four days curled up in a cold flat with nothing to eat or drink. Which is precisely where he has been. Without a penny to his name, he has had to wait for Mike Butterworth to pick him up today for this interview. He clutches a carrier bag full of Special Brew which Mike has given him. Pulling one open he coughs again.

'I've been flat on my back in my room for four whole days, without even enough to buy a stamp,' he says, shaking his head and slurping his beer. 'I've lost my house! No more phone, no more electricity, and they've cut my water off. I've been through hell.' And not for the first time.

'I've had to go through four days of withdrawal, all by myself, and that's very, very dangerous. You can have a heart attack. I didn't know what I was going to do. I kept repeating to myself, I can make it, I can make it . . . but I really didn't think I could.'

He takes another slug of beer. Today's intake will consist of the cans of Special Brew, a bottle of cheap white wine, and a bottle of Canadian Club mixed with half a litre of Seven-Up; and then of course he'll more than likely want to go out in the evening.

'I was so desperate for a drink I was gonna pawn this ring [brandishes ring] – it's the last one I got. It's worth quite a lot of money, but I don't give a shit. But I couldn't get out of bed.'

Proby's face doesn't just look lived in, it looks as though that same person died in it too. He's still got his Texan drawl, and though he mumbles unevenly, it's with determination. He's a sad figure, a broken old man, and you feel a bit ghoulish for treating him like a freak. But undoubtedly, his behaviour during the past five years has turned him into one. When everyone else has left the room, he makes his feelings known about the 'freakish' records he's made with Savoy.

'I think they're awful, I think they're the worst things I've ever done in my life. They're goddamn awful, they don't say anything, they're rude, they're vulgar, they're not commercial – no station will play them. I like "Heroes", the Phil Collins thing and the Prince song's OK, but most of the stuff I've done is too filthy to be played. And you know what? I wrote it all. They'd call me up and say, "Write some more filth, write us some more dirt!"

'But Mike and Dave, they're my friends. Ever since I met them they've been very kind to me. Every time I've been really down they've always helped me out financially, giving me five or ten pounds or something like that. When I was living up on the mountain, out in the country, in the winter when there was five feet of snow outside my door, I'd have to call them and they'd come up in a Land Rover with food and money.

'But why did I make the records? Money. My wife and I were starving. Why does a whore fuck on the streets with a mattress on her back with rollerskates underneath – she's hungry.'

Proby says he'd like to get into a studio with a proper orchestra and record country songs, but not only can Savoy not afford this, they don't think it would work anyway. 'He'd either never turn up,' says Britton, 'or he'd try and conduct, or he'd get into a fight, or if he organised it, no one would turn up. We tried it a few times, but it was a nightmare.'

After 20 years of failure and missed opportunities, Proby knows more than most about that real nightmare, that huge abyss of regret, into which everyone peers occasionally.

'If I had everything I had between . . . say '64 and '66 . . . along with all this computer bullshit, well, I'd be better than anybody. It's difficult, but I could do it. All I need is one hit record, just one hit . . . but nobody will give me a chance. Those years, I didn't give a shit. I was making a name for myself instead of living up to one. Now I have to live up to something that's already in the past. In the old days, if nothing happened, nothing happened. Who cared? I could always go back and be a stunt man or ride my motorcycle . . . But I can't do that because P. J. Proby was born and now he's my responsibility.'

How would he describe himself today?

'I'm a very jaded person, but not to the point of hate towards the many people who took advantage of me. Bitter? I don't feel bitter, I just feel sad. Jack Good invented me, and if he'd stayed with me and guided my career instead of going back to America, none of this would ever have happened, and Tom Jones would still be in the working men's clubs.'

Seemingly oblivious to his own shortcomings, he continually mentions the managers, the agents, the promoters, the friends, the lovers and the record companies who let him down. He tells me his biggest regret, though you feel the answer was different yesterday, and will be different tomorrow:

'I think back to 1957, when two guys came to my house on Mulholland Drive and wanted me to sign up. I said, "Why me, I'm nobody? Wait till you've got a product to sell." They said they wanted me right there and then. Well, I regret not signing with the mafia, I really do regret it. At the time I was 19 and my idea of the mafia was big men stomping on little men, killers and everything like that. My Hollywood mind was going back to the days of Capone. I'd forgotten it had become very, very big business. That was the biggest mistake I ever made. I should have signed up, because almost everyone is now. If I'd signed I'd have had great representation, great management, no matter how they got it for me ... and I'd have had someone working for me. I've never in my life had someone working for me, except myself, and I've had to learn the hard way. I've had to bullshit since I was 17. I was thrown in at the deep end too soon, with no guidance. That's the main word of my life – "guidance", no guidance. I've had to play it by ear all the way.

'What I really wanted out of showbusiness, the reason I put so much of me into it, I never got out of it. I'm not talking about money, I'm talking about a stable marriage, a home, and children. Those were my goals. You can tell that by how many times I tried – six times.'

Three years ago he flew back to Texas, to die. Ten days later he was back in Manchester. He had been arrested for vagrancy, and his stepmother had put him on the next plane for Britain. To his family Proby is an outlaw, an embarrassing drunk. He wants to be buried by his father in Texas, something his stepmother apparently opposes.

He's been diagnosed as having some form of stomach cancer, and, though his liver is shot, he refuses to give up drinking. The rest of him is in remarkably good shape, but you wonder for how long. He's been drinking every day for the past 35 years, a staggering amount of booze which would have killed stronger men. All the other big boozers of the Sixties, people like Peter O'Toole, Richard Harris, Richard Burton, have either stopped, or are dead. All except P. J. Proby. His drinking has affected him so much that his vision of the world bears no resemblance to reality. There doesn't seem to be much that is dignified about the decay of Jim Proby.

His anecdotes, like his muse, are on tap, though they're largely unreliable, as they start and finish (if they finish at all) in different decades, different countries and often involve different people. He can be lucid, and some of the early stories – like how he initially met Jack Good – have been honed to a fine art, but they've been embellished so much that it's impossible to decipher the truth.

'I'm a very unhappy person, but a person who's ready, in a couple of months, to check out.'

It's unnerving to sit in a room with someone who's telling you they're going to kill themselves, but as Proby has said this before, to other journalists, it's difficult to take him seriously. 'I'm gonna blow my head off on stage. Elvis was gonna do that, but he died on the toilet, ha, ha, ha! Elvis planned to die on stage, but he had a heart attack and keeled over. *I* wanna die on stage; I'm just gonna end it with the greatest stage finale the world has ever seen. And this will be in about two months . . .'

He's talking about a forthcoming date at a nightclub in Wakefield, though the Savoy bunch seem convinced it will never happen. 'He's working out his set for the night, writing down all his favourite songs,' says Dave Britton, 'but it'll never happen, he'll have forgotten about it next week.'

'You know,' says Proby, 'I don't fear anything any more. I've had too much of life to fear. I've had everything. I've had it all . . . but no guidance to keep it all. It will be a grand finale . . . it will be the happiest place I've ever wanted to be in my life.'

He coughs one last time.

'Right up until the end I had a deal with [British] *Vogue* – they were selling these exclusive little P. J. Proby shirts for the men and nightgowns and false hair extensions for the girls, and buckle shoes for boys and girls. I became a designer label. But when the pants split they dropped me like a hot rock. These days, the more clothes you wear the less you get paid. These days, the boys all wear ponytails and all the stuff you see in *Vogue* magazine is ripped anyway. Every mistake I made is now a design.'

Copyright © Dylan Jones, 1989

The Curse of the Pub-Human

Why the British Public House Must Die by Geoff Deane

November 1989

THE GOOD LORD BLESSED ME with a pronounced fondness for alcohol consumption. When a publican looks at me his seasoned instincts crank into action and neon pound signs start to flash before his smoke-filled eyes. I am the gear box in his E-Type, the gold strap on his Rolex, the poolside terrace to his villa in the Algarve. I am money in the bank. I am a punter. Or so he thinks.

In fact I detest pubs with a passion and avoid them like the plague. I would rather drink in a bar, a club or a gutter than waste my time in these tawdry establishments. They may be part of Britain's heritage but they are a part best scheduled for demolition.

Remember, the pubs grew out of this country's bizarre licensing procedures; not just anyone can sell alcohol in Britain. Those that are permitted to do so have long believed that this alone is sufficient to keep their customers satisfied. For their part, pub customers became so accustomed to feeling gratitude at being allowed to actually buy a drink that they were prepared to turn a blind eye towards an establishment's shortcomings. What other explanation can there be?

With the advent of the package holiday Tommy Brit started to spread his wings and soon discovered what he'd been missing. He could drink around the clock in comfortable surroundings or just sip a coffee. He could even get a decent bite without having to shift his flabby white buttocks from the chair, and little Norman could sit on his lap throughout, a 7-Up in his grubby little mitt. So much more civilised than relegating your child to a pub doorway. So much more civilised, period.

Not that Tommy always knew how to behave himself in this utopian environment. After years of deprivation what else could one expect? Sadly, excess is a trait that has never died out. The long-term effect of foreign travel, though, has been to bring about a more cosmopolitan outlook.

As wine consumption grew, wine bars sprang up in every high street, and semi-decent meals were offered which seemed positively *cordon bleu* after years of dreaded pub-grub. Then came cocktail bars and the rise in popularity of the private members' bar, based around the service and atmosphere one would expect to find in New York or Paris. Tapas bars and brasseries followed closely behind. All in all, one's options increased tenfold. There is now a far wider choice of watering hole, offering a higher standard and greater variety of service than ever.

One would have assumed that breweries and pub landlords would have learned something from these developments, but progress has been painstakingly slow. If you drink wine, the choice is anonymous white or red, both lovingly stored at room temperature. If you want entertainment there's the pool table or video game. How thrilling. And if you're hungry, perhaps sir would care for a packet of exquisitely prepared pork scratchings?

When you walk into a pub you enter the world of the lowest common denominator. Sloppy management runs sloppy pub attracts sloppy customer. Order a screwdriver and they think something's wrong with your table. Ask for a vodka and orange and they reach for the bottled Tree-Top. You want ice? You're a communist. Would it be too much for the people selling the drinks to know a little about the correct serving procedures?

During the recent hot spell I found myself in dire need of a drink. As I happened to be passing a well known East End public house I decided to chance my luck. First impressions were favourable. The decor had improved since the days when Jack 'The Hat' McVitie's entrails provided the focal point for the saloon area. It was now yuppies, yukkas and Continental lagers. The sign said 'You Can't Top A Grolsch' and I tended to agree. It was lovingly poured. It was raised to my lips. It was luke warm. I made for the exit. As I walked home I pondered on life's great unanswered questions: Is there a God? Why are we here? And why are lagers stacked on a shelf behind the bar instead of being kept in a fridge?

The question of decor unrolls a whole new sheet of crimson and gold flocked wallpaper. Most pubs are basic, which in practice verges on the sub-functional. Where an effort has been made it is usually in the direction of mock-Tudor or, worse, mock-Stringfellow. Fine for Rotary Club regulars and Wayne & Company, but if you happen to be a member of the human race, forget it. I live on the front line of East London's disco pubs, surrounded by place names like Razzles, Gigilo's and Nipples. They all have stupid canopies outside, they all play Stock, Aitken and Waterman's greatest aural atrocities, and they all think the ability to mix a decent cocktail revolves around sticking a bloody toothpick with a hat on into your glass. I would rather spend a weekend in Beirut than a solitary night in one of these places.

But I shouldn't complain. A little further down the road you can sup your pint peacefully while enjoying the compelling visual spectacle of some ageing hag displaying her sagging breasts and varicosed legs to the flagging interests and comatosed brains of a beery one and all.

Don't fancy that? Well worry not, just pop into the rough-house around the corner and relax to the soothing harmonies of the Country and Western band whose only claim to fame is the fact that two of its members died at birth.

A pub is the place where a hen-pecked Sid James can take refuge from a nagging Diana Coupland while she prepares the dinner for which he will return home late. Or where Terry and Bob can arrange to meet their dates on a Saturday night, only to discover that they are in fact mother and daughter. Still never mind, they'll be laughing about it come Sunday morning. Over a drink. Daarn the pub.

Get the drift? The pub is an embarrassing remnant of a Britain long gone, OK for those that set their sights below knee level, inconceivable to those that don't. To them a pub is just one more outmoded bastion of male braggadocio. Game of arrers, give it a portion, and a large dose of '*Djoo sbill mar pint?*' A place where a single woman cannot feel comfortable, a place where you can get well tanked-up before going on to terrorise the local Indian restaurant. With these credentials the only pub improvement I'd recommend is a major league torching.

I know that many people swear by public houses. That's fine, I've no gripe if you've been fortunate enough to find this quaint little pub somewhere in Upper Wallop, where the landlord's wife does the business with a leg of lamb and no one wants to stick a glass in your face. Great. But not for me. I hate the country. It gives me a migraine and makes my shoes dirty. And I hate country pubs. They're like all pubs really, they're just in different places.

Brewers and alcohol manufacturers spend fortunes projecting a more glamorous, up-market image. State-of-the-art advertisements are now common-place. You'd have thought they would have noticed that their products are being sold in places that are completely at odds with their marketing strategies. But they haven't. You know why? 'Cos they're all down the bloody pub, that's why.

Copyright © Geoff Deane, 1989

The Real Thing

The Greatest Football Match Ever Played by Neil Lyndon

November 1989

MY BROTHER AND I WERE ALONE in the house that evening. He was 17 and I was 13. My mother was taking a rest cure for her varicose veins in a BUPA clinic in Hove and the old man had driven his wallowing Jaguar Mark VII down to visit her, stopping off at The Plough on his way home, leaving us alone with our homework and the telly. He would have given two of her legs to have seen the vision that we witnessed. Nobody had the remotest understanding or expectation of the miracle about to be conducted through the ether into our presence – one which would live in our imagination for the rest of our lives and which would permanently alter those lives.

The earliest moments of the 1960s were not rich in the promise of glamour; that was to be found only in the arenas of sport. The political world was in the hands of soldierly grandfathers – Eisenhower and Macmillan, Adenauer and De Gaulle. Pop music was in the hands of phoney colonels and robber barons who rolled the cigars in their mouths around a lachrymose appeal for 'the all-round entertainer' and who wanted Cliff Richard to sing Rodgers and Hart songs to families at Blackpool. Eddie Cochran was dead. The most adventurous stylists of dress were villains like the Kray twins in their boxy little jackets with their slim-jim ties. Not a promising time to be young and on the look-out for excitement and inspiration.

In the first 18 months of the Sixties, however, there appeared a succession of miraculous sporting manifestations which seemed to light the way to a new world, a parade of heroes of such irresistible magnetism that you felt, watching them go, that the moment you had been waiting for – not knowing what it was – was coming, and that the people you wanted to be like were at last declaring themselves.

Herb Elliott, the first athlete you ever saw who might have been a film star or a rock singer, ran away from the toiling prefects of the old school through the floodlights of the Rome Olympics. And the gold medals in the 4×110 yards relay were won by the fabulous Tennessee Tigerbelles, led by Wilma Rudolph, the first all-black women's relay team from the USA, who were also the first women you ever saw run so fast that they had to bank their bodies through the turns. In the spring of 1961, the princely Wolfgang von Trips and the Steve McQueen-ish Phil Hill emerged in the shark-nosed rear-engined Ferraris, so neat and yet so menacing, to blow the world away on the Grand Prix circuits.

Those were glorious surprises enough to turn a boy's head; but nothing matched the appearance of Real Madrid in the 1960 European Cup final. Nothing in a post-war childhood in England had prepared us for an apparition of such other-worldly grace and ferocity, for a sporting performance of such comprehensive and unanswerable skill, power, wit and glamour.

We had, after all, hardly ever seen a back-heel played with professional purpose, nor an overhead bicycle-kick placed with the deliberate accuracy of a penalty. Those flourishes, first glimpsed when the Brazilians turned them on in the 1958 World Cup, were banned by sports masters throughout the land and, if they were attempted on English League grounds, were greeted from the terraces with choral jeers of 'nancy' and 'get rid of it'.

Our idea of raffishness in sporting dress was the thuggish appearance of Sheffield Wednesday's Peter Swan, with his black bloomers rolled up in scrotum-strangling tightness; or of Ron Flowers, centre-forward for Wolverhampton Wanderers and England, wearing a new pair of the cut-down 'Continental' boots your father wouldn't let you buy because they exposed your ankles and had no reinforcement in the toe-caps (and which did nothing to stop Ron Flowers from playing as if he thought he was Ted Drake). We were impoverished. Our imaginations were still held tight in the austerities of post-war rationing; we had nothing to share but dim and unrealisable yearnings.

And then, out of the greyness of that time and the monochrome of the cathode ray tube, came Real Madrid. It was as if the heavens had opened and angels of light had descended to earth, to Glasgow of all places, still a ship-building town swathed in the smoke of Players Weights a quarter of a century before its reincarnation as the Florence of Caledonia.

Before that evening, we had never seen Real Madrid – already four consecutive times winners of the European Cup – play a full 90 minutes. We knew, vaguely, who they were and we had been struggling for years with the pronunciation of their names (my friend Barry Harmer called Di Stefano 'Die (like Princess Di) Stevano'; to my father, Puskas was Puss-Cass). The European Cup did not, however, interest us very much: all we knew was that it was won by dirty wops who kicked shins and pulled shirts.

For the first 20 minutes of the 1960 final, we wanted Eintracht Frankfurt to win. The instinct was partly racist (they were, at least, manly Germans – whom we knew as squareheads – rather than pansyish greasers showing off their bottoms and their tans in natty whites); it was also fired by the allegiance of the 130,000 crowd at Hampden Park.

The Glasgow crowd was on Eintracht's side because, in an earlier stage of the competition, Glasgow Rangers had been stuffed, home and away, by Eintracht, who had won 12-4 on aggregate.

For the first 20 minutes, it looked as if Eintracht would slug out a deserved victory over the Spanish team. Indeed, they scored first, with a goal by Kress. I wouldn't have remembered that fact if I hadn't just read a couple of old cuttings about the match.

I do, however, remember what came next, for it came with such a thump of emotional shock and thrilling engagement that I can recall the impact now, 30 years after the moment. Real Madrid responded to Eintracht's goal like a boxer who has been laconically sparring with an inferior opponent and suddenly, to his surprise, tastes a drop of blood dribbling from his nostril. After the Kress goal, Real Madrid gathered their powers together and – like the moment when Muhammad Ali decided to stop dickering with Jerry Quarry and let him have it – with a fury controlled by *hauteur*, the angels in white cut loose.

The next 70 minutes of football changed the world. For one thing, Real Madrid put on the greatest display the world has ever seen from a club team (in fact, the only football performance fit for comparison was the Brazilian victory in the World Cup final 1970). For another thing, two young boys in a suburban villa would never again be able to see the world through the eyes of the Attlee generation, would never again believe automatically that Anglo-Saxon virtues were supreme, and would, in future, be able to imagine that it might be more satisfying, from every significant point of view (appearance, passion, ability, grace) to be a foreigner – preferably a dark-haired, olive-skinned foreigner.

Now we saw, for the first time (and saw at their best), the astounding skills of Di Stefano, Puskas, Gento, Del Sol, Canario, Zarraga and Santamaria (the names of Real's defending four players faded from Kenneth Wolstenholme's unsteady narrative and disappeared from memory: we couldn't remember them the next day). Real Madrid equalised, with Di Stefano's first goal, in the 26th minute. Three minutes later, the Argentinian scored again and Real Madrid took the lead.

He was so grand! We had never seen a player so commanding in his demand for the ball, so majestic in his delivery of passes to his team-mates. We had never seen a player to whom squad discipline and the orthodoxies of positional play meant nothing, one who might gather the ball from a scrum in his own penalty area, rap an exchange of passes in midfield, gather a return and accelerate through defenders in their own half to drive a shot which came off his boot like a pinball from the striking hammer.

A few players in the past 30 years – Best, Pele, Maradona, Gullitt – have been called 'complete'. Alfredo Di Stefano was the first we ever saw and the only one to whom a club team filled with internationals and major stars unquestionably deferred.

Ferenc Puskas, after all, was one of the greatest football heroes of the postwar era. Everybody in Europe had known his name throughout the Fifties, since his Hungarian team had humiliated England at Wembley in 1953. Puskas, now comically portly but still the most powerful and decisive goal-scorer in the world, knew and kept his subordinate place alongside Di Stefano. Gento was just the greatest winger ever made – breathtakingly fast, dazzlingly deft and capable of delivering flashing crosses with the accuracy of a snooker cue. He took his lead from Di Stefano.

The detailed record of the match doesn't matter any more. I shouldn't pretend that I remember every move and each of the ten goals scored that night. If I tried to recount them here, I would have to borrow from the published record. So you might as well look it up. Or get the tape.

What matters, historically, is that my brother and I spent the *whole* of the second half standing up in our living-room yelling at the screen. We became delirious with entrancement. Anybody who saw that match remembers what we felt. They shared it, too.

The swirling white spectacle of Real, advancing through flicks, back-heels, overhead kicks and a complete unity of individual skill and team purpose imprinted itself upon our consciousness as an image of perfection. (It certainly imprinted itself on Don Revie, who, when he took over the management of Leeds United later in the decade, threw away his struggling team's royal blue shirts and gave them an all-white strip like Real's, just to boost their self-esteem.)

Nobody who saw it expects to see its like again. The final score was 7-3 to Real Madrid. Puskas scored four, Di Stefano three. When the team paraded the cup around Hampden Park, 130,000

Glaswegians rose to them in thunderous applause, as did the whole country. The yearnings had found a focus. The stifling disciplines of the bombadier lance-corporal had been sundered. Nothing – not just football – would ever look the same again. The Sixties had begun.

Copyright © Neil Lyndon, 1989

Punchlines

A Day in Front of the Amstrad by Geoff Deane
March 1990

A T 7.30 A.M. I AWAKE. I arise carefully taking care not to stir the sleeping she-goddess. If she does not enjoy her full 14 hours the she-goddess tends to get a little 'ratty'. With correct nurturing this later becomes a fully grown 'ratty'. And with my 35th birthday looming I have become far too attached to my genitalia to consider risking even the briefest of encounters with this most fearsome of species, size notwithstanding.

Actually I tell a lie. There is one exception to this rule. When she has her period she is 'ratty', _period_. How 'ratty'? Well, if I were to wake her with breakfast in bed, tell her she's the most beautiful woman in the world, and then toss her the keys to a new Mercedes Sports she'd probably reply by telling me that she thinks I've put on a little weight.

7.45 a.m. Sandblast my epidermis to smithereens beneath the shower then top up my caffeine and nicotine levels. This routine achieves the expected results. I feel like shit.

8.15 a.m. Check the answerphone for last night's messages. There are none, other than a dictum from my mother on the subject of neglect. To my mother the answerphone is a blessing. A surrogate son, there to be chastised, reproached and scorned in the absence of the real thing. 'Please leave any guilt you may wish to inflict after the forthcoming high-pitched tone.' She did.

8.30 a.m. Check the mail. One letter from Amex threatening legal proceedings. Another letter from Amex inviting me to apply for a gold card. Then another threatening more legal proceedings should I ever dare apply for a gold card. An invite to an exhibition on modern plastics. An invite from my bank manager to attend an interrogation at his place, at my earliest convenience. He and I get on like a house on fire. If only he were in it. He is about 26 years old but already looks more like a bank manager than anyone else in Europe.

9.00 a.m. Read the papers.

9.01 a.m. Risk life and limb by taking in tea to the sleeping she-goddess. I try to awaken her gently but to no avail. I then yell, scream and perform an impromptu clog dance around the bedroom but she remains stubbornly insentient.

10.00 a.m. Switch on the TV for my daily dose of Kilroy. *Oozing charm from every pore he oils his way across the studio floor.* Mornings just wouldn't be the same without Kilroy. I watch in awe and marvel at his ability to appear so dreadfully concerned all the time. 'Really my love?' Concern, concern. 'Has anyone else in the studio audience suffered like poor Sheila?' Concern, concern. He must be one of the most concerned men in the world. A sort of macho Mother Teresa for the Grecian 2000 set. If Kilroy had a pound for every ounce of sincerity in his soul he'd be worth almost 50p by now.

11.00 a.m. The phone goes.

11.15 a.m. I track it down to a run-down bar on the corner of 42nd and 3rd.

12.01 p.m. Decide that work cannot be put off any longer.

12.02 p.m. Decision reversed after a recount.

12.15 p.m. My agent calls. He's had a good reaction to my screenplay. Would I be prepared to work in Hollywood if push came to shove? What? Move from Bethnal Green? Me? Perish the thought. As an agent my agent is good. As a purveyor of *dumshmuck* questions, he's exemplary.

12.30 p.m. Phone rings again. A magazine wants to know if I'd like to interview Emma Thompson. I stifle laughter and replace the receiver.

1.00 p.m. Work. I switch on the Amstrad Personal Bastard 8256 Word Processor with the special built-in sabotage device that loses all of your work at the end of the day. The screen is blank and my mind complements it perfectly. Nothing. Nisht. Nada.

I need inspiration. So I smoke like a *kamikaze* lab rabbit whose wife is currently giving birth for the first time, and drink sufficient coffee to keep me buzzing well into the next millennium. Still nothing.

1.30 p.m. I hear a noise. The sleeping she-goddess (as was) sticks her head through the door.

2.00 p.m. Am still removing splinters from head of said she-goddess when she suddenly utters the word 'lunch'. In yet another bold display of masculine bravado I nod both subserviently and repeatedly. Lunch with the she-goddess is usually a simple affair consisting of a short phone call, followed by a longer taxi ride and rounded off with a large bill. Today is no exception.

2.45 p.m. Lunch. Enjoyable, though marred by a waiter sporting a dyed blond crop and a sphincter made to measure for somebody much smaller. To say his attitude was offhand would be a little like describing Islamic fundamentalists as 'tetchy'. We eat, and I pay. A tip? Don't tempt me.

5.00 p.m. Back in front of the Amstrad Safety Hair Trimmer And Combined Personal Cocktail Cabinet. This machine is not so much user-friendly as user-smug. How come you can never find a Luddite when you really need one?

5.30 p.m. I am slumped over the desk, mentally fondling my dejection when the she-goddess walks in. She then makes the sort of gesture that could get a practising freemason into a lot of trouble with an alert, investigative journalist. Suddenly the mystery of the capless toothpaste, the hairs found clogging up the bathroom sink and the endless Luther Vandross tapes all fall into perspective. I understand everything and the answer is beginning to manifest itself prominently in my loins.

5.45 p.m. With the crowd behind me I perform a perfect Triple-Lutz into the thick of the mêlée. I wade my way through the Kama Sutra with all the enthusiasm of a latterday Errol Flynn but none of the bad publicity. Trains enter tunnels, pistons begin to thrash, but unfortunately my reputation as something of a speedreader begins to preceed me. I turn to the final chapter somewhat ahead of schedule. Then the phone rings. Instinct says leave it. But it might be my agent. It could be impotent. I mean important. But it won't be. But it might. So with as unpointed a moot as one could ever expect to own, I go to answer the phone.

6.00 p.m. Hello mum. No, don't worry, you're not interrupting anything. Why did she stress the word 'anything'? I swear the woman is psychic. Where does it say in the _Talmud_ that sex with a gentile woman shall _always_ climax with a phone call from your mother? Would I like to come round for dinner? Actually mum, I've eaten. Oh, it's my favourite is it? And it would be a shame to waste it . . .

Alright! I'd love to come to dinner, mum. Yes, of course I'm sure. No, of course it isn't any trouble. No, of course you're not putting me out. I'll see you later. Bye.

6.15 p.m. Phone rings again. Honestly mum it's no trouble. Bye.

6.30 p.m. The she-goddess enters and gives me one of those looks that can sink a thousand ships. It's wasted on me. My galleon is already well and truly scuppered.

6.32 p.m. One final confrontation with the Amstrad Motherfucker 8256. Nothing happening. That's it, I've had enough for the day. Turn off the Alan Sugar Dust Collector 8256 and sulk. Final word count – zilch. I kick around the idea of writing about a day in the life of a writer. Dismiss it as unrealistic. Who'd be interested?

6.45 p.m. Go round mum's.

Copyright © Geoff Deane, 1990

The Euroman Cometh

The New Breed of Business Internationalist by Rob Ryan
March 1990

WHILE EVERYBODY ELSE on Swissair flight SR 831 from London Heathrow to Geneva is busy tucking into the complimentary Charles Heidseicker, the man in 14A is resolutely sticking to the orange juice, busy keeping himself as sharp as the crease in his trousers. Together with his seat, his clothes and his attitude, this is another tiny corroboration that *he* is the one I have been looking for.

I had first marked his card when, between stowing his briefcase and taking his seat, he glanced around the cabin at his fellow businessmen and, for a fleeting second, unsheathed The Smile; the smile a small furry mammal with precognisance might have made when it observed the dinosaurs strutting around as if they had an indefinite tenure on the planet; the kind of smile a Cro-Magnon Einstein flashed at his low-brow buddies when they warned him that messing with fire wouldn't get him anywhere.

14A smiled The Smile because he knew that this cabin-full of fellow Brit businessmen in their dandruffy charcoal and navy-blue M&S suits have as many prospects as the Triceratops. 14A has seen the future of Europe, and he isn't diffident in claiming his position at the cash-face of commerce. The Smile betrays an absolute confidence, a certainty in this manifest destiny: not for 14A the I'm-not-foreign-I'm-British haughtiness UK citizens usually inflict on their Continental peers around the conference table. Nor the let's-assume-we-all-speak-English arrogance of the linguistically incompetent. And certainly not the dressed-in-the-dark crumpled look that has the French and Italians sniggering about the British business uniform.

In fact 14A doesn't even consider himself to be British any more – he is Euroman, the perfect Nietzschean product of late-twentieth-century economic eugenics, primed and keyed for the Single Market. If he were to need an anthem, he would unhesitatingly go for 'Tomorrow Belongs To Me'.

I am not alone in my curiosity about this particular species of Business Class pedant. If they were here, the representatives of Price-Waterhouse, John Coultis and Saxton Bampfylde would share my interest in 14A. Companies like these are the great white sharks of the business world: cruising for fresh meat, armed with hefty salaries and comprehensive benefit packages, golden hellos and silver have-a-nice-holidays. These days they call themselves executive search consultants, but their old epithet is far more apposite – headhunters. The heads they are most concerned with right now belong to the likes of 14A: Pan-European Executive, Euro-crat, Euro-Yuppie or, more simply, Euroman.

Euroman is the current Holy Grail of the executive search world. Endless reports are written and profiles drawn of who, what and where he will be when the Big Day comes (oddly enough 1992 actually starts on Jan 1, 1993, when everyone of course, will be on holiday). The argument for finding and holding on to Euroman goes like this: when the trade barriers come down to create the single market, much of British business will be caught with its trousers in the same position; those companies that have not trained their personnel adequately to take on the other eleven countries (and Sweden and Switzerland, who are poised to jump into the new fiscal romper-room feet first) will need executives well versed in other business cultures and markets.

He will know not to do business over lunch in Rome, will know that Germans are always paid 13 monthly salary cheques a year, that the relaxed clothing code of the French masks a rigid pecking order, that the concept of the understatement is alien to the Spanish. In short, they will need Euroman, the Lone Ranger of '92.

Those who have such people, those who *are* them, will be able to demand a very high premium indeed.

14A is certainly promising Euroman material, which is something of a relief – finding the perfect specimen has so far proved rather difficult. Not that there has been any shortage of volunteers: the hotel bars, Club Class lounges and duty-free shops of Europe are teeming with fresh-faced pretenders to this new business throne. They drop foreign phrases into the conversation, are learning to prop up a bar with a Gallic slouch, perfect Continental affectations such as ordering 'two drinks' by signalling with thumb and index finger, and generally treat Europe as a pick'n'mix cultural bazaar.

And they always have that whiff of superiority, sardonically flashing The Smile when they see their less fortunate compatriots coming unstuck with the local language or customs. Look them in the eye and challenge, 'You are Euroman and I claim my 50 francs' and they will unflinchingly hand over the cash. These people don't subscribe to hiding their light under a bushel (or 36.4 cubic metres as they would doubtless prefer to say) – they have no doubt that a Euroman is a credible aspiration.

However, those most keen to establish their credentials prove woefully inadequate when the criteria of true Europeanisation are applied. I soon came to be cautious of those who thought an electronic diary that keeps time in 260 cities and a shopping spree along New Bond Street for a Hermès tie and a Loewe briefcase is all that is needed to create the consummate Euroman.

Nor did I have much joy trawling the beds of the multinationals in search of our mythical Euroman: the IBMs and Fords of this world tend to operate within a US-spawned Corporate Culture that is adapted to operating globally, an extension of the Holiday Inn principle. Too long in such a system institutionalises the executive. Euroman will have to work outside such a cultural cocoon.

But my money is on 14A being the full bhuna. Witness the seat positioning. Euromen fly often enough to cultivate favourite seats, and Row 14 on the Swissair Airbus is generally considered to be prime real estate: plenty of leg-room (no row 13 – who would have thought the Swiss superstitious?), not too near the toilets, and with the preferential disembarking that Business Class enjoys. The Euroman can be in the hire car while Scum Class punters are still waiting for their baggage.

Not that Euroman will have any baggage, of course. Hand luggage only – usually a folding 'suiter' or a voluminous shoulder-bag plus briefcase. Euroman seems to have adopted an aphorism culled from Harry Tuttle, De Niro's character in _Brazil_: 'Get in, get out. Travel light. A Man Alone.'

Apart from the lack of luggage, clothes remain the greatest signifier of a man who has successfully submitted to the cultural Robochef. Euromen are gradually casting off the shackles of the drab business dress. There was a maxim in the old days at Morgan Grenfell that went: 'Never trust a man who wears slip-on shoes or whose tie is lighter than his shirt.' This sentiment is still engraved on most British businessmen's wardrobe doors, but not so the pioneers of _affaires sans frontières_.

For starters Euroman has discovered the lightweight Italian business suit, or – at an even greater level of advancement – that the wearing of a tasteful blue blazer with slacks does not cause mass cardiac arrests in European boardrooms. 14A has not yet progressed quite that close to Euro-perfection, but the brown Cerutti is certainly a bold statement in the murky sea of navy and charcoal that surrounds us.

I'm worried about his raincoat, though. Euroman must have a Euromac. The Germans, Italians and Swedes tend towards their green Loden coats, which look as if they have been cut from army-surplus bivouacs. There are rumours of English Euromen, too long in Düsseldorf or Hamburg, finally succumbing and going native by adopting the Loden. They are to be treated suspiciously – it could be lederhosen next.

No, the true Euromac has the cut of, say, an Aquascutum or Burberry trenchcoat. If I'm not mistaken, 14A has opted for a Ralph Lauren, which is the right shape but lacks the epaulets Europeans favour. Still, close enough – more important for our man is getting the contents of his wallet right.

The wallet should contain a mixture of currencies: Kroner, Deutschmarks, Swiss Francs (tipping and taxis must be done in cash), and a selection of plastic money. There will be telephone cards from several countries. A stack of business cards for the ritual exchanges that open up any meeting is essential. Euroman has cards in several languages – the more advanced have even progressed to colour coding them: green cards have French backed with English, blue German backed with English and so on.

Euroman is also out to give the lie to the cliché about the English and foreign languages. He will speak one fluently and have a smattering of two others. Of course English is the international business language, thanks to the Americans and computers (whose programs rarely use anything else), but Euroman despises such linguistic imperialism. Better to flatter and impress the clients by speaking his own language. He has even learnt a few Eurojokes which can be quickly translated and will even make the Germans laugh.

The current favourite on the circuit is about Europe 2000. If it is Heaven the police will be British, the cooks French, the lovers Italian, the workers German and it will be organised by the Swiss. If it turns out to be Hell, the police will be German, the cooks British, the lovers Swiss, the workers French and it will be organised by the Italians. Of course the subtext for Euroman is a rubbishing of national stereotypes – only in his darkest moments will a rogue doubt enter his mind that the joke may hide an immutable version of reality.

14A has got his briefcase down – a bomb-proof Hermès Espace, no less. Why would a British businessman fall for an expensive bomb-proof carbon-fibre briefcase? It could be a sensible precaution; in some parts of Europe they treat their captains of industry with slightly less respect than the City of London. Think of Dr Alfred Herrhausen, head of Deutsche Bank or Hans Tietmeyer or Karl Heinz Beckhurts or Hans Zimmerman, all subject to assassination attempts, some of them successful. Perhaps 14A has nightmares that one day the Red Army Faction will sit up and take notice. A bomb-proof case ensures that at least the appointments diary will survive.

No, the Hermès is a present, I'll bet. Euroman by definition needs a second cultural input into his life, ideally parents of two different nationalities, but that is rather difficult to arrange retrospectively. Failing that, wife/girlfriends in Paris or Zurich or Amsterdam will do nicely.

Out of his case comes a stack of reports; judging by the mass ploughing of paperwork going on around me, it isn't the Business Class passengers who are responsible for emptying the Skyshops of the Deightons, Krantzes and Archers. They are too busy, like the Navy Blue Suit next to me, reading reports on the future of plastics in the automotive industry.

But 14A ditches the folders and from the carbon fibre confines produces the magazines *L'Express* and *L'Oggi*. What is this: Euroman relaxing with recreational reading? Not a bit of it. Euromen scour such publications for conversational grouting to work into the cracks of the forthcoming meeting: how did Denmark do in the European Ice Hockey Championship, and will Prime Minister Schlueters succeed in re-organising the tax structure for 1992? Will abortion be legalised in Belgium? A little local colour inserted for when business talk is not appropriate. Euromen are big on satellite dishes, for the same reason: cultural nuances. So perhaps they do end up watching stripping housewives, but even that does wonders for their colloquial Italian.

Eventually Euromen tire of flights from Heathrow every second day, or even the best Business Class food, and sooner or later run out of space for all the complimentary champagne bottles (Euroman does not drink *en route* to meetings, but on Swissair and BA you can opt to take the champagne away). Their thoughts turn to a permanent bolt-hole on the Continent, nearer the girlfriend perhaps, or an apartment in Sydney, a good base for those holidays in the Solomon Islands they talk about or, anything other than face Terminal 2 Heathrow again.

God knows, they need a holiday – being pan-European is a full-time occupation. A litany can be produced mimicking the mournful one of the Magnificent Seven when they discuss the price of being a gunfighter. For a Euroman it runs: Social Life – none. Hobbies – none. Friends – few they get to spend much time with. Books read recently – none that weren't job-related. Sights seen in cities visited – none. Films enjoyed – none, they only catch in-flight movies, and nobody ever enjoys them.

Euromen do not even get to luxuriate in expensive hotels, opting instead for a Sofitel or an Ibis: clean functional room, shower and a bed – they are rarely in it long enough to need anything else. Any extra expenses go in upgrading the hire car. After all, the client rarely sees your hotel room, but they may be watching you drive up to the meeting.

Of course there is the nagging doubt I could be wrong about 14A. He could be a cuckoo-clock importer going to Geneva to check the birds come out of the doors smoothly. My reverie is interrupted by the prepare-for-landing announcement and 14A is forgotten. When it comes to air travel, taking off is fine, but I am not a good lander.

Twenty minutes later, on a train out of Geneva, I discover I'm not wrong about 14A. Well, some of the details perhaps. The briefcase was a present from a delighted client in Paris, there is no Parisian girlfriend (although the idea does appeal to him), he does not yet have multilingual business cards (on the agenda), but yes, he considers himself a Euroman. His destination? Like me, he has business at IMEDE, one of Europe's principal schools for the production of Euromen.

True Euromen may be born to those bi-cultural parents, but reasonable facsimiles can be made, and they are made at places such as INSEAD at Fontainbleu and IMEDE in Lausanne. These schools teach 22 different nationalities, examining the national stereotypes and resultant cultural barriers that often impede business. Apart from any other benefits, here the budding Euroman also builds up his Network.

In his office overlooking Lake Geneva, Dominique Turpin of IMEDE brandishes three hefty albums full of business cards. 'This is my Network. Mostly from my time in Japan. Over there they always open any meeting with an exchange of business cards, which they take very seriously. When you swop cards you are saying, "Call me if I can be of assistance any time in the future." ' Turpin makes it sound like the Masons without the trouser-rolling. 'Increasingly, the same is true here. So when British people come to IMEDE or INSEAD, rather than the London Business School, they miss out on building up a domestic Network, but they feel they are compensated by having contacts across Europe.'

Apart from membership of this card-trading cadre, INSEAD and IMEDE also offer the ultimate Euroman qualification, the MBA – Master of Business Administration. Both schools accept only high flyers for this course – they must have four years' experience and the motivation to spend one year (and £12,000 in course fees) to achieve the MBA. 'The most valuable thing about the MBA,' says Turpin, 'is the months spent working out management problems with other nationalities, and realising that your way of thinking is not the only way.' Such Euro-competence is so valued by multinationals that the MBA graduates are subject to fierce headhunting, and 40 per cent of them end up working in countries other than their native ones.

Chris Parker is a psychologist from South Shields who teaches Executive Development at IMEDE. Parker is contemptuous of those who think they can re-invent themselves as Euroman simply by picking a few accessories off the Continental shelf. He is adamant that Europeanisation requires more of a cerebral adjustment than a sartorial one. 'The true European manager is more concerned with the variations in how a country's culture affects its business dealings. It is the diversity at the level of values and beliefs that needs to be appreciated,' says Parker, 'knowing how the French or the Germans approach negotiations.

'My nightmare is that this international businessman everybody wants to produce will turn out to be some neutered, castrated, bland and boring guy with no real identity at all. What we try to do here at IMEDE is not get people to give up their national characteristics but to exploit the synergy you get when different nationalities work together.'

Parker's premise is that a management team of 'castrated' Euromen will lack the inherent conflict necessary for creativity. A board of Euromen would rapidly fall victim to what he calls 'organisational decay'. And anyway, if there *has* to be a Euroman, Parker feels, 14A and his UK friends have a lot of catching up to do. 'The Swedes, the Swiss and the Dutch have been able to compete across Europe for years. They have had to learn other languages, have had to expand because of small home markets, and have got no hang-ups about their own cultural superiority.'

The other threat to Euroman comes from outside the tariff-free zone. Many of the Japanese business behemoths have had small offices in Europe for ten or more years – Kao, for example, the biggest cosmetic company in the world, and Dentsu, the biggest advertising agency. They have been losing money for those ten years, just doing their homework, rather like the little men in white lab coats with clipboards who visited the Isle of Man TT races in the late Fifties, and suffered ridicule until the worm turned and wiped out the British motorcycle industry.

These slumbering giants are stirring. Kao has recently swallowed a German cosmetics company, Dentsu considered (but eventually declined) buying part of the beleagured Saatchi empire, but has announced it will be on a shopping spree for other agencies this year. The Japanese don't need Euromen – they use their own Japanese management, overseeing executives native to the country they are operating within.

Partially because of this Japanese connection, IMEDE expects 1992 to see a new clarion call from the headhunters – Go Global. The executive of the mid-Nineties will not only need to take Europe in his stride, but be able to operate on the Pacific Rim and understand both the Oriental and Occidental business mentality. After World Music, the World Businessman. The irony could be that, within five years, Euromen may seem just too parochial.

On the way back from IMEDE I spent two hours in the Business Class lounge at Geneva Airport. This is one of the major capitalist crossroads of Europe, through which sooner or later all currently extant species of businessmen pass. At the complimentary drinks counter I chat with Hans Nijpels, a Dutchman. He speaks four languages, has worked for Agfa in the UK and Belgium, and is now employed by a French consultancy specialising in European markets. He has been in Lausanne giving a presentation at the headquarters of Tetrapak, the Swedish drinks packagers. From his clothes (the familiar Hermès, Burberry package, but worn with an élan most Brits would be hard put to match) to his impressive command of frivolous gossip, he has poor 14A beaten hollow in the Euroman stakes.

I put IMEDE's theory to Herr Nijpels that our vision of 1992 is simply too myopic, that beyond Europe the World beckons. He smiles, dips into his pocket and brings out a business card printed on one side in English, the other in Japanese. 'The secret,' he says, 'is to always be one step ahead.'

14A, look to your laurels, because somewhere out there is a Businessman's Boot Hill, full of New Generations that had a brief flowering and died when their shortcomings became apparent: Meritocracy-man, Room-at-the-Top Man, Mid-Atlantic Man, and, freshest flower on the grave, City-Oik Man. I have a feeling that one day they will be chiselling a new headstone:

EUROMAN! 1990–95
IT SEEMED A GOOD IDEA AT THE TIME

Copyright © Rob Ryan, 1990

The Last American Class Act
Paul Newman by Nick Kent
March 1990

T HEY'VE BEEN CALLING him 'America's premier superstar' for eons now, ever since *Time*, *Newsweek* and all the other big guns first caught wind of that plummy word back in the mid-Sixties. So I guess it's taken as law now. Paul Newman, the great inscrutable American, at 65 resembles less the Greek God statue come to life, and more a walking monument to righteous living and stoic endeavour. Still eerily 'forever young' in his demeanour, still sexy, though now in a decidedly crumpled way, still replete with that bedevilling 'I can't help it if I'm lucky' smirk of a mouth, Newman is still more than capable of laying on the charm with a gilded trowel.

'I'm actually looking forward to this,' he says although he is referring to his next film, not to the interview. 'See, I'm very close to Mr Bridge. He's pig-headed and opinionated. He's a very moral man. He believes in hard work and providing for his family. He doesn't know how to do anything else. I mean, he's not a poet . . .'

And here he pauses, dropping the one-to-one eye contact that leaves you momentarily spell-bound (his eyes *are* incredible close-up, two perfect weapons of lethal seductiveness), and looks off into the ether (if this was schtick, it was great schtick). And then, 'I mean, I can certainly understand a man like that.'

It was late, languorous August and we were all in Paris in an appropriately 'classy' ('class' and 'the Newmans' being inseparable concepts) restaurant, we being a profusion of international journalists, Newman, his indecently radiant wife, Joanne Woodward, the director James Ivory (casting a condescending glare over proceedings) and Ivory's Machiavellian producer, Ishmael Merchant. The following day shooting would begin on *Mr And Mrs Bridge*, a Ruth Prawer Jhabvala adaptation of two novellas by the Kansas writer Evan Connel dealing with a Midwestern family's insular odyssey from 1917 to the early Forties, with Newman and Woodward 'reunited' in the title roles. Not that they've ever really been apart. 'Well we did *Harry And Son* together only five years ago,' Joanne Woodward would later reminisce. 'And I only remember that because that's when I got my dog . . . This new film just sort of providentially happened along, really. You see, film-acting is something I haven't been doing that much of, for quite a while now (pauses). I think it's just nice to do one together because we can spend the time together. Last year Paul was on location pretty much all the time.'

'If you want to get anywhere with him, be interested in her,' a press agent advised, and although it turned out to be unnecessary advice (they were placed at separate tables for interview purposes), it shows just how dependent and deferrential Newman is on, and to, Woodward when they're together. ('He's constantly trying to provide a setting where the world can see what he sees in her,' the screenwriter Stewart Stem, a Newman colleague of long-standing, once observed). You'd catch him sometimes, panic pinching at his features, glancing over across a crowded room until his eyes received their due reassurance from hers and he'd mellow back. 'That's my lady over there,' he'd mutter, addressing no one in particular. It was cute as hell.

Any bold image of Newman being one of those take-charge kind of Hollywood heroes-made-flesh had been banished anyway from the first second the little beehive of paparazzi outside the bistro had opened up and the press got their first glimpse of the great couple. When that glimpse came, one thing became immediately apparent, that Newman and Woodward as a screen couple are the perfect paradox, in that while the former is an instantly recognisable screen presence in every film, his wife, technically a far greater actor than he, is almost unrecognisable from one film to the next, so deeply immersed is she in the chameleon process of character projection. Here together *au naturel*, Newman might have been looking sleek like an old grey seal, but the class act was Woodward – six years his junior, granted, but with the more 'charismatically radiant' physical presence, by a clear country mile.

She was in charge anyway, and firmly so, leading him by the arm through the photographers, shepherding him along like a mother navigating a disorientated schoolboy through a long, dark tunnel. For all his stealth and outward vigour he still looked out of it, an impression strengthened by the fact he was wearing his dark glasses hanging down around his chin like he was understudying for Steve Martin's role in *The Jerk*.

Anyway, they lined up the press so the great couple could make that 'all-important initial acquaintance' with the folks who would be grilling them over lunch. Woodward does this sort of thing regally, but Newman isn't up to it at all. He managed to squeeze off a couple of pained smiles to the first two journos in the queue, gave the third a blank stare . . . by the time they got to me, he threw me a look so downright cold that I thought that he thought that I meant to mug his wife or something.

The last time I'd seen those impossible blue eyes boring a hole in my face had coincided with my first real introduction to the great screen phenomenon of Paul Newman and his perfect visage. I must have been all of 11 when *Hud* came to my town and everywhere you'd see the same huge daunting bill-poster; on it Newman's face was cast in granite, his cobalt eyes at their most enticingly 'low and mean'. Above him in extra-bold letters were writ large the words: 'PAUL NEWMAN IS . . . HUD, THE MAN WITH THE BARBED WIRE SOUL!' Then and now, in both instances, it was some introduction.

Later, in one of his more telling exchanges, Paul Newman would seize upon the subject of that 1963 film – one of his most celebrated – wringing his features fretfully as he berated it for being 'the biggest godamned mistake of my career. You see, we started out with noble intentions – we took this character, Hud Bannon, from a Larry McMurtry novel ("Horsemen Pass By"); he played no real part in the book, but we took him and made him into . . . the most selfish, vain bastard that had ever hit the screen! A guy that had all the superficial graces . . . all that external beauty Tennessee Williams used to say Americans always place such a godamn high premium on. And all the artificial, superficial aspects of Hud . . . well the young people just ate them up. It was meant as a condemnation, but the kids were absolutely captivated by it all. I'm saying I think we made a big mistake bringing that to the screen.'

Hud's popularity in the early Sixties brought Newman face to face with his great limitation as a screen actor: his looks make it impossible for him to play unsympathetic, dark or villainous types convincingly, simply because audiences find his very presence too infectiously likeable.

Newman came up at the time of Brando and Dean (he attended Actor's School in New York with Dean and later introduced him to Pier Angeli when both were installed in Hollywood) and in fact suffered through most of the Fifties from criticisms of being a Brando look-alike ('I've signed as many Brando autographs as Brando,' he said at the time. 'Sure, it's frustrating. You're in this business to promote your own personality'). But Newman was always more of an old-school pro movie actor type, harking back to stoic American charm-school leads like Ronald Coleman, Clark Gable (_Hud_ was very much in the Gable mode), or Cary Grant (whom Newman would seemingly go out of his way to emulate in the Sixties with a brace of lamentable comedies).

When he was rebellious it was animal energy and high spirits, not neurosis, that motivated him towards calamity. 'He's one of the few stars we've got in a normal emotional range,' Pauline Kael once wrote, '. . . He has grown by going deeper into the emotions of ordinary men.' Which isn't to say that Newman didn't make it as a 'leading protagonist in contemporary American themes' like Brando. There's a difference between the latter's gut 'instinct' and the former's reliance on 'technique' to call his shots for him, but Newman has a way of getting next to an audience's heart, of making his struggle, when it pays off for him, a shared triumph for all of us.

After commencing the Seventies with two of the biggest box-office successes of all-time – the Redford collaborations *Butch Cassidy* and *The Sting* – his star slumped badly through the rest of that decade with each subsequent ill-conceived vehicle (*Pocket Money*, *W.U.S.A.*, *Sometimes A Great Notion*, the empty Altman artiness of *Buffalo Bill* and *Quintet*) bombing with the new movie audience. But in the Eighties he reaffirmed his status first, in 1981, with a sly, compact performance in Sydney Pollack's *Absence of Malice* ('Newman gives even "revenge" class so we can all enjoy it' – Kael again) and five years later when he superbly reprised 'Fast' Eddie Felson and his continuing pursuit of excellence 25 years on from *The Hustler* with Martin Scorsese directing in *The Color Of Money*. Saddled with an over-energetic, dorkish Tom Cruise, Newman still pulled out all the 'class' stops in this film, finally winning an Oscar for his pains after six unsuccessful nominations.

Most agreed he had deserved the award three years earlier for *The Verdict*, when he took over from Robert Redford to play Frank Galvin, a down-and-out attorney desperately trying to break away from his own seediness and establish himself as a figure of some weight and integrity in the courtroom.

Here Newman really broke new ground for himself, finally getting to well and truly 'crawl out of his skin' (his own pet term for the transcendent acting moment) on the big screen. Galvin as played by Newman aches all the time all over, like an all-purpose sufferer for TV commercials; he can't ever seem to hold back the bad taste constantly welling up in the back of his throat and so is perpetually locked into himself, claustrophobic in his own body and sensibility. This finally *was* great acting, not just great screen technique, and apparently it's only this sense of continued 'risk-taking' that motivates Newman back out under the sulphur to ply his trade.

For the past 18 months, though, he's been on a roll, working first with Roland Joffe on *Fat Man And Little Boy* (released here in March as *Shadow Makers*) down in Mexico, then over to Texas, where he played the flamboyant Louisiana Governor Earl (brother of 'Kingfish' Huey) Long in *Blaze*. *Mr And Mrs Bridge* was his third back-to-back project, although Newman went so far in another of the day's interviews as to intimate that it might be his last. Even Woodward confided at one point, 'Less and less is he as interested in acting as he once was. Actually I wish Paul would retire from acting altogether and just direct films. Acting for him now is one little segment, while he's more concerned with the overall view.'

* * *

'Don't call me an actor. Just say I'm a man who sells salad dress-ings!' Newman told a writer from *Today* later in the afternoon. He was referring to his range of Newman's Own food products; his big kick in the Eighties seemed to have been inventing phenom-enally successful recipes for salad dressings, spaghetti sauces, popcorn and lemonade. ('If you're going to commercialise yourself, then let it be in the most obvious way possible,' he added. Joanne Woodward, too, had started doing advertising, specifically for Audi cars in 1987, and Newman himself has just signed a $5m deal with American Express.) I asked him at one point whether he felt his greatest roles had helped – like Brando's and Dean's – to shake up the culture and create a climate of change, but he wasn't having any of it.

'Well, I don't think we really preceded anything so much as we just reflected it . . . [he pauses] Actually I've never felt actors had that kind of power . . . Now, music . . . that brought about the kind of changes you're probably talking about . . . the drugs and all that . . . That was [dismissive sweep of the hand] those music guys . . . Elvis Presley and the Beatles . . .'

Newman has little sympathy with such icons, it appears. In recent years he's tried single-handedly to block Madonna from joining the Screen Actors' Guild of New York (of which he is a director). He also tried to have Iggy Pop 'removed' from his two-second cameo in *The Color Of Money* back in 1986. This con-siderable antipathy may well stem from one root cause: in 1978 his only son, Scott (Newman was married once before, to Jacqueline de Witt with whom he had three children. Scott being the first) died of a drugs overdose at the age of 28. Newman, who was es-tranged from his son at the time was devastated for several years and still plainly carries a terrible burden of guilt around with him. As one of America's great national heroes, the image of him finally as a man chasing his own tail relentlessly trying to save the world with high-minded thoughts and noble deeds who nonetheless was unable to save his own son from self-destructing is the most haunt-ing and may prove the most painfully apposite. Newman Jnr was known to resent his father's celebrity status and, prior to his death, often publicly berated it for having messed up his life. Others of Newman's brood have complained of feeling like disorientated ciphers next to their father and mother's perfect, thrusting super-star vitality.

'Oh my God, do they ever complain?' Joanne Woodward admit-ted. She has three daughters from the 31-year-old marriage. ('An ornithologist, a jazz singer, and the youngest is flirting with going to drama school. It's always such a big deal in our family.') 'All the time. I finally turned on one of them and said OK . . . but Paul and I are the parents you've got. So live with it! It could've been worse!

'There just isn't any way out with parenthood, is there? You simply can't win. I have to be honest, I think I did them no favours by staying involved in my work. If you're going to have children, stay home and raise them. Otherwise, why have them? I mean, it's not like we need 'em to work on the farm, God knows. And just having them as an extension of our own egos – well, we all know, once they arrive, that's not a good reason . . .

'But you have to understand about Paul and I,' she said. 'We're from a very different age. We come from the "interim" generation, the generation between Mr and Mrs Bridge, and what is taken as the present generation. It's been disorientating . . . for both of us. Different values, different moral codes . . . It's been hard to keep up.'

Newman said something, then let his impossibly blue eyes settle mistily on the red wine in the big old glass he tenderly clasped before him. For one moment he even let his fingers dance a tentative pirouette around the neck of a near-by wine bottle. In reality it was only Paul Newman doing his 'little ole wine drinker me' schtick, because I'd seen him employ all the same mannerisms in old films of his, specifically in the mock-drunk scene with Shelly Winters in *Harper*, not to mention Eddie Felson's booze-play in *The Color Of Money*'s early sequences.

He wasn't really drunk though – more jet-lagged (he complained of 'not travelling well' these days). An hour before he'd appeared scattered and uptight. Now it was clear Paul Newman was feeling no pain. What he was feeling – and right off the bat one couldn't help but pick up on it – was authentically shy, and it was this highly charged diffidence he projected so guilelessly, far more than his appearance, that made him seem so eerily, irrepressibly youthful to all of us. He'd be talking away like some concerned senior citizen, then suddenly lighten up by making a hopeless remark like 'Hey . . . don't mind me, I'm a dinosaur.' And then he'd let go with that bashful schoolboy smile and the generation gap of up to 40 years separating him from the rest of his interrogators would evaporate, like ice-cones in hell.

It was a rather spooky phenomenon to witness so close at hand. Surrounding the two of us, I should add, were six other supposed journalists – all of them foreign, all of them young and quite hope-less. Most of them couldn't make themselves understood in English and so they arranged themselves around the long table like human cushions, utterly useless but blessedly non-verbal. The verbal con-tingent appeared to consist of two feckless girls in their early twenties – one, a _Vogue_ correspondent, was quite brazen, the other simply lent her support by giggling a lot – who seemed bent on vaguely flirting with the venerable superstar.

Newman for his part seemed to be enjoying it – maybe it was the wine mellowing him out – because he was sporting with them, although, ever the wise old oracle, the sporting involved playfully chiding the pair for smoking. Newman started waxing expansive about 'tics' and such-like, like he was the Elmer Gantry of alter-native medicine or something. 'And AIDS OK.' He was even using his hands now – this is great to watch ... '... Intravenous drug users, right ... the needle ... just one tic rubs off on that needle, OK, it's a killer. Now you smoke cigarettes ... Yeah? Ho, ho, ho! Oh boy ... Whatever you're putting into your body, OK, with cigarettes is 50 times more deadly than what a tic or an Aids virus can do.'

'Well so what!' the brazen girl replied, while her friend's violent laughter at this utterance visibly fractured even Newman's mellow routine.

'Well I don't say "so what",' he lumbered back as gracefully as he could. 'I'm one of those people ... see, you've got to appreciate there are people who are athletes, people who are great lovers who take great pride in their bodies and how they treat them. They treat their bodies with respect. I just think it's so amazing that we are so disrespectful of this thing that we inhabit that we'd actually even think of abusing it. I mean, you don't drive your car 90 miles an hour into a brick wall ... do you?'

'I don't drive.'

'Well you know what I mean. You must take some sensible pre-cautions, right? All I'm saying is that you're entitled to disrespect your health if you want to, but there are people who enjoy being reverential. That's all ... So don't smoke, OK!'

'But you drink ...' someone else offered.

'Yeah, drinking's fine,' muttered Newman. 'In moderation.'

'You race cars ...'

'Hey, everybody's got to have their own brand of poison in this life. What can I tell you? Mine just hasn't poisoned me yet.'

* * *

You've played some great American bastards in your time, I begin. Some great self-destructive figures . . .

'Well, self-destruction to America is its own attraction, I guess.'

You played Buffalo Bill . . .

'Now he *was* a bastard.'

And you played Billy the Kid, who was a psychopath and a killer.

'Well, so was Ronald Reagan!'

Virtually everything I've read about you seems to contain a reference to you as the Last Great American Class Act. How do you carry that weight?

'Let me tell you about class acts and America . . . Old Duke Wayne . . . OK, I always slightly envied him, y'know, the way he got to shoot up the whole town in his films. Not that that's my style, really [laughs]. But, as you can probably imagine, John Wayne and I were from totally opposite ends of the fence politically. We'd even exchanged correspondence during some of the grislier parts of the Fifties. But basically I always admired his integrity and I think he admired mine.

'Anyway, at the Carter Inauguration, for some reason they'd asked Duke Wayne to make a speech and as this was being televised, we somehow ended up sharing the same dressing room. After that, all I gotta say is . . . the class act that night was Duke Wayne. He wrote it. He delivered it. It was only 45 seconds long, but he was the great American class act that night. Yes sir. All he really said was that he represented the loyal opposition and he'd never see eye-to-eye with what the President would recommend the country do. But that he was still in the service of his country, albeit as a red-blooded Republican. It was touching as hell.

'See, the problem with American politics now is that no one is prepared to campaign on a slogan of "Identify the Enemy". And even if they *find* the enemy they're not going to admit that it's the enemy. America is altogether too comfortable, it's like an old married couple. Stubborn and unthinking.'

What do you identify as the enemy?

'Well . . . it has something to do with a shorter attention span . . . it has a lot to do with television. And the ironic thing, last year I made this film *Fat Man And Little Boy* that's basically a history of the creation of the atomic bomb, and it was then that it finally dawned on me: the atomic bomb, which was going to cause the wholesale destruction of this planet, now looks as though it might have actually saved us all. Or at least saved the savages from unleashing it in the first place! And the thing that was going to save the planet – television, this perfect educational tool – has probably done more than anything else to ruin human minds and the quality of thought among people! And *that*, let me tell you, that's the work of the devil right there!'

Someone starts blathering on about 'the effects of American downfall syndrome' before Newman quite sensibly cuts them off:

'We're in very complicated territory here. No really . . . If you want to talk about the mass sterilisation of the American mind, then OK. We'll discuss that. We can talk about that in relationship to films, or to government. Or if you want to discuss it in terms of acceleration of "time" and "change", the acceleration of "change" in human beings' lives, then sure . . . You can also discuss it strictly in terms of relatives and absolutes. The idea that secular absolutes are now beginning to inform fundamentalist and religious thinking, the arrival of fundamentalist/religious thinking into government. But you can never discuss it head-on.'

You once said you wanted written on your tombstone, 'He was a part of his time.' I'm interested in whether you see yourself still being able to reflect this kind of cultural turmoil in your film work.

'Well, OK . . . see, for me *Mr And Mrs Bridge* represents a microcosm of what's about to happen to the American family – this concentration simply on a feeling that possession without education can be a family salvation. But you look at the family. OK, Ruth, the eldest daughter is off in New York headed for disaster and, it's intimated, a life as a high-class call girl. The younger daughter's marriage is faltering. Only the son has stuck to his own goals and sense of values. Meanwhile Mrs Bridge has spent her whole life being "agreeable". In the book she even faces her death agreeably. [In a high squeak of a voice] "Hello, hello, is anybody up there?" Wonderful. The movie's not the same, of course. Meanwhile Mr Bridge is rather stoic in his values about what constitutes a good American life and is bewildered by all the change that's happened. It's not a film about "family" so much as it's a film about Americans and it's a film about "life".'

In the script there's a scene where your character, Mr Bridge, is intimated to have strong incestuous longings for his daughter Ruth . . .

'Oh it's more than intimated, I think. It's pretty upfront. But I like that.'

I was just wondering how you intended to play that scene . . .

'Right now I'm thinking of just taking off all my clothes and playing it that way.' (Newman's jokes are never funny. But then humour isn't their specific function. They serve to stop furtive and unpleasant probing dead in its tracks.) 'Joanne asked me to be in this project and I just said, "Sure". But there was no way *then* that I thought it *could* really translate into a film. But ... this lady, Ruth (Prawer Jhabvala) ... I mean, she comes from India, right, and she's trying to write abut Kansas in the Fifties ... Not a snow-ball's chance in hell, I thought. Then I read the script. What an achievement! She'd captured two whole lives and she'd done it with "essences" that are non-specific. Everything happens indirect-ly to the Bridges, if you notice. They go through the Depression, which is a period of American life I was born into and I remember only too well – but the Depression itself doesn't touch them, it doesn't impinge directly on their lives at all.

'It's all down to the right script for me. Always has been. And that's why it's so hard these days ... I mean, Joanne and I have been looking for a project like this, something good that we can both get our teeth into, for 13 or 14 years ... We're always look-ing for something. (Robert) Redford and I have been looking for something for 12 years, for Christ's sake.'

Surely, you've been offered another Sting?

'I don't know if I'd ever read that script,' he mutters abruptly. 'No, we'd need something solid, something to stretch us ... I still don't think people understand what *Butch Cassidy* was all about. It was successful because it successfully presented on the screen a love affair between two men. That's all. The so-called chemistry between me and Redford was always secondary to that. And *The Sting* – the thing I always believe that sold that film was that the audience got to witness this whole new extravagant con-man kind of lifestyle going down. That's what really suckered them.'

For me, your finest films have been about individuals who've dogmatically refused to have their spirits broken.

'Well, I'd probably agree with you wholeheartedly there. If you're asking a question, then yes, I think it's absolutely critical to stress such things. But that's not to say that every film you do should adopt that attitude, mind.'

The attitude you adopted in Absence Of Malice, *that kind of one-man media revenge squad, was roundly criticised by some sec-tions of the press. Haven't you gotten a little high-handed with the media at times? After all they haven't caused you that much per-sonal grief ...*

'Listen, what they do to me is irrelevant! I just don't think the press is cracked up to be the institution it's supposed to represent. In America the press is the largest unregulated business in the USA. They are arrogant beyond belief! Free speech is a tremendous privilege and when it's abused and when papers invent sources and put things in people's mouths just to sell newspapers we're all diminished. For instance, the press was frightened of McCarthy. I mean, *that's* absolutely diabolical and chickenshit. They were frightened by Reagan's popularity, too. Reagan was allowed to function as he did directly through the generosity of the press. What they allow to happen is . . . I mean, no White House correspondent is ever going to ask the President an embarrassing question. 'Cos if he did he'd be shipped straight back to Detroit or wherever!

'And let me just add here that I think the tabloid press in England is a complete *obscenity*! In the medical profession now they have what is called an ombudsman. That's what the press needs. Internal regulation.'

It sounds like you're getting more conservative in old age.

'Conservative?' The word makes him flinch. 'Never. No, I'm becoming an anarchist now . . . Well, not really. But hell, it's not inconceivable.'

Seriously.

'Well, I like to think I can summon forth some kind of optimism. I mean, I despair for everyone's country, not just mine. But yes, I despair more for mine because I think we should always be in the forefront of "the battle". And instead we're just dragging our heels . . . There are a lot of explanations about the state of America today. A lot of explanations. But no excuses.'

You said earlier that Hud *was the biggest mistake of your career . . .*

'Yeah, but I don't feel responsible. I mean, I don't regret making *Hud*, no. I don't have to feel responsible for the idiocy of the audience or the idiocy of my government. All you can do is do your work, y'know, and if the audience reads it the wrong way, well, that's not the artist's fault. It was Winston Churchill . . . he was accused of something going wrong in the government. Taxes or something. Anyway he said, "I simply cannot be held responsible for the idiocy of every civil servant in the British Isles." Something like that. That line has a good ring to it.'

You've reprised only two characters in what could be defined as sequels. You did Ross McDonald's super-hip long-suffering private detective, Lew Harper, first in Harper *and then in* The Drowning Pool . . .

'Well, I loved the original Harper. Lew Harper was such a wonderful character for me because he seemed able to accommodate almost any improvisation I was able to come up with.'

And then there's Eddie Felson, of course ...

'Well, *The Color Of Money* wasn't so much a sequel to *The Hustler* as it was a follow-up. It was 25 years later and the character had never really been completed in the original film to begin with. In the story, Eddie Felson was a man forced to give up on his own field of excellence, who then became excellent in another more materialistic arena. But once he really saw "excellence" again and confronted it on a daily basis, he couldn't escape the pursuit of it anymore. He wanted to be a player. He'd forgotten what it was like to be a contender.

'And, to answer your question, that is also the role of the actor I suppose. To pursue and illuminate his own particular brand of excellence any way he can. So, yes, sure I can relate to him. But I'm not Eddie Felson. I'm not any of the guys I've played.'

Paul Newman is summing himself up and once more I've got to give him full marks for knowing how to cap things off just so. 'There's a wonderful quote in "Billy Bathgate", the new E. L. Doctorow book. One of the fictional characters – a gangster who's just about to be executed – is talking to a kid about his life. And he says, "I know when they call upon my gun that it's *my gun* that they're asking for. I love to wine and dine women. I like to walk thru' a dining room and cut a swathe. But more than anything else I love the fact that they recognize *my reliability*." And that's what set him apart. He was clean. And neat. He was efficient. And he didn't bully the victim (laughs). He just did it.

'Now I see a lot of parallels to be drawn between me and that character, don't you. Because, yes, I am responsible. Yes, I am on time. I'm punctual. I . . . I don't ever laugh at the material. I try to be prepared. I try to do the best thing I can do. See, maybe there is a premium to be placed on reliability. And if that's what it takes to be an American superstar or whatever damn term they choose to hang on me, then . . . so be it.'

The Race to Offend

The Ultimate New York T-Shirt by Alix Sharkey
May 1990

T HE T-SHIRT is the essential New York garment: direct, practical, blunt, singular, utilitarian. Like New York, the T-shirt pervades twentieth-century existence. Like a T-shirt, New York has four holes – the Lincoln, Holland, Brooklyn-Battery and Queens-Midtown tunnels. Sloganeering is an American art, perfected in the glass towers of Madison Avenue. Therefore it follows that T-shirts and New York slogans go together like hit-and-run.

The classic New York T-shirt slogan is graphic designer Milton Glaser's I LOVE NY design, which first appeared in the mid-Seventies and has been plagiarised and distorted a billion times. The only problem with Glaser's seminal logotype is its earnestness. The man was *serious*. He really wanted to wear his heart on his Fruit Of The Loom XOS.

This is not appropriate for the average New Yorker, who cherishes his indifference above all else. Closer by far to the city's true ethos is BEFORE YOU ASK THE FUCKING ANSWER IS NO, which speaks volumes about that world-famous New York social skill, *attitude*. Indeed, you can now buy a T-shirt bearing the legend I LOVE MY ATTITUDE. Talk about going down on your own Trump Tower.

Hail a cab in New York and chances are you'll get a driver who has survived that fabled Manhattan institution, the stick-up. The victim will be an Egyptian living in New York. His assailant will have got in, held a pistol to his head and demanded his takings, a lousy $35. Later that day a new T-shirt slogan will catch your eye. The words NEW YORK stand proudly over a smoking handgun; beneath this, the legend IT AIN'T KANSAS. You'll wonder if the cab driver would appreciate this philosophical nicety. CAIRO – IT AIN'T THE VALLEY OF THE KINGS doesn't have quite the same ring to it.

New York was once the refuge of the poor and hungry, welcoming the 'huddled masses, yearning to be free' in their millions. The extent to which times have changed can be gauged by the solemn WELCOME TO NEW YORK, NOW GO HOME, an increasingly popular slogan.

But if a new mood of selfishness is manifesting itself, there is some way to go. Surprisingly, Gekko's *Wall Street* maxim GREED IS GOOD has yet to be immortalised on a Hanes Beefy-T. Meanwhile the city's legendary fatalism is enshrined in that old standby, LIFE'S A BITCH – AND THEN YOU DIE. And there's not another metropolis in the world where the citizens would dare to wear T-shirts that say FUCK YOU VERY MUCH. Such a crass pun, such a brilliantly dumb slogan. Sheer alchemy.

Despite its vintage, SHIT HAPPENS is still good value for money. As long as masonry falls from skyscrapers and subway trains burst into flames, as long as planes crash and gunmen go berserk in crowded restaurants, this stoical gem will remain with us. Shit is big in New York.

So is work. The two come together in SAME SHIT, DIFFERENT DAY, an old favourite among slogan-hunters. Yet another aspect of the city's legendary work ethic is illustrated by the increasingly prevalent YOU MUST HAVE MISTAKEN ME FOR SOMEONE WHO GIVES A SHIT. These feculent prizes are obtainable in all sizes from various tourists stores around Times Square.

A recent trip to New Jersey confirmed a nagging suspicion. Take a 20-minute train ride from New York in any direction you choose, and you'll find yourself in another country – the USA. Manhattan is just Europe on steroids, but New Jersey is *terra incognita*.

For example, there's Hoboken, birthplace of Sinatra. A small seaport, Hoboken has always been a workers' town. The slow trickle of New Yorkers looking for cheaper rents and safer neighbourhoods has probably diluted the civic character a little, but not noticeably. Hoboken has that honest, down-to-earth feel of a town run by concerned citizens. It goes without saying that they are most concerned about all those filthy perverts and barbarous ethnic minorities – Jamaicans! Haitians! Puerto Ricans! *Britons!* – just across the Hudson.

Here I found the ultimate New York T-shirt. It isn't funny, it has no swear words, and it certainly isn't from New York; but it kills all other wise-ass T-shirts stone dead. It shows a dead cockroach lying on its back, and is emblazoned with three-inch caps that say HOBOKEN EXTERMINATING. Not impressed? Well, you have to read between the lines. Roughly translated, this means HEY DUDE, I'M FROM JERSEY – IT AIN'T MANHATTAN – MY SHIT IS BADDER THAN YOUR SHIT, LIFE'S A BITCH

AND I WILL FUCK YOU VERY MUCH IF YOU DON'T GIMME WHAT I WANT AND GET OUTTA MY FACE *NOW*! THANK YOU. OH, AND HAVE A NICE DAY. OR ELSE.

It's a great T-shirt, and people are always asking me where I got it so they can get one too. I tell them before they ask the fucking answer is no. They sometimes get upset, but I just reply they must have mistaken me for someone who gives a shit. I feel like a Hobokenian in my cockroach T-shirt, and the people of Hoboken have got attitude down to a fine art. Just ask Ol' Blue Eyes if you don't believe me.

Copyright © Alix Sharkey, 1990

Essex, Innit?

A Native's Guide to Cortina Country by Mick Bunnage
July 1990

N MAY 1986, FOLLOWING a few unexpected modifications to the UK tax laws, gravel-voiced lad's lad Rod Stewart, 43, ended his self-imposed Californian exile and bought a £1.2m spread on the exclusive Copped Hill Estate, Essex, from used-car dealer Terry Clemence. Rod was well pleased. He'd had his eye on the property for some time and fought off heavyweight competition from, among others, ex-King Constantine of Greece and Seventies fork-twisting psychic Uri Geller. 'He may be able to bend spoons,' said Rod's agent, Annie Challis, 'but Rod got the house.'

And like many a supertaxed millionaire Cockney geezer before him, Rod slipped into Essex country life with predictable ease. 'I love the place,' he said. 'I'm especially fond of the local boozer. I've spent a few bob in there. The local people say, "Hello Rod", as if I've been living there for years.'

Vain, good-natured and painfully rich, a big fan of football, fast cars and blonde, leggy women with big tits and exotic accents, Rod is perfect Essex material. Because Essex is the spiritual home of Lad; a jacuzzi for the soul. Although more of a legman, Rod knew instinctively that he'd finally found a bosom he could call home.

London's version of New Jersey and the butt-end of much sniggering, Essex is a county loaded to the brim with boy racers, footballers, villains, ex-villains, popstars, popstars' parents, more footballers, hairdressers and taxi-drivers – people like Rod. The county crest isn't three swords on red but two dice on fun-fur and a legend that reads 'Stroll on!' It's all true. Well, most of it. And best of all, Essex doesn't give a damn.

Folk here like to do things in their own time. Full of homespun, crackerbarrel commonsense, large shots of Cockney fatalism and a big dollop of TV culture. Homelovin', homeownin' and sentimental, Essex is Sainsbury's Homebase heartland. A county built on Artex and DIY. Loves Country'n'Western, shopping malls, sunbeds and a packed freezer in the double garage. Indulgence is the keyword because this is the wealthy South East. Tebbit Country. A Tory block vote.

Growing up in Essex leaves an indelible mark on your mind. Have the attitude and you'll be irresistibly drawn there, just as Rod, and hundreds of self-made Cockney millionaires, have been.

Essex has been exporting its particular brand of laddish redneck individualism worldwide for hundreds of years, giving it an influence out of all proportion to its size. Believe it or don't, the Pilgrim fathers met in Billericay before leaving for the New World, and their boat, The Mayflower, was built in Leigh-On-Sea, just up the road. George Washington's family came from Maldon and George Bush's from Colchester. Just a couple more Essex boys who made good.

And when they make it they don't forget it. Barking-born Billy Bragg was so haunted by the space, the big blue polaroid skies, the low buildings, the sprawling flat land, the sheer *Americanness* of southern Essex, that he mythologised it to the tune of 'Route 66': '*Now if you should ever have to go to Shoeburyness/Take the 'A' road/The OK Road/That's the best/Go motoring on the A13.*' Get Cortina'd up and take a trip on that two-lane blacktop to the coast. Essex is the unofficial 51st state of America.

But despite the huge contribution Essex has made to the arts, there's no poncy subsidising here, just plenty of your get-up-and-make-a-million determination. If you can paint you can probably decorate as well, make a few bob for yourself. Essex spent just 9p per head of its population on the arts last year, compared with Hammersmith (£9.97), or, even worse, Westminster (£22.56). Not that they're against the arts; it's just that they know a place they can get it cut-price. There's many a fine statue in the garden-centre-Greek-style gracing the front lawns of Essex, and the odd Botticelli original (well, y'know, original oils anyway) in the lounge. Bit of culture. Upmarket, innit? Well tasty.

But naturally the Essex bent for creativity has its darker side, and the county's reputation for providing a pleasant home to East End villains is backed up by official crime statistics and the occasional episode of _Police 5_ (more people plead Not Guilty in Essex than anywhere else in England and Wales, and there are more burglaries, serious woundings, frauds and conspiracies there too). Yes, Essex lives it large – the place where people do what they want to do; and if they've got the dosh they just do it bigger.

Rod's pad, for example, is a Jacobean-style mansion designed in 1898 by William Morris to include six guest bedrooms, a rose garden and stables for the horses. The Jacuzzi and helicopter pad were pencilled in while Bill was off choosing the wallpaper. Blue plaques dotted around the drawing-room walls celebrate a host of other superstars who have lived here. Winston Churchill used the house as a campaign HQ when he was MP for Wanstead and Woodford. Locals have dubbed the place 'Fort Rod'. Security-conscious Rod has staked the place out with video cameras, heat-sensitive pads and some state-of-the-art cross-fire sensor beams, all on a hair trigger with a direct line to the local copshop.

One of the rooms in Fort Rod is given over entirely to Rod's model railway and model city. 'He built every part himself and even painted all the little roadsigns,' according to his agent. 'It's something he likes to do when he's thinking about material for his new songs.'

For a choice selection of 'Essex Rococo' take a poke around Havering Atte Bower and Emerson Park on the borders of Romford and Hornchurch. This is dreamland for every Plaistow plasterer's mate who ever aspired to a Dallas/Dynasty lifestyle within range of his favourite fish'n'chip shop. After all, conspicuous wealth is the only sort of wealth worth having.

Every luxurious house off the dappled tree-lined avenues of the two square miles of Emerson Park has a swimming pool. A 35-footer if possible. Stone lions on the manicured lawns, a snooker room, personal gymnasium, chandeliers, plenty of pillars, and at least one bar. Six cars per house essential. BMWs or Mercs preferred. Not as a style statement, but because everyone knows they're bloody expensive. Besides, this is Essex and there's a by-law against taking yourself too seriously. Every car – Porsche or Roller – must have a Garfield on suckers in the side window. 'Look at this Babe,' says Leslie Grantham's character in the supposedly South London, but in fact cosily Essex, underworld TV series _The Paradise Club_, surveying his newly purchased Georgian terraced house. 'This spells taste. T.A.S.T.E.' Essex achievers don't want out, they just want up, and success is literally just around the corner.

When Julie Burchill, surely the most unlikely resident of Billericay ever, described Essex as 'a footballer's idea of the countryside', she obviously had Chigwell in mind. At one point during the Sixties all three of the big West Ham and England superstars – Bobby Moore, Geoff Hurst and Martin Peters – lived in the same street in Chigwell, Manor Road. And they all drank in the same pub, The Bald Hind, just up the way from Bob's house. Now the landlord's regulars include Angela Rippon, Dennis Waterman and Rula Lenska, and a whole bunch of Page 3 girls.

Chigwell is home too for darts player Bobby George, TV's Mr Science Raymond Baxter, Jimmy Greaves and David Sullivan. In fact, 40-year-old bachelor, soft-porn merchant and *Sunday Sport* publisher Sullivan is so thoroughly Essex that it would be almost impossible to imagine him living anywhere else. Like a fat, happy tom-cat curled up in front of the fire, in interviews he radiates the values of Essex lad. He's tapped the very source and made it pay. 'Deep down I'm still a mummy's boy. She's very proud I'm successful. I speak to her five nights a week,' Sullivan told a *Mail On Sunday* reporter. Rumoured to be worth a staggering £100m, he relaxes in the vast seven-sofa living room of his Edwardian mansion. Everything is red, black or white, there's a huge open swimming pool next to the dining room and a whole fridge packed full of chocolate and cakes. 'I read that red meat is bad for you. So now I eat fish and chips,' said Dave. 'I work very hard and pay my tax, I have a drawer full of cheques that show I've paid over £30m in tax. I ask for the cheques back because I want to paste them around the loo to show what a good citizen I've been over the years. I have very establishment views, deep down. I believe in tolerance and moderation.

'I've never taken a drug or smoked a cigarette in my life. And I can have up to three women a day, but some days I don't have any.'

Yup, true Essex, and more than that, every Essex boy's hero. Flash motor and down the disco every Friday night. Hollywood in Romford is a good bet. The archetypal Essex disco in flamingo pink and silver, its only real rivals are Dukes in Chelmsford and Charlie Chan's, situated directly under Walthamstow dog track. Both are guaranteed pulling establishments, but Hollywood, I'm reliably informed, is the only one with, y'know, class. Ten-foot-high neon letters and on a Friday night a queue that stretches round the car park by 9.30. The uniform here is straight down the line white shirts and black trousers (boys), stilettos and underwear (girls). Everyone has a name with four letters in it, one syllable. Simple rules, easy to follow. No weapons. No denim in the Directors' Lounge.

The penguin-suited bouncers mix stocky menace with a little *bonhomie*, carry walkie-talkies and run an airport-style metal detector over you as you go in. 'What you packing sunshine, Semtex?' There's a box-full of confiscated Swiss Army knives, bottle openers and flick-knives at reception. 'He looks like a blademan, dunne!' says the happy bouncer, taking a two-inch cocktail knife from one confused punter. 'Fuck me, *Lethal Weapon II*.' Inside, at one of the many bars, a punter pulls out 25 quid and orders nine Grolsch and a straw while two semi-naked chicks, hired by the management to work the crowd into a frenzy, do a bump and grind to a house mix of the *Neighbours* theme. Everyone is busy pulling everyone else and nobody is drinking the local brew, John Bull Bitter, which catapulted Romford to fame with the help of some saturation TV advertising. 'Get it down yer neck, and shut yer face,' was the general marketing drift.

Not surprisingly locals stick to lager. Hofmeister seems to have struck a chord, probably because Essex geezers have a way of walking which brings to mind those dodgy 'Follow The Bear' ads. A bow-legged, rolling gait which serves to emphasise the impressive weight of Ford Escort car keys, collected over the years and left clipped and dangling from the belt of baggy, stonewashed denims. For out of towners who wish to appear *au-fait*, this curious 'big trouser-snake' trundle, with its low centre of gravity, can be simulated by clenching rolled up mortgage papers between the buttocks. If you've got one, think hard about your crotch. And persevere. You'll get the hang of it.

Perhaps because the Ford works company town of Dagenham has always supplied the area with a steady stream of fresh new motors, Essex is a car-based culture supreme, a fact celebrated by another Essex lad, Ian Dury: '*A thing that Blockheads often acquire are black and orange cars/premature ejaculator drivers/They often have roll bars.*' For Essex lads a car isn't a Freudian extension of anything in particular. A car is too important for that. Your average Essex lad would willingly trade his wedding tackle for something with four wheels and white-wall tyres. Something he could park outside the house. And perhaps, in the only ironic twist on offer here, there is no greater compliment you can pay your much-admired XR3i than to wrap it around a tree on a Friday night, pissed out of your skull, foot stamped down on the mat, doing 80-plus round the pitch-dark and murderously twisting country lanes with the headlights off to add a bit of an edge. Next day you get another one. Try getting thrills like that with a 4oz floppy bit of genitalia.

It's easy to see why Rod feels so at home here. It's his sort of place: ruggedly individualistic; straight up; a place where you can be proud of your achievements and show off what you've got; where men can be lads and women chicks. Rod is frequently seen at the local Chinese restaurant with his girlfriend Kelly Emberg, and the landlord in the local pub plays only Rod's records when he's in the place. The neighbours seem thrilled. 'We're all hoping he'll settle down and start a family here.' Domesticity can be a great thing, and Rod's all for it. But superstars operate on a tight schedule. 'Of course I would like more children,' he says. 'I will definitely be having some more. It only takes me a couple of minutes.'

Mick Bunnage was born and raised in Ilford, Essex, where his neighbour was the drummer in The Rubettes. He now lives in Brixton but phones his mum every week.

Copyright © Mick Bunnage, 1990

Tie Me Up, Tie Me Down!
New York's Favourite Dominatrix by Rob Ryan
July 1990

TIME IS DRAGGING. I've been waiting in one small room of a mid-town Manhattan apartment for 20 minutes and the air has grown stale. Over in one corner an androgynous blonde girl is ignoring me, watching re-runs of the Flushing Meadow tennis championship on a mass of video equipment. When I try to open a conversation she grunts and cranks up the volume. I am left to stare at the walls.

The decor, I note, does not go with the location – we are in prime interior designer territory, a few hundred yards from Carnegie Hall, yet this place is out of the SOFAS-R-US school of decoration. Mind you, most people who come here don't take time out to admire the furnishings – not the ones in this room, anyway – and the only real hint of this apartment's purpose is the painting of a leather strap on the wall, and the largest bottle of baby oil I have ever seen. The sole reading material seems to be the *Dominatrix Directory International.*

The door opens and my interview whisks in, apologises for being late, offers a firm handshake and sits beside me. No such acknowledgement is made of the tennis fan's presence, who snorts in disgust and makes a showy exit. Ava Taurel shrugs and offers an explanation: 'She is my slave girl. I got her from Xavier Hollander during a party in Amsterdam. She wants me to humiliate her but' – a weary sigh – 'I'm really not interested any more.' Having spent the past half-hour wondering how to broach the tricky subject of Ava's profession, it appears that, along with the blonde, any need for circumspection has gone out of the door.

They say you can get anything you want in New York if you have the dollars or the plastic to pay for it, and the right contacts. Even if you don't have friends in the Wrong Places, the enormous Manhattan *Yellow Pages* acts as a comprehensive introduction to New York's This-Town-For Hire philosophy. For instance under 'Escorts' there is a full-page ad of women drawn in the exaggerated style of those ads for lingerie catalogues. It modestly promises nothing less than total fantasy fulfilment and gives a phone number. At the end of the line is the recorded, accented voice of Ava Taurel, my hostess, describing herself as a 'blonde Norwegian lady in her mid-forties', explaining that her organisation is not an escort agency; nobody will be going anywhere with anybody else, and sex is not on the agenda.

What is on offer is, 'risqué role playing', which translates into domination – whips, leather, bondage, rubber and associated paraphernalia. If that is your bag, and you are in NY, then Ava is generally considered to be *the* person to check out.

If the idea of a dominatrix conjures up images of Streatham and Luncheon Vouchers, consider that this apartment is just one of *four* pieces of prime real estate that Ava leases to carry on her activities. This operation is neither furtive nor bargain basement.

Ava settles down for the interview. In the harsh sunlight she looks like she has past the mid-forties mark, and there is something hard and steely and masculine in her features. She begins by begging me not to ask the 'usual boring questions'. I ask what sort of questions she means, but she shrugs unhelpfully. I get the feeling she'll let me know if she gets bored.

I start with one that she is bound to have heard before: where do her clients come from? 'Oh, ads in the *Village Voice*, in the *Yellow Pages* and in specialist magazines, but more and more by personal recommendation.' And does she accept anyone? She shakes her head. Clients, she says seriously, must be vetted. For what – the size of their wallets? No: 'To make sure they aren't dangerous.' This is a business, it seems, that can easily get out of hand, and Ava has never been one for taking chances.

'Three years ago when I was working by myself, the clients would stand on the street corner and I would look at them through binoculars to make sure they were correct. If they were, I would go down and frisk them for weapons. Then I would put glasses on them, only they weren't glasses because the lenses were painted black and you couldn't see through them. Then I would lead them to my space. Nowadays we don't need to do that, unless I don't have their full name and address.'

Ava delivers all this in a deadpan monotone, as if she were just an over-cautious home manicurist. Her manner only becomes animated when we discuss the identity of the clients, and her conversation is peppered with veiled hints about the movers, shakers and flagellants who pass through her rooms – film directors whom you have known and loved, bankers, publishers.

But did Ava wake up one morning and decide, 'Hey, I'll get into domination and make a few bucks'? Not at all. 'When I came to New York City I was introduced to this by an old friend, who had been in some S&M stage shows. People who had seen her had asked for private sessions and she invited me to watch. At first I thought it was so decadent, but I realised that I was repelled because I was secretly quite attracted to it. When I accepted this I tried it and I found it fun. This was quite late in life, I was 35 when I found this subculture existed in New York.'

Ava glosses over her life before S&M – au pair, model, dancer at the Folies Bergères, film actress, can-can girl in Canada. This snippet of a CV is interspersed with how she realised a little slap and tickle – with the emphasis on slap – could enhance her sex life. It was only in New York that she found she could combine business with pleasure for fun and profit.

She explains the ground rules for anyone wanting her services. 'What we do here is consenting sado-masochism, with no abuse. I am very much against anything that involves violence or coercion.

I have seen stage shows where they simulate cutting up a woman, and I think there is a sickness in that, even if it is simulated. I make sure my clients respect women. Also we have to be careful not to come into conflict with the law. Specifically no genital or oral contact between the mistresses and the clients, otherwise it is prostitution.' So no sex? 'No sex. And no drugs; in fact I don't even allow smoking on the premises. We are not an escort agency, we are involved in fantasy role-playing. People come to me because here they can live out their fantasies in a very safe, controlled, and discreet environment.'

Ava's outfit is so legit that it is even registered for tax – she is not about to repeat Al Capone's mistake – and goes by the name of the Taurel Institute. Hence her stressing the 'no sex' angle, something which, as a relative S&M *ingénue*, worries me – surely the fantasies are intimately intertwined with sex. If no consummation takes place, don't the customers leave more frustrated than when they arrive? Ava dismisses such thoughts as naive, and repeats that no sex is involved. You could be forgiven for thinking: well she would say that, wouldn't she?

So, apart from the celebrities, what walks of life do the fantasy-fixated clients come from? 'Lawyers, real estate, bankers,' a smile, 'then journalists and writers in the fourth category.'

So here I am, I postulate, new boy on the block, Category IV, nervously eyeing the baby oil, what happens next? 'For $50 you get a consultation, which means we go through what you might like to experience. I ask questions such as, what sort of clothes turn you on – leather or latex or lace; whether you prefer women in boots or shoes, or uniforms or black stockings. I might suggest a few things – a little light spanking. Perhaps some torturing and teasing – verbally I mean. Everybody likes a little of that.'

She thrusts a hefty photo album on my lap. 'And then we will select one of the mistresses for you. Each has their own speciality, so it is important we get you the right one.' The album features poses by a dozen or so women, all kitted out in their working garments. I recognise the tennis fan, dressed in a baby doll nightie, transparent enough to reveal the boyish body underneath. 'She is one of the few submissives we have,' says Ava.

The other members of the team have mostly only their height in common. Few are conventionally attractive, certainly not facially, although a number have bodies that could stop clocks. The predominant image is of tightly bound, rubber- or leather-clad torsos, high heels and loftly elevation – *real* power dressing.

'This girl here is British, an actress, very good at verbal stimulation; this lady is a body-builder, some clients like her for wrestling or muscle-worship; this one is very tall, six foot one in her stocking feet and men just melt when they see her. This is Greta, also very tall, and a singer. She is my star of the moment. All the men want her.'

Where do all these lanky amazons come from? 'From friends, or recommendations. I tried advertising, but it doesn't work; people have to have lived this in their private lives to understand it. And they have to be very intelligent, because they need a lot of imagination. Some clients come with three- or four-page scenarios to be acted out; they might want the Queen of Sheba or a futuristic goddess, or the head of a prison camp.'

The mistresses are what Ava calls 'independent contractors' brought in for their specialist skills, and their motive, like Ava's, is to combine business and pleasure. But do they come ready to be unleashed on clients? 'No, sometimes they need training. I have a male bondage trainer who comes in and teaches them how to tie a selection of knots' – somehow Ava makes this sound like the Sea Scouts at work – 'and they will tie him up and he will give them feedback. The training takes varying periods: Greta, for instance, had already dominated her boyfriend, so she only needed polishing.' Now, fully buffed, Greta has a long list of clients who insist on her personal service.

Does Ava herself still get involved, or is she just some sort of *Maîtresse d'*? 'I only give sessions when something highly technical is required, such as a complete submersion in latex, with double inflatable hoods and breathing tubes.' She adds, with a smile, 'It is mainly the British who want such things.'

In a comfortable room the whole milieu seems natural and unthreatening. Faced with the tools of the trade in the nearby apartments, the reality is a little more daunting.

A five-minute walk and we are in an apartment whose corridors are crammed full of wardrobes and storage areas, where costumes, painful accoutrements and even personalised enema bags are kept ('We have to be careful since AIDS'). The rooms, in contrast, are relatively empty – mirrored walls, and often with beams and shackles decorating the ceiling. Any furniture is purely functional – one room is dominated by a massage table with cut-outs in the groin and chest regions: 'Here we can put on the nipple clamps or the testicular weights.' Sorry, Ava? 'Testicular weights. Weights on the testicles.' This seems to me to qualify as genital contact, but I let that one slide.

Ava fetches another popular device: 'You have to be careful not to beat them while they are wearing this one.' I have some trouble figuring out how it fits – Ava holds the garment against herself; it turns out to be a needle-lined jockstrap.

Some rooms, Ava explains, are dark ('the dungeons') because clients like privacy, others are bright and open to prying eyes. 'Some people enjoy the risk that they will actually be seen in women's clothing.' Does Ava think she can cater for _all_ men? 'No, no – just those with these particular needs. That is not all men by any means.' I remain sceptical: exposure to the wilder shores of the male psyche must have left her convinced that we all have some unrealised concupiscence. Perhaps she is right.

Still, I'm pretty sure there is no place in my fantasies for the room that features a giant mechanical hoist more usually applied to lifting out car engines. 'Clients can be bound, lifted up and left to dangle,' explains Ava, cranking the handle. Judging by the dents on the ceiling some of the mistresses are a little over-enthusiastic with this one.

Ava does have a separate private life, another name and even another profession – video, which explains the rather complex set-up being used to watch old tennis matches. But still, she obviously enjoys her bondage business immensely, and like any conventional entrepreneur, complains about overheads. 'I have to import a lot of the equipment from England. For some reason the English make most of the items I require. And of course they absolutely make the best canes. Then there is the upkeep on these apartments. And I pay a lot of tax.'

Still, business is booming. The Taurel Institute has 1,700 clients on its books, willing to pay up to $300 an hour to be 'tortured and teased' by one of her mistresses. It is easy to dismiss Ava as a product of New York, but only the openness of the operation is idiomatic of that city. As Ava herself admits, 'The best operations I have ever seen are not here, but over on your side of the Atlantic.' And who form the main clientele in the UK? An elusive grin. 'You would be surprised.' After two hours with Ava, I don't think I would.

Copyright © Rob Ryan, 1990

The Taming of the Superbrat

John McEnroe by Kathryn Flett

July 1990

I N 1981 I WAS as obnoxious and self-absorbed and vulnerable as only 17-year-olds are entitled to be. In the ongoing search for an adolescent niche I didn't have very far to look for yet another anti-establishment role-model. On an overcast Saturday afternoon in June I found a soulmate: undoubtedly obnoxious, self-absorbed and vulnerable, he was also possessed of a towering talent.

Picture the scene. It is one set all and a 22-year-old John McEnroe is 4-5 down in the third set against Bjorn Borg in the Wimbledon final. The score is 15-30 and McEnroe is serving to stay in the set and, psychologically at least, the match. McEnroe serves what he considers to be a winner. It certainly looks it. The umpire overrules the linesman and calls it out. McEnroe sinks to his knees in desperation. It is a pivotal moment – McEnroe has been living a lifetime on every point and it's all there in his eyes. You are forced to live it with him and it's painful, often unwatchable, stuff. Quietly McEnroe gets to his feet and questions the umpire's decision. There are no histrionics – earlier in the tournament spectators were, after all, witness to the legendary 'Pits Of The World' tantrum, heralding the arrival of the tabloid Superbrat – but the umpire sticks to his decision and McEnroe now has two set points against him.

From somewhere deep down he delivers a crunching smash followed by another textbook serve. Deuce ... Advantage Borg ... set point again ... McEnroe serves, volleys and crushes ... Deuce ... Advantage McEnroe ... Deuce ... Advantage McEnroe and, finally, game McEnroe. At five games all there is now a tie break, but Mac is back and finally takes the set 7-6.

It is an exact reversal of the 1980 final, when Borg led 2-1 after the third set. In the final set McEnroe comes back from 3-4 down, with Borg serving, to take the set and the title: 4-6, 7-6, 7-6, 6-4. I punched the sofa and cried like a baby and gave my heart forever to McEnroe that afternoon. Generally considered a classic match, it was tennis – indeed sport – as it should be played. Athletic, cerebral and gladiatorial in equal measures, it still sends a chill up my spine.

I may have given my heart to McEnroe but I didn't stick him on my wall. He was, after all, an American (still deeply unfashionable in 1981) and he had a dodgy haircut. But I felt sure we could work it all out.

Post-Borg, John went from strength to strength. No Samson he, a haircut actually seemed to help. Connors may have despatched him in an epic five-setter in '82 but it was only a temporary hitch – Mac was back on top where he belonged in '83 and '84. In the '84 final in particular, McEnroe was at his most ruthless, seeking revenge against Connors. 'McEnroe seems to be quite unplayable,' mused Dan Maskell as John blitzed through to a 6-1, 6-1, 6-2 victory in an hour and 20 minutes, having dropped only 11 points. 'One of the greatest displays of tennis I've ever seen,' conceded Dan when it was all over. McEnroe went on to win the doubles and later in the year the US open. A man at the peak of his powers.

Despite his five consecutive Wimbledon victories, Ice-Borg's clinical, bloodless game always left me cold; Connors' EEEUUUAAARGH! serves merely irritated and Nastase was all mouth and no trousers. More recently Becker's teutonic grunts, thighs and invisible eyelashes turned me right off, while Stefan Edberg and Ivan Lendl both appear to have had a total personality by-pass. Only Pat Cash, Yannick Noah, Henri Leconte and Andre Agassi – merely excellent players as opposed to tortured geniuses – had enough attitude to make you really care if they won or lost.

Only McEnroe had it all ... even sufficient good taste to stay just the right side of the sartorial baseline. Tennis is a golden game and the glitz of the Wimbledon trophy has often vied for attention with the players' 18-carat obsessions. McEnroe, happily, has never succumbed to a tournament tint or grand-slam tan and only briefly gave in to the lure of the status chain (ironically in 1985, when he lost to Kevin Curren), and we fashion types who care about such things are grateful.

When it became obvious that the closest John McEnroe and I were ever going to get would be to spend a fortnight in the same city once a year, I was happy enough to relinquish him to Tatum. The marriage of the 'Superbrat' and 'Tantrum' O'Neal – the perfect love match – was clearly one prophesied on papyrus many millennia ago. Except that it soon became apparent that Tatum and progeny were distracting John from taking care of business. As John's centre-court appearances petered out altogether, it was a cruel blow. Had he lost it? Was he happy? Was he ever coming back? Would it be too late?

But last summer as I took the phone off the hook at 12.55, poured a stiff Pimms and settled back for my annual 14-day fix, he was there. I think I shed my first tear in the first game of the first round.

The serve; the transcendental cross-court volley; the sublime backhand return of service down the line – they were all there, alongside the semi-sneer, nervous shrug, obsessive brow-wipe on the sleeve and pre-serve racket-tapping. John McEnroe and I are both marginally less obnoxious, self-absorbed and vulnerable these days, but last summer I wallowed in long-forgotten hero worship, punched the sofa and cried like a kid when he lost in the semi-finals. It was the inevitability of it all. Neither John nor I are getting any younger and, while Tomorrow Belongs To Becker, in June Mac and I will get to be brats again.

Copyright © Kathryn Flett, 1990

Less Than Zero
What Men Tend to Know About Cunnilingus
by Jessamy Calkin
November 1990

CUNNILINGUS. GOING DOWN. There's not even a hip word for it. The thing about cunnilingus is it's still not that *cool*. If you were a Hell's Angel in the Seventies, the process of getting your wings included giving head to a chick. Red wings entailed giving head to a menstruating chick. Along with doing a ton up on the Golden Gate Bridge and biting the head off a live chicken. That's how cool cunnilingus is.

It is a term which probably reached the height of fashion in the Sixties. As did 69, a rather gimmicky concept that involves a lot of clambering and manoeuvring and is aesthetically wholly unacceptable. And 69 *is* rather extraordinary behaviour; the one position where, if you don't know your partner very well and you haven't been transported into ecstasy in the first five minutes, you really stop and think what the *hell* am I *doing* here? It is not an erotic moment. But 69 has a sense of humour; cunnilingus doesn't. If it's done well, there's probably nothing better to break the ice. If it's not done well, it is a serious drag. 'I think it's a bit annoying,' says one philosopher I know. 'It would be all right if your top half was being entertained, like if you were having your hair brushed at the same time. Or if you've got the telly on. The worst bit is if you look down, and they look up, and they've suddenly got a beard . . .'

There're a lot of head fans in the classics. Virgil was very keen. In more contemporary annals, there's nothing like the Marquis de Sade. A few pages into his magnum opus, *Juliette*, we have a Mother Superior indulging in a bit of 'cunt-sucking'. The good Marquis does not beat around the bush in his choice of terminology. He had his finger on the G-spot long before *Cosmopolitan*: 'You'll not leave my clitoris unattended, will you? 'Tis there the true seat of woman's pleasure: rub it, worry it, I say, use your nails if you like . . . Christ's eyes! I am jaded and I require to be dealt with stoutly: I want to melt absolutely into fuck, fuck I want to become, if I am able I want to discharge 20 times over. Make it so.'

The male often experiences a blow job through the metaphors of dominance and submission – what could be more submissive than a girl on her knees with your dick in her mouth? On the other hand, if she's got sharp teeth, what could be more threatening? But the male who likes cunnilingus often experiences it through similar sensations of power – there's an element of control; the female is essentially vulnerable with a head between her thighs, and the sense of control is arousing in itself. Cunnilingus has a more *invasive* quality about it than fellatio.

'*Girls are better at it because they get the right bit. Most boys tend to just stick their faces down there and hope they don't throw up*' – bisexual hairdresser, 30.

Shere Hite's *Report On Male Sexuality* found that cunnilingus was the second most popular sexual activity, after straight intercourse, with over half the men questioned. Reservations about smell and taste ranged from 'Darndest thing: women taste so sweet down there,' to 'It's ghastly. I tried it once and barfed all over my wife.' One fellow wrote: 'I ate one girl who later said she was menstruating at the time, but I guess I was too wrapped up in it to care. Blood, blood, I had enough of it on me in Vietnam not to worry about it.'

Although it used to be considered 'a crime against nature', along with sodomy, cunnilingus is most popularly practised in the Western world. In a tribe called the Ponapeans, the men enjoy the rather salubrious custom of placing a fish in the woman's vulva and then gradually licking it out before penetration. This would appear to be gilding the lily. Which brings us to the inevitable hackneyed joke section. Like the range of flavoured creams available to make the process more enjoyable, and the Polish man who bought tuna fish flavour. I mean there aren't even any *good* jokes about it, and there are a lot about fellatio: 'What's the ideal woman? Three feet high, no teeth, and a flat head so you can rest your drink on her.' Brilliant.

The fish phenomenon, by the way, is widely misunderstood. It is the *combination* of sperm and female secretions which produces this particular odour, and not, as is widely perpetrated in chauvinistic circles, the girl on her own.

'It beats all that eating at Greens and Chez Moi,' says one restaurant critic. 'It's rather similar to eating oysters – a soft, slightly gelatinous feel with a definite structure, easy to manipulate with the tongue. Oysters are directly sexual – you have to prise them open, like a pair of legs, to reveal their soft and delicious inner core. I can't eat oysters in a restaurant without feeling giddy and slightly high.

'It's best to work your way down, taking a sufficient amount of time to travel. The inner thigh is very much a point to be taken into account, and the perineum is important (between the anus and the pudenda). That usually does it. It's all rather like washing your face with a very soft flannel.'

Yeucch. There is an alternative approach, in the words of a Geordie maintenance man from Harrods: 'Why didn't God invent women who taste like strawberries? I can never do it unless they've had a bath. This is the trouble with picking up girls from Harrods, you know they've been in their tights for eight hours, so I'm thinking of having a sheep dip installed outside my front door so they can't get in without going through it.'

This is largely the reason that some women don't like it, because they think men don't like it. On the other hand, some women really *don't* like it.

'It's revolting,' says a 29-year-old female journalist. 'I mean the *physical* discomfort. The blankets always come off so you get cold and it's just incredibly *embarrassing*. I mean think what it *looks* like. And there's nothing more unsexy than his stupid head appearing from between your legs, picking a pubic hair out of his teeth. And the next thing you know they want *you* to do it to *them*, which is completely out of the question.

'It's not so bad if they eat things out of you – tinned fruit and ice-cream, things from the sweet trolley. But then what are you supposed to do with your *hands*? You use them to push his head away, that's what. Or carry on building your matchstick cathedral. I mean who *invented* it, anyway? Someone very rude and foreign probably. You can bet that it wasn't a girl. Why on earth do boys *like* it? If they want to give a girl pleasure why don't they just take her out to dinner and buy her a nice frock.'

There are cunnilingus girls and penetration girls, and there are those who like both. It's probably less emotional than penetration, but on the other hand there's something more intimate about it. It has totally different connotations to fellatio. *Supping on the old furry mug, eating pussy, dining at Y's, chewing the beef curtains*: there are boys who think doing it means you could be a fag, and there are girls who think *not* doing it means you could be a fag.

Gives good head. What is good head? There are no hard and fast rules. Just try and remember that the clitoris is a delicate and sensitive item, and not a hamburger. Approach with caution and finesse, pay attention to the surrounding areas, and don't forget to breathe.

Copyright © Jessamy Calkin, 1990

Auto-Erotica
Women & Cars by Jim McClellan
December 1990

F ORGETTING ALL THE STANDARD ideological objections, there are practical reasons why mainstream pornography is a somewhat flawed product. The main problem is that its banal fantasies of bedroom bliss are, in theory, denied to the person they're seemingly designed to satisfy – the pizza-faced pubescent male whose sex drive is more developed than his awareness of sexual politics (and whose complexion and personal hygiene generally put the real thing out of the question). Feminists might argue that these conditions continue to apply to most men long after the wet dreams of overheated adolescence have dried up. But for most men, by the time you can buy it, you don't want to.

At an age when you do want to buy it though, you can't, so generations of horny adolescents have sought stimulation elsewhere, developing a keen interest in literature (Henry Miller, de Sade), film (late-night art movies) and photography (mags devoted to coaching the amateur snapper in techniques of shooting the nude), studying the latest swimwear as previewed in the Sunday supplements, and, as a last resort, buying the *Sun*.

But if you grew up in the Seventies, there was another source of pseudo porn – car culture. Auto porn kicked into gear at the Motor Show of 1969, the first occasion here when a female model was so enraptured by the sleek lines of a new model Jag that she felt compelled to remove her top and buff up the chrome with her cleavage. In the years that followed, naked blonde babes dry-humping Triumph TR7s (or whatever excuse for a sports car the British motor industry was flogging that year) became a routine sight, and the Motor Show became a major source of totally gratuitous nudity in the car mags (always, of course, justified by a jokey column about promotional excesses).

Alongside the upmarket auto glossies at the respectable end of car culture pornography, you had ads that slyly massaged the middle-aged male ego. For example, the campaign for the Ford GT 40 depicted the suggestively sleek curves of Ford's answer to Ferrari with the slogan 'Would You Let Your Daughter Marry A Ford Owner?' Most famously, auto porn aspired to the status of art with the tasteful kitsch of the Pirelli calendar – leggy models, exotic beaches, name photographers and definitely nothing as vulgar as a car, a set of tyres or visible pubic hair in sight. At the bottom end of the market, you had car-spares calendars featuring buxom girl-next-door types apparently reaching orgasm in the presence of crankshafts and spark plugs.

At the very bottom you had something like *Custom Car* magazine. With its back-page garage ads – pics of suspendered women accompanied by *Carry On* innuendo ('She wants to help you with your parts') – and its centrefolds of women wrapping their legs around the latest piece of customised, airbrushed, phallic baroque, it was hard to differentiate from regular porn mags, which have always used cars as erotic props and filled leftover editorial space with hymns to the forgotten glories of the Hillman Imp.

Things have been tidied up now (the boys still get their tools out in *Custom Car*, but the girls keep their kit on) and it's tempting to write off the excesses of Seventies auto-eroticism to the laddishness of an age that had experienced sexual liberation but not yet discovered sexual politics. But really it was just the most extreme manifestation of male fantasies fuelled by the car over the years. Think of pop songs like Chuck Berry's comedy of frustrated teen desire 'No Particular Place To Go' or Prince's less reticent 'Little Red Corvette', and Grace Jones' lewd manoeuvres in 'Pull Up To My Bumper' ('and drive it in between').

Think of the original peroxide blonde, Jean Harlow, vamping away in the backseat of her V12 Cadillac, or Diana Rigg playing Emma Peel, her skin-tight shiny leather jump-suit matching her Lotus Elan. Think of *American Graffiti* and the mobile American courting rituals it documented, in which the convertible became both the expression of teenage libido and a place away from the parental home where it could be satisfied. Sit through any Sixties Brit-com movie and the dolly birds in open-topped MGs start piling up. More recently, think of Laura Dern wearing lingerie and a sports convertible in *Wild At Heart*, or Dennis Hopper's *The Hot Spot*, which features Virginia Madsen parading about as an American *femme fatale*, all peroxide curls, pink Cadillac and a skirt that just can't help riding up as she works the gear shift.

Ever since the Italian futurists got weak at the knees at the sight of all those throbbing pistons under the bonnets of their Bugattis, cars have been fixed in the male imagination as inherently sexual. Hardly surprising, really. Extending the limited capacities of the (desiring) body, cars transport their users in more ways than one. Driving fast is a physical high, an adrenaline kick, an engine-powered endorphin rush with a thrill quotient boosted by the knowledge that you're exceeding social as well as physical limitations. Controlling this extension of the body is a power trip for lots of men, a sign of male prowess. Sterling Moss once accurately suggested that 'there are two things no man will admit he can't do well – drive and make love.' The two pursuits have become so linked in male machine dreams, that the former is seen as a quick route to the latter.

This may all be a matter of fantasy, but you're kidding yourself if you think there was ever a time when men thought cars were just for getting from A to B, rather than getting off. The horseless carriages of the 1890s may not have had curves or speed, but the ads that pushed them still used sexual imagery to articulate the thrill of the new technology. A turn-of-the-century poster for the Société de Construction de l'Ouest, a French manufacturer of cars and bikes, featured a male driver hunched over his steering wheel, impressing three female passengers with the way he handled his big rig. Meanwhile, in the foreground, a kind of mechanical goddess kitted out in jewellery made from cogs and gears struggled to keep her dignity in a see-through chemise.

The first 'babe on a bonnet' appeared in the Twenties in illustrations in Italian car magazines that showed flappers perched on new saloons, dresses riding up to reveal stocking tops and suspenders. In many ways, all women-in-car fantasies since then have been versions of the babe on the bonnet – enraptured to varying degrees by the size of a man's motor, just passive sexual trophies designed to impress other men.

By the Thirties the racy women in Italian car ads even managed to get the Pope's blood pressure up. The campaign pushing Fiat's 508 Ballila showed a low-angle back view of a woman dressed in tight blue evening wear slinking purposefully toward her matching blue motor. After complaints from the Vatican that the woman's rear was too ample, too plumped up with desire, her cloak was extended to hide the offending curves. Of course, this ruined the desired effect, which was to link the woman's sharp dress sense and curvacious figure to the Ballila's shapely bodywork.

From the Thirties through to the end of the Fifties, ad men and art directors tried, with less Papal interference and consequently more success, to forge this particular look in the minds of male customers. They didn't have to try too hard in the case of the convertibles that began rolling off the production lines of post-war Detroit. Stylists like General Motors' Harley Earl dressed them up with all manner of suggestive curves, ducts, flares, fins and vents, and the result recalled a strange hybrid between a jet plane and the female body. Where Bugattis were upper-class vamps, Earl's creations were flirtatious floosies, all motorised wiggle and chromium bump and grind.

But you had to be careful not to take all this too far. When the Ford Edsel bombed with the public, market researchers floated the idea that it had failed because its newly aligned radiator grille reminded some people of a vagina. The Edsel certainly looks a little odd, but it's hard to take some of its critics seriously, particularly the lawyer who, while getting crotchety about the Edsel's front end, also revealed that the Studebaker's shape reminded him of 'male testicles'.

However, it is true that the American cars of the Fifties didn't just recall the female form, but swung both ways – most being endowed with an enviable phallic length. The car that took this particular strand of imagery to productive extremes was the E-type Jag, perhaps the ultimate example of the sports car as penis extension. The E-type proved so potent and profitable when it appeared in the early Sixties that most sports cars followed its lead, dropping the fussy feminine curves of Fifties America to become more straightforward expressions of phallic intent. As a result the babe on the bonnet changed. As the cars became motorised sex toys, she changed from Fifties fashion accessory whose clothes matched the upholstery, to pornographic centrefold. Where once she showed a hint of leg, as she perched demurely on the front bumper, by the end of the Sixties she was spread out against the windscreen.

It's easy retrospectively to ridicule the excesses of Seventies auto porn, but in one way it seemed to be the response called for by such obvious design. Just as ridiculous were ad men's attempts to sell the sexless small cars of the Eighties as chariots of desire. In 1987, Austin Rover tried to sell the boringly boxy Maestro by showing it picking up four female hitchhikers then racing off, front wheels raised, all accomplished by the slogan 'Get Up To More In A Maestro'. But the award for the most misguided campaign has to go to Fiat. In the early Eighties they tried to revive the 'car as sexy woman' stereotype to sell the Fiat 127 by suggesting 'If it were a lady, it would get its bottom pinched.' The graffiti reply scrawled on the posters – 'If this lady were a car, she'd run you over' – nailed it perfectly.

In the no-fun Nineties, pleasure for both sexes may be forced to take a backseat – cars are increasingly depicted as a family business. If you gun your motor down the road these days, you're usually on the way to the hospital to see your new-born baby. But sex hasn't completely disappeared. All those Audi ads might rely on the thrills of Teutonic hi-tech, but they make sure to flash a bit of leg as well. The 'babe on the bonnet' was even restyled (albeit jokily) for the post-feminist late Eighties, with the 'Love It' campaign for the Peugeot 205, which depicted a model clad in body-conscious fashion slinking up to her car, extending her lipstick and sensuously inscribing a heart on the source of her joy. In the controversy that followed, feminist critics filed the predictable objections to the crosscutting between female flesh and gleaming bodywork while the female writer of the ad argued that it was actually an expression of female pleasure. But perhaps the most ridiculous thing about the whole business was the idea that anyone could get sensuously carried away by something as boring as a Peugeot.

An E-type Jag or Ferrari is a different matter altogether. Perhaps you'd be hard-pressed to find a woman who wouldn't find a fast ride in a low-slung, well-sprung mobile erection an exciting proposition. Perhaps ... However, it's certain that most women passengers probably wouldn't get half as turned on as some male drivers. The truth is that cars don't always function as a prelude to sex; for some men they're just a straight substitute for it (the car as mistress, bit on the side, an alternative thrill for the middle-aged man afflicted by waning libido and the predictability of married life). However, women still have to be there in the passenger seat or doing the splits on the bonnet to both stimulate and disguise the essentially masturbatory pleasures offered by cranking your 'little red loving machine' up past the legal limit.

The reason? Car culture is basically homoerotic boy's own stuff – the people most impressed by the size of what you've got hidden under your bonnet are other men. But admitting this comes dangerously close to swerving off the straight and narrow, hence the existence and persistence of the babe on the bonnet. She isn't the final destination for all those rolling phallic symbols, the endpoint of all those wheelbound fantasies; she's just the necessary alibi, an excuse which allows men to hang out at the garage with other men, getting their kicks by tinkering around with the real object of their desire.

Copyright © Jim McClellan, 1990

Havens of Comfort, Pavilions of Splendour

The Best Hotels in the World by Jon Futrell
March 1991

L ET'S FACE IT, THERE IS LITTLE that is romantic about travel – the taxis, the airports, the shrink-wrapped food and the endless waiting. Romance begins in hotels, along endless corridors and beneath high ceilings, a long way from home.

Hotels are for those of us who either can't or won't go home. They're cocoons of intimacy, discretion and anonymity, reduced to four unfamiliar walls, a view, a suitcase or two, a bunch of keys, a street-plan, an address book, a telephone, and the most potent symbol of travel – the right number to call. Now that's romance.

Hotels are theme parks for itinerants, where time stands still, home is a memory and a signature is all you need to get by. Where grown-ups are permitted, even encouraged, to express their dreams of power and success. People escape to them, and succumb to their mystery.

We do funny things in hotels; sometimes strange, unnatural things. Sid Vicious killed his girlfriend in one. Sirhan Sirhan shot Bobby Kennedy in one. Bert Stern's final tragic photo-session with Marilyn Monroe was shot in one (a three-day session commissioned for _Vogue_, less than two months before she overdosed on barbiturates, began on June 23, 1962, in the Los Angeles Bel Air), as was Madonna's latest video (the Royal Monceau in Paris). There are still some Beatles fans who book months ahead to stay in John and Yoko's 'bed-in' suite in the Amsterdam Hilton. In the Mint hotel in Nevada, Hunter S. Thompson refined Gonzo journalism while purging himself of fear and loathing. And while the Israelis blasted their way into Beirut, the world's press gathered around the pool of the Commodore Hotel and threw empty beer cans at the grey African parrot mimicking the sound of incoming shells. You can buy a lot of humanity for the price of a room key.

Once, in a room in a small and very discreet hotel just off the Boulevard Montparnasse, a voice on the other end of the phone asked me what room I was in. It then instructed me to slide my hand behind one of the overhead timber beams and pull out what I found. Sure enough, there it was, a packet of Bolivia's finest marching powder, one of several emergency packets squirrelled away in hotels throughout the world. This must be why rock stars are forever hurling electrical equipment and pieces of furniture out of hotel windows; they're hunting their stash by a process of elimination. And I always thought it was good PR. A friend of mine, a former employer even, once dropped his mini-bar seven floors on to a hotel courtyard in Tenerife over a dispute about mineral water. Not mineral rights mind you – I could have understood that – but a bottle of Perrier.

Others are not so lucky. I cannot imagine Washington's former mayor Marion Barry busting himself to get back to room 727 of the Ramada Inn, the theatre of his great transgression, or that John DeLorean ever wants to set foot inside room 501 of the Los Angeles Sheraton Plaza.

Women unpack, but what does a man do the moment he enters

a hotel room? Switch on the television, make a bee-line for the mini-bar, and with an iced beer in one hand get straight on the phone to tell everyone at home what a great time he's having? This is not uncommon.

I spent 24 hours in an un-air-conditioned room in the Hotel Condes, Barcelona, one very hot and uncomfortable day in July and managed to empty the mini-bar and run up a phone bill the size of the Third World debt talking to answering machines on three continents. It helped to, well, pass the time. But mini-bars ought to carry government health warnings: at breakfast the morning after I'd emptied one at the Aberdeen Holiday Inn I ran into some co-ordination difficulties with the conveyor-belt toaster – I fused the machine with a bread knife and unwittingly hurled a flaming slice across the crowded dining room.

With such fond memories I was looking forward to The Hilton Blue Lagoon, in Miami. I'd stayed at Hiltons before, and knew that they were mostly unimpressive affairs designed to appeal to out-of-town sales executives; but the Blue Lagoon had an address that reeked of glamour and room service. As the great iron bird made its final approach among the condominiums, stretch limousines and pools of south Florida I juggled images of sunshine, long legs, and long drinks with pink parasols on top.

In fact The Hilton is not much to look at from the outside; a towering block of prefabricated concrete hemmed in by water, palm trees and busy dual carriageways. The lobby is like all other hotel lobbies – full of agitated people waiting for something to happen or somewhere to go. People in clothes you wouldn't want to be seen dead in, complete with shoulders like surfboards and ties like tablecloths. They pretend to read *Time* or the *Herald Tribune* and effect a calm but not totally unnatural cosmopolitan air, though one that cannot mask a certain shiftiness. Like members of a cosmetics convention queueing for the dentist – over-dressed and agitated.

But the air-conditioning in the Blue Lagoon hit me like an arctic storm, and I immediately felt good about being in America. Checking in was painless, and after I'd validated my status, the spiky-haired young man in the salmon pink jacket behind the reception desk handed me two plastic credit card room keys and a metal security key to operate the lift. The lift wouldn't budge without it. It means thieves have to use the stairs.

Blame it on the 11 hours of travelling, or the litres of complimentary Pan Am Californian Chardonnay, but I couldn't get any joy from the lift, or the door of my room, come to that. This reminded me of the famous Charles Laughton quote: 'I've lived 26 years at the Algonquin. I've spent seven of them waiting for the lift.' And to make matters worse the bureau de change didn't have any small notes, and every door that was ceremoniously opened for me by someone in a salmon pink jacket cost me a ten dollar bill. As I picked the broken remains of one of my credit card keys out of the lock it occurred to me that when the bell-hop eventually arrived with my luggage I would have to ask him if he accepted Visa (thankfully he didn't).

My Blue Lagoon television, complete with satellite and movie channels, snapped into life at the touch of a button, but the mini-bar remained firmly shut. International hotels tend to provide their guests with more en-suite reading matter than most libraries, and the Blue Lagoon was no exception; but nowhere was there any hint of how to get at those cold beers. Downstairs, sun-tanned Don Johnson lookalikes and their female companions were jet-skiing in the lagoon, while I was on the 13th floor hurling abuse at a refrigerator. To the south, black storm clouds were rolling in from the Bahamas.

Tired (but not yet emotional), I applied my full concentration to finding the light switch in the bathroom instead. In the gloom I could see acres of marble, a bidet, a bath and shower, a toilet, another television that flickered into life when I hit what I mistook for the light switch, and enough shampoo, soap, shoe-shine, sewing kits, shower caps and hair and body gel to spruce an entire army. Every guest amenity it was possible to imagine, but no light switch.

I resigned myself to either a bath in the dark, or *Die Hard II* on the pay channel – Bruce Willis, or the risk of slipping in the marble blackness and leaving the Blue Lagoon in an ambulance. Besides, showering in the dark is dangerous; the temperature of every hotel shower I have ever encountered has gone from below freezing to scorching in less than half a turn. I was once told a (surely apocryphal) story about the marketing chief of an insurance corporation who took a shower in the dark. He grabbed a 'guest amenity' package and scrubbed himself clean with the shoe-shine. It was probably the same fool who turned up for breakfast the next morning with his complimentary bedtime mint welded to the side of his head.

Hotel ablutions are a headache. Somebody once asked Conrad

Hilton the one thing he would like all his guests to remember. The great man paused for a moment, adjusted his silk tie and formidable Texan brogue, and said, 'The shower curtain goes inside the bath.'

Those few choice words could have been aimed at the Japanese, whose obsession with personal hygiene is costing hoteliers untold millions. At London's Forum Swallow International, at Claridge's ('the Royal Family's living room'), and thousands of other hotels around the globe, the Japanese custom of standing in the middle of the bathroom and pouring bowls of water over their heads is ruining ceilings, carpets and entire electrical systems.

Dirty and dry I called down to the Hilton's front desk to ask if anyone knew why I could see terrorists and 747s going up in smoke on my television, but not hear them. The night porter – grey hair, blue suit, and an expression forged from many years of dealing with disgruntled, drunk, or just plain stupid guests – told me the video repair man would not be back until the following morning. It was at that moment that I realised why people throw themselves out of hotel windows.

It was revenge. The god of hotels was getting even with me for doing a midnight flit from the Holiday Inn on Sunset and Vine in the days when I still enjoyed airline food. But it must have escaped his memory that in my haste to leave LA without paying I had forgotten I'd given my suit to room service to be dry-cleaned.

The Hilton Blue Lagoon was simply not co-operating the way a five-star hotel should. Hotels ought to be calm refuges of comfort and pleasure, where every whim is met and invisible staff shroud their guests in discretion. This, after all, is why we rendezvous, honeymoon, conference, escape, have affairs and sometimes even sleep in them.

In a distant land, with nothing to impress strangers with apart from the cut of your suit and the choice of a wine, the right hotel, a temporary address, can be vital. Conducting business in a suite at the Regent Beverly Wilshire says more than the fact that you have arrived in Los Angeles – it says you have *arrived*, that you are a *big* person with access to *big* money.

And staying in the right room is just as important. There are supplements on single rooms despite them being cramped and uninviting. Years ago I learnt to always book a deluxe double, a shade more expensive than a standard double, but with twin beds the size of snooker tables. Inform the hotel manager well in advance that you expect to be entertaining some business associates in your room, and with any luck you will be upgraded to a suite, with a bottle of Moët thrown in for good measure.

As a rule, most of the classic hotels – the Grand in Rome, the Imperial in Vienna, the Cipriani in Venice, the Ritz in Madrid, and the Berlin Savoy – were built at the turn of the century, before the advent of lifts. Unlike modern hotels, where the best suites are always the penthouses right at the top, away from the hoi polloi, the best bedrooms in *fin de siècle* palaces are on the first floor, and usually at the front with a balcony or veranda.

I know a man who demands that floor plans of hotels are faxed to him before making a reservation. That way he can be certain of getting maximum floor space for the best price.

Should the receptionist insist that all the best rooms are taken, your only course of action is to turn to the concierge or hall porter for assistance. The one to look for is a member of the Clef D'Or. He will be wearing them like a brace of Victoria Crosses in each button hole. They mean he has been a concierge for at least five years, and boasts an impeccable service record good enough to admit him to an international 3,000-strong masonic order. Get in with him and you will travel in style for ever more.

A Clef D'Or concierge will be dressed up to the nines, have immaculately groomed hair, the posture of a grenadier and speak with the deliberation of a high-ranking civil servant. More to the point, he is unquestionably the best connected man in your neck of the woods. He will arrange cars, restaurant and theatre bookings, and provided he takes a shine to the cut of your jib, secure that room with a view just about anywhere in the world where there is a Clef D'Or member. And should you call him after midnight and ask for 'an extra pillow', you will inevitably be offered something rather more intimate than a sack of goose feathers. Of course his undying loyalty and assistance is not cheap, but only a fool believes the best things in life are free.

Just moments before three bullets were pumped into Special Agent Cooper's metal vest at the Great Northern Hotel in *Twin Peaks*, he whispered to Diane via his mini tape recorder, 'Twenty-four-hour room service must be one of the premier achievements of modern civilisation.' He's not wrong: it's no fun stuffing lavatory paper into the bathroom air-extractor at six in the morning to steam the creases out of a suit for a 7.30 breakfast meeting because the hotel valet is tucked up with the wife.

The Sterling Hotel at Heathrow's Terminal Four – a sort of Comme des Garçons shop inside an aircraft hangar – has around-the-clock room service and a computerised billing system so advanced that guests can see the price of their assault upon the minibar flashing up on their TV screen bottle by bottle. It keeps them abreast of flight details, too. The snag, according to the hotel, is that guests simply refuse to check out on time if their flight is delayed.

At New York's Paramount, from the same team that transformed Morgans and The Royalton, a choice of videos and music cassettes are just a phone call away, catering for those of us who have the occasional four-in-the-morning urge to listen to Van Morrison or watch *Taxi Driver*. And room service at the Yesil Ev in Istanbul can arrange for a masseur to knead those parts of you that you cannot manipulate yourself at all hours of the day or night (in your very own en suite Turkish bath, no less).

Discretion is the key to a pair of 'love' hotels in Barcelona. Casita Blanca and the Rosaleda are designed for couples whose other desire is anonymity. Guests pay in advance and may only arrive by car or taxi. A green light at the entrance means the coast is clear and a solitary porter, invisible on the other side of a screen, takes couples to rooms filled with water beds, velvet drapes, four posters – in fact anything reckoned to give *that* moment an extra bite. The lights go out as couples proceed along the corridors just in case anyone should emerge from another room and catch a glimpse of them.

The Gramercy Park may have the best views in New York, but it is the Chelsea that attracts expense-account Bohemians, lured by the ghosts of Wolfe, Thomas, and Behan. According to writer Gene Krell, who has lived there and knows, the Chelsea 'is the only hotel where I am scared of being mugged by the chamber maids. Not even Tom Waits will stay there.'

Recently, the readers of *Condé Nast Traveller* voted Hong Kong's Oriental Hotel 'The Best In The World' for what seems like the umpteenth time. Intrigued – from the outside it just looks like another slab of prefabricated concrete – I asked a regular guest why the Oriental gets consistently good notices. He told me about the elegance and comfort of luxuriously appointed suites named after celebrated authors and travellers, among them Conrad, Le Carré, Coward and, believe it or not, Cartland. He said he was impressed, even touched, when the bell-hop noticed a few jars of pills in his bathroom and asked if he wanted to see the hotel doctor. But most of all, he said, he liked the fleets of almond-eyed beauties who work in every oriental hotel and who provide that singularly Eastern obsequiousness, the kind that unhinges arrogant Western emotions.

Hotels offer us a roof over our heads and the opportunity to be nursed and cared for by people who neither know nor judge us. Loose for a few hours in a palace of mortal delights, we presume to be emperors and indulge ourselves anything our egos will allow.

'Some people think hotels are just a stack of bedrooms in the sky, but they are much more than that,' I was told firmly. 'They are like theatres. The guests as actors and the staff the stage managers, making certain that each performance runs smoothly.' I neglected to ask this man, a former manager of The Ritz, whether he had ever stayed at the Blue Lagoon.

Copyright © Jon Futrell, 1991

Male Order

The Specifications of the Ideal Man by Jessica Berens & Jessamy Calkin
May 1991

YOU ARE SITTING in a fashionable restaurant, the Caprice, say, or Joe's. You have just eaten one button mushroom on a bed of warm radicchio, paid the bill, and are enjoying a Lucky Strike. Suddenly, from the table to your right, comes the nasally pious tones of one whose anal retention will undoubtedly culminate in a painful colonic operation. You turn around to see a man in a denim jacket and fashionable Cutler & Gross spectacles. He is waving at an invisible cumulus. 'Do you mind,' he whines. 'I am eating.' As you are wondering if your legal position is indicated by a 'No smoking' sign, the hushed atmosphere is shattered by the sound of breaking glass. You look up to see a person with a physical configuration similar to that of Arthur Miller. In one hand he is holding a blowtorch. He stares into the condensation that has gathered on the whining retentive's spectacles. 'You don't like smoke?' he enquires, aiming the torch. 'Try this.' At this point the table, denim jacket and half the restaurant are consumed by a conflagration.

Meet the Ideal Man.

The archetypal warning about the ideal man is delivered by Blanche Dubois in *A Streetcar Named Desire*. 'May I speak plainly?' she says. 'He's common. He's an animal. There's even something sub-human about him. Thousands of years have passed him right by and there he is, Stanley Kowalski, survivor of the Stone Age . . . Maybe he'll strike you or maybe grunt and kiss you . . . don't hang back with the brutes, Stella.' Enter Marlon Brando covered in axle grease and wearing a grin that could melt tarmac.

The ideal man is a member of that fantastic sub-species that exists in our dreams but rarely graces reality. Why? The answer is, of course, that despite the fact that men have invented God, painted 'Guernica' and accomplished all kinds of wondrous things, one basic truth still evades them. They have no idea what women find attractive.

Here we come to the first of many anomalies, because the ideal man, in fact, doesn't care what women find attractive, blessed as he is with an alluring mixture of subtle self-confidence (not to be confused with egomania) and insouciance.

Some misguided geeks, bless their Bass Weejuns, have recently voiced the opinion that the cool white woman has been outmoded by hot ethnic chicks. But the ideal man is not the victim of any such silly separatist ethos. He can be any colour – as long as it's not denim.

Mysterious but not necessarily beautiful, the ideal man can look like Popeye as long as he is funny and complicated and does not smell of Paco Rabanne. He has the demeanour of Peter Cook (as the Devil in *Bedazzled*), the attitude of Dennis the Menace, the voice of Leonard Cohen and the unpredictability of a Vietnam vet. He is Jimmy Nail and Ayrton Senna; he wears *GoodFellas* cardigans and appears in the works of J. G. Ballard. He is *not* Lou Reed, Martin Amis, Kevin Costner or Kenneth Branagh.

Photographers have been responsible for a warped aesthetic which forgets that chiselled features, highlighted hair and polycotton sportswear portrayed on unlikely cyborgs will bring no flush to the female face. Furthermore, modelling, like television presentation and professional golf, is not an acceptable profession for the ideal man.

There are four ideal men in America. They are Nicolas Cage, Afrika Bambaata, Denzel Washington and Tom Waits. The list would be longer but Muddy Waters and Neal Cassady are dead.

The ideal man is biologically unusual in that he has neither a mother (whom he might have killed) nor children (so far as he knows). The lucky visitor to his bedroom will note that he is not a reader of men's fashion magazines. *Autosport* lies beside his bed, as does a video of *Two-Lane Blacktop* and a small handgun. There are no mementoes that might illuminate his background. This might be because he has been in prison, of course, but, in general, the ideal man does not curse one with photographic evidence that there have been (or are) other women in his life.

He has three attributes that guarantee his pulling power:
1. A 1968 Dodge Charger sports coupé.
2. A very nice doggy.
3. A slight stutter.

The perceptive will note that money is not on this list. The ideal man knows that it is not how much you make but what you spend it on that counts.

On matters of sensual gratification opinion is divided. There are some for whom the ideal man was the late Danish millionaire who, after he was married, paid women £1,200 to sleep with him, thus giving his wife something of a break (this is a very satisfactory arrangement that would enable one to read books and watch *Lovejoy* without fear of being forced to wear lingerie). Others say the ideal man is very good at it due to fearlessness, imagination and an immense physical stamina honed by a life-long habit of entering houses via windows.

Although he is not a show-off, the ideal man will do anything, for he is possessed of an unassailable *sang-froid* that is as at home putting in an offer for a Richard Dadd as it is chained to one's bed.

He loves women and he particularly likes you.

Physically he should try to be taller than 5′6″, unless born with a devastating sense of humour (which rules out Prince and most of the Rolling Stones). The best ones are a little grubby and look as if they have been up all night, because they have. Their coiffure is usually disarranged and they can drink an enormous amount, but they are never ever drunk. They are basically kind, but this is camouflaged by a facial expression that seems to harbour a desire to blow things up.

The best way to judge whether you have found yourself an ideal man is to look through his pockets. Here you will find any or all of the following – keys; cigarettes; Valium; starter-motor; switchblade; £750 cash; an indoor firework.

The ideal man knows everybody.

He doesn't do the washing up.

He has never been in the Groucho Club.

He was sad when Alex Harvey died.

He has been known to be three days late for dinner.

He never asks permission.

The ideal man, then, is a cross between Billy the Kid and Dario Argento.

Come in all Italian cowboys. Your number is being called.

Copyright © Jessica Berens & Jessamy Calkin, 1991

Muscle Building
The Penis Expander by David Bowker
May 1991

L AST DECEMBER I entered a bleak sex shop on the Holloway Road, where a nervous-looking man – sitting, somewhat incongruously, in a garden chair – handed me a brown paper package containing a device that has haunted the imagination of schoolboys for two decades.

The so-called Chartham Method Of Penis Expansion is actually a simple device, consisting mainly of a suction tube designed to increase the length and girth of the penis. It first came to my attention when I was a first-former at secondary school. In those days penis expanders were like girlfriends: none of my friends possessed one but they all claimed to have friends who did. Now I own my own penis expander. I have become the friend I tell my friends about.

The booklet accompanying the Chartham method outlines the principle behind penis expansion. The penis is composed of tissue that is full of holes like a sponge. When the vacuum developer is applied to the penis and expands the spongy tissue, a maximum amount of blood flows into the holes in the tissue and stretches them, thus enlarging the penis.

'The pressure of the blood in the holes will in time bring about permanent enlargement of the tissue and thus of the penis itself.'

But the Chartham method does not merely involve the use of the infamous vacuum developer; if optimum penis potential is to be achieved, daily expansion must be augmented by a rigorous programme of exercises.

The student must first learn to contract 'the muscles which force the semen out of the penis during climax . . . No one can tell that you are doing this, so you can do it standing at the bus stop, sitting in the car, standing at the work bench or sitting behind your desk.'

The purpose of this, apparently, is to strengthen the muscles of the penis to such an extent that during contraction the erect penis will eventually 'jump backwards towards the belly in an arc of anything up to an inch. If you contract [these muscles] when the penis is in the vagina, the jumping of the penis will add to the sexual excitement of your partner.'

What kind of sexual partner would be excited by a jumping penis, you wonder. What kind of man would wish to make his penis jump in the first place?

The course booklet contains a number of similar exercises, asking us to believe, for example, that rotating one's hips and performing a variety of naked cycling exercises in the air will lead to greater control over one's organ. ('DON'T DO THESE EXERCISES IF YOU HAVE A HEART CONDITION,' warns the instruction manual.)

Part two of the course instructs the would-be expander to wrap a hot flannel around his member. I'm not sure what the point of this is, and the manual offers little explanation, although it does usefully warn, 'It is essential to see that the water is not so hot that it scalds the penis.'

But perhaps we're getting a bit a, er, head of ourselves here. Before you actually use the vacuum developer, it is necessary to 'massage' the penis. This involves greasing the palms of the hands with cold cream and stretching one's organ manually. 'Hand should follow hand in a rhythm, so that the penis is always stretched to a maximum. It is rather like milking a cow.' It is also rather like having a bit of a wank.

At this stage of the proceedings, the penis seems to take on an eerie intelligence. Initially, penis massage will probably result in 'climax', but 'after three or four days the penis begins to realize what you are doing and stays soft' (clever dick).

Only when the penis has been thoroughly massaged, is it ready to be inserted into the vacuum developer. This resembles a large test tube with a pipe attached to a rubber bulb at one end and an entrance for the penis at the other end. A pierced rubber base is provided, which, when greased with cold cream and placed over the entrance to the tube, creates a vacuum between the tube and the erect penis.

I inserted my reluctant member into this rather unlovely device, and squeezed the rubber bulb as directed in the instructions. Air was immediately sucked out of the perspex tube and I was rather alarmed to see my hitherto disinterested penis charge down the tube like a performing eel. Then it abruptly jerked to a standstill, as if awaiting further instructions. I depressed the bulb again and my penis inflated in width. It was rather like receiving a blow-job from a half-hearted ghost. Not a pleasant sensation, but not altogether unpleasant either.

I noticed that after the bulb had been squeezed six or seven times, it took its time to re-inflate. The handbook states that 'this is because the Developer is deliberately constructed so as not to create too strong a vacuum, which could be dangerous'. In other words, a strong vacuum would cause the penis to explode. Try explaining that to the nurse in casualty.

Although ingenious in conception, the Chartham method is hardly an aesthetic triumph. It is difficult not to feel foolish with a giant test tube stuck to one's end. And the instructions fail to point out that if the penis is not inserted into the tube at the correct angle, the head of the penis can be sucked against the sides of the tube. This can be rather painful and, when it occurs, the crown of the penis, its opening distended by suction, tends to resemble a coy and blushing animal, staring up at its owner with a baleful solitary eye.

Another drawback is that in use the apparatus is far from silent – a major design fault, as the user of a penis expander hardly wishes to draw attention to the fact that he is unhappy with his allotted meat ration. When I visited my parents over Christmas, I locked myself in their bathroom with the vacuum developer. My bemused mother knocked on the door and asked me if I was pumping up a bike. As if this was not bad enough, failure to repress the developer tightly over the root of the penis causes air to escape, making an urgent, high-pitched farting noise, leaving the sensitive user feeling incontinent as well as perverted.

Let us not, however, split short and curlies. Anyone interested in this device will be far more concerned about its effect on the penis than in the way it looks or sounds.

The first noticeable effect is that even after the expander has been packed away and hidden under the socks in one's bottom drawer, the head of the penis continues to feel as if it were being expanded. This is an odd sensation, quite distinct from the pressure of an erection, and, although the penis was unchanged in appearance at this stage, it felt curiously bloated.

After three weeks of twice-daily expansion, my penis did seem to have grown. Although its dimensions during erection were more or less the same, it began to look much larger in its flaccid state. It had become the kind of phallus that long-distance lorry drivers pee with in the lavatories at motorway service stations. However, this effect only lasted while I was using the expander daily, and after five days of abstention, my penis returned to its original state.

However, this should not be taken as a criticism of the Chartham method. The developer's own instructions recommended that it be used twice daily for three months if any enlargement of the penis is to be permanent.

I have neither the time nor the inclination (my penis is already three feet long) to investigate the method thoroughly), but, in the tradition of *Blue Peter*, allow me to produce a penis that was expanded earlier.

The penis in question belongs to John, a friend of mine; the only man I have ever met who has freely admitted to feelings of penile inadequacy. 'I used the expander every night for about three-and-a-half months,' he said. 'I'd say it added about a quarter of an inch to the length of my cock, which I reckon is pretty good going for three months' work. The trouble is that it also expanded my foreskin, which is now a bit on the droopy side. It also made the veins on my penis stand out to a worrying extent.'

As far as the medical establishment is concerned, there is no such thing as a penis expander. The authors of sex manuals generally take the view that the size of the penis is unimportant, advising that, 'The vagina will expand to accommodate a large penis and contract to envelop a small one.' All very well, as long as the small one doesn't belong to you.

I took my vacuum developer to my local GP and asked her to comment. She looked horrified. 'You have got to be joking,' she said. 'This is simply going to irritate the penis. If the penis is exposed to excess friction or pressure, it may swell temporarily. It won't grow.'

Doctors will sometimes prescribe hormone injections to promote the growth of a penis, but only in extreme cases. The Chartham method has never been available on the NHS.

Because of this lack of official recognition, devices like the Chartham method, which retails at around the £20 mark, are only advertised among the inflatable dolls and the virility pills in less reputable men's magazines, and perhaps this is their rightful home.

For my part (*fnaarr, fnaarr*), I find myself reluctant completely to dismiss penis expanders. While in use, the Chartham method certainly made my penis look and feel larger than usual. Perhaps, as my doctor believed, this was because the vacuum developer worked by irritating my member. Even so, this could well be the kind of irritation that a man with a small penis could happily live with.

Copyright © David Bowker, 1991

Here Comes the New Lad!
The Unreconstructed Man by Sean O'Hagan
May 1991

L ATELY, I'VE BEEN THINKING about that stillborn species, the New Man. I've been wondering if, behind the myth, beyond the advertising concept, there was ever any real possibility of such a creature actually existing. A sensitive, caring, emotionally balanced, non-sexist, non-aggressive male? And what's more, a sensitive, caring, emotionally balanced, non-sexist male who wasn't simply a wimp.

The answer, as we all know by now, is a resounding no. It seems blindingly obvious, with the benefit of hindsight, that the New Man was simply a specious advertising construct catering to female wish-fulfilment and male wishful thinking. Today, the New Man is a figure of fun, sniggered at by men secretly relieved by the acknowledgement of the impossibility of such a concept, laughed at by women who always recognised the implausibility of such a conceit.

But, just because the New Man doesn't exist, that doesn't mean things haven't changed between men and women. Indeed, the death of the New Man has coincided with the birth of an identifiable, though slippery, sub-species which has emerged as a muted response to the embarrassing vacuum left by the New Man's ignominious non-appearance. In fact what we are dealing with is a hybrid – a would-be New Man who can't quite shake off his outmoded, but snug-fitting, laddishness.

This half-(new)man, half-lad is a tentatively positive reaction to three decades of feminism. Initially, he was a by-product of collective male guilt and the power of positive polemic, but, gradually, as the shrillness of sisterhood subsided, he has gestated into a more confident, not to mention more complex, being.

Let's see if we can pin him down. First up, he tends to be part of the thirtysomething generation – educated, stylish, more often than not well groomed and totally in tune with the shifting codes of contemporary culture. His character has, to some degree, been moulded by prolonged exposure to today's tastemakers – magazines, music and the entire spectrum of post-modern media spill from David Lynch to _The Late Show_.

We are looking at an intelligent and articulate gent here, particularly when he is in the company of intelligent, articulate women with whom he can broaden his cultural constituency even further and talk with confidence about such selfless topics as sexism in advertising, chauvinism in the workplace and a woman's right to choose.

In short, he is well versed in the language, and protocol, of post-feminist discourse and he will never, _ever_, even after a few post-prandial brandies, slip into Sid The Sexist mode like a regular (Jack the) lad might. Of course, he may tell the odd dubious joke, but he'll preface it with the words, 'You'll probably think this is a bit sexist, but it's dead funny,' just so you know that he's aware that he isn't trying to be New Mannish (ie boring, right-on), but is actually acutely aware of, and can even relish, his ideological shortcomings. And besides, the joke _is_ funny. Does this guy sound like you? Yes? Good, cos he sounds like me, too.

I've been trawling about for a generic term to describe us. We're nowhere near ideologically sound enough to qualify for New Man status, but we can't simply be dumped into the old unreconstructed Lad category. What we are dealing with here is the New Lad, a rather schizoid, post-feminist fellow with an inbuilt psychic regulator that enables him to imperceptibly alter his consciousness according to the company he keeps. Basically, the New Lad aspires to New Man status when he's with women, but reverts to Old Lad type when he's out with the boys. Clever, eh?

The New Lad is undeniably a perceptive soul, someone who has sussed out the fact that most women actually share his reservations about the New Man – the main one being that if he did exist, he'd be so terminally right-on, so awesomely aware, that he'd be a total turn-off. 'If men try to be too good,' a woman journalist confessed recently, 'they turn into such bores. Women actually enjoy some element of – I've got to be careful here – wickedness in their men. They don't want loud-mouthed lads and they certainly don't want neurotic wimps who are convinced that they're New Men. There has to be a happy medium.'

I have to admit that the last sentence was said with a distinct air of weary desperation rather than in gratification for the emergence of the New Lad. For, although New Lads see themselves as the epitome of nouveau-male cred, women see us as, at best, deluded souls and, at worst, charlatans. They also detect an element of male manipulation in all this.

'Initially, when a woman meets a New Lad,' another woman friend confided, 'they think they are meeting an open, communicative, emotionally balanced bloke who might just be responsive to the things she wants. And they think this, time and time again, against overwhelming evidence to the contrary, because they want to believe it. Basically, women are incredibly optimistic when it comes to men, and men have learnt to exploit this.'

Which introduces a new element to the New Lad's psychological make-up – the possibility that he, unconsciously or otherwise, preys on the progressive woman's need for a sensitive, caring, dependable soul partner. Maybe the New Lad's tentative grasp of feminist theory is simply another element in the psychology of seduction.

'They know all the right buttons to push,' insists another of my female sources, 'so they can tell you how misogynist the new David Lynch film is *and* they've read *The Female Eunuch*. But when you scratch the surface, you'll find the same old sexist attitudes lurking underneath. If a pretty girl walks into a restaurant, he won't ogle her openly like the Old Lad, but you will catch his eye clocking her as she walks past. And, somewhere underneath all his surface good behaviour and carefully observed protocol, you suspect that he's probably wondering if he can eventually get you into bed.'

Outside the elaborate codes of the courtship ritual, the New Lad retains a chameleon identity. Among unavailable women or in mixed, convivial company, he has a tendency to overstate his non-sexist sensibilities to the point where the women present don't get a word in. The more deluded New Lads – those who actually think they're New Men – tend to get totally carried away with the extent, and exclusivity, of their emancipation. You shall know *them* by their wholesale appropriation of female issues; they will even go so far as chastising women for what they perceive as casual sexism and/or will give you a blow-by-blow account of the recent birth of their offspring while the woman who actually gave birth to said sprog is relegated to the sidelines.

'The thing that really irks me most of all is the fact that if I confide some emotional problem to any of my men friends, they nod in sympathy then start talking about their own problems. Women can confide, men demand an audience.'

Which is why the New Lad is not really that different from the Old Lad and why, indeed, he can metamorphose, at the flick of his psychic switch, into an Old Lad when he's in the company of his ideal audience – his mates. The bottom line with male bonding is that boys will be boys. If six women have dinner together they will, at some point in the evening, talk seriously about the things that really matter. Put six men in a room together and they'll talk, loudly and at length, about anything _but_ the things that really matter. And they'll talk against each other – 'Your team were crap the other night', 'Are you wearing that suit for a bet?' – or in praise of their communal excesses: 'God, me and Steve got wrecked last night.' Cars and girls, sport and booze are still the staple ingredients of the lads' night out. The only difference with New Lads is emphasis – they're not quite as boorish/tribal/drunken or loud as their prehistoric predecessors. And, if someone pulls them up on their double standards, they are immediately able to couch their laddishness in political/sociological terms – 'I know that football is a tribal ritual but it's one of the few remaining outlets for working-class communal expression,' or 'I wasn't out on the piss with the lads last night, I was actually engaging in a new form of positive male bonding very similar to women-only groups insofar as it provides a productive environment for communal self-analysis. Now, where did you say the Paracetamol was?' The beauty of being a New Lad is that there's always a get-out clause.

But, maybe I'm being too hard on this new species. More to the point, maybe I'm being too hard on myself. After all, we have to put the New Lad in perspective. I mean, he may be pretty flaky but he's a damn sight more fun than the New Man and a damn sight more progressive than the Old Lad, who, incidentally, is still going strong – loud, proud and utterly unreconstitutable. Or, as one of the many women I talked to while researching this article put it, 'There are some positive aspects to the New Lad. I mean, he's not sexist to the core.' And, he can be fun in his endearing naîvity, his misguided self-righteousness, his brazen double standards and his utter, unshakeable conviction that he's a one-in-a-million catch for any intelligent female.

Ultimately, however, there is something sad about the New Lad and that something is tied up with the utter dismissal of the New Man – not the New Man as advertising construct, nor the New Man as neurotic right-on wimp, but the New Man as a potential role model. Basically, we just didn't have the will, nor the nerve, to seriously consider such a radical shift in our consciousness. For now, to steal a recent advertising slogan, the New Lad is 'the best a man can get'.

Copyright © Sean O'Hagan, 1991

The Mad Bastard Capital of Australia
Kalgoorlie by Douglas Kennedy
July 1991

THE TAXI DRIVER wouldn't let me sit behind him in his cab. He also wouldn't let me enter his vehicle by the door directly behind the driving seat – a door he kept permanently locked.

'No one uses that door, mate,' he said as I struggled to open it. 'Haven't let a bugger through that door in years. Y'wanta ride in this cab, you go round to the other door.'

I did as I was told, but then made the mistake of sliding across the backseat.

'I'd stay on the left side if I was you. Won't allow anyone t'sit behind me. It's simply not on, y'understand?'

'Whatever makes you happy,' I said.

The driver gunned the motor and we flew at low-altitude out of the motel car park. As we chewed up the tarmac on this suburban desert road, the cabbie – a sinewy dude with eyes as frozen as a lake in winter – kept up a steady stream of twitchy rapid-fire repartee.

'Bet you think I'm a mad bastard,' he said. 'Bet you think I'm one sandwich off the full picnic.'

'Now why should I think a thing like that?' I said, noticing that we were clocking 70 in a 25mph zone.

' 'Cos I wouldn't let you sit behind me. But, like I said, no one sits behind me. No one! Know why? 'Cause everyone in this town is a wanker.'

'Really?' I said, trying to maintain a neutral, anything-you-say tone of voice.

'Yeah, Kalgoorlie is the wanker capital of the world. And that's why I won't let anyone sit behind me in my cab.'

'Because they're wankers?'

'No – because they might punch me.'

'Why should they want to punch you?'

'Because that's what people do in Kalgoorlie – they punch each other. It helps pass the time.'

Kalgoorlie. Look at a map of Australia and let your eye roam its vacant midsection. This is the place they call The Dead Heart – a 2,500-mile geographic void. A non-stop vista of empty wheat fields, supplanted by empty prairies, supplanted by empty desert. A relentless red desert that appears almost molten. It takes over two days by train from Sydney to traverse this topographic *tabula rasa*, and the last 16 hours of the journey are spent in this empty quarter. No trees. No fauna. No elevation to the landscape. No signs of life, barring a village for railway employees called Cook – a nowhere hamlet of six houses and no discernible boundaries, as it simply floats like a bizarre little island in the midst of all that blankness.

After watching this lifeless vista hour after hour, you think – this is no mere barren landscape; this is Genesis 1:1. The beginning of the world. Or the end of it.

But just when you start to wonder if you will ever escape this prehistoric expanse, just when you've come to regard this desert as a hostile no-man's-land ready to swallow you up, the train sheds speed. It begins to coast into something that looks like a proper town, and you heave a major sigh of relief. This is the payoff for all those days in the void. This is a return to civilization. This is a place called Kalgoorlie.

Kalgoorlie. A name which is afforded near-mythical status in the Australian consciousness, as befits a centre of human endeavour in the continent's Dead Heart. Australia, after all, is a coastal society (with over 90 per cent of its 15 million inhabitants strung out on either the Indian or Pacific seaboards), so places in that vacant zone are regarded with a certain degree of suspicion. Not only are they considered frontier outposts; there's also a general belief in the rest of this hyper-urbanised country that you really have to be something of a 'mad bastard' to live in a spot so deep within that out-of-bounds realm they call the Never-Never.

And Kalgoorlie – I was warned before I left Sydney – was the 'mad bastard' capital of Australia. An outback mining community perched on the edge of nothingness. A one-horse town still enveloped in a distinctly Wild West ethos. A place where men were men, boys were boys, and wankers were wankers.

So I took the train west. Sixty hours later, I was in a Kalgoorlie motel room. When night woke up, I called a taxi and made the acquaintance of that manic cabbie who had a thing about people sitting directly behind him. And when I asked him to take me to the centre of town, he said, 'I'll drop you in front of the world's tallest litter bin.'

And he did just that.

The world's tallest litter bin was, verily, the world's tallest litter bin. At least I'd never seen a litter bin so tall before. According to a sign posted by the bin, it was 16 feet high, making it the loftiest rubbish receptacle on the planet. Why someone had gone to the trouble of manufacturing such a thing – and what it was doing here – was not explained. Then again, how could anyone supply a rational explanation for the fact that the World's Tallest Litter Bin could be found at the end of the main street in Kalgoorlie?

Besides the bin, the other notable commercial feature of this central drag – known as Hannan Street – was the large number of shops that advertised themselves as 'Authorized Metal Detector Dealers'. It was a reminder that Kalgoorlie was, first and foremost, a gold mining town. It has been a gold mining town ever since a trio of prospectors (led by a certain Paddy Hannan of Hannan Street fame) struck a nugget in 1893, sparking off a major gold rush. Before then, Kalgoorlie was nothing more than a squalid mining camp – a toxic waste dump of shanties, with no running water and a proliferation of raw human sewage decorating its two or three dirt streets. There was no such thing as fresh food, and water was regarded as such a luxury in this nowhere corner of Western Australia that many a prospector took to bathing in champagne – which was cheaper to buy in this bivouac than *eau naturel*.

Three years after Hannan's legendary strike, however, gold had turned Kal into a boom town, complete with all the gimcrack trimmings: saloons, gaming parlours, whorehouses, a lock-up, and a handful of hard-working undertakers – in short, all the basic necessities of life (and death) required by the sort of self-deluding, self-destructive fantasists who look to the earth's veins for an instant fortune.

I stood by the bin and took in Hannan Street. It was a half-mile vista of Victorian High Noon architecture – ornate hotels with cupolas and wrought-iron balconies; saloons with swing doors; wide protective verandas shielding the pavements from the white-hot morning sun. This was no ersatz backlot set for some fettucini western. This was the real thing – an extant relic of the Australian Old West.

It was an hour or so before noon, and the mercury was already punching three figures. Along this main street, clusters of derelicts were stretched out on the pavements, courting heatstroke. They were a scraggy melting-pot of whites and Aborigines. Seen against the backdrop of this 1890s honky-tonk town, with their four-day beards, their sweat-soaked grandfather shirts, their dust-laden stetsons, and their sunken eyes, they were like figures in a sepia daguerreotype. It struck me that had you been in Kalgoorlie nearly a century ago, you would have seen a comparable collection of forlorn figures sprawled on the streets, with that similar haunted demeanour of men who'd been on a month-long binge and were wondering where their next beer would be coming from. Boom towns, after all, are always convention centres for life's certifiable no-hopers.

I stopped by the oldest hotel in town, The Exchange, for a beer. The saloon doors flapped behind me as I entered, and I was carefully eyed up by a dozen or so customers perched on bar stools and already engaged in the business of drowning a few brain cells before lunch. There was a pair of off-duty miners – beefy gents with faded tattoos and biceps that appeared to have been bred on steroids – engaged in an analytical discussion about the personality deficiencies of their pit foreman.

'The bloke's a complete fuckwit,' one of them said.

'Too right,' said his mate. 'And he's also got a head on him like a robber's dog.'

There was also a pair of burnt-out housewives – dyed-blond hair; faces that were elaborate bas-reliefs of premature age lines, and dripping pancake make-up; cigarettes between their teeth:

'Told Geoff I simply wasn't going to take it anymore. Told him I was going to piss off back to Perth and leave him holding the bloody baby.'

'How'd he take the news?'

'Split my lip, the bastard.'

And finally, there was Robbo. He was sitting to the left of my elbow at the bar – an ageing Boy of Summer, pushing 30, dressed in shorts and a polo shirt, drinking vodka on the rocks with beer chasers. Like myself, he was a newcomer in town.

'Just pulled in last week. A real brass razzo, Kalgoorlie. A serious dump, if you ask me. And I'm signed on for a two-year stint down the mines here. Two bloody years in the fag end of the universe . . .'

Robbo called for another vodka and beer, and told me he was a mining engineer from Queensland. Ah, Queensland – mile-upon-mile of virginal beaches; of big Pacific breakers rolling in with metronomic regularity; of surfing safaris and lazy-hazy-crazy-days-of-summer; of blonde golden girls who liked to park their shoes under the beds of blond, golden guys like Robbo.

Listening to Robbo speak of Queensland was like listening to one of Chekhov's Three Sisters spout on about Moscow. Queensland, to him, had become the Xanadu from which he'd been exiled. It was, however, a self-imposed exile, as he'd voluntarily come to Kal to work in a proper mine for two years and thereby gain an additional qualification as a mining engineer – a qualification which would mean another $10,000 a year for his next job.

'I came here because I thought the experience in the mines might mean more money later on. But, I'll tell you something – after a week in Kal I'm ready to throw in the towel. I mean, you don't know what it's like here. A 12-hour shift down the mine, and then bugger all to do back above the surface, except get drunk or get into a fight. I mean, the nearest beach is in Perth, which is only something like 600k from here. And when it comes to women, your only option as a single bloke is Hay Street.'

'What's Hay Street?' I said.

'Brothel Boulevard – the place you go to buy yourself a ride. It's all legal here, y'know. And the girls get a regular going over by a local quack, so there's no chance of picking up a dose, or anything worse. They're kinda nice girls, too. I mean, this is my eighth day in Kal and I've been to 181 twice already, which everybody says is the best whorehouse in town.'

'Why do they call it *181*?' I asked.

'Simple, mate. That's the metric for 69.'

I took a walk down Hay Street. It was, at first sight, nothing more than a wide, rather tumbledown boulevard, two streets away from the main drag. On closer inspection, I noticed what looked like an aluminium-sided shed on which a signwriter had crudely daubed the words: 'Come Meet The Girls – Sherri, Jasmine, Cilla, Sia, and Nee. Open 12pm Daily.'

This was 181. It was currently 11.30 and the shack was shuttered. However, as I turned away from the building, a woman headed towards the front door. She was in her mid-twenties; a petite blonde woman wearing dark glasses and carrying a small briefcase-like bag with her. She looked like someone on her way to work – which, of course, she was.

'G'day,' she said. 'You waiting for us to open?'

'Just passing by,' I said.

'Window shopping, eh? Come back in a half-hour, we'll see you right.'

'Do you get many customers at midday?'

'Mainly blokes coming off the night shift who can't sleep,' she said, stepping into the portals of 181. 'Listen, got to go. Like I said, it's only 30 minutes till we're ready for business, so why don't you get yourself a beer and drop by later, OK?'

I wandered down Hay Street to another aluminium structure – a place that looked like a small collection of out-houses clustered together. In front of these cubicles was a woman in red hot pants and a matching halter. A fine trickle of sweat cascaded down her pretty, if somewhat hardened, face.

'Feel like a party?' she said.

'It's a little hot for that, don't you think?'

'Don't worry about the heat, mate. Got air-conditioning inside my humpy here and a fridge full of tinnys, so you'll be nice and cool.'

'Think I'll pass,' I said.

'Well, if you're in the mood later you know where to find me.'

What was fascinating about Hay Street was its matter-of-fact, business-like approach to prostitution. A service was for sale here – and it was sold to potential customers in a no-nonsense fashion. The citizens of Kalgoorlie, in turn, accepted the brothels as an intrinsic part of the town's commercial and social landscape – something I discovered when I got into a chat with a waitress while having lunch. She asked me what I thought of Kal and I mentioned that Hay Street struck me as a rather unique institution.

'You know, the local bloody bible-thumpers are always going on about how Hay Street is the wages of sin incarnate,' she said, 'but theirs is kind of a minority view in Kal. And I'll tell you why. Because – thanks to Hay Street – there hasn't been a rape in this town for 12 years. And in a mining town, where there's a definite shortage of women, a place like Hay Street keeps everybody nice and docile. Anyway, the houses are very much part of the life in town. I mean, 181 sponsors the local Australian Rules rugby team.'

I asked if the houses competed with each other in the commercial marketplace when it came to the rates they charged for services rendered.

'Nah,' the woman said, 'they're all pretty standardised.'

'Like how much?'

Without batting an eye, she said, 'Fifty for regular, seventy-five for French.'

Fred believed there were two types in this world – those who worked below the surface and those who worked above it.

'Like, you're an above-the-surface man,' Fred told me. 'So, in my book, that means that you'll never really understand me, since I'm strictly a below-the-surface bloke. Gives you a different perspective on things, spending your whole working life down a mine.'

'What kind of perspective?' I said.

'Put it this way,' Fred said, 'if you spend ten to twelve hours a day down a dark, dangerous hole a couple hundred feet underground, you're going to want to raise a little hell once you get back above the surface.'

Fred and I had this conversation several hundred feet *below* the surface. He was a miner – a fleshy gent around 50, with a hangdog moustache – who agreed to show me around the place where he dug for gold. And equipped with a borrowed hardhat and a pair of coveralls, I rode with him in the tiny cage-like lift that dived 300ft into the Kalgoorlie lower depths. Had I been claustrophobic, that five-minute plummet straight down a meagre shaft would've turned me into a candidate for a straight-jacket. As it was, our little walking tour through the narrow, dank tunnels of the mine was merely a little disquieting for someone unused to this subterranean netherworld – especially as the deeper down we climbed the more I realised that my one link to the world above was a rickety lift which made asthmatic noises as it creaked up and down its shaft.

Fred, on the other hand, treated this expedition like a tour of his office. And since he had a captive audience on his hands, he talked non-stop. As we negotiated the black maze of excavated rock (where the temperature was around 70°F cooler than on the surface), he told me how Kal was going through something of a mini-boom at the moment, thanks to the worldwide increase in the price of gold and the fact that nickel was also mined here (there being a big demand for nickel these days, owing to NASA's use of the metal on its high-flying expeditions). He also told me that he wished he'd been a miner back in the 1900s – the early days of the

Kal gold boom – when the town was so wealthy that one saloon apparently braided its staircase in solid gold, and one prospector who hit a big stake went on a month-long binge, squandering $4,000 in 30 days on champagne (a sum equivalent to $30,000 today). He told me he hadn't spoken to his daughter in ten years, ever since 'she'd gotten knocked up by some Darwin bastard'. And that his wife left him in 1980 after he lost an entire month's wages playing 2-Up.

'What's 2-Up?' I said.

A big smile appeared on Fred's face. 'Let's go back above-the-surface,' he said.

We drove in Fred's arthritic Holden – the Australian version of a Chevy – to a dirt track on the outskirts of town. At the end of this track was a crude amphitheatre made of aluminium siding. Inside, two wide circles of plain wooden benches faced a dirt pit. This was the '2-Up School' – a makeshift gambling arena; an Outback variation on a Las Vegas theme.

2-Up, Fred explained, was essentially a more elaborate version of the heads/tails coin game. Here's how it works: two old Australian pennies – each with a white cross painted on one side – are placed on a small hand-held plank and then tossed into the air. The thrower keeps tossing until both coins turn up heads or tails. Before the toss, however, everyone in the arena bets against each other. So a punter will shout 'Twenty heads' and drop a $20 bill on the ground, and then another punter will signal him that he'll take up the challenge and bet on 'Twenty tails'. Meanwhile, the thrower is also gambling, because every time the two coins turn up heads his money doubles. This means that a thrower who starts off betting $20 can see his winnings rise to $320 with four consecutive throws of heads. It also means that if he gets too cocky or greedy, all the money he's accumulated can vanish with one toss of tails.

There must have been 100 people crammed into that amphitheatre – a disparate array of off-duty miners, housewives, ranchers, Aboriginal workmen, and the occasional besuited local businessman. Watching the interplay between gamblers – the way a bet was shouted out and a response to that bet signalled back – was like watching a very basic version of the same sort of speculative game you see on the floor of a commodity exchange or money market. The roar of the gamble in motion.

But what was most fascinating about the 2-Up School was not only the trust involved in the betting (and the way everyone always honoured their losses); it was also the way 2-Up was considered a community activity, played every afternoon from Monday to

Thursday, with 'school' suspended on Friday, as that was pay-day, and even Kalgoorlie didn't want to see its miners squandering their paychecks on the spot (though Fred had managed to blow four consecutive paychecks – and, in turn, his marriage –by convincing his employers to fork over his wages on Thursday afternoon, so he could hit the 2-Up School before it closed for the weekend).

The more I considered Kalgoorlie's libertine attitudes towards prostitution and gambling and the inherent right of a man to roll in the gutter if he so desired, the more I realised that I had landed in a corner of the world with a unique rough-and-tumble morality. Fred really was right – if you worked below the surface, your natural instinct was to raise some hell once you got above ground. But isn't that the reality of all isolated, elemental outbacks? They are so cut-off from the big metropolitan wheels around which so much of contemporary life revolves that they simply don't have to worry about society's ethical niceties or moral posturings. They can re-write the rule book. And in this neck of the Outback – 'a place where crows fly backwards' – there was a general unspoken acceptance of the fact that man was in a fallen state of grace – so why not cater to his most basic instincts?

Fred was also right about another thing – he was a perennial loser when it came to 2-Up. I watched as he seized the opportunity to be the thrower, and, plonking down $30, threw four heads in a row. Suddenly, he had $480 to hand. But instead of cashing some of his winnings – as is allowed according to the rules of 2-Up – he plonked down that $480, hoping to increase it to $960 with one more throw of heads.

And, of course, when the coins landed in the dirt, they both came up tails.

Fred said nothing as we drove back to the centre of Kalgoorlie, his hangdog moustache now augmented by a hangdog demeanour. It was dark by the time we reached Hannan Street. And as we pulled up in front of a local saloon, a voice could be heard from within: 'Up you for the rent, dickhead . . .'

Accompanying this was the sound of fisticuffs. And glass breaking. And more voices being raised to a level somewhat above a normal conversational tone.

Night had come to Kalgoorlie. And when I turned to look at Fred, I saw that he was smiling again.

Copyright © Douglas Kennedy, 1991

All Boys Together

The Myth of Male Bonding by Peter Howarth

July 1991

THERE IS A THEORY that goes something like this: men like each other, they like to spend time together; for men, the company of other men is something profound, mystical, a heightened experience quite distinct from the company of women. Above all, this brotherhood is something to be celebrated.

Look at those men over there – in the pub, in the restaurant, City types with portable phones and hand-tailored suits, or lads in polo shirts and denim – either way, it's the same story. As the rounds are bought, the courses served, a curious ritual unfolds. Horseplay, joshing, back-slapping, pawing, heads-down huddle followed by raucous laughter. Boys together. Sincerely.

In its true form, male bonding has been around for centuries, a phenomenon born of life and death situations. Hannibal's elephant riders, fresh from Africa, crossing the Alps in 15 days; Scott and Amundsen's crazy frost-bitten polar explorers; teenagers scrambling their Spitfires into action with only a handful of flying hours behind them; the first astronauts, circling the earth in what were potentially nothing more than fancy hi-tech coffins; and, perhaps the ultimate example, Nelson at Trafalgar – 'Kiss me Hardy.'

These are men who have experienced real bonding. They know the value of contact with their fellow men. And in their shared experience of being on the edge, the bond is forged; a bond of respect, a bond of love. It is the intensity of this experience that justifies a celebration of unifying, sustaining maleness – for it is maleness which they pitch against a world of danger and hazard, a world which at every moment threatens to break the bond, and to tear them apart.

But this is not what we see in the hurdy-gurdy high jinks in today's pubs and restaurants. Self-conscious in the extreme, this is a pale imitation of the original, the style without the substance.

There lies the problem. Robbed of its rationale, and reduced to mere social toasting of male sexuality, bonding becomes a sham. Because away from danger, in the quiet lull of peaceful normality, there is one immutable fact about heterosexual men: they do not like each other. In fact they make each other nervous. They don't

167

want to spend time together. What they really want to do is spend time with women.

Men are highly competitive animals. You see it whenever two meet for the first time. What happens? A gesture of welcome, followed by a frank, candid exchange of views? No way. Bowie got it right: 'When you're a boy, other boys check you out.' They sniff around each other, flash some plumage, clash their antlers.

It's a primal thing. Ever since he was a hunter-gatherer sharpening the flints, man's been out there, demarcating his territory, establishing his status. Apart from getting together to do battle, commit genocide, and subjugate their enemies, men also meet to do business – which is really only competition in the name of commerce. Then there's sport. This is self-evidently competitive: there are winners and losers, and there is an opposition. But think of what's going down on your own side. When the big sweaty jock walks into the showers and says, 'Well played, lads,' what he really means is, 'You played well . . . but I played just that little bit better.'

Finally, men get together to hang out and shoot the breeze. Once they've thought of a reason (they wouldn't feel comfortable just popping round for a chat), whether it's poker or pool, shooting or fishing, or simply a boys' night out, then they meet, supposedly at their most relaxed.

Even here, the competitive edge won't lie down. It's not just a question of how much money you've won, or how many grouse you've bagged. It's what and how fast you're drinking, how funny you're being, the quality of your anecdotes, the twinge of jealousy you feel at the news of another's success, and the stab of delight when you hear of some poor bastard's failure. Men are not generous to their comrades.

It's for this reason that they find it hard to really get to know one another. It has nothing to do with communications. Men don't really talk to each other, they talk *at* each other – an inexhaustible stream of banter, in-jokes, in-references, jargon, code, nicknames, and wind-ups. Much of the subject matter is pre-determined (cars, girls, sport, work) in order to avoid anything too revealing. These exchanges are calculated to reveal *nothing*. Nothing personal, nothing intimate and nothing that could be used in evidence. Shooting the breeze is the verbal equivalent of putting up a smokescreen.

This is not a good basis for lasting relationships. As Robert Louis Stevenson, writing on the subject a hundred years ago, put it, 'A man who has a few friends, or one who has a dozen (if there be any one so wealthy on this earth), cannot forget on how precarious a base his happiness reposes; and how by a stroke or two of fate – a death, a few light words, a piece of stamped paper, a woman's bright eyes – he may be left, in a month, destitute of all.' Men's bonds are easily broken.

Women are different. Once out of pigtails, women are forever more grown-up than their male contemporaries. It's a fact, so let's face it. Women are capable of deep, loving, loyal, and relatively selfless relationships with their fellow women. Perhaps it's a result of the raw deal they've had, the kind of siege mentality which causes men to band together in times of stress but which has been felt by women throughout their oppressed history. Whatever the reason, women can see male bonding for the insubstantial thing it really is. A woman I know recently expressed a fear that, should she leave her boyfriend, he'd have no one to turn to. 'He has no male friends he could really trust, really talk to,' she said. I had to tell her that he was no freak. He was just a man like other men.

Last week, on the occasion of a friend's stag night, and his girl-friend's corresponding hen party in Wales, my girlfriend set off for what turned out to be a weekend of good company, good food, walks, wine, and healthy sex-talk. She returned on Sunday night full of the joys of sisterhood.

This is what the boys did:

Saturday morning was spent in a greasy spoon off the King's Road – fried bread and lots of eggs – and then it was off to Stamford Bridge, where the team played like a bunch of concrete-booted apprentices, and were deservedly whipped 2-0 by the Saints. Johnny, the groom and a keen Chelsea supporter, was distraught, so we took him to a local for some liquid consolation. There were 12 of us, and we were in high spirits. A couple of hours later, we sat down to a first-class blow-out at a dining club in Kensington. We toasted Johnny, drank a lot of vodka, and made the required lewd suggestions to the waitresses. Like Chelsea, we didn't score.

Around midnight, we stumbled, bug-eyed, into Johnny's Brixton flat, discovered a couple of guitars among the crates of beer and set about serenading each other with every piece of Seventies pop nonsense our addled brains and tired throats could muster. At about three, Johnny turned the colour of his buttermilk woodchip wallpaper, and went to bed.

We were just congratulating ourselves on how civilised we'd all been – no debagging, no handcuffs, no strippers, no blow jobs – and wondering what to do next, when someone suggested that we take a look at how Johnny was doing. The next thing I knew, we had all piled on to Johnny's bed, and were playing castanets with every spoon the kitchen could furnish, singing 'Viva España!' at the top of our voices.

Johnny was not amused. In fact he was very ill. He threw up. He even threw a few desperate punches in our direction. Then he collapsed. But now we had a new game. On the quarter hour, every quarter hour, for the next six hours, we stole into his bedroom, guitars and spoons at the ready, hit the lights and blew his head off.

Back at home, on hearing my girlfriend's account of her Welsh weekend idyll, I was seized with remorse. I picked up the phone. 'Johnny?' I asked, 'is that you?' There was a silence. Then came the reply. 'Peter, you old sod. Great night!'

You might think that this sounds like a good night out, that the boys had fun. And yes, with the probable exception of Johnny, we did. It was great, it was brilliant, but it was also kind of nothing. I can't speak for the others, but it left me with a hollow feeling. Is that all there is to *having fun* with the boys? What, after 18 hours of close confinement, did we know that we didn't at the outset? What had we learnt apart from the lyrics to 'Billy Don't Be A Hero', 'Tiger Feet' and 'Glass Of Champagne'? Kind of nothing.

Of course, there are those who will tell you otherwise – men who believe in an easily accessed brotherhood of man – men like American playwright, David Mamet. Not long ago, Mamet wrote an article for *Playboy*, in which he argued that men have a special affinity for one another. Men's and women's emotional make-ups are quite different, he said. To illustrate his point, he supplied the following anecdote:

'I was sitting at a bar in Chicago many years ago. It was late at night and I was drinking a drink. An old waitress came over to me and guessed the root of what she correctly took to be my state of the blues. "Look around you," she said, "you have more in common with any man in this room than with the woman you'll ever be closest to in your life." '

Now I don't think this is anything to boast about. Because what exactly was it that Mamet had in common with his fellow men, if not his loneliness and isolation? It took a woman to come and offer him some kindness. The men in the bar knew a loser when they saw one, and stayed away.

Copyright © Peter Howarth, 1991

Kiss Kiss! Bang Bang!

Robert Bly & the Men's Movement by Mark Cooper

December 1991

HE INSTRUCTIONS FROM The Open Gate, organisers of the Robert Bly weekend, were quite clear: 'Please bring a drum' and, later, 'Bring your own towel'. The towel was easy enough, but I hadn't owned a drum since childhood. I passed on a pair of gleaming congas set in a metal stand as too professional and set off for Dorset on Thursday afternoon with an ancient, leather-thonged hand drum in the back of the car and Primal Scream on the stereo. By the time I got to Gaunt's House, a converted ancestral seat near Wimbourne, I was seriously spooked.

Billing the weekend as 'The Shadow and The Soul', The Open Gate's brochure promised lashings of the kind of soul-mining most of us work hard to avoid. One hundred and ten men had coughed up £300 each, ditched their responsibilities and come to Dorset in search of something missing.

The presence of Bly, 'star' of the American Men's Movement, seemed a guarantee that this would be the real deal. Bly is a prize-winning poet and has been holding men's workshops since 1981. In his best-selling bible of the Men's Movement, *Iron John*, Bly argues that men have lost touch with their wilder instincts and that we lack the mentors who used to teach us how to be men. To Bly, manhood is a quest. The Open Gate's prospectus likened him to a surgeon with a sharp scalpel, cutting 'into the long bag that we drag behind us, exposing the repressed world that is meowing, snarling, rattling, clanging, wheezing and rotting within us'.

The shadow sounded bad enough, but the scalpel sounded much worse.

The American media have had a field day with the Men's Movement's blend of mythological/New Age language. Tales of naked computer programmers yelling and screaming in the woods have already become a source for jokey asides in sitcoms like *Cheers*. British reviews of *Iron John* have been similarly sniping. Much as feminism was reduced to bra-burning in the early Seventies, the Men's Movement has already been dismissed as a mixture of drumbeating and self-pity.

Like the rest of the men *en route* to Gaunt's House, I wanted

171

to see for myself. Ever since the Seventies, I've been wondering about why it seems easier to talk to women than men, why my childhood struggles with my father still dominate so much of my emotional weather. Yet, after an initial burst of enthusiasm for my women friends' feminism, I'd simply put a question mark over the whole area and let it ride. Occasionally I heard about a men's group or glimpsed a copy of *Achilles Heel* on a magazine rack, but the kind of discussions feminism provoked in the Seventies seemed to fade away in the Eighties. I felt I'd opened and closed a book without ever reading the contents. Working away and bringing up two sons with my partner, I'd almost stopped bothering about any interior life. I wanted a bit of my soul back (at *Arena*'s expense).

Soon a small group of us were queueing before the theatre at the side of Gaunt's House, used for all manner of New Age activities. A man with long hair and a headband in the manner of a Hollywood Red Indian stood guarding the door with a gnomic air of spiritual superiority. Drums pounded from within as men were shuffled through in groups of four. Eventually a few came wandering back around the side of the building, studiously avoiding the beseeching looks of the remaining initiates shuffling about like small boys waiting to enter a Ghost Train. The drumming swelled. I wondered anxiously how far it was to the nearest pub.

Once in the door, the tension eased. We were directed inside small booths to choose between the Lion Clan ('Lions rise proudly from the earth . . .') or the Raven Clan ('The Raven's work is to make sure that the dark side of things is clear'). In the theatre proper some 30 men were drumming away with concentrated bliss as we made our way to either the Lion's or Raven's table to pick an additional small group for the weekend. I turned over a scrap of paper to discover the phrase 'The Unblinking Guardians'. The panic had now subsided, but I was beginning to worry that this was going to be like spending three days reading fortune cookies.

The dinner-table talk is wary, the food vegetarian. Most of the men are in their late thirties and early forties, many are therapy veterans, the majority are middle-class, and a surprising number have been what one man later calls 'expensively deprived' at public schools. Overall, the group has the slightly rundown look of men growing older in teenage clothes – jeans and T-shirts, thinning hair, a fair share of beards, lots of glasses.

At my all-male school I grew strong on the weakness of others, the ones we called 'creeps' or 'spastics'. I keep wondering if the rest of the men here are 'creeps'. Coming to Gaunt's House seems like an admission that something isn't working, an admission of failure. Right now, I'd prefer it if that sense of failure belonged to somebody else.

After dinner, we fetch our drums and head back to the theatre. A rhythm builds quickly and soon men are pounding away with a hungry urgency.

Bly and the storyteller Michael Meade take their seats on a small dais with a minimum of fuss. Bly is wearing one of his trademark waistcoats; his white mane makes him look every inch the poet. Meade is dark, almost cheeky looking and resembles an Eskimo. Bly is of Scandinavian stock. Meade has Irish roots. They tease each other mercilessly all weekend. After they have recited a few poems, Meade sets up a rhythm on his drum and begins to spin the yarn around which the weekend will be threaded.

Like *Iron John*, Meade's story is a folk tale, with a not-entirely unpredictable cast headed by a young pig herder and including a beautiful young woman, a castle with a forbidden room, a bird thrice nailed to the wall who asks for water, a hunter with a three-legged horse and, of course, a witch. Very soon we are enraptured.

'Mythology is ahead of psychology,' says Bly, and he and Meade teach via myth, story and poetry. Metaphors seem to dig deeper than the abstract language of therapy or psychoanalysis. The tests that face the tale's young hero are constantly offered back to the audience, his dilemmas presented as struggles in the male psyche. On the first evening, Meade leaves the hero in a castle, standing outside the only room he has been forbidden to enter by his beautiful young hostess. Meade has told the story so well that every one of us is inside that castle with the young man. Later, when we stand up and describe our images of what the room contains – devouring mother figures with empty thrones, a cobra, dragons, a snakewoman, a baby with an old face – Bly and Meade help 'read' the images and explain how the stories work. 'These tales have been honed down over 20,000 years. Their images and devices are a condensation of human wisdom about the psyche. What you see in that room is what's trapped inside you.'

When the story is over for the evening, Meade divides the hall into Lions and Ravens. As the drums pound, we square off like rival Maori tribes, each tribe chanting as men take it in turns to front their clan in a pantomime of movements. There is nothing particularly elegant about the gestures, which are full of crude contempt for the rivals; noses are thumbed, arms flapped, fingers given. Some hurl themselves in front of their group with a giddy abandon. It is like a dam exploding. I am shifting from foot to foot at the back, arguing with my own embarrassment, my awkwardness in groups.

Exhausted, we retire to our bedrooms. I share a room with two others. Pinned to the door is a sign bearing the legend 'The Unblinking Guardians'. The following two nights we won't be able to stop talking, but that first night I fall straight to sleep.

At 8.30 the next morning, straight after breakfast, the drums begin again and Meade takes up the story. Each day the sessions last from breakfast until 10.30pm. Bly and Meade warm to their theme of 'father-hunger'. Talk is of the shadow that falls across our wilder, masculine identity, of the bag in which we bury those parts of ourselves rejected in childhood. He elaborates on the 'shadow' of the weekend's title, 'The Shadow and The Soul': that area of repression, shame and denial into which we must plunge in order to become whole.

Bly's ideas are rooted in his studies of the mythologist Joseph Campbell, but also in the AA movement which has become such a pervasive force in American society over the last decade. Young men may be cool and strong, says Bly, but all men's hearts are broken by the time they reach 35. Then they grow empty and, eventually, hungry. He talks about how his own life 'stopped working' in his forties when he realised he couldn't write poems about his alcoholic father. He describes how he realised that he could no longer continue to visit his parents, talk to his mother and leave without speaking to his (now sick) father. According to Bly, Western culture is sick because we have done away with fathers and all they can teach us. Fathers have become a source of shame and the root cause of the silence between men. When Bly got past his mother and entered his father's room, the American Men's Movement began in earnest.

Bly's story strikes a deep chord in his British audience. There is talk of men dying in the Great War and of the English cult of the stiff upper lip. An Italian stands up in the corner of the theatre. He is boiling with rage. 'Ever since I came to live in this country, I was treated like a second-class citizen by your motherfucking, self-satisfied arrogance. I've been waiting for years to be in a room with 100 Englishmen so I could tell you all to fuck off!'

It is the first real gust of deep feeling to come from the floor and the whole theatre shudders: from the truth of the man's complaint and the sheer resentment that seems to drive it. Throughout the weekend, men seem compelled to contribute something of themselves to the discussions. Often they end up saying more about themselves than they realised they knew.

A South African in his forties gets up and explains that his estranged father died the day he left on the retreat. Everybody breathes in. He cannot grieve for his father because, even when he confronted him, his father would neither acknowledge him nor confess to the terrible things his son knew he had done.

The subject of fathers hangs heavy in the air for the rest of the retreat. Men talk repeatedly of how they either long to forgive their fathers, or have their blessing. Many will sob, broken by the wall of silence their fathers present in life or in death. Some of the stories are truly terrible.

A man stands up one night and explains how he is being divorced by his wife for 'unreasonable behaviour'. He describes waiting for his children on a station platform, prior to taking them on a caravan holiday. Before the children arrive, he is gripped by an overpowering conviction that he is going to abuse them. The fear sickens and haunts him throughout the holiday. Somehow he manages to survive the claustrophobia of the caravan and the children return safely to their mother. The fear leads to his discovery that his father abused him as a child. Suddenly his whole body shakes and he bellows, 'That behaviour is fucking out of order!' Then he takes a deep breath and sighs. 'But I'd also like to say that I love my father.' Over the weekend, Bly and Meade will try to teach us how to work through this long legacy of love and hate.

No matter how extreme, the stories never sound as if they belong solely to someone else. If the stories are particular, the sorrow is mutual.

Late on Saturday morning, Meade suggests an exercise. We will sit opposite the man next to us, one hand on a shoulder, one on the heart. I am standing next to a small wiry man who looks both clever and hunted. I have not spoken to him before, but soon we are sitting opposite one another, speaking of our deepest wounds, wounds that seem to begin in adulthood and then suddenly lead us further back, into early childhood. We trust each other completely and barely speak again all weekend. Like hitch-hikers, we are able to speak freely.

My own embarrassment never disappears completely, but I begin to understand that the old contempt for other boys and men is a kind of self-hatred, a kind of shame. Almost overnight, the group has turned into a kind of safety net. All around me, men are hurling themselves over their own personal parapets: they have found somewhere to fall.

As the weekend unfolds, the theme of distant or unforgiving fathers merges with repeated tales of cowed men dominated by their wives and mothers. There is no animosity towards women and no lad's talk, but these men want to reclaim some of the emotional ground ceded to women during the Seventies and Eighties. They want to stop being ashamed of men.

Bly describes the 'soft' or 'naive' man who has emerged in response to the Women's Movement: a man who sees his masculinity as something to apologise for and who longs for a New Age full of spirit, but curiously lacking in soul. 'You're with a woman who's sticking you full of lances and you're proud of the blood!' snorts Bly. His idea of a complete man is a warrior: neither an aggressor nor a soldier but a man who will not be shamed and who will stand his ground. Bly has little time for the New Age, and he and Meade complain about the vegetarian menu all weekend.

Between story sessions and exercises on the lawn, we gather in our smaller groups for more personal discussions. The Unblinking Guardians turn out to be mostly gentle, professional men, many of whom are already involved in therapy. All are dogged by a numbness, a sense of frustrated desire. Many have powerful female figures in their lives whom they long to match. One man reveals that his wife has decided that she's had enough of their marriage and wants him out of their house. He has spent years commuting between Suffolk and London, working to support their three children. The group urge him to hold his ground.

On the first day, a man stood up to say that he felt frightened being in this large group of men. Bly responded that anyone who did not feel afraid in a room full of 100 men is crazy. 'And that's the man we're all afraid of,' said Meade. Some of the men seem to swell with an almost ungovernable burden of rage. On the last day, they turn some of that rage on Bly, who has played the father figure to the hilt.

On Saturday afternoon, the Lion Clan gather on the lawn to create a shadowplay. Like all the other groups, The Unblinking Guardians fashion an uncomfortable purging of male violence. The group forms a circle and then each in turn plunges inside to bellow and gesture at the circle that holds him prisoner. Some bounce around inside the ring, others bare their teeth. I lose my voice and feel a terrible claustrophobia. The blind desire to strike free seizes me for a second, then I'm back in the circle and another man is raging at his captors. At the end of the exercise the circle falls over backwards, arms outstretched. The demons we have conjured up are supposed to exit skyward.

Soon after this we are in the library with Bly. He has talked a lot about the King figure who doubles as our unshamed self and as the mentor we most admire. We are then asked to write down a meeting with our King. A few minutes later I am scribbling furiously but am quite unable to picture any King. Instead I am ten or eleven again, and out on a cricket pitch. It is a pleasant afternoon but I am stonewalling the bowling. My father is slow-handclapping. I do not acknowledge him. I want to please him by scoring runs. I don't want to fail him by getting out. I have stalled.

Saturday night is for silliness after all the grieving. Bly recites poems by Rumi, the Sufi poet, and laughs. He winds up dancing in front of the group with the man who has lead most of the exercises out on the lawn. The weekend has been planned like a journey and now Bly is celebrating a Blakean kind of desire, the joy that passeth understanding.

By Sunday lunchtime we are all exhausted. The story's hero has completed his quest and is united with the beautiful young woman. Many of the men are nervous about going home. They wonder how what they have learnt will survive in the real world. Before lunch, we gather in a circle out on the sunlit lawn. Bly, then Meade, then those next to them peel off and walk by the others in the long circle. We stand like cricketers waiting for royalty at Lords. Grateful cricketers. Bly looks carefully and lovingly into my eyes and kisses me lightly. He moves on. I lean forward to kiss Meade. He looks a little embarrassed. Perhaps I got carried away.

A few weeks later, I am still wondering about how much I learnt from the weekend, how much it meant. There's a kind of glib emotion that comes with being able to talk freely to strangers in a protected environment. I have no real desire to see the men I met on the weekend again, and I've yet to talk to my dad about any of it. Yet the richness of the weekend – the talk, the poems, even the drumming – is still with me, still stirring. Things matter again.

On the way home I looked forward to seeing my two sons and their mother and felt a deep calm in my stomach. I picked up a hitch-hiker, a young guy who'd been working on a pig farm and was heading for Devon. His hands were large and mudcaked, his eyes wild. When we passed a particularly heavy lorry, he reached over and rested his hand on the steering-wheel as if to grab it. He seemed angry about something and he muttered to himself constantly. Ten miles later I dropped him off.

There are some wild men out there.

Copyright © Mark Cooper, 1991

In the Presence of Royalty

Prince by Simon Mills
December 1991

F IVE THINGS *NOT* to say to Prince: 1. Word up, shorty! 2. Nice shirt. Buy it new? 3. Did you really sleep with Sheena Easton? 4. Aren't you the guy from *Diff'rent Strokes*? 5. The new album's a lot rockier, isn't it?

I still don't know how it happened. I'd managed to avoid the first four OK. It was the last one, the killer 1974 *Melody Maker* question: 'The new album's a lot *rockier*, isn't it?' I didn't actually use those exact words but I may as well have done. I blew it. I had my chance and I blew it. I'd been waiting years for the opportunity just to hang out with Prince. Interviewing him wasn't such a priority – I thought we'd just, y'know, talk – but I wanted to see him recording, I wanted to find out exactly what he smelt like, I wanted to get 'tight' with him.

I'd literally dreamt about stuff like this, and as the big day approached friends started to notice subtle changes in my behaviour as my Prince obsession reached its inevitable climax. I took to wearing leotards, sitting in front of the mirror with my tongue hanging out for sustained periods of time and saying, 'Just gotta go work on that zipper, baby', when all I wanted to do was go and pee. It was ridiculous – like Zelig The Rockumentary (if you will).

What does one wear to meet Prince? I considered this carefully after I was given the final 'yo' from Paisley Park in Minneapolis to come and visit. At first I set aside my fabulously sexy purple Vivienne Westwood suit. Prince would, of course, immediately identify with me, I thought, and talk for hours, giving me the beef on the Kim Basinger/whipped-cream story. No he wouldn't. He'd think 'Ohmigod. A fan. Get me outta here.' After more careful thought, I settled for 501s and an old cowboy shirt. In the end I could have worn a Christian Lacroix ball gown for all he knew.

Before I knew it I was in Minneapolis giving good meet 'n' greet to Paisley Park employees in Armani suits and cowboy boots, and being ushered through the corridors of Prince Inc (nice enough, but not exactly *Homes & Gardens* material if you know what I mean). Having endured all the usual Hannibal Lecter-style preparatory shenanigans ('Do not touch the glass. Do not approach the glass' – only kidding) there he was. 'Hi, I'm Prince,' he said, with a surprisingly firm handshake. It was probably the best quote I got.

He looked amazing, of course. Bright yellow shirt (tied at the waist), with a black lacy vest thing underneath, cobalt-blue trousers, matching high-heeled ankle boots and . . . shit! He ain't got no underwear on. As I sat down on the sofa (he remained standing) I could see that Prince dresses *sans* Calvins and to the right.

I wanted to ask him so much. I'd prepared loads of deep shit about lyrics, the synergy of sex and religion in his songs, where he gets his inspiration from etc, but it was like one of those nightmares where you can't talk, walk or run. I wanted it to be so deep, but it came out dumb. Everytime I asked him a question he'd just grin or grimace or roll his eyes. He actually laughed at one point. *At* me, not with me. But he seemed like a nice guy to me. Give him his own stool next to Norm and Cliffy, I say. Not shy or weird or unfriendly, just very focused and . . . well, short.

The problem was that I just couldn't hear what he was saying and he could hardly hear what I was saying. His band were tuning-up in the background; I was sitting down, he was standing up and of course my questions were lousy. I was feeling like a complete schmuck when the guy from *Playboy* (sitting next to me, like Woody Allen without the self-confidence) asked Prince an even more embarrassing question – you know, dumb, but with a Harvard degree. It relied heavily on the experiences of the taxi driver this guy had travelled with from the airport, and how he couldn't sleep because he was so obsessed with Prince etc. Anyway, when he was through, Prince just rolled his eyes and said: 'I'll have to get back to you on that one.'

I'd just started to feel better when Prince bent down toward me and, nodding toward the stage, said: 'Do y'all wanna try my trampoline?' Now call me childish, but it was a truly magical moment. 'Do y'all wanna try my trampoline.' Wow! I was already structuring the quote into a legendary dinner-table anecdote when I noticed that he'd gone. Now I'm convinced that someone like Prince doesn't walk any distance further than a few yards – he must energise or teleport or something, because throughout the rest of my time with him he would just ... appear, and then vanish. It was really quite odd indeed.

I've danced near Madonna, been pretty close to Michael Jackson, kissed his sister Janet, but nothing is quite like meeting Prince. It's like reaching your thirties and being told that Santa Claus *does* exist. He's a very special person. And I can rest assured that I scooped the world with my Prince interview. I found out that his favourite colour is yellow ('Sick, right?' he joked) and that the new album is a lot rockier. So that's OK. And bouncing on his trampoline ... well, you really had to be there.

Copyright © Simon Mills, 1991

Rare Proofs

The *Arena* Literary Parody by Tony Parsons, Steve Beard, Marek Kohn & Dylan Jones
January 1989 & May 1992

Less Than Typing by Brat Hardon Hopeless

When I regained consciousness I was back in LA. I take the keys to my brother's Porsche, smoke a joint and drive to the party of the Freshman I fucked last week. She was a JAP from UCLA and we had taken STP that we bought with her mother's gold AMEX, listened to REM, watched some MTV with the sound turned down while I nearly sliced off the top of my dick on her IUD. Or was that someone else?

The party is up in Beverly Hills. It is the annual Dress To Get Raped party that we have at the end of every winter term when we come home for Christmas to our rich and broken homes. I am Dressed To Get Raped as a cheap, seat-sniffing tramp in a bar. I am not into the situation. It is sort of nothing.

Some Freshmen I know are on the front lawn drinking beer, smoking joints and torturing the Spanish maid. I am about to go over and join in when the horse tranquiliser I jacked up in my room listening to Elvis – we all love Costello, man, New Wave is where it's at – suddenly hits me and I black out at the wheel. When I come to I park my car with difficulty. The long sweep of driveway is full of stoned kids with the weight of the Western World on their shoulders.

'Those starving Biafrans and like Asians, man,' says this bleary-eyed Valley Girl sitting on the hood of a Ferrari. 'They don't know how, like, lucky they are, dude.'

Inside the party I see over by the Christmas tree someone I wish to avoid like the clap. It is the roommate of this really stupid girl I fucked who had some really cool Paracetamol. She jerked me off while we listened to Fear, Plague, Famine and Tense Nervous Heartache on a compilation album called 'The Best Of LA Thrash.' It was kind of blank and nothing and, anyway, she ended up stealing my Pretenders CD and my copy of _One Hundred Years Of Solitude_ and told everyone I call out 'Mother!' when I come. Weird.

I head for the keg where some guys I knew in High School are drinking beer, smoking a joint and staring at the wall. Toke – not his real name – looks at me with mad, bulging eyes and spit on his ski-tanned chin. 'Hey, dude,' he sneers. 'So what's it like at Harvard?'

I pop a mushroom. Led Zep are blaring from the speakers of my mind.

'Harvard?' I say meaningfully. 'It's the same as here.' I sip my beer. 'Except different. How's Yale, Toke?'

He stares at his shoes. 'I forget,' he says.

I turn to his companion, a skinny kid called Snort whose father owns IBM or Ford or something.

'Everything is like, you know, kind of _nothing_, man,' Snort says. 'It's like Kennedy, man. He got shot and, you know, wow, it blew our mothers' minds. The inner psyche of their wombs could, you know, sustain life, man, but not _hope_. Dig? And Kennedy, wow, he's kind of, you know, sort of _dead_.'

Dear Kennedy, I muse. For he's a jolly good Jello. The beer tastes old and sour on the back of my tongue. It tastes of lost dreams and of betrayed innocence and of that awful toothpaste with the green stripe in it.

'I'm, like, going to the bathroom to slash my wrists,' Snort says. Toke and I smirk at each other. Another suicidal Freshman, we are thinking. Please.

'How's Laura?' I say. Laura is this crazy girl whose mother owns Gulf and Western or Mastercard or Ohio or something.

'The bitch is pregnant, dude,' Toke says. 'But that's OK. I enjoy abortions.'

'How do you know it's your kid, dude?' I leer.

'What do you want me to do?' Toke snaps. 'Draw you a diaphragm?'

We banter like this until I pass out again. When I wake up I am in the triple garage giving head to this Mohawk girl with I LOVE YOU BUT YOU'RE DEAD tattooed on her upper thigh. Her stepfather owns Belgium or something. We start taking off our clothes.

'Do you have herpes?' the bitch asks.

I am semi-appalled. If I wasn't so massively drugged, I might be offended. 'What makes you say that, man?'

'The Freshman you buggered in Double Math told me and some other girls that you might have herpes.'

'No, dude, I don't have herpes.'

'Oh.'

'What I have is gonorrhoea,' I say.

'Right,' she says, and we take off the rest of our clothes. 'What's your name again?' she asks me.

My generation, I think, as passion, like a bad drug, feebly begins to take its effect. People try to put us down, I reflect, just because we could use a credit card before we could crawl. A new wave no wave no count blank generation, as washed out and faded as the winter sun over the Hollywood Hills. Lost souls who see their reflection in the smashed chrome, glass and metal by the side of the Los Angeles freeway. Round round get around, we get around, our spirits writhing in mute, MTV-watching agony, impaled on the gold tie pin of American affluence. Or something.

'You can't come in my mouth,' the Mohawk says.

'Then forget it, bitch,' I tell her.

And when I woke up I was back in my room on campus.

Transcribed by Tony Parsons

From Broadway to Soho by Demon Onion

One morning along about two bells, I am standing in front of The Slounge Club in Dean Street with a guy by the name of Omo, who has this name because it seems he wins the Omo account the day before the advertising agency he works for falls by the wayside, and can never forget it, which is maybe because it is the only very large account he ever wins in his life.

Now, Omo is always short of potatoes, and this morning is no exception, so I agree to stand him the price of a San Pelligrino or two, with maybe a little medicinal chaser thrown in, purely on account of the temperature, what with it being December, and sub-zero, and nearly Christmas, and all that.

The Slounge is a very high-class trap which is patronised only by the better elements of rumpots and general newspaper guys. There is no band or floor show to speak of, but a good enough selection of fair-looking dolls, even if they are often accompanied by ugly-looking scribes. In fact The Slounge has just about everything a man can wish for a good time. Personally I never go there much, because I do not care for such places, what with the liquor being nothing extra at all.

There is a lot of racket as we come in, a lot of single-handed drinking going on and a lot of types with whom it isn't wise to be seen in such an establishment. Everyone in Soho is here: Harry the Horse, Mickey the Finn, Erik the Viking, even Attila the Pun, fresh from a poetry reading at Bar Italia sponsored by a doll calling herself Lady Lydia Folkestone-Hovercraft.

Inside we meet a certain party by the name of Steadicam, the copywriter. Of course this is strictly the phonus bolonus as Steadicam is not a copywriter, and never is a copywriter, and he is 100 to one in my line against ever being a copywriter, but he calls himself one because it pleases him. Personally, I never have any truck with anyone pretending to be in advertising, but Steadicam has some serious import-export connections, in kumquat, star fruit, pau-pau, custard apple and certain prescribed goods, and is a person to know, if you get my drift. I know him from around and about the drinking clubs, and other deadfalls, for Steadicam is such a guy as loves to mingle with the public in these spots, as he picks up much business there, and sometimes a fair-looking doll, too.

But tonight Steadicam is in no mood for dolls. In fact Steadicam is not really in the market for any kind of mood at the moment, particularly one which involves dolls of any nature whatsoever, in fact, indeed.

Naturally Omo and myself are most concerned over Steadicam's lack of mood, and try reviving him with a few San Pelligrinos and purely medicinal chasers thrown in for good measure. It seems Steadicam's ever-loving doll took off when she found out his lenses weren't exclusively focused on her, what with him being head-over-heels with a doll of a different nature altogether. Naturally, and furthermore to boot, Steadicam feels like a one hundred per cent heel, and sees no percentage in doing anything other than drowning his sorrows in a few San Pelligrinos with purely medicinal chasers thrown in for good measure.

So, after consoling Steadicam, and not finding any prescribed goods about his person, myself and Omo take off into the night – up Dean, down Frith, across Old Compton, round Brewer, up Broadwick and out on to Oxford, in desperate search of a moral. Naturally, we didn't find one.

Transcribed by Dylan Jones

Kerbside Quiche by William Burrows

So the nurse look at me funny like we've met before and says, 'Not you again. What is it this time?' I cough and explain how I got to see Doctor Feelbutt on account of this virus I got just yesterday. Maybe I got throat cancer or something.

So I am screaming at the nurse about how I am dying and she makes like she is completely unimpressed. She gives me this form and says, 'You are a pain, aren't you?' Which is one of my old aliases from way back. The government think they got me taped but I am too smart for them. Officially, I don't exist. They don't call me The Man Who's Not All There for nothing.

Sneak past the nurse and burst into the surgery, the virus going to my head. Doctor Feelbutt look at his intelligence file on me and sighs. 'Another fatal disease?' he says. 'What happened to the radiation poisoning from last week?' I tell him it mysteriously cleared up. Now I got some kind of special cancer. What I don't say is how the military-industrial complex have been fucking with my ectoplasm. I'm not crazy. He could be in on it.

Recollect when I am working with Mister Know-It-All, best informed buff in the business. We is rolling the drunks in the Groucho Club, looking for the secret papers on who killed Kennedy and how come there's never a cab when you need one. And Captain Headwank (he got that moniker hiring himself out as a sex aid at college parties) shows up and says: 'How many conspiracy theorists does it take to screw in a light-bulb? Two. One to screw it in and the other to find out who really screwed it in.' The Captain always was a real asshole.

So Feelbutt agree to give me the works and tell me to drop my trousers. What happens next looks to the casual observer like a homosexual practice but is one of those medical examinations they have in the secret service. Then he give me some new junk called Placebo. (Note: junk is old beatnik slang for cool drugs.)

'There is absolutely nothing wrong with you,' he say. I understand how he has to talk in code because of the aliens and take the news real well, considering: 'That bad, huh, doc?'

So I'm hanging off of his neck, trying to make him spill it, when he turns into a giant insect. You know the type comes on to the US Army like a cheap special effect. I seen that one before.

'Lighten up,' he chirrups, dismissing me with a curt wave of his feeler. I know the next line off by heart: 'At least you still have all your arms and legs.' It's like I tell the Paraplegic Kid. Some people will say anything to get you off their back.

Transcribed by Steve Beard

Infinity's Bollocks by Martin Aimless

Darren Spandex knew instantly his father had been shagging his granny because Dad's cock tasted all funny. And the wind, the wind howled and the sky bled, the poor abused sky was shagged out. The sky had shot its lot. The sky was knackered. The sky had nothing left. The sky was fucked, as fucked as Debbie Stocking-Top when she woke up in the ditch with every orifice full of something white. White and sticky and fucked. 'Well fucked,' leered Darren, smelling of damp dog, pressing the fast-forward button on the _Carry On Swedish Nymphos_ video, his mouth full of 'farm fresh' cottage pie and Bogies-U-Like.

Notting Hill Gate. The shadow of the poor, fucked Westway winding like a grey trouser snake above the sad, shagged city. Darren eased his Vauxhall Mysterioso down Westbourne Park and stared with uncongealed hostility at the spade dealers who loitered with intent. His mind – so full of arrows and World Wrestling statistics – clicked like a pacemaker in a fucked heart. Black guys, Darren thought. Big knobs. Good fighters. Offer you out just before closing time at the Rat and Trumpet and then pull your jacket over your shoulders before you can reach for the cosh. Slam their black, salty foreheads against what was left of Darren's yellow, rotted tombstone teeth. His teeth were fucked.

A black chick walked down the street – her big round black chick ass rocking like jelly on a plate. 'Sit on my face and I'll guess your weight,' leered Darren, coughing up a lump of phlegm the size of a fist. 'You stinking bitch.'

Debbie Stocking-Top was waiting at his sock, his trouser turn-up, his pit, his pile, his shoebox full of shit.

'Where's me dinner, you posh bint?' shouted Darren, casually cuffing her across the mouth. It was the kind of mouth that doesn't look right unless it has a pair of testicles hanging from it. Darren Spandex ran into a lot of women with mouths like that.

'One doesn't have dinner until night time,' said Debbie, running a tongue the size, colour and scent of a spawning salmon along the velcro-fly of Darren's boulder-rubbed denims, which sagged wantonly over the cleavage of his Lethal Brew-gorged buttocks. 'It's time for *lunch*. Didn't your Mummy teach you anything?'

Darren Spandex remembered Violet Spandex, his poor fucked mother. What had the star of the Earl's Court International Escort Agency – with her vodka and limes and polyester uplift bras and endless line-up of 'uncles' – taught him? To thieve. To cheat. To lie and con and stink. And to give rich bitches like Debbie Stocking-Top what they were asking for, begging for, taking out classified ads with a special box number for.

Darren had come a long way from that semen, beer and pizza-splattered hovel in Earl's Court. A long way – and all of it in his Vauxhall Mysterioso. All of it on the Westway. The poor fucked Westway weeping for the sad, finger-fucked, hand-jobbed, gang-banged, weeping-for-mercy city. 'Did you hear the wind last night?' sang Debbie. 'Oh my fucked, funny Valentine – I think there must be a hole in the End Zone.'

'You mean *ozone*,' snapped Darren. 'Now get yer smackers on me knackers.'

And then he tossed her aside. Like a salad.

Transcribed by Tony Parsons

Jesus Christ! What Happened? by Albert Golddigger

'My career is over!' cried Jesus. 'The bastards are trying to crucify me!'

The disciples, or Bethlehem Mafia, exchanged anxious looks. Life with the self-styled Son of God had become a waking nightmare. The former mild-mannered carpenter had shot like a Zen arrow to become the idol of millions. But with celebrity came only horror. Once tanned and slim and gorgeous, the so-called Messiah was now bloated and impotent. He had taken to wearing long white dresses and poncing about at all hours of the day and night trying to get crowds of strangers to follow him.

'What hotel you stay?' Jesus would ask them. 'You like sucky-sucky? You maybe want to enter the Kingdom of Heaven?'

Despite all his boasts, the disciples knew that Jesus could now only achieve satisfaction with lepers and sheep. And, on top of everything else, his hair – once so shiny and nice – was a mess. He was basically a spoilt little rich bastard who would never have got anywhere without his daddy wiping his bum from dawn to dusk. And you should have seen his fingernails – they made you realise the sermon on the mount was an overrated pile of camel shite.

This Last Supper had been planned long ago as a party to celebrate Christ's tour of the Canaanite Empire. But the tour had been a disaster, an endless round of provincial one-nighters and crowds who screamed so loudly that Jesus could not hear himself preach. It was perhaps just as well – his voice was shot and, like a falling Zen arrow, his routine just wasn't what it used to be. The willing Jewish girls who flocked to touch the hem of his women's clothing had not helped deaden the pain. Time and again, the Bethlehem Mafia had pulled him back from the beckoning black brink of suicide. He was lucky to be alive. He longed for death. He ached for it, wished for it, prayed for it. Death would be a blessing, a relief, an executive hand-job. His hair, as I mentioned, was just a complete mess. And now the Last Supper, like the pathetic Prophet himself, was coming apart at the seams.

'Get a round in, you tight bastards!' screamed Jesus at his anxious entourage of pissed apostles. 'And I'm *not* picking up the bill this time, you circumcised tossers!'

'Cool it, Boss,' said Peter, one of the founder members of the Bethlehem Mafia, the motley crew of psychotic sycophants who catered to the Christ's every whim.

'Ah yer buncha dirty Roman-noses,' Jesus said, slurring his words as he reached for another flagon of wine. 'What am I – black?'

'Take it easy, Boss,' said Peter. 'And later we'll play "hide the tabernacle".'

'The wine is my blood and these little biscuit things are my flesh,' snapped the drink, drug and herpes-ravaged Prophet. 'My father will ruin you, you slag. You'll never work in the Promised Land again.'

'Like mellow out, Boss,' said Paul. 'And maybe you should put your sandals back on.'

'Bollocks to the lot of you,' shouted Jesus. 'I'm gonna find me some tarts. Really dirty ones that will let me do anything I want. Bring my donkey round the front.'

'I'll get it,' volunteered Judas, quick as a Zen arrow.

Transcribed by Tony Parsons

My Life As a Bog by Heinous Blarney

Bog, bog, sodden bog,
How lonely I wondered as a bog,
Oh dead oak, dead dog,
Bloody bog

Clear water and gifts of rain,
Cloudbursts and the like,
Feeding yonder black pie earth,
Dark juices now at work

Riverbank and ditch,
Hollow trunks and swallowing sea,
I am of the bog,
The bog is of me

Oh black dead birth,
Down below my feet,
Tell me, Seamus, is it Dud?
Or is it Peat?

Transcribed by Dylan Jones

Fax by Nicholson Streetfinder

'What are you reading at the moment?'
He said, 'I'm reading Czeslaw Milosz's *The Captive Mind*. Re-reading it, that is. Also Flaubert's letters. How about you?'
'*Skinhead Escapes* by Richard Allen. He's a British writer. From the terraces. Out of print. I'm thinking about buying up his back catalogue and putting it out as trade paperbacks. Matter of fact, I was thinking maybe that's the way I'd like to see you go . . .'
'On to the terraces?'
'Not quite. But, you know, more visceral. Juicier.'
'I have a problem with that stuff. I see these college girls and office women on their lunch breaks in the park and they're reading these *wads*. Shall I tell you what I did once? I bought one of those wads, a hardback. But it was just too big. Then I thought, you could have a book that was the right size – slim, hard, literary, like one of mine – but it could have that special thing that the SF ones have.'
'You mean . . .'
'Right! Gold lettering! So I took the jacket off the big one and

wrapped it round one of my own. It was like getting the stockings off a lady blockbuster novelist and putting them on myself. It felt good!'

'I could give you that, you know. Forget about the "S" and just do the "F"; that'll keep it slim, and just add some aphoristic details about contemporary technology. Between us, we'll reinvent publishing.'

'A genuinely literary work designed to produce . . . well, masturbation.'

'I don't especially care for that word. Call it "critical acclaim".'

'But the most important thing is . . .'

'Gold lettering, I know. OK, let's put some flesh on it. We'll go for a hardback plus trade, 216 by 135 millimetres, title 72 points, in gold.'

'Fax to confirm?'

'Right away.'

'I suppose yours is a plain paper one. To me, that missed the whole beauty of the fax. I love to watch the paper come scrolling out with that brothel-creeper noise it makes, and I love the way it's just a little shiny and just a little yellow. It's like a sleazeball private detective, with his tobacco stains and his greasy suit. All the marks and transmission fuzz you get on the copy, it's like he's gumshoeing through the alleys and dives, and he's covered in _life_ by the time he gets to you.'

'That's nice. Put that in.'

'Great, then we got a title . . . And how about this? Spot colour – bright purple, say – for the "F", and gold for the "AX".'

'Nick, I think we've got a classic on our hands.'

Transcribed by Marek Kohn

A Time to Do the Dirty by Mervyn Braggart

My darling Sharon – light of my life, fire in my trousers. Let me now speak of love. And though the hour is late and the bottle is almost empty, permit me, my working-class spicy dumpling, to speak of your bush. Your pelt. Your minge. Your shaved triangle of folds and creases and petals and effluent juices of desire. Pelt, I think, describes that secret place best. There. I've said it. Pelt. Your sweet pelt, my Sharon, warming itself in front of the open fire in that somewhat self-regarding hotel in Catford. 'Whooah, I feel really pissed,' you said.

Was it only last summer that your pelt welcomed my prick, my shaft, my willy, my ting-a-ling? There. I've said it. Big fat penis and hairy bollocks. Fifty years as a chartered accountant have not made it easy for me to use these words. Was it not Byron who said that when a man speaks of sex, he makes of himself either fool or cretin? Hang Byron! Hang this small town and the rough boys who jeer at me in the street, knowing of my shame. But what do they know of my love? I remember walking into the golf club with you, my sweet Sharon. You wore a tiny leather mini-skirt, white shoes, fishnet tights with holes in, a see-through blouse from Miss Selfridge, suspendys and a bra.

'Fuck me,' you said. 'I'm a bit overdressed for this gaff, mush.' They stared at you, my sweet Sharon. Oh how they stared at the foolish old man and his young l-o-l-i-t-a. But to me you were the loveliest thing in all creation. The fag that dangled from your red lips only affirmed your love of life, your love of the things that I had missed all those years in my office. Your pelt, your bush, your snatch, your purse. Did my invalid wife ever have such a pelt? I think not. And though they mocked, my precious Sharon, was it not Shelley who said that he who comes first, comes fastest?

How you must hate me. How you must detest hearing me speak of your bush, your pelt, your firm breasts with their jutting nipples screaming lick me, bite me, eat me. Is there no love left in your young heart for this old fool? The hour is late and the bottle is empty and the cat is out. But still I hear your sweet words to me during those precious, precious minutes of love that we spent pressed up against the dustbins. I feel your breath, I hear your words. Will hear them forever – my Sharon.

You're a dirty old git, ain'tcha?' you said, laughing. Oh how you laughed! 'Well, you're not coming in me mouth, grandad.' The days are short and the nights grow long, my sweet, seat-sniffing Sharon. Your brothers came round and gave me a good kicking. But was it not the Great Bard himself who said that a bird in the bush, the squeeze box, the pelt is worth one in the hand? I suppose one in the hand is completely out of the question now? I can still hear your sweet voice, so full of the land I love and the pelt I long for, will long for forever. 'Have you finished yet?' you said.

Transcribed by Tony Parsons

Fields of Dreams
Baseball's Spring Training by Robert Elms
September 1992

LORIDA IS A GOOD PLACE for mobile homes. Most of the inhabitants of this flat, scrubby sunshiny state seem to live in the kind of sedentary, ramshackle mobile homes which aren't going anywhere, fast or slow. Away from the glamorous beaches and keys of the south, Florida is a dreamy desultory kind of place where there are huge areas of nothing much, between towns which really aren't all that much anyway. Better, I guess, to sit still in your mobile home and enjoy the fact that it's snowing like it's never going to stop up in Boston and New York. But then the men of Boston and New York, of Baltimore and Philadelphia, of all those tough, freezing Eastern Seaboard towns are down here now. They're here because it's spring, the time when things start again. And the thing that starts here in sunny scrubby Florida is baseball.

Baseball is the great American pastime. That name not only denotes its place as the premier sport, it also points out the unique position that this game of bat and ball plays in the mythology of the nation. A democratic, meritocratic sport where a player of any shape or size can rise to the top, where quick wits and sharp eyes are your greatest assets and where stealing is all part of the game; it mirrors the image that America would still like to have of itself. But baseball is also the great American pastime because the rhythms of its 162-game season act as a metronome. Starting day is the beginning of April and there are contests every day throughout the long summer, pounding towards a climax in the pennant races and the mesmerising week of World Series games in October. Then, like most sensible summer animals, baseball hibernates, to be born again when the spring comes. And the place where spring comes first is Florida.

The tradition of decamping to sunnier climes, to warm up lazy bones and get in shape for the long haul to come, started when the Baltimore Orioles first built a training camp in St Petersburg in the north west of the peninsular, way back in Babe Ruth days. Soon the whole state was dotted with little club houses and ramshackle stadiums. Throughout March, ball players would gently go

191

through a few exercises, throw some baseballs about and play a series of half-hearted exhibition games against their near neighbours, watched by the ageing dozing residents of those mobile homes. But it's not like that anymore.

Spring training has become one of the great rituals of American life, and like most things in American life it's also become an industry. All of the teams from the Eastern leagues (the new boys over in the West, like LA and San Francisco, have a similar set-up in Arizona) now have large, elaborate camps full of the latest fitness technology and shiny stadiums. And those exhibition games occur in front of sell-out crowds, with TV cameras beaming the action to snowbound northern towns. Those games are known as the Grapefruit League (it's the Cactus League in Arizona) and they mean millions of dollars to the tourist industry of the Sunshine State.

But despite the commercialisation, despite the fact that you now have to buy tickets for the big games in advance and share your place at the after-game bar with a Yankees fan who owns a condominium in Miami and flies down for the games in his personal jet, despite all that, spring training still retains enough of the pastoral past of baseball, enough of the soporific ease of pre-season pre-tension sport, that it is one of the *great* sporting pilgrimages. Sitting in the early-morning sun in the bleachers in somewhere called Joker Marchant Field, watching a man just a few feet away with the name of Bobby Bonilla swing gracefully at loping pitches, while trading jokes with his team-mates as they mess about at the start of the day, is a rare thrill. Bobby Bonilla has just been bought by the Mets for $29 million. Once the season starts in earnest I won't get this close again and Bobby Bonilla won't do much messing about.

If you're not a committed partisan of one team, the best way to approach spring training is to base yourself in one of the hotbeds of Florida ball; St Petersburg maybe, Sarasota or Clearwater, where there are half a dozen teams within easy freeway distance, and go to them all, depending on which team is visiting for an exhibition game that day. And the best time of day for spring training is early in the morning. The fans – the young kids with their mittens and their balls, and the old men with their memories – start arriving at about 9am. This is when the players begin to drift in and it's a good time for the true romantics to cadge an autograph, trade a story or just stand and gaze in awe at these multi-million dollar men.

Proximity is a big part of the thrill of pre-season baseball, it's why the kids get so excited by it, and also why it attracts a coterie of fans who would be train spotters if their country had a decent railway system. An anorak is still an anorak, even if it does have a St Louis Cardinals emblem on the back. So there are a few inadequate souls who hang around trying to poach some glory from the passing ball players. Sitting watching the Yankees warm up one day I found myself next to a man who insisted on plaguing Don Mattingly, their star first-base man, as he was playing catch nearby. 'Don, you remember me, I'm the friend of your orthodontist,' he would cry every time his hero came within earshot. Finally Mattingly was forced to come over and shake the guy's hand just to get him to shut up.

But the train spotters are far outnumbered by those who just love the core of this beguiling game. And at around 11am when the teams are out there on the diamond running sprints, catching fly balls and practising double plays, swinging bats and talking tactics, the essence of baseball is laid bare. The best part of spring training is definitely the training. That's when you see just what magnificent athletes these men are, just how fast the ball flies, how precisely they throw. The almost overwhelming grace of these fellows, who become superstars once the season starts, is made all the more powerful by the fact that they are just out there on a field doing things which we could all do. But we couldn't do them like that.

And if you can get behind the scenes it becomes even more potent. It's in the gyms and net-covered practise areas that the real work is done. Suddenly I notice that the man with a look of pain on his face and his leg stretched up on to the shoulder of a coach is Lenny Dykestra, the former Mets terrier, once my favourite player and a man I still like even though he's now hitting for the Phillies. Wandering over to where that demon pitching machine is pumping out fast balls at 100mph I catch a glimpse of Wade Boggs, the Boston club's mighty opening hitter, trying his best to swipe these missiles away with a tiny round bat. And what's more he's succeeding. Then you understand why this is the highest-paid team sport in the world. It is so damn difficult, and they make it look so damn easy.

Backstage you also get the real earthy flavours of the game, hear the curses from the coaches and the rumours from the assembled sportswriters who are also busy renewing summer acquaintances. It's here, where the smell of sweat and leather hangs heavy, that ancient leathery men with white hair and in full uniform spit out dark balls of tobacco juice and utter their wisdoms. Sparky Anderson, manager of the Detroit Tigers says, 'Spring training is the worst time for some of these guys, the ones who don't know if they're going to make the team. This is tough for them, they're fighting.'

But for the fans beginning to gather for the game outside, $6 tickets in hand, the only tough part is the decision about whether to have lunch now or wait for a hot dog and a pretzel inside. This is whitebread family America, nice people only slightly overweight and still in love with the pastime.

Spring training games used to be dominated by old-timers, many of them former residents of those hard northern towns who had retired to the sun and adopted the local side. They are still there and so are the local kids (you can tell the two apart because the old ones wear their baseball caps the right way round), with thick, slow Florida accents getting their one chance a year to see the big names.

But now there are organised tours bringing die-hard fans down for a week or two. So you get taciturn New Englanders doomed to die loving the Red Sox, the Lords of Disappointment. You get smiling, gauche Canadians for the Toronto Blue Jays' game and serious big-city boys for the New York teams. The atmosphere is different when the Mets or the Yankees are playing, with singing and shouting and even the occasional insult for the opposition, which would seem entirely out of place in the more sedate parks.

For the most part though, pre-season games are still wonderfully inconsequential. Roger Angel, the poet laureate of baseball, wrote, 'Spring baseball is all surmise.' And it is indeed a wonderful kind of guesswork, full of the anticipation of a season yet to come and free from the bitter letdowns of real sporting life. Only one of these teams can win the big one; the rest will inevitably be failures. But for the month of spring training, hope springs with every hitter at bat and every pitcher at the mound. All the talk is of possibilities as you watch the greats to see if they still have it, and study the youngsters to see if they're ever going to get it. Promise of the right stuff is what you're looking for in the spring.

Watching those cursed Red Sox (they haven't won a World Series since 1918) one afternoon, the old guy next to me suddenly turned round and said about their all-star pitcher: 'Watch Roger Clemens, if he's really got his stuff, if he's throwing heat, he will take a little tour of the sidelines after each inning to milk the fans. If not, it's straight into the dugout.' And he was right. But then he's been watching this team for nearly 60 years. At times like this it feels like you're in some great American fantasyland. That feeling grows when the two old vendors in front of you, one black, one white, suddenly burst into a rousing duet of 'Sixteen Tons' before going back to their chants of 'Beer Here'. This is like all the corny baseball movies you've ever seen.

As many of the games trail off into a kind of drowsy insignificance, the occasional spot of extra entertainment is welcome. But then that's the beauty of them: they aren't significant, and they don't really matter. They are sport as fun, which is a rare thing indeed. Then suddenly, just as you're about to nod off somewhere in the bottom of the ninth innings, the peace is shattered by one of those rumours from the ranks of the sports-writers. It seems that three Mets players, including their ill-starred genius of a pitcher, Dwight Gooden, have been accused of gang rape. A Florida girl has claimed that during last spring training three of the team raped her in Gooden's Florida house and that she has kept the semen-stained clothes in her freezer for a year as evidence.

This bizarre story, which is taken seriously by the police in the light of the recent Tyson conviction and the fact that the girl's father is a cop, is a sharp reminder of the warped world of moneyed licence and intense media scrutiny that these young men live in (though they later decide not to press charges against any of the players). Suddenly the whole roadshow turns a little sour as teams of news reporters hit town and besiege the Mets camp. Another troubled young pitching star, David Cone, is followed at night to a bar full of girls by hacks eager for some salacious stories. As a result the media is banned from the training camp where the New York ball players now work out behind closed doors. Spring training wasn't meant to be like this.

And most of the time, thankfully, it isn't. Baseball in the spring, in the Sunshine State, is still an elegant, easy way to slide into another year of this great sport. It is a reminder that even in the days of multi-million dollar deals and tabloid scandals, there remains a thread which links young to old, past to present and fan to star. Out there on those small-town diamonds it is still possible to believe that people play and watch baseball because they love it, still possible to believe in this green and lovely game.

Copyright © Robert Elms, 1992

────────

Porn Again

What Women Really Want From Erotica by Jessica Berens
September 1992

F EMALE SEXUALITY, like America, has no history.
    The components of Her carnal character eluded every-
body for centuries as men, so good at invention and
discovery, failed to observe physiological facts that stared
them, literally, in the face.

It wasn't until 1918 that Marie Stopes popped up and declared
that the female libido had been warped by years of silent acquies-
cence. Her book, *Married Love*, announced (hold on to your hats)
that women, like men, had 'a reciprocal need for enjoyment and
benefit from sex union in marriage distinct from the experience of
maternal functions'.

This simple notion revolutionised thinking for 20 years. Ideas
evolved, but the clues were shy. It seemed that they could not bear
to reveal themselves. Even in the Sixties your average yippy appreciated that women enjoyed an orgasm as much as men, but he
did not really know what women found attractive – he just hoped
it was him.

The Mrs Yippies, when asked, offered individual thoughts, but
there was no common thread. And collective enlightenment was
hampered by the tension between the permissiveness granted by the
Pill and aggressive egalitarianism. Hip ladies were told to fight the
very person they were indulging in free love with on the bean bag.

Progress was further sabotaged by the fact that women are always sexually competent whereas the poor old hero is beleaguered
by a litany of potential handicaps. Too much angst. Too much
beer. He is so easily useless, no wonder he wants to retain control.

It was only four years ago that *Time Out*'s art critic Sarah Kent
wrote of the prejudice that greeted women who exhibited an overt-
ly sensual perception of the male physique. Roberta Juzefa, for
instance, having produced photographs for a calendar of male
nudes, could not find a printer to work on it. And there was the
fear and loathing, from male critics, that greeted the ICA's exhibition of male nudes by female artists. 'Our sexual appetites,' wrote
Kent, 'as far as we are acknowledged to have them, are assumed
to lie elsewhere ... while campaigning to have offensive images

made illegal, women should not lose sight of the larger battle to have the right to explore their own sexual proclivities.' _Four_ years ago.

Erotic equality then, as a concept, does not enjoy the security of tradition or the empirical experience that often provides clarity. It is immature, new-fangled even. Consequently it is surrounded by confusion and incompetence and nowhere is this more apparent than in the development of pornography for women.

For Women magazine is viewed by some as a thrusting projectile of modernity. Its first issue boasted a circulation of 400,000. There are others, however, who resent being informed that the Dreamboys, a glistening loin-clothed dance troupe featured there, are their 'idols of erotic fantasy'. There are many things left to do with one's life, but paying 48p a minute to ring up Dreamboy Trevor ('my private striptease will drive you wild') is not one of them. Centrefolds displaying pouting Tonys and Kevins who have spilt a pint of milk over their bottoms prove that _For Women_ has not appreciated that too much time spent in the gym, too much hair-brushing and too much ortho-dentistry are not the agents of stimulation.

A man with the voice of experience, strength of character and looks that suggest he has spent three days being dragged on a rope behind the Marlboro Man's horse. This is a turn-on. A man whose jokes are like a poke in the ribs. This is a turn-on. Luke Perry with a gun? The jury is still out. Ray Liotta? _He_ encourages the sin of Onan.

Why, the gentle consumer may ask, is she still being presented with crass images and unintelligent ideas from people who have underestimated her complexity? She likes looking at women, prefers most men with their clothes on, and thinks that clitoral stimulators look like the medieval torture equipment used to wrench confessions from witches. Pornography comes from the Greek word meaning 'the writing of harlots', which says it all. Fiction, ultimate source of cerebral infinity, lies at its centre. Does it have to be stupid and lewd? Could it not be clever, funny and exciting? The female inclination to fantasise offers limitless potential. Olive Schreiner, who gave the prescient sex psychologist Havelock Ellis many of his ideas, was right when she said, in 1886, that a woman's sexual being should not be divorced from her personality. When a man touches a woman, she wrote, it is not just her body that he is touching, 'it is really her soul . . . her creative power . . . It is putting his fingers into her brain . . .' It's a head thing. And the traders have not cashed in on this.

There are glimmers (rather than rays) of hope. Candida Royalle's videos are (according to her) 'Quality Award-Winning Erotica Made by Women For Women'. Debbie and Tina have opened Libido, a fetish clothing store in Camden. Penny and Kim run Sh!, a porn shop in Shoreditch where coffee drinking and house-party chat are encouraged. It is a good idea to provide a safe atmosphere for women to choose their toys, but it is undermined somewhat by the fact that the composition of these toys has not changed since their inception.

Penny may show you 'Jessica Rabbit', a vibrator she believes must have been designed by a woman because it is soft, provides stimulation in two areas, and bears a nice smiling face. In general, though, Sh! is forced to stock the same ranges as other High Street porn stores. And these are still full of oversized Dildos from Hell, distorted prosthetics created by minds constrained by the male obsession with size, an obsession that has, of course, lurked in history since Dionysus was honoured with parades of gigantic phalli. Do women still want these frightening things? These double-ribbed torpedoes? 'Oh yes,' says Angela Wood, who chooses the marital aids for Ann Summers. 'The big ones do sell. They are doing very well. We wouldn't put them in the shops if they didn't.'

The female customer is wrong, then, to conclude that if Freud was correct and man is propelled by narcissism and sexual drive, the veneration of a totem-phallus is the logical artistic by-product of these drives – a male idea conceived for the benefit of other men. Perhaps, in fact, the successful survival of cock culture relies on its appeal to what the good Doctor called 'polymorphous perversity' – the male and female in us all.

She may reflect, with a smile, upon lager-flavoured Booby Drops and Vie en Rose Action Cream. She may survey corsets, archetypal symbols of oppression, whose power has not necessarily been diffused by this fashionable freedom to choose. It is a brave woman who confesses to a desire to be sexually submissive, whom some would say was beautifully politically correct (she says what she wants) and others would damn as sadly incorrect (her libido impelling her to surrender personal responsibility).

The cumulative effect of women becoming rude is an atmosphere that encourages one to avoid cooking while never turning off the heat. Sexual assertiveness is the new ethos. It is symbolised by modish fetish-wear and promulgated by everybody from female rap groups to the Pussy Posse, who hold 'raves' for those who believe that it is essential to combine unashamed flaunting with the sticky protocol that surrounds safer sex. The men of this vision are appropriated rather than seduced, handcuffs click like castanets and porn slithers easily into the life of the predatory diva. There is no reason why women should not practise recreational sensuality ('I want to fuck you, not marry you'), but the flaw of these messages is that its harbingers assume that all men wish to sleep with them. They do not address the risk, the fear, the devastation of rejection.

The future may reveal magazines devoted to the delights of tumescence (_Vast Dicks_, the brother magazine to _Big Jugs_), streets full of male prostitutes (yes please) and clubs full of Dreamboy clones (no thanks). As men exploit themselves they may suffer the derision that greet women who have chosen to do the same; but if the womens' market booms, will it redress the balance? It might be great to swan out and wolf-whistle at labourers, but is revenge progressive? The female customer will not be able to help wondering whether the sisters are legitimising the lamentable messages they have shrieked against for so long. 'What's wrong with you?' says he who wanks over the photograph of the spread-eagled _Penthouse_ Pet. 'You've got your own now.'

She has indeed.

The woman in the sex shop may stride to a corner where, next to Debbie ('she never says no') is an inflatable man. Black Macho. He costs £47.95 and is portrayed on the box wearing white swimming trunks. A girl in a rubber dress, hair lacquered into a shrub, has her arms around him. Bold letters describe the contents: 'A brand new dark-skinned dusky male doll with erect ready and willing vibrating penis guarantees full satisfaction.'

Then, at the bottom, a more cryptic communication: 'WARNING. Do not use on unexplained calf pain. Consult a doctor.'

It is natural to wonder if a White Macho is also available. It turns out that there is, but he has sold out. He has been very popular, you see, since he was introduced last year. With men or women? 'Both,' says Angela Wood. 'We cater for every type of person.'

So the lady customer may buy Black Macho and take him home with her on the tube. Seated on the Central Line she will feel an interesting sense of superiority as she looks at the Selfridges carrier bags of other passengers. Their shopping doesn't contain an unstoppable sex machine.

At home she will unwrap him from his discreet grey and white striped paper and pull him from his box. Ensuring that the neighbours' faces are not pressed against their windows, she will lay him on the bed where he will recline in a deflated slick of crumpled rubber – a cross between Jimi Hendrix and a Lilo. His head, with its jaundiced eyeballs, is rather disproportionate to his feet, which are square and devoid of toes. His hair, the victim, perhaps, of sensible budgeting, is confined to a fringe of curly black nylon. The back of his skull is entirely bald. His face, which seems to have been stuck on separately, bears the expression last seen on the police identikit pictures of the Cambridge Rapist.

She places her mouth to the translucent nozzle in his back and blows him up with the cardiovascular difficulty of one who cannot give up smoking. Chest first. Legs. Arms. And there he is, in all his pneumatic splendour; little curly fronds painted unconvincingly on to his chest and an odd pink pocket in his groin. Something is missing here. Surely the £47.95 covers an appendage of some sort? She turns the box upside down and out falls a brown fissured object similar, in appearance, to a log.

Closer inspection reveals this to be attached to a unit. She shakes the box again. Batteries Not Included. Cursing, she runs, legs blurred by speed, to the shops, buys two Duracells and galvanises the log into action. It hums like a Hoover.

She notices that Black Macho does not come first.

She introduces him to her girlfriends. They scream with laughter, ask if she needs a puncture repair kit, and say he's funnier than the Chippendales.

She introduces him to her ex-boyfriend.

He tells her she is a very lonely and sick person and she should see a doctor.

Copyright © Jessica Berens, 1992

Dressed to Frill

Why are Rock Stars So Badly Dressed? by Mark Edwards
November 1992

LET'S TALK ABOUT EXCESS. Tattoos, badges, cowboy boots and far too many zips; make-up *sans frontières*; jeans too tight to mention; T-shirts with interesting messages; T-shirts with interesting stains; a tendency to squeeze into things that used to fit, oh, five, six years ago; colours imported from a parallel universe; floppy scarves; too much suede; and a lurve thang with sequins.

What are we doing here? Exploring bad taste in clothes? Or just running through the basic elements of rock'n'roll fashion? Why, both, of course.

Ever since Mr Rock met Mr Roll, the resultant music has been at the forefront of fashion, spreading the looks that swept through the emergent youth culture. The connection was obvious. Both the new music and the new fashions replaced old class divisions with a new age structure. If you listened to *the* music and wore *the* clothes you were a member of the new aristocracy. When Mary Quant's husband Alexander Plunket Greene declared of her clothes that 'many items should not be worn by people over 28', his statement was but a microphone's throw away from The Who's '*Hope I die before I get old*' and the wise rock adage that you should never trust anybody over 30 (age or waist measurement).

Greene was – well, he would be, wouldn't he? – 33, when he said it.

Throughout the Sixties, Seventies and early Eighties designers fed off pop and rock and fed it back the next big thing. But the next thing couldn't get to be big without the rock stars and the size of their audience. As designer John Richmond says: 'Rock doesn't create fashions, but it does make them happen. Fashion designers don't have the ability to do that, except in a very limited, cliquey kind of way.' Thus, Elvis, The Beatles, Bolan, Bowie, Malcolm's Sex Pistols all influenced (virtually determined) the way a generation dressed.

But while rock and fashion have pursued this symbiotic relationship – with rock stars acting as patrons of the most inventive designers of the era – rock has also thrown up some of the most absurd, tasteless and just plain embarrassing looks imaginable. For every Bowie there's a Numan, for every Bolan a Sweet, for every Elvis a Cliff.

So, what's the visual difference between Bolan and The Sweet, the Pistols and The Cars, mod-revivalist The Jam and Teddy boy revivalists Showaddywaddy? Why does one work and the other suck? What's the difference between a look that inspires a generation and . . . Spandau Ballet?

Well, it's *not* the clothes. Not primarily, anyway. No rock star is going to affect the way anyone dresses unless they first affect the way they think and feel, and they're not going to do that unless they first make them either (a) dance, or (b) scream, or (c) nod wisely along to the enclosed lyric sheet muttering 'yeah, right'.

In the world of rock fashion there is a thin line between icon and wanker. Having removed the power of the music and the shocking effect of the attitude (as hindsight can), the clothes stand, as it were, completely naked, and they can look more than a little silly.

Which is why the first law of rock fashion states: 'Rock's main influence on fashion is its attitude, not its taste.'

The second says: 'To create a truly influential look, an artist has to pull together attitudinal, musical and fashion influences from the two extremes of safe pop and dangerous outlaw culture.'

A shocked contemporary commentator once described The Twist as 'half Negroid, half Manhattan'. This mix of acceptable society with wrong-side-of-the-tracks is at the heart of all rock fashions. Presley was 'half Negroid, half Redneck', fusing the wildly clashing musical styles of establishment country and western and dangerous rhythm and blues – the showbiz aspect of the former's clothes making the loose, flowing, rhythmic, *sexual* cut of the latter's more obvious and more prominent than ever before (and flaunting it in the face of a white middle-class audience).

The Beatles were blessed because the conflict existed within the personalities of Lennon and McCartney. The conflict was then given a visual outlet as Brian Epstein took his drug-fuelled, denim-clad and leather-jacketed rockers down to Dougie Millings' shop in Soho.

The *Daily Mirror* summed up the outlaw-made-acceptable look in 1963: 'They wear their hair like a mop, but it's washed and superclean.' Oh, that's all right then.

Marc Bolan pulled together the hard grungy riffs of nascent heavy metal with the sugary strings and massed backing singers of the conventional pop single. He also pulled together the dangerous hair, flares and sexuality of hard rock with the (by then) safe pop dandyism that had developed from the mod groups of the Sixties.

Bowie also used the mods/dandies as his safe ingredient, adding a dash of outlaw Iggy and The Velvets. Note also that in British society the drag queen somehow manages to fit neatly into both mainstream popular culture and right out there on the wild side.

Rock's *worst* moments come when – stumped for their own look – a group borrows the clothes of one of the style-setters without having either the music or attitude to back it up. In *Awopaloobop Alopbamboom*, Nik Cohn quotes PJ Proby answering a spectator at one of his shows who's asked Proby how he 'does it'. 'Mister,' says Proby, 'I don't do. I am.' Essentially rock's best dressed are the stars who are; rock's worst dressed are those who merely do, and try and do while wearing the former's clothes.

At this point – the point at which the original *attitude* behind the clothes has been removed, the sometimes dubious *taste* of the clothes themselves is revealed. Search out a copy of 'The Hollies Greatest', just for the cover shot: a group who'd put on the psychedelic clothes of the time, but haven't quite managed to pull it off. The frilly lace down Allan Clarke's shirt looks like it's trying to get off him. You won't see another group looking quite so uncomfortable in their new look again until ... Ure-era Ultravox ('Yeah, I know you explained the rationale behind the flying goggles to me once, Midge, but just run me through it again').

Check out The Cars and see the sad spectacle of a good ol' American AOR band got up in punk duds because that's the way they think they're *supposed* to look. Look even at Dave and Annie unhappily acting punkish in The Tourists before they realised that the right look for them was the look-at-my-new-look look.

Marvel at the other members of The Jimi Hendrix Experience as they bravely opt to shop at the same places Jimi does. Poor Mitch Mitchell *looks* as hopelessly stranded as he *sounds* trying to play behind Hendrix. Step back in amazement as *every* heavy metal group after, I suppose, Black Sabbath, opt to wear the same bloody outfit.

You could argue that heavy metal's uniform is the perfect representation of the music, because its music is no longer rebellious, anti-social or even exciting. Maybe what we need is a heavy metal band wearing suits, and then ... oh, no, perhaps not – that's sort of Tin Machine, isn't it?

The metal bands, The Hollies – all of them are caught in the audience-led stage of a music star's image cycle, as laid out in the third law: 'A group/artist's career will tend to go through the following phases: original naive look; manufactured look (imposed by manager/record company); moment of freedom as group/artist gets too powerful to be controlled; return to manufactured look (this time imposed by the demands of the audience).'

The Beatles looked uncomfortable in their Cardin-style suits. Even the 'penchant for pinstripe' that Freeman remembers them displaying is rarely allowed to punctuate the carefully composed black-on-black look of the time. Their moment of fashion freedom comes (as it does musically) at the time of 'Revolver', when they begin to explore and indulge in the fashions of the day in a fairly random way.

But by the time of 'Pepper', they've entered the second manufactured period. By now the audience (the media?) expects them to wear something outrageous, and they duly comply. And at least 75 per cent of the group knows how dumb they look.

There are plenty of exceptions to the third law (Sheena Easton blows a big hole through the middle of it), but it holds true for most of the major figures. In punk's case it works nicely for the movement as a whole, all four stages of the process being whipped through in about 18 months.

The last stage is a nasty one, as rock stars come to terms with the obligation imposed on them to be fashionable.

The number of column inches spent describing Van Morrison's scruffy appearance (and complete lack of interest in doing anything about same) very nearly exceed the amount written about his music. When Lou Reed played the Hammersmith Odeon earlier this year, the national press based their reviews not on Lou's astonishing guitar sound or epic tales of cancer-ridden friends but on the fact that he wore his jacket sleeves rolled up. It may have been poet-designate Lou's elliptical reference to TS Eliot ('*I grow old, I grow old, I shall wear the sleeves of my jacket rolled*'), but the trivial, style-obsessed English press saw it merely as an appalling fashion *faux-pas*. Oh, and perhaps we should re-examine just how good 'Sweet Jane' is, if the man who wrote it can wear his hair like Ian Botham.

Lou obeys the fourth law of rock music fashion, which states: 'The longer an artist/group takes between records, the worse their image becomes.'

And if that one holds water (Elvis, Jackson, The Beatles, Costello, Dylan, shell-suited Lydon, 'Ironic' Bono . . .), it's essentially because the more time they have between records the more time they have to think about their look, and the more they think about it, and the more other people who become involved think about it, the more they add to it, and the more they add to it, the worse it gets.

It makes you wonder what Bryan Ferry's going to look like when he finally gets his next record out. Or worse still, what would happen to Prince if he ever took a day off?

With time and money on their hands, perhaps rock stars are simply committing the same crimes against good taste that most of us would. Designer Nick Coleman says, 'The thing is most people dress badly, and rock stars are people, so they tend to have bad taste. There's no reason why they should be more clued-up than your average person.'

Designer Paul Smith echoes Coleman's sentiments, and adds – as is his wont – a new twist: 'Nearly all rock stars are badly dressed,' he says, 'but then most fashion people are badly dressed too. The thing with rock stars is that so much of what they do is for the stage. That either means something that's very extreme, something that's overtight – because they think that's sexy – or something bright, which makes a lot of sense at a stadium concert.'

Bowie, a champion of the bright suit for the big gig, is a Paul Smith client, but the designer says, 'With him, it's probably Mugler for stage, Paul Smith for reality.'

Even those with taste in rock don't feel that a rock star has any business being understated _in public_. The obligation to stand out has created a species of rock star that spends as much time searching for the ultimate pleat as for the ultimate riff.

Increasingly it looks like displacement activity: it's _easier_ to buy another shirt than come up with another song. The most extreme example is probably Eric Clapton. He kicked heroin only to become addicted to alcohol, and now he's given up alcohol only to become hooked on clothes. He goes through life searching the racks for the pure, uncut fabrics. ('I don't know what it is – Versace just doesn't give me that rush anymore.')

Still, the flight into designer suits is a better way of growing old gracefully in rock than the Mr Showbiz route taken to its wildest extreme by Elvis. But does the audience care about the sartorial fool The King made of himself in his later years? Or is the public all too ready to latch on to rock's periods of bad taste? The phenomenon of Presley imitators and lookalikes suggest they are.

How many of this unhappy breed have taken the ultra-cool Elvis of the Fifties as their role model? How many have even gone for the still-just-about-groovy leathered-up Elvis of his TV comeback show? And how many have chosen the mutant crossing of Liberace, Superman and Sindy that strode the Las Vegas stage like a colostomy bag, sorry, colossus?

Early estimates suggest those numbers are none, none, and far, far too many.

Every now and then some group comes along and drags rock back to the basics – it may be the Pistols, it may be Nirvana – but sure enough it goes off again into art-rock or New Romanticism, adding more chords, notes, tracks, months in the studio, years between records. The clothes, inevitably, get equally bloated.

The New Romantics were, simply, the inevitable result of punk. They were a fashion accident waiting to happen, another spin on rock's continual cycle of constraints followed by indulgence. At its root, it's human nature wedded to each generation's desire to not do what the last one did.

But if rock continues, and continues to have any influence on culture as a whole, then certainly bad taste will continue too. Let's face it, Emerson, Lake and Palmer have reformed, and if we can't get rid of drum solos, we certainly won't improve the clothes.

Although there is one pocket of sanity, of simplicity, of clear-thinking: the only part of the rock world to feel an obligation to dress down, not up (so as not to upstage the band). Which is why the final law of rock fashion states: 'On any given stage, in any given town, in all probability, the best dressed people will be the backing singers.'

Copyright © Mark Edwards, 1992

Male Rape

The Love Which Dare Not Speak Its Name by Marek Kohn
November 1992

A MAN WAS PUSHED INTO a toilet cubicle at knifepoint by three men and brutally raped in the latest of a spate of horrifying indecent assaults on males, police revealed today.

'The latest attack is the sixth homosexual sex assault in London in the past three months.

'The 28-year-old man, from Middlesex, who works in the security industry, was attacked at about 10pm in the Underground toilet at Piccadilly Circus . . .'

All of a sudden, male rape has made the news.

It took eight days before the Piccadilly victim could bring himself to report the crime. The following week, he appeared in silhouette on BBC's *Newsroom South-East*, and described what had happened. 'He put the knife up to my throat and I said, "All right, take the money . . ." He said, very calmly, "We don't want your money." '

The attackers dragged him into the toilet cubicle, and pushed his head into the toilet bowl. Two of them held his arms behind his back, while the one with the knife pulled down his trousers and raped him.

Afterwards, he was sick. 'I jumped straight into the bath, because I felt so dirty . . . I just wanted to wash everything off, and wash off how I was feeling – and of course you can't do that.'

A thousand women could have said the same thing. Rape victims experience the same feelings, the same reactions, whether they are male or female, straight or gay. And before we go any further, let's note the second paragraph of the wire report. It illustrates one possible reason why the Piccadilly victim did not report the attack for more than a week; and why many more men may never reveal that they have been sexually assaulted. It was a 'homosexual' assault in the literal sense that the attackers and the victim were the same sex. But the victim was heterosexual, and the chances are that the attackers saw themselves as heterosexual too. Male rape is a crime perpetrated by both straight and gay men, against both straight and gay men.

A heterosexual victim may fear being thought to be gay. A gay victim may fear that the police and courts will disbelieve him, if not rub salt into the psychic wounds. However, a couple of recent developments have improved the prospects for men who come forward to report sexual assault. The first is that since the beginning of August, legal anonymity has been extended to all victims of sexual assault, not just women who report rape. Unfortunately, the second applies only to London: in May, the Metropolitan Police set up a Male Rape Pilot Project.

And it was around May that the first attacks to receive wide publicity occurred. A man in his mid-twenties, travelling to meet his estranged wife, fell asleep on a Tube train. Between London Bridge and Angel, he woke up to find a man's hand on his groin. There were two attackers. They laughed as they knocked him to the floor and sexually assaulted him. A few days later, in Streatham, a man of 22 was indecently assaulted by a man who attacked him as he was walking home. The following month, a 35-year-old man was raped in Finsbury Park. In July, a man of 20 was grabbed outside Leicester Square Underground station, driven to a derelict building and raped at knifepoint. The following month, in central London, a youth aged 17 was indecently assaulted by two men, who also slashed his legs and stole his wallet.

The general view among police officers and people who work with victims of sexual violence seems to be that there is probably nothing new going on here; rather that the publicity surrounding one case has led to a string of others coming to light. This also seems to be the view from the street, according to Tony Whitehead of Streetwise Youth, an organisation that works with rent boys in the West End. 'The talk here is that such cases have been going on for some considerable time,' he says.

Streetwise Youth was founded by the late Richie McMullen, who also helped establish Survivors, the voluntary agency which helps male victims of sexual assault. In his book *Male Rape* (Gay Men's Press, 1990), McMullen analysed the phenomenon in the only terms that make sense: as an act of power, rather than a sexual act. He asserted that, 'Males who rape other men are, more often than not, heterosexual.'

The statistical basis for this claim was slender to say the least, since the only data cited came from an American study of just 16 male rapists. Subsequently, work by Ford Hickson at Project SIGMA (Socio-sexual Investigation of Gay Men and AIDS) has produced a more rounded picture. Hickson is disturbed by the assumption he detects in gay press coverage that rape is committed solely by heterosexuals. 'It's replacing one myth with another,' he says. 'In the past, any male rapist would automatically be labelled homosexual. It's been replaced with, "It's only nasty heterosexual men; gay men couldn't do it or wouldn't want to do it."'

Hickson's findings suggest that the pattern for gay male victims is similar to that for women: they tend to be attacked by men who know them. A quarter of the participants in his investigation reported that they had been sexually assaulted at some time in their lives. Of the men assaulted when they were aged 21 or over, two-thirds were attacked by regular or, much more commonly, casual partners. Only a sixth of all victims were attacked by total strangers; their average age at the time was 14.

A major study published in 1990 by Dr Richard Hillman supported the idea that boys at the highest risk of sexual assault were aged between 12 and 15. Hillman became aware of male rape about three years ago, when working at the STD clinic in St Mary's, Paddington. There was hardly anything in the medical literature on the subject. He contacted Survivors, and combed through the group's anonymous records.

Survivors emerged, about six years ago, from the painful public recognition that child sexual abuse is widespread. Eighty-five per cent of the cases in Hillman's survey concerned attacks on boys and adolescents under twenty. But more recently, Survivors' records show that the proportion of adult cases has risen to nearly 40 per cent of the total.

Dr Hillman observes that where US counselling agencies are open to both male and female rape victims, typical findings show that ten to 20 per cent of the clients are men. 'My feeling would be that the proportion is likely to be of that order,' he says. 'Male sexual asssault has been looked at most closely in the context of children. That's because of the relative ease of access, not because it shows any great degree of similarity to it. It has closer parallels to female sexual assault.'

This also seems to be largely invisible: surveys suggest that only a quarter or a fifth of female rapes are reported. A *World In Action* survey two years ago found that a quarter of the adult women in its sample said that they had been raped. Of those, only one in fourteen were attacked by strangers.

Nonetheless, many people refuse to believe in date rape. A study carried out by Lancashire Polytechnic's psychology department found that only one in five believed it was possible to rape a woman with whom the rapist had previously had sex by consent. Unlike teenagers, it seems adult women are expected to go all the way, or none of it.

Male rape victims face similar prejudices and misconceptions. Gay men, Ford Hickson says, often assume that gay victims were really asking for it. The rape of a heterosexual male may be taken as evidence that he is actually gay. Many men may not even realise that it happens at all, other than in a prison context. One or two only find out when it happens to them.

Rape victims are supposed to fight. If a woman can't show wounds, she may not be believed. But it isn't expected of her to win. A man, on the other hand, is supposed to be able to defend himself. Rape may make him appear less of a man in the eyes of others, or to himself. 'Men need to stop pretending that it can't happen to them,' says Harvey Milnes of Survivors. 'It only takes a guy to walk up behind you, knife at your throat, "Drop your trousers." Doesn't matter how big you are, forget it. Once your trousers are round your ankles, you can't move.'

Paul is 31; outwardly cool, self-possessed, successful. He tells me what happened when he first came up to London at the age of 20, 'to join the big wide world'. He was working in a nightclub; one night, a man he knew started fondling him while he was playing Space Invaders. The man had previously given the impression he was heterosexual. 'He was always talking about girls, and he had children.'

Paul knew that he himself was gay, but he was inexperienced. 'I thought, "Well, I've got to find out, I'm 20." So I had sex with him, and he fucked me. I didn't like it. It was the first time. I said, "I want this to stop", and he did.

'The next night, I was feeling very lonely, and I thought it would be nice to just be close to someone, be intimate. And I remember thinking, "This is dangerous, because maybe it's sending out the wrong messages."

'He said he wanted to do it; I said, "No, I don't wanna do it." He started to get on top of me; a fight broke out. He got my pants off, and the phone went, and he went to answer, and I pulled them back up, as though that was going to protect me or something. He came back in and I was out of the bed.

'The most humiliating bit was me fighting with my underwear, trying to keep them up, with him trying to pull them off, and over-powering me and raping me.'

Paul said no. He struggled until he was overpowered. He continued to protest while he was being raped. Yet he still blames himself. 'It was my fault. I shouldn't have been there in the bed. It was so humiliating that I just pushed it away.'

There was much more. Paul had been sexually abused as a child, by a children's activities leader. He had been in care. In recent years, he has had counselling in which he has talked about some of these childhood traumas. Yet he never spoke about the rape until two months before our conversation, when he saw his assailant in the street. He went back to work and told his colleagues. 'It was the first time I felt really angry. I had to talk about it; I had to say to the guys, "I was raped once, I just seen the guy that did it." I've learnt that you can't push things down, they don't disappear, you've gotta actually deal with shit. But I don't *feel* that I have got a right to complain about it. I *know* I've got a right, but internally it's like – I can't put it into words.

'Well, no one's going to believe you anyway,' he says.

Paul doesn't have relationships and he rarely has sex; when he does, the encounter is fleeting. He is afraid of intimacy. It is easy to imagine that such an attack would set the seal on what a young man, already abused and lonely, understood about what happens if you go looking for comfort and warmth.

The most disturbing psychological legacy of the assault emerges shortly before the tears, when I ask whether the rape has affected his sexual behaviour. 'I was listening to the radio about a week ago, and I heard that somebody had been raped in some Tube station,' he answers. 'And to be honest, it turned me on.'

It's worth pointing out that if Paul had gone to the police, he could have risked being arrested for under-age gay sex. And as far as the law is concerned, male rape does not exist. There is only buggery or indecent assault; the definition of rape is restricted to forcible vaginal intercourse.

And if the law doesn't recognise male rape, the public is less likely to do so. In a contribution to a recent book edited by two leading British experts on male rape, Dr Gillian Mezey and Dr Michael King (*Male Victims Of Sexual Assault*, Oxford University Press), Zsuzsanna Adler concludes that while the law on sexual assaults against females is primarily concerned with protecting victims, the law regarding assaults on males seems to be largely about curbing homosexual activity. The offence of buggery, for example, is subdivided into no less than 11 categories, only three of which specify assault or lack of consent. In 1990, there were 33 recorded cases in these categories, out of a total of 334 buggery offences.

The police themselves don't see a problem. 'We're quite happy with the terminology, and with our powers,' says Detective Chief Inspector Steve James, manager of the Met's Male Rape Pilot Project. The important thing, he argues, is to understand how grave an act male rape is.

James represents the new model Met officer. 'Like any company, before we offer a product out on the market, we want to make sure that it's being done right,' he tells me.

'You're not going to use the word "customer" in a moment, are you?' I enquire.

'I realise I'm talking to a professional here,' he answers reproachfully. 'They are technically customers of ours, but they are victims of crime as well.'

Pretty soon the dictionary entry for 'Life' will read 'Obsolete term for shopping'. But grotesque as customerspeak can be – and describing a rape victim as a customer is pretty high up the scale – it should not detract from the quantum leap in sensitivity and care that the Project represents. Through it, male victims can now be assigned 'chaperones', officers handpicked for their sensitivity. There are 26 of them so far (compared to 1,200 trained to work with women), aged between 25 and 35, half of them male and half female.

So far, they have seen seven victims. 'Obviously we're a bit disappointed with the slow take-up,' DCI James says, adding that they are going to expand the scheme according to response. 'Gut reaction is that there are still major cultural difficulties, apart from us, which are stopping people reporting it.'

A conversation with one of the chaperones, Detective Constable David John, confirms that the Project has its own cultural set sorted out. A former Baptist pastor, and the officer who looked after the Piccadilly victim, DC John knows that rape is about power rather than sex. 'There's certainly no suggestion that this is in any way connected to the homosexual community,' he assures me.

Both John and James deny catching any flak from the macho attitudes found in the police forces' canteen culture. As far as the victim is concerned, in any case, the chaperone should shield him from reactionary attitudes. Outside London, regrettably, the chances of being taken under the wing of a PC DC are not so good. Richard Hillman suggests that if a victim does not want to deal with the police, it may be a good idea for him to talk to his doctor. Alternatively, he may find that staff at STD clinics are able to offer counselling.

Survivors remains the only voluntary agency dedicated to helping male rape victims. But with only a few local groups, a meagre budget, and a national phone helpline operating two evenings a week, it cannot hope to meet the demand. Even under ideal circumstances, building up confidence and a sense of trust in the victim is a precarious business. 'It sometimes takes a few phone calls before somebody'll meet us,' says Ian Warwick of Sheffield Survivors.

Sometimes the victim can't face the meeting. One man phoned Ian Warwick two or three days after being jumped and raped by three men in Tenerife. He had never heard of male rape. 'For him, it was like meeting aliens from Mars,' says Warwick. 'It was an experience that wasn't in his realm of belief.'

He was due to get married the next weekend. He couldn't decide whether to go through with it; he eventually did, but kept the attack secret from his fiancée.

'He was desperately searching for what messages he'd been giving over,' says Warwick. 'He obviously hadn't. He didn't even know whether he'd seen them before. When something like that happens to you, the fear is that it's going to happen again, because you think, "I'm obviously giving out some messages that are going to make me a target."'

Even more disturbing is sexual arousal. It sometimes happens. According to Dr Hillman, it's a physiological response; a matter of friction against tissue. Harvey Milnes says that some rapists set out to induce it. 'Imagine the power that a man will feel degrading and humiliating a child, or a woman, and think how much more power they'd feel doing it to another man – especially getting the man to ejaculate.'

Another sadistic embellishment of rape is the threat of HIV infection. In Richard Hillman's survey, such threats were made to one in five of the victims.

A man who rapes men poses a challenge to conventional notions of sexuality. 'I've worked with quite a few queerbashers,' says Jim Wilson, a counsellor at Bolton MOVE (Men Overcoming Violence). 'Their homophobia is a straightforward beating, grind them into the shit, and that's it.' Rape, he believes, arises from 'instability in the perpetrator's own sexuality'. In other cultures, by contrast, men are classified into those who fuck and those who get fucked. Homosexuality becomes a matter of sexual acts rather than identity; a macho man will 'conquer' women *and* men.

Whatever the psychology of the attacker, there is no doubt that rape puts the identity of the victim into crisis. Dr Gillian Mezey has concluded that men, like women, suffer disbelief, fear, humiliation and rage. Whether he is a straight man jumped by a gang in a public place, like the Piccadilly and Tenerife victims, or a gay man raped by a casual sex partner, like Paul, a male victim is likely to feel humiliated by being overpowered; is likely to suffer for years unless he is helped.

There is one major difference between the rape of men and of women. Rape is in the background of all women's lives, shaping everyday choices about where they can go and what they can do. It's worth noting that on last year's averages, 1,000 rapes or sexual assaults against women would have been recorded in London during the period when half a dozen male rapes made the papers. The rape of a woman acts to shape society as a whole, whereas male rape only has a function in prisons or similar institutions.

That is of no comfort to the victims, though. We don't yet know whether the half-dozen reported cases are the tip of an iceberg. What we do know is that men do get raped, and they are devastated by the experience. And whatever the numbers, the victims needs far outstrip the supply of help available. Rape is not something a man just gets over. 'There's an old saying that time's a great healer,' says Ian Warwick. 'It wants kicking into touch. We find ways of coping, but we don't actually heal.'

Copyright © Marek Kohn, 1992

Dino!

Dean Martin by Kevin Jackson

November 1992

'LIVING HIGH IN THE DIRTY Business Of Dreams', leers the subtitle of Nick Tosches's book *Dino*, like a doorman trying to entice the rubes inside his joint. You can understand the need for such a salacious come-on. These days, the name Dean Martin probably carries about as much clout with the public which buys most of the records and sees most of the movies – and, come to that, reads magazines like *Arena* – as Perry Como or Al Jolson. Without the promise of some outstandingly juicy scandal and inside smut, you might wonder why anyone under 50 should want to read this biography.

Unlike some other big stars of the Fifties, he didn't die young enough to be petrified into an icon of seductive insolence for rising generations; and unlike his old Rat-Pack buddy Frank Sinatra, he didn't manage to ride out the waves of popular taste into a triumphant late period. Most of his 60-odd movies are too rotten to be shown anywhere outside the dead zone of mid-afternoon television, and the last time his slightly smarmy, half-cut vocals tickled the public's ear was in Cher's romantic vehicle *Moonstruck* when his cod-Italian number from 1953, 'That's Amore', played over the credit sequence. ('*When the moon hits your eye/Like a big pizza pie . . .*')

It's a cruel reversal. Dino used to be huge. By the late Fifties, he held the high ground of mass entertainment in America, the first man ever to have enjoyed stardom on all four fronts of stage, records, television and films. (Sinatra, his nearest rival, never quite cracked television, and looked up to Dino with almost fawning admiration.) A decade of unbroken success later, he was one of the most highly-paid performers in the world, pulling down $15 million a year – which, as the seriously rich say, was quite a lot of money in those days.

And Dino's ascendancy wasn't wholly founded on work that now looks or sounds embarrassing, either. If, like so many other greying men in tuxedos, he was reduced to drawling out the mandatory cover version of 'Tie A Yellow Ribbon (Round The Old Oak Tree)' by the early Seventies, his earlier recordings are still insinuating enough for us to understand how they helped clinch a few million courtships: 'Memories Are Made Of This', 'Volare', 'C'est Si Bon', 'Everybody Loves Somebody'. And with one of his signature songs, 'Little Ole Wine Drinker Me', Martin shrewdly turned his highly-developed fondness for the sauce into one big, open joke – though if he had been somewhat more frank about his intoxicants of choice, he might well have recorded a sequel, 'Little Ole Percodan Popper Me'.

As for all those films . . . well, despite all the turkeys (*Cannon-ball Run II*, anyone?), he managed to turn in some good work in a handful of enduring, maybe even great movies: Howard Hawks' Western *Rio Bravo*, in which (the Big Boozy Joke again) he played an alcoholic deputy, Billy Wilder's sour *Kiss Me, Stupid* and Frank Tashlin's *Hollywood Or Bust*.

No less an arbiter than the *Nouvelle Vague* director Jean-Luc Godard thought that Tashlin's romp was one of the ten best films of 1957 – although, to be strictly accurate, his compliments to Martin were a shade left-handed: 'To have turned Dean Martin into a comedian is feat enough to rate his director a place at the very top.' (Luckily for Jean-Luc, the Mafia, who lapped up Dino's stage act, didn't subscribe to *Cahiers du Cinema* at the time). Later critics have been warmer. In his magisterial *Biographical Dictionary Of The Cinema*, for example, David Thomson sums up Martin's screen work in the admiring general maxim that, 'No idler works harder, no drunk retains such timing, and no womanizer seems so amused by sex.'

But more directly, Dean Martin was a star not just because he could sing well or act appealingly but because he was the epitome of relaxed, funny sexiness – in a word that first came into vogue during his rise, he was *cool*. Tributes to both the humour and the cool echo throughout Tosches's biography. Martin's one-time partner Jerry Lewis – the demented chimpanzee who somehow managed to steal the spotlight away from Martin's urbane organ-grinder (much to the latter's disgust) remarks, 'There are some people born with the genius of time. And he had not just a sense of humour, he had a sense of humour that applied to anyone and everything around him. And it was brilliant. It was right on the money. I was in awe of his ability to make you laugh.'

And there can't be a much crisper account of Dino's other major asset than a remark by one Tony Torcasio, who recalled Martin's sangfroid from the early years of his nightclub act: 'He pissed ice water.' To this extent it looks as if Tosches is on to a real winner with his subject, and that his *Dino* is a timely and strenuous attempt to pull Martin's reputation out of the archives, dust it down and push it back towards centre stage.

What's more, that drooling subtitle isn't a complete con. Whatever you think of Martin's tunes and shows, there's just about every last sleazy element here that the most prurient browser could crave. Sex and drugs and . . . well, actually, rock'n'roll played only a slim and mildly incongruous part in Dean Martin's career; his generation never quite got the point of guitars and amps.

But, yes, the tale certainly oozes with semen (Dino's hyperactivity between the sheets makes Don Giovanni's score pale into monkishness) and it's certainly pumped full of drugs, like the aforementioned and highly addictive painkiller Percodan. There's a hefty subplot about gangsters – Dino was on chummy terms with the Mob from his earliest days – and the walk-on roles are great, too: Marilyn Monroe, Sinatra and Jack and Bobby Kennedy are all part of the plot.

More innocent, but no less seductive, is the Horatio Alger side of the Dean Martin story: he was the son of a modest Italian barber from Steubenville, Ohio, where the infant crooner-to-be was baptised Dino Crocetti in 1917. In short, it has all the classic stuff of pulp biography. But the running isn't quite as smooth as it may first appear.

For one thing, Tosches had no direct access to Martin, who has only given a couple of bland interviews in his life and is now a reclusive old man, more and more deeply in the grip – if the impressionistic final pages of *Dino* can be taken literally – of Alzheimer's disease.

For another, Dino was nearly always discreet in his philandering, and his women were persuaded to follow suit: 'Any broad who went public with what happened behind closed doors, well, as far as he was concerned, that broad had spent the last dollar of his that she would ever see and drunk the last ounce of his fame and spratz as well. He was notorious for that: his song of songs was a blowjob and a fare-thee-well. "You wanna talk, see a priest," he would tell the girls in Vegas.' It seems to have worked: Tosches keeps up some dutiful running hints about Dino's many conquests, but the rutting and the fellations in *Dino* all take place offstage, so there's no point hunting for the dirty bits.

Finally, there's something as much routine as classical in the trajectory of Martin's flight from Ohio to Hollywood: modest beginnings, a few odd jobs, early triumph, the big breakthrough, later triumph, old age and decline. No surprises there, and, despite the gangsters, not that many arresting anecdotes either.

Yet these and other obstacles in Tosches's way are relatively trifling; some of the best biographies have been written under similar restrictions. His main problem is more serious. Whatever may have been going on behind Martin's slurred delivery and easy smirk, the man who saunters through the pages of *Dino* is a man who made such a virtue of not giving a hoot that he ended up with no real inner-life – if he ever had one in the first place.

The dust jacket of *Dino* brags dutifully of Martin's 'inner demons', but that's just a publicist's blague. Dino didn't need an exorcist; he was scarcely in that major league of performers who owe much of their dazzle to neurosis, and whose ranks include Monroe and Dean. Come to that, he wasn't even in the same troubled league as Jerry Lewis.

Lewis's sporadic presence in *Dino* tends to be a good deal more vivid than Martin's – but then Tosches managed to secure an interview with the comedian. There's something appealing about Lewis's enduring sense of astonishment at the ridiculous ease of their ascent: 'Can you pay two men $9 million to say "Did you take a bath this morning?" "Why, is there one missing?" – do you dare contemplate such a fuck-and-duck? Yet that's what we did. We did that onstage, and they paid us $9 million.'

Unfortunately, as Tosches rightly points out, there aren't any accurate records of the duo's stage act to corroborate Lewis's memories of what a wow they could be, or his enraptured view of Dino's comic gifts; just the statistics of frenzied crowds packing into their nightclub shows and huge box-office takings. Their act had to be bowdlerized for radio, and their movies, something of a specialist taste nowadays unless you happen to be French (bafflingly, Parisian intellectuals have always had a regard for Jerry Lewis, just as their grandfathers swooned for Edgar Allen Poe), flattered Lewis more than Martin.

And Lewis gives no hint that Martin's clowning was of the tormented type. On the contrary, Lewis was drawn to the older man because Martin 'possessed all the strength and security he so desperately lacked. The distance, the *lontananza* that others found chilling, he saw as a stole of nobility, and an air of self-sufficiency and self-assurance so profound that the dismal burdens of his own anxieties and fears seemed to lighten in its presence.'

There are less flattering ways of putting that same thought.

Beneath Dean Martin's flip, insouciant exterior was . . . well, maybe not quite a flip, insouciant interior, but definitely a personality that could be thought of as unreflectingly shallow, not so much self-sufficient as self-centred. No fool, surely, but sometimes not so very far from an oaf. A more representative summary of Dino's habitual mentality other than the cliché about 'inner demons' is Tosches's account of his indifference to the big events of his time.

'The Trojan war, World War II, the Cold War, what the fuck did he care? . . . His uncaring air of romance reflected the flash and breezy sweet seductions of a world in which everything came down to broads, booze and money, with plenty of *linguine* on the side. There was a beckoning to join him in the Lethe of the old way's woods that appealed to the lover, the *menefreghista*, the rotten cocksucker, the sweet-hearted dreamer in everyone.'

Dino's simple-minded greed for 'broads, booze and money' reads like the hallmark of a spoiled brat, not a grown-up, and time spent with any overgrown infant soon becomes pretty tiresome unless they have compensatory charms. In life, Dino was handsome, cheerful and no doubt extremely good company. On the page, without the grins and the nods, his celebrated insouciance is more like the affectlessness of a zombie, and his conduct that of a taciturn, somewhat boorish man whose only U-rated pastimes were playing golf (he joked about preferring golf to sex) and watching old Westerns (which he genuinely preferred to meeting his buddies).

To be sure, Dino's lack of perceptible adult interests wouldn't be any obstacle for an aspiring biographer had he been a straightforward man of action – a soldier, a politician, a tycoon. His principal claim on our interest, however, is that he was an artist of sorts; and yet he exhibits almost no sign of the motives which fuel and shape creativity of any order. From childhood, Martin hardly ever showed strong feelings (unless you count the night early on in his career when he beat up a heckler: 'Dean looked into his fat fucking cunt-eating face. He needed this drunken bastard like he needed another fucking hernia . . .'), never made particularly close friendships, never fretted about anything much, never opened a book.

Most damning of all, he seems to have been indifferent to the popular arts he practised. Maybe it was a pose at first – an exercise, as his kinder critics have suggested, in making the difficult look effortless. But even in his best years he began to lapse into sloppy delivery and often could barely be bothered to finish the song he had started. Studied nonchalance slid towards a barely veiled contempt for his material and, finally, for his audiences.

Tosches describes an unpleasantly revealing moment from his 1988 tour of America with Sinatra and Sammy Davis Jr: 'He looked long and hard at the faceless sea beyond the stage. What the fuck was he doing here, and who the fuck were these people? He took a final drag from his cigarette and flicked the burning butt into the crowd.' (At least Johnny Rotten's fans had already been given some clue that their idol despised them.) Camus once summed up the futility of an unengaged twentieth-century life in the sour epitaph: 'He fornicated and read the papers.' Tosches's Dino is a man who fornicated and sang some songs.

All of which helps account for the biographer's weird narrative method. He knows he has some good scenery, but his leading man appears not to be a great deal more animated or complex than your average showroom dummy. So he casts the usual biographical scruples to the winds. The result is less an orthodox biography than a kind of non-fiction novel, which, to be sure, keeps doggedly to the public record as far as main events are concerned, but which takes off on flights of wild conjecture when it comes to Martin's presumed response to those events. Dino had no perceptible inner-life, so Tosches has invented one for him.

Take the book's opening page: 'It was like the guys from the other side used to say: *La vecchiaia e carogna.* They were right: old age is carrion. He was only 54; he would turn 55 a month from this day. But he felt like an old man, like the carrion those old men spoke of in those days of shadow and sunlight; felt as if he had skulked and staggered and stridden through three lifetimes, been wrung and wrecked and worn down by them . . .'

It's a shame that Tosches has yielded to the temptation to play Great American Novelist in this way, because in some respects his work is commendable, not to say outstanding. The sheer quantity of research recorded in his notes puts many academic biographers to shame, and it isn't just the usual taped interviews and cuttings from *Variety*, either.

Tosches has looked into every area that touched Dean Martin's life, from the history of Italian immigration and the development of the recording industry to the proliferation of the Mafia. He has looked at court records, statistics on the Ohio steel industry and the Steubenville City Directory, and his bibliography includes such oddities as the autobiography of Mozart's librettist da Ponte and *The Everlast Boxing Record Book*.

Given a less ponderous touch, this diligence might have yielded fresh and enlightening angles on some perennially beguiling subjects. Uninspiring as Martin's temperament may be for a writer, the man's life does offer a ready pathway into such areas as, for example, the ties which bind the entertainment business to the underworld; the struggles of loyalty and prejudice which made and ruined Kennedy's dream of Camelot ('Dean saw what Sinatra was too blind to see: there was no place in Camelot for wops'); or the democratic paradox of modern entertainment, which allows men of no very startling abilities to live like feudal lords if they happen to be in the right place and the right decade.

Tosches makes a stab at all of these areas, particularly the last – in fact he nudges us roughly towards it with his choice of epigraph: 'There can be no question that fortune is supreme in human affairs. It is a capricious power, which makes men's actions famous or leaves them in obscurity without regard for their true worth.'

Yet, thanks mostly to the author's addiction to his own version of the Grand Style, there's far more sound and fury in *Dino* than significance. Take this early passage on the theme of entertainment and the dreaming masses: 'The funhouse was a vast and wonderful place of imaginings and greed. One entered for a nickel, the twentieth part of a dollar. Even in this century, the painted face of a laughing man on the great Western wall, faded and excoriated by the seasons of a century or more, could still be discerned; the slick black hair parted in the middle; the eyes wide and transfixed as if in the throes of an ecstasy more terrible in its emptiness and endlessness than agony; the thin-lipped, rollicking cancerous grin of metastatic delights . . .'

Tosches's accounts of how and why Martin managed to woo his public at various times can be highly acute: Martin began, Tosches suggests, by breaking with conventional wisdom and addressing his songs not to his female fans but directly to the men who paid their nightclub tabs: 'He sang to them as if only they could truly understand him. Other singers worked to seduce the women in the audience. To him, that came naturally. He worked to seduce the men, winning them, bonding them to his side with the illusion of camaraderie . . .'

And later, when he was a big star on television, Dino played a similarly wild card, treading along that narrow borderline between raffishness and sneering which he later slouched heedlessly across. For every prissy television critic who hated his programme, 'There were thousands of others who loved what Dean was doing. He was not spitting at them; he was spitting for them. His message was clear: all this fake-sincerity shit that was coming through television – not only through television: the newspapers, the pictures, every politician's false-faced caring word and grin – it was all a racket.'

This rings true enough, and if Tosches had kept his habit of fanciful conjecture within such a plausible range he would have had a less risible book on his hands. Before very long, you start to feel an unexpected sense of sympathy for the poor soul whose life is being buried under the avalanche of humbug, and who, for all we know, after turning the final page, may well be a decent enough bloke. Early on in his career, Dean Martin had to suffer the indignity of being upstaged by Jerry Lewis, the man who was supposed to be his stooge. Now, in his sad old age, he's suffered the even worse indignity of being upstaged by Nick Tosches, the man who was supposed to be his biographer.

Copyright © Kevin Jackson, 1992

Single File
The Bachelor Decoded by Neil Spencer
December 1992

'FUNNY HE NEVER MARRIED . . .' The hetero put-down is aimed at the discreetly closeted, but these days it applies equally well to that other perennial feature of male single life, the bachelor. Once held up as society's dominant life form, hymned in novel and film, analysed in colour supplements, by the Nineties the bachelor has become an endangered species.

The very term is a throwback to a former age; only the spouse-trading pages of blue-blood glossies like _Harper's_ still prattle about 'eligible bachelors'. Elsewhere single men are hunks, unmarried, divorced, available . . . 'Bachelor', with its connotations of perennial, predatory singledom, is hopelessly tainted, as outworn as Sean Connery's 007 hairpiece.

What happened? Feminism, of course. Far from being admired, the condition of being an unattached male is now held to indicate a major psychological deficiency. Rampaging misogyny perhaps, or terminal halitosis. Or at the very least, a divorce or two. Single

men are expected either to have girlfriends or to be 'between relationships' as Woody Allen-speak has it. If he's available, runs the
female line of reasoning, there must be something wrong with him.
He may even turn out to be, horror, a *bachelor*.

Rather than a thrusting, independent soul, a bachelor of the seductive arts, a solo man is now tagged by the shrinks a *puer
aeternus*, an eternal boy, unable to cut the apron-strings that tie
him to mother and make a mature commitment to another
woman. He is forever sampling, never satisfied.

Like the dinosaur, the bachelor roamed for a long age before ex-
tinction. He first showed up in the Middle Ages, when 'bachelor'
came to describe a squire-at-arms, a young man who fetched lances, carried armour and mulled the wine for questing knights. The
term also referred to university students taking the first step to
their master's degree. Later the word was applied to any unmarried
man, and by the eighteenth century had acquired the connotations
it still carries – a single man past the normal age of marriage, either
a well-off professional or a man of independent means, who is
committed to life as a rake, a 'gay blade', a *bon viveur*. Or, alternatively, to a life where women are few and distant. (Bachelors are
invariably middle- or upper-class; single working men have always
lived, not in bachelor flats, but with their mums.)

By contrast unattached women were 'spinsters'. Far from being
romantic, a spinster was an unwanted, probably unmarriageable
woman, left with nothing to do but spin yarn. It was a term for an
'old maid' who had been 'left on the shelf', a figure who, for all of
feminism's advances, still haunts present-day folk wisdom, though
terms like Bachelor Girl and Career Woman have helped relegate
the spinster to history.

Bachelors have always divided into two broad categories: confirmed
and eligible. The confirmed bachelor emerged in late Victorian times, a
mature, if not crusty, sort who had successfully eluded the womanly
trap of marriage. Unencumbered by frivolous female chatter and
bickering, his income untapped by a wife's insatiable demand for new
hats and dresses, not to mention the needs of a nursery full of tiresome
brats, the confirmed bachelor could get on with the important tasks in
hand. Often these were professorial pursuits: enumerating different
species of butterfly, or detailing the migratory habits of the Lesser Auk.

Mr Chips, the public school housemaster who showed up one
term with a young wife in tow, was one such confirmed bachelor
who unexpectedly succumbed to marriage. Professor Henry Higgins, of *My Fair Lady* via Shaw's *Pygmalion*, was another, with his

celebrated complaint that he'd 'prefer a new edition of the Spanish Inquisition than to ever let a woman in my life'. Later, of course, after prolonged exposure to the charms of cockney waif Eliza Doolittle, the prof's resolve weakened. Grown accustomed to her face, he joined the ranks of the vanquished.

If not confirmed, then bachelors are eligible. This can mean they are stuck so deep in male pursuits – rebuilding the Great Western's lost branch lines in the loft, following United to every away game – they have failed to notice there's another, deeply fascinating breed of human beings running round the planet. Or an eligible bachelor may be so damnably aw-shucks shy in front of women that he needs a particularly un-shrinking Violet to frogmarch him to the altar. Thirties Hollywood abounded with this type. Cary Grant often took the improbable role of a fellow so innocent he didn't realise he was the world's best looking, best dressed man, and couldn't understand the female fuss surrounding him.

Usually, though, the eligible bachelor is racy. Pre-World War II, while no innocent, he was essentially a decent chap, and certainly not the womanizing cad he would later become, and whom he would most likely biff on the jaw. His solo style was often dictated by a job demanding lengthy absences from home on important missions. He was a soldier, a detective, an adventurer, a pilot, a spy. Richard Hannay, hero of John Buchan's *Thirty-Nine Steps*, is typical of the breed. Away in colonial Africa involved in diamond mining, he never had the chance to meet a good woman with whom to settle down in a rose-frilled Sussex cottage. Sherlock Holmes, Bulldog Drummond, Sapper, Biggles; these were all stout fellows whose lack of female company was easily explained by their commitment to a masculine profession.

The immaculate bachelor lifestyle of those other tireless fighters against injustice, Superman and Batman, was likewise necessitated by their vocation as superheroes, leaving female admirers like Lois Lane in frustrated pursuit of their eligible everyday alter egos.

Almost by definition, of course, screen cowboys have been bachelors to a man. Obsessively courteous to the fairer sex, they took their pleasure with the whores in the local saloon, while reserving their heart for their horses. Only occasionally would John Wayne stop his tumbleweed-roving to settle down with the school-marm at the end of the picture. Otherwise cowboys remained Lone Rangers.

For many years, eligible British bachelors had craggy jaws, smoked pipes, and rattled along country lanes in flying jackets and open-top MGs painted British Racing Green. Later, in their Fifties incarnations, they acquired Triumph TRs, Austin Healey 3000s and lounge suits of daringly slim cut which they wore with suede shoes. Lesley Charteris's Saint character was a copybook bachelor, so was television's one-armed detective Mark Sabre – men who lived alone in swish London flats. Laurence Harvey as Joe Lampton in *Room At The Top* was a bachelor in style if not attitude.

The post-War bachelor breed reached its apotheosis in James Bond. Not so much the upper-crust killer of Ian Fleming's Fifties thrillers but Sean Connery's inspired Sixties screen incarnation. It wasn't just that Bond was surrounded by scores of wilting dolly birds – Pussy Galore! – he had the car, the pad, the cool. And of course the job, secret agent, which stopped it being funny peculiar that he never married.

Bond spawned action-man clones by the dozen in what was to prove the last great spasm of bachelordom before its abrupt demise in the Seventies. There was Robert Vaughn as *The Man From Uncle* with his sidekick Ilya Kuriackin; James Coburn in *In Like Flint*. Even avuncular types like John Pertwee as *Dr Who* and Patrick Magee were given a rakish tinge. Most of all there was crafty cockney Michael Caine as Len Deighton's Cold War spy Harry Palmer, loading button mushrooms into his shopping trolley as he makes a meet with his controller.

In real life, too, Caine came to typify the bachelor in his last golden age, with the Harley Street knocking-shop he shared with Terence Stamp as one of the last great bachelor pads. The bachelor apartment had acquired a life of its own by then. Bare and mannish, it came with copies of *Playboy* on the coffee table and a fridge containing only vodka and ice. Jack Lemmon had an archetypal bachelor pad in *The Apartment*, and was forced to keep renting it out to a pair of adulterers with nowhere else to do their stuff. James Fox had an East End version in *Performance*, a film that encapsulated the collapse of bachelordom's pretensions and driving forces under the onslaught of Sixties sexual bohemia.

Nowhere was the bachelor pad and lifestyle promoted so self-consciously as in *Playboy*, where, like publisher Hugh Heffner, men were ever eligible, never married. Its hard-drinking heroes were men like rat-packers Dean Martin and Frank Sinatra (who kept forgetting bachelors aren't meant to fall in love or get married), macho writers like Norman Mailer, or movie studs like Steve McQueen (that sports car again).

Alas, when the sexual revolution called for in the 'Playboy Philosophy' arrived, access wasn't restricted to members of its but-toned-down, dry-Martini'd world. The sexual conquests that had been the more or less exclusive province of bachelordom were sud-denly available to all, even to women, who by the end of the Sixties had established a philosophy of their own.

The vulgar, rock-sodden, unisex Seventies scrambled the codes that had shaped bachelors past. Studs like Warren Beatty and neur-otics like Woody Allen were the new breed. And if the bass player of a third-rate heavy-metal band was getting laid more than James Bond, something had clearly died.

Bond himself had moved on, or rather back, to the old-school asexuality of Roger Moore. Secret agents just weren't what they had been; John Le Carré had seen to that. Smiley's people weren't smoothies but Cold War crazies, twisted, lonely and bitter, be-trayed and compromised. Other real-life adventurers also trashed old ideals. There were no single men in space, for example. To have the right stuff, astronauts had to be happily hitched, mentally stable.

It's been downhill for the bachelor ever since. Even the Eighties couldn't resurrect him; no wardrobe of designer clothes, no acre-age of matt-black dream home could ever make the 12-hour day of a futures dealer seem more than an over-paid, mundane job. Even on screen the bachelor failed to hold up; while Stallone and Schwarzenegger played killer robots, single yuppies like Griffin Dunne in *After Hours* lived out bachelor nightmares. Only Indiana Jones – a clever blend of Professor Henry Higgins and Rider Hag-gard, of crusty and confirmed and adventurous and eligible – bucked the trend.

The smooth bachelor lifestyle has now given way to the idiocy of *Men Behaving Badly*, up to their lying teeth in take-away car-tons, warm lager and women who are too smart for them. Hemingway's supposedly noble concept of 'Men Without Women' is likely to refer to rugby hooligans or a Robert Bly weekend. If the old bachelor notions have gone anywhere it is, in fact, to women. In film and fiction alike it is the single woman who is the creature of fascination now. And the ultimate bachelor pad of the age? Why, owned by Madonna of course, a woman resolutely in charge of her single life.

Copyright © Neil Spencer, 1992

———————————

This Gun's for Ire

The Legend of the Colt .45 by Rob Ryan

May 1993

THE COKE BOTTLE got one. So did the tampon and the Volkswagen Beetle. The lumpen fax machine even got one. And the M25, f' crissake. But the Colt .45 Auto will probably never get its own BBC2 or Channel 4 programme. It may be an archetypal example of its ilk, but that ilk has the drawback of comprising very large, nasty guns, and it just isn't done to discuss them in polite producers' circles.

Yet the Colt .45 Auto *is* a design classic. It has all the attributes, including longevity (the basic design can be seen in John Browning's patent of 1897; it had evolved to its present form by 1911; the gun is still in production today) and an integration of form and function that Walter Gropius or Dieter Rams would envy.

But suggest that you admire the engineering and aesthetics of a handgun and acquaintances start whispering 'Helter Skelter' behind your back and decline to give you their address.

Yet even in this gun-fearing country, shooting is a popular pastime. The tiny gun lobby here reckons that two million people enjoy shooting as a hobby (presumably this figure excludes armed robbery). This makes it second only to angling as a participation sport, although something tells me that there will never be a Redford-esque homage to the sport of the *A 9mm Hollow Tip Runs Through It* kind.

If they ever did get round to doing a programme on the classic gun, they would, of course choose the wrong one: the only gun to make people misty-eyed in this country is the Auto's predecessor, the Colt 1873 revolver that is laughably known as the Peacemaker.

This is The Gun That Tamed The West, the gun that could be used in a noble cause (eg Gary Cooper, Alan Ladd and other reluctant *pistoleros*), an anachronism that, like muskets and flintlocks, can be safely consigned to history (even though it was the official US Army revolver up until 1945, and General George Patten toted a pair of ivory-handled Colts across Europe).

In fact the role of the Peacemaker as we know it exists only in Hollywood's parallel world version of the West. Samuel Colt's baby (and one he didn't see – he died in 1862) was just one of many handguns knocking around the frontier at the time. Jesse James was actually shot with a Smith & Wesson Model 3; James himself owned a S&W Schofield .45, Frank James preferred a Remington M1875, Cole Younger a .32 S&W. Even Wyatt Earp was reported to have used a S&W in the gunfight at the OK Corral (which actually lasted some 121 minutes less than the film of the same name – that is 30 seconds). It comes as something of a relief to discover that Pat Garrett used a Colt to kill Billy the Kid, another .45 fan, at Fort Sumner. At least Peckinpah got this detail right in his 1973 film of the duelling duo (James Coburn v Kris Kristofferson), albeit more by accident than design.

But Peckinpah, fond of the revolver as he was, also appreciated the significance of the Colt .45 Auto in a Western as a nail in the coffin of an era. When the doomed Wild Bunch stage that opening bungled robbery, it is a shock to see a cowboy film in which the protagonists draw their guns, and instead of the familiar curves of the 1873, there are the square, brutal lines of the M1911 Colt-Browning. It was one of the earliest visual clues that the film concerned the bitter after-taste of the Old West rather than the real thing, that the days of gunfights and gunfighters had long gone. Who, after all, could imagine the classic mainstreet stand-off where the duellists are wearing automatic weapons? By the time the Auto appeared, the gunslinger was history. Colt Autos and pump-action shotguns were used to underline a similar theme, the end of the romantic notion of the frontier, in *The Professionals* with Lee Marvin and – ahem – the very wonderful Robert Ryan.

But if the Peacemaker's ubiquitous presence is phoney, the Colt .45 has much more claim to being *the* iconographic firearm of fact and fiction, although of the twentieth rather than nineteenth century. How many sidearms get to be the central character of a novel (*The Pistol* by James Jones, although, of course, the Winchester '73 got a whole, eponymous movie to itself – starring James Stewart)? And also become important accessories on movie stills and posters (Humphrey Bogart, Edward G. Robinson and Lauren Bacall in the *Key Largo* poster; Susan Sarandon blasting the tanker open in *Thelma and Louise*; the hideous gun-with-dummy poster for *Man Bites Dog*)? When Abel Ferrara called his revenge movie *Ms .45* there was little doubt what hardware she would be packing. Sean Penn, Brian Denehey, Steven Seagal – there are few action actors who haven't struck that macho gun-clasped-to-chest-in-both-hands pose with a M1911.

There were even a few glorious months back in the early Forties when the prime exponent of the fists-not-firearms philosophy strapped on a Colt .45 and let rip. Forget the Dark Knight, these were the golden days when Batman was a *real* vigilante. I seem to remember his comic-strip companion, The Phantom, had a penchant for the Colt as well, but I cannot recall him ever using it. And such was the Duke's association with the gun that those purveyors of good taste, The Franklin Mint, once produced a 'John Wayne Armed Forces Commemorative Colt .45 Wall Plaque' for $79, complete with – a nice touch this – a posthumous signature.

Of course, there are some who have strayed from the path. Dirty Harry had an unhealthy obsession with .357 magnums that would blow your head clean orrfff. James Bond had the opposite problem from Clint's testosterone-inflated muzzle velocity: both his early Beretta and the later Walther PPK 7.65mm were what Sean Connery would doubtless describe as poo-see. And although that looks like a .45 Auto on the *Lethal Weapon* posters, it is in fact one of its many, many clones (the words imitation, sincerest and flattery spring to mind), the Beretta 9mm. The neat S&W .40 Auto, another variation on the theme, is also putting in a strong showing.

It is interesting that some people think that even a passing knowledge of weaponry propels you straight into the John Milius/ Hunter S. Thompson one-round-short-of-a-six-shot mould. Personally, I have no desire ever to shoot a handgun, either at a person or a cardboard image of a person, and only a mild curiosity to take pot shots at little clay discs spinning through the air. I had almost convinced myself a few weeks ago that it was possible to have a cursory, but nonetheless healthy, interest in weapons.

And then I bought a copy of *Guns & Ammo*.

I bought it because it contained a feature that proclaimed the ageing Colt .45 was still King of the Auto Handguns. In the interests of research, you see. I honestly think there would have been less reaction in the till queue at WH Smith's if I had walked up with a copy of *Beasts 'n' Babes Monthly*. Did I want it in a bag? asked the cashier. The other customers shuffled their *Evening Standards* and doubtless thought of Hungerford. No, before you ask, Michael wasn't a blood relative.

But reading the piece on the .45 brought me up short. One of the picture captions read: 'The author's choice for all-round handgun would be his old Colt Government Model . . . the Federal Hydra-Shok loads should give him better than 90 per cent stopping efficiency.'

I re-read this to make sure this was stopping and not shopping efficiency. No, it refers to the fact that 90 per cent of all people hit with a bullet from a Colt .45 (and that is a *big* bullet) will go down and not get up again too readily. They may not be dead, of course, but what they won't do is claim it is just a flesh wound and light up a cigarette.

Elsewhere in the magazine, a columnist tried to explain in sincere, caring tones that you should only shoot intruders and muggers as a last resort. And another writer had devised a particularly elegant solution to food-looting gangs in Somalia: every mother should be issued with a rifle before the US withdraw. Just what Africa needs, several million more weapons. And, of course, there were the usual anti-Clinton and gun control diatribes.

I was left feeling that if you ever get bitten by a member of the National Rifle Association (and if you have ever spent time in bars in the deep South, you will know this is not as unlikely as it seems) you had best get a course of injections before you find yourself up a clocktower surveying Saturday shoppers through telescopic sights. 'Rabid' just doesn't do justice.

Guns & Ammo brings home the difference between a trainspotting ability to recognise the make and calibre of a gun, and the desire to have about your body something that can put a half-inch hole in somebody. And, if the statistics are anything to go by, probably in someone you love. Possibly even yourself.

Much as I appreciate John Browning's design, I don't actually want one. I mean, I also have a soft spot for the B-29 Superfortress – it must be some childhood trauma caused by it being the sole Airfix supermodel I never built – and the Mallard steam train, but I don't want to own either of them (God knows, parking is bad enough for a car).

No, the nearest I like coming to weaponry is Row D of my local cinema. And in case you think this hides a desire to witness vicarious bloodshed, my all-time favourite .45 scene isn't, say, the one from *Reservoir Dogs* where Harvey Keitel, twin Autos blazing, takes out the cop's windshield, or the bloody debacle at the end of *State of Grace*. It's when Jack Nicholson walks into a bar in *The Last Detail* and tries to get Randy Quaid a drink before he goes to the brig. The barman refuses because Quaid is under-age. He threatens to call the shore patrol. Nicholson's face contorts into an early work-in-progress version of the 'Heeeeeeeeere's Johnny' look, whips out a Colt and slams it into the bar. 'I *am* the mutherfuckin' shore patrol,' he leers.

And he *still* doesn't get served.

The barman obviously didn't recognise a design classic when it was right under his nose.

Copyright © Rob Ryan, 1993

The Man Who Came in From the Cool

Donald Fagen by Barney Hoskyns

May 1993

A S ANY SELF-RESPECTING rock legend will tell you, sabbaticals have become essential career moves in today's music business. Put out an album every year and you blow all credibility; wait five and the world will be salivating.

Still, few legends have taken quite as much time out as Donald Fagen, erstwhile frontman with the indisputably legendary Steely Dan. Over a decade has now elapsed since Fagen released his masterful solo album, 'The Nightfly', and in that time there's been scant word from the man: a short-lived column for *Premiere*; the soundtrack to the lame *Bright Lights, Big City*; a low-key reunion with his old partner Walter Becker on flame-haired Rosie Vela's 'Zazu' album. But nothing substantial until his appearance as ringmaster at the festival circus that was 1991's New York Rock and Soul Revue, an all-star live affair on which the likes of Boz Scaggs and old Dan hand Michael McDonald applied their chops to Fagen's favourite R&B/soul chestnuts.

So what in God's name has Donald Fagen *done* for ten years?

'Well, the Eighties weren't very inspiring for a start,' says the unassuming-looking character who sits opposite me in lopsided wireframe glasses and a pair of shoes that definitely do *not* become a legend. It's as if I'm meeting the man Donald Fagen could so easily become: a fortysomething Jewish academic on some upstate liberal arts campus, not the singing half of the most brilliant rock duo of the Seventies.

'More to the point,' he continues, 'I'd used up all I knew on "The Nightfly", and I had to live another ten years to write a new album. Basically, I was just trying to get a life, having been a workaholic ever since I was in college. I'd never been able to figure out what to do with myself when I wasn't writing or recording, and it was time to learn. You know . . . getting into relationships . . . getting out of relationships. I even practised the piano a little.' He manages a faint smile and sinks into the black leather sofa in his publicist's office. Outside, high above Broadway, on an early March afternoon, snowflakes whirl ineffectually through the sky, failing to settle on the window ledge as on the blustery streets below.

This 'new album', for those of you who've given up keeping tabs on the activities of Messrs Becker and Fagen, is the intriguingly-titled 'Kamakiriad', on Warners – a company which wisely agreed to let Fagen take his time when they signed him back in 1981. ('I told them there was no way I could be sure of meeting any particular deadlines,' he says.) Produced by Becker and recorded over a period of two and a half years in New York and Hawaii, it's an extraordinary 'comeback' for two principal reasons: first, because it is set in the future, towards the end of the millennium, thereby dashing the hopes of anyone counting on some retro-*nuevo* reprise of 'The Nightfly'; and second, because almost every one of its eight tracks boasts the kind of kick-ass funk grooves that were only ever implicit in the music of Steely Dan. Rhythm one expected of Donald Fagen, a virtual *dance* album comes as something of a shock.

'It's a little more aggressive than anything I've done before,' concedes the man in the wire frames. 'Dance music to me is still the soul of the Sixties and the funk of the Seventies, and that's kind of what I wanted to capture on the record – funk based on sixteenth rather than eighth-notes, everything from Sly to Earth, Wind & Fire. I was writing the album at the time when we were putting the Rock and Soul Revue together, and that whole experience had a major impact on the songs.'

The marriage of Fagen and Becker's nouveau Nineties funk with Fagen's inspired sci-fi imagery – the Kamakiri of the title, for instance, is a steam-driven car with its very own hydroponic vegetable garden! – makes for some bizarre listening. Take 'Springtime', a close encounter between Philip K. Dick and early Marvin Gaye in some twilight-zone timewarp:

'*Easter Break '66*
A shack on Cape Sincere
Mad Mona bakin' gospel strudel
It was a radical year . . .'

Or 'Tomorrow's Girls', whose glorious pop chorus marks it out as a potential hit single of the order of Fagen's classic 'I.G.Y.': the B-52s meet *The Stepford Wives*, anyone?

'They're mixing with the population
A virus wearing pumps and pearls
Lord help the lonely guys
Hooked by those hungry eyes . . .'

Clearly Fagen's prodigious lyrical gifts have not deserted him, but what's it all about?

In the album's brief sleeve-note, Fagen explains that 'Kamakiriad' is the story of a journey in which 'each song is a charming detour or dangerous adventure along the way'. Slumped on the sofa opposite me, he adds that his peripatetic hero is 'kind of a fuck-up, but with excellent intentions': 'As in all the grand old myths, he only really discovers his destination as he continues along. The journey can be taken on different levels, of course: the literal level of the action, and then a deeper psychological level.' Fagen further contends that 'Kamakiriad' 'completes some inherent trilogy, with "The Nightfly" being the past, the Steely Dan records being about the present as it unfolded, and this album being about the future.'

Whether any of that will make the record less bemusing to the world at large is hard to predict: I fear Fagen may lose hardcore Dan fans without gaining a substantial number of new ones. (I also have reservations about Walter Becker's production: perhaps it's the hand of Dan/'Nightfly' producer Gary Katz that's the major missing ingredient here.) For the sake of sabbatical-taking iconoclasts the world over, I hope I'm wrong.

Whatever one's feeling about Fagen's new music – and an initial disappointment is perhaps inevitable after the pristine perfection of 'The Nightfly' – it is hard to begrudge the man his new spirit of celebration. (There's a deliciously desolate jazz ballad that dates back to the 'Nightfly' era – 'On The Dunes' – but the remainder of the songs are all upbeat.) It would seem that, for Fagen, 'getting a life' has partly entailed the thawing-out of everything that was so coldly aloof about Steely Dan, a process which began with the Rock and Soul Revue and now continues with the kinetic workouts of 'Countermoon' and 'TransIsland Skyway'. Certainly the Revue was hardly something that Steely Dan, those malcontented New York misfits let loose in Hollywood Babylon, would have had much truck with. But Steely Dan never had much truck with anyone but themselves.

'In Steely Dan we were very arrogant kids,' says Fagen, 'and when life starts to kick you around, you have to swallow your pride. See, there was a real family feeling about the Rock and Soul Revue that I'd never experienced before, and certainly not in Steely Dan. In a way, people from my generation have had to create new families, since their own families have so often failed to satisfy the needs that a family historically provided.'

Donald Fagen, a Dysfunctional Family man? I never thought I'd live to see the day. So is he repudiating the blistering cynicism, the merciless irony, of the great Becker/Fagen songs?

'No, because it wasn't like we were promoting or endorsing that cynical attitude. We were just reflecting the *Zeitgeist*, talking about the way the world seemed to us in the Seventies. But by the end, when we were making 'Gaucho', I think both Walter and I were down and depressed, and both of us really had to make changes.'

In Becker's case, the changes included the termination of a hazardous drug habit and the adoption of an idyllic Hawaiian lifestyle that, in Fagen's words, 'is very amusing to me, and to him as well'. In Fagen's case, the changes have simply been about coming in from the cold.

That Fagen has begun to *join in* is evident from his appearance several hours after our interview at a sub-Rock and Soul Revue hoedown at the Lone Star Roadhouse on West 52nd Street. This 'New York Night', like the Revue itself, is the brainchild of Fagen's companion, Libby Titus, who I suspect has had to push her reclusive paramour into having the kind of sloppy, informal fun for which all these all-star Lone Star jams are renowned. 'The whole thing started when Libby asked if I'd do a jazz evening with Mac Rebennack [Dr John],' says Fagen. 'I then helped put together a show celebrating the songs of Bert Berns and Jerry Ragovoy, using all the great New York musicians who'd played on their records – like Paul Griffin and Jerry Jermott. The evenings got so popular we ended up at the Beacon Theatre.'

The trouble is, the moment Fagen walks on, unannounced, to take his place alongside such luminaries as Al Kooper and Elliot Randall (the almost-legendary axeman who soloed on 'Reelin' In The Years'), he looks distinctly out of place. In straining to get down with these dishevelled old lags, he only accentuates the distance between himself and rock'n'roll in general. For the fact is that Fagen is not a joiner-in, even if Libby Titus has managed to convince him that he is, or that it's somehow good for him. Nor are his makeshift renditions of 'Green Earrings', 'FM', and 'Josie' far short of torturous, since Fagen is barely able to stay in tune on any of them. Only when Chuck Jackson, that now-forgotten legend of the uptown New York soul which Fagen so loves, strides on to sing Leiber & Stoller's wacky 1963 beat concerto 'I Keep Forgettin'' (covered by Bowie on 'Tonight') does out hero's face momentarily light up.

As I watch him, I'm asking myself whether this is supposed to be some sort of therapy for the man who called a halt to all live performances after the ill-tempered 'Pretzel Logic' tour nearly 20 years ago. And I'm wondering if, after all, the point of Donald Fagen doesn't lie precisely in his detachment, his distance from such beery gatherings as this 'New York Night'. Yes, Steely Dan were cold, soulless, fetishists of the studio and 'funked-up muzak'. But next to all the phoney passion and bravado of most rock music, that in itself was bracing. In the wake of The Great Grunge Overkill, moreover, we have much to learn from the classicism and strategy of vintage Becker and Fagen. Moreover, I'm far from convinced that whooping it up with clapped-out Al Kooper and Co – or exhuming soporific Seventies jazz-funk on 'Kamakiriad's' 'Florida Room', come to that – is really the answer for Fagen himself. At the Lone Star Roadhouse, he doesn't look too convinced either. Perhaps that's why he failed to mention the show during our interview.

'*You take a walk on Bleak Street, tonight could be the night you crash*,' Fagen sings on 'Teahouse On The Tracks', the album's spirited finale. '*Then you turn and stop, start to fingerpop . . .*' Perhaps this is what Fagen himself has done: turned and stopped, picked up some life-affirming beat. '*From somewhere deep inside you*,' he sings, '*some frozen stuff begins to crack.*'

Me, I miss the frozen stuff of Steely Dan's glory days – the grim comedy and clinical precision that sheared away all the bullshit of rock'n'roll. I just hope Donald Fagen doesn't thaw out completely.

Copyright © Barney Hoskyns, 1993

———————————

It's a Man's, Man's, Man's, Man's World

Heroes by Alan Moore

September 1993

M Y NAME IS ALAN, and I am a heroholic. I've been straight
for years now, but some scars never heal. Before I
allowed relatives to enter me in a 12-step programme,
I was one of the worst, a hero-broker, fencing fantasies
to a ring of teenage addicts.

Down at the Dream Distillery, I hung with a hardcore crowd. I
had dinner with Jerry Siegel, the writer who created Superman,
and I gave a goodnight peck on the cheek to his wife Joanne, the
original model for Lois Lane. Tim Burton bought me lunch and
sought my advice on how to handle Gotham City in his then-forth-
coming first Batman movie. I was asked to write *Robocop II* (but
declined, having begun by then to come to terms with my problem)
and still consider myself a close friend of the Teenage Mutant
Ninja Turtles.

I first heard the alarm bells clearly while I was working on the
Watchmen graphic novel with Dave Gibbons. We'd created a character named Rorschach with the intention of satirising the obsessed
vigilante-type prevalent in comic books back then and still wildly
popular to this day. We portrayed the character as a slum-dwelling
paranoid, a right-wing borderline psychotic with no friends, no sex
life, a complex about his size and a lax attitude to personal hygiene. What we had obviously failed to consider was the fact that
a large section of our audience, adolescent boys unencumbered by
girlfriends or the concept of intimate freshness, would see this as
heroic rather than satiric.

The key element, naturally, was the violence: Rorschach, as a
character, was presented as being totally dysfunctional in any social sphere other than those connected with physical retribution.
What we'd overlooked was that to a contemporary audience, this
is *no bad thing*. Ask Arnold Schwarzenegger's accountant and he'll
tell you just the same. It doesn't matter a jot that the hero has no
verbal or social skills; that he has no opinions whatsoever about
art or music; that his range of emotional responses is inferior to

that of the average kelp bed. The important thing is that he kicks ass and isn't frightened of anything. Unlike us. In the majority of ass-related exchanges, we are more likely, on balance, to be the kickee rather than the kicker, and as a result we get frightened all the time.

I believe the phrase I'm looking for here is 'Revenge Fantasies of the Impotent'. I saw it on a T-shirt last week and it has the ring of truth. It might be argued that heroism doesn't have to be based on revenge, or violence, or indeed upon anything physical at all, but while I'd certainly agree in theory with this, it takes only a cursory glance around modern culture to confirm that this theory is not widely applied. While there is an undeniably heroic glow surrounding Stephen Hawking, I'm willing to bet good money that Norman Schwarzkopf's biography makes it to the big screen first.

The problem is probably not so much with heroes as with the political, social and market forces that inevitably manipulate them. You'll note, as a for instance, that I have not bothered to employ the feminine form of the word 'hero' thus far. This is mainly because heroism, as currently defined by our media, is an almost exclusively male preserve, the current rash of quasi-feminist adventure movies notwithstanding.

Films such as the *Terminator* series are allowed to have female leads as long as they behave exactly as a man would do in the same circumstances. Sigourney Weaver is allowed to take centre stage in *Alien III: Sinéad O'Connor Goes To Hell*, but only on the condition that she has an androgynously muscular physique and dresses like someone who shifts cement blocks for a living. Even dear old Thelma and Louise emerge from beneath their veneer of social relevance long enough to blow up a couple of petrol tankers and go out in a blaze of glory that Butch and Sundance would surely have approved of.

Heroes are boys. Moreover, they are tough, physically active boys who reach for their Browning when they hear the word 'quiche'. The only other qualification is that politically, they should be somewhere to the right of General Franco. This last point was probably the one responsible for the second, decisive stage of my conversion.

After *Watchmen*, I handled a documentary project entitled *Brought To Light*, being a history of the activities of the Central Intelligence Agency from the end of World War II up to the present day. In many ways, it wasn't that much of a departure from the earlier super-hero work: both, after all, featured blackly comical parodies of the traditional hero figure.

The difference was that in *Brought To Light*, those parody heroes were real flesh and blood people: nun-slaughtering Contras hailed by former cowboy hero Ronald Reagan as 'freedom fighters'; Oliver North, a middle-ranking army officer with a history of mental instability who, incredibly, was able to emerge from the sleazy, blood-spattered corruption of Irangate as a full-blown American icon in the tradition of Davy Crockett. Here were Dirty Harry and Batman, somehow escaped to the real world with their B-movie morality and their comic-book solutions intact.

This political point is important: we get the heroes that we are allowed. The young man turning back the tanks in Peking was allowed to be a hero, just as Jan Pallach was allowed to be a hero for immolating himself before the Russian tanks as they rolled into Prague, just as Lech Walesa was allowed to be a hero for standing up to communist authorities in Gdansk. Anti-communist heroes, even suicidal ones, are permitted. The unemployed man who burned in his car at the bottom of Downing Street towards the end of the Thatcher years, however, was an anti-monetarist hero and is thus forgotten.

Hero worship is a dangerous thing. Ronald Reagan's white stetson did more to get him into an equally White House than his political acumen ever did. Anti-war campaigners in America during the Eighties gave Sly Stallone's *Rambo* series a major share of the credit for that decade's bulge in the army enlistment figures. Hitler, Thatcher, Charlie Manson: they were charismatic heroes all, revered in certain quarters to this day. Heady and intoxicating as a hero-binge can be, the effects can prove to be harmful to our health, both as nations and as individuals. Next time somebody tries to sell you a hero, just say 'no'.

Tell 'em that a shuffling derelict with a haunted look and a threadbare Spiderman costume said so.

Copyright © Alan Moore, 1993

Gender Benders

Why Women Shouldn't Drink by Tony Parsons
November 1993

W
HY SHOULD A WOMAN never get drunk? Because being drunk makes you loud, obnoxious, sentimental, self-pitying and stupid. And of course most women are like that when they are completely sober.

There are some things in this world that women do better than men. Shopping, weeping hysterically and cleaning up around the house – women do all these things brilliantly and we should go down the pub and let them get on with it.

But one of the things that women should leave to men is getting drunk. Being drunk is like having a moustache. It looks good on a man and terrible on a woman.

Drunkenness does not suit all men, of course. After two cocktails, a few beers and half a bottle of Chardonnay, most men do not become better people. In fact, they are far more likely to become troglodytes who swear eternal friendship one minute and threaten to punch your face in the next. But while some men make bad drunks, *all* women are bad drunks.

The dark side of drunkenness is raised voices, casual violence, crazy laughter, unwise sex – it makes a man look like a fool. But it makes a woman look insane.

There are some men – the urbane, the sophisticated, the lovers of life – who can handle getting drunk. After a hard day at the office, a little bacchanalian excess actually improves a few of us. After the pressures and stress of the working world, with a few drinks inside us we become more relaxed, more open and more talkative. But did you ever meet a woman who needed to become more talkative? Too much drink tends to remove a woman's dignity, pride and underpants – usually in that order.

And alcohol is powerful stuff. It can bring you down. Sometimes you have a few glasses of vino and soon you are pondering the very nature of existence. This kind of philosophical, moody introspection does not suit women. Because they are intuitive rather than cerebral creatures, it makes them sad and bitter. It makes them think too much – and that is not what they are best at.

After a few drinks, a man will say something like, 'If God really exists, then why does He allow so much suffering in the world?' But a drunken woman is far more likely to say, 'My mother warned me about you and she was absolutely right, you filthy bastard!'

Drinks tends to emphasise all that is unpleasant about a woman. If she is a bit of a slut, then getting drunk will find her offering a blow job to the wine waiter. If she is over-emotional, then getting drunk will find her overturning tables, throwing plates and cutting up your clothes with a pair of shearing scissors. If she has a rather melancholy personality, then getting drunk will make her suicidal. Drink is poison to the female heart. No matter what her personality is like, it will be made much worse by drinking alcohol.

Some men look wonderful when they are drunk. I have a friend who, when he is really smashed, leans back in his chair, develops this glassy look in his eyes and gets this little secret smile playing around the corners of his mouth. About two minutes later he usually falls off his chair but in that short time before he disappears he is a charming and delightful companion.

But his girlfriend drinks just as much as he does and it doesn't do anything for her. She suddenly develops this uncontrollable urge to discuss French cinema. As you can imagine, this completely spoils the evening.

There are approximately ten million wonderful women in the world. But not one of them is made more interesting, more attractive or more loveable when she is drunk. It doesn't matter if she is a high-powered career woman with a university degree or a suburban _hausfrau_ with a gold ankle chain, drink brings out the worst in her. There is something sluttish about a pissed female. A drunken woman seems – and tends to act – like a waterfront strumpet. And I don't feel like discussing French cinema with her. I feel like selling her to a couple of sailors.

And though some men are made more charming, extrovert and garrulous by drink, in all honesty alcohol usually just makes us behave badly too. We try to get total strangers to go to bed with us, we get into arguments with their boyfriends, we piss out of the windows of train. OK, we have all done it. _But there is not a woman alive who looks good trying to piss out of the window of a train._

There are men who get drunk and become sentimental, depressed and incoherent. It certainly doesn't look good on them. But it looks far worse on a woman. And if a man wants a sentimental, depressed and incoherent woman, he can always stay at home with his wife.

Drinking is a man's world. Pubs, bars, clubs – these are the hunting grounds of the male of the species. It's good that women are there but if they are talking too loudly, making fools of themselves and making stupid jokes – if they are drunk – then it spoils the fun. Who wants women to act exactly the same as us? Who is wearing the trousers around here? Who is paying for the drinks? OK, OK – so the modern woman pays her way. But heterosexuality is a celebration of differences. A drunken woman acts like a bad imitation of a man.

Alcohol is a powerful drug and nobody can truly predict the effect it is going to have. After the third bottle of sweet dessert wine, there is just no telling how you are going to feel. The roulette wheel of intoxication – you never know where it is going to take you. You never know if you are going to spend all evening laughing, or get into a fight with a policeman or wake up naked in an alley tied to a lamppost only a few postal districts from where your friends have hidden your clothes. And no woman should ever be that out of control. I am with Camille Paglia on this one – it's too dangerous for women. We are equal but different.

I am not advocating that women should abstain from alcohol. Far from it! Women should all be able to drink a little bit. Like knowing how to massage and sew buttons and change the wheel on a car, drinking in moderation is one of those skills that every woman should have – just as a man should know how to cook, take care of babies and operate the washing machine without a phone call to his mother.

Women should be able to take a sip of spritzer or even – on very special occasions – a small glass of white wine. Because there is nothing worse than going out for dinner with a woman, ordering a bottle of wine and then having to drink it all yourself. When a man goes out with a woman who doesn't drink at all, he always gets far drunker than he intended to.

But the trouble is that women either drink too little or too much. They either can't smell a barmaid's apron without getting completely drunk or else they don't know when to stop. When a woman starts ordering aperitifs, a second bottle of wine and a cognac, you should immediately throw away her telephone number. She will be boring to talk to and equally boring in bed. Drink is *not* an aphrodisiac, not for any of us. Drink is not like having Spanish Fly – it is more like having hermetically sealed pyjamas.

Although when we were teenagers we tried to get local girls

drunk so that we could stick it in them, there is actually little joy to be had from making love to a drunken female. We only did it when we were teenagers because there was no other kind available. But in bed a drunken woman is either completely inert, laying there like a dead fish, or else she goes to the other extreme and imagines she is in a remake of *Fatal Attraction*, bouncing around on top of the dishwasher until she starts turning green and asks you, 'Quick – where's the bathroom?' Either way, you are not really fucking her. You are only fucking some drunk.

But if there is one thing uglier than a drunken woman then it is a woman with a hangover. A hangover – the dry mouth, sore eyes, bilious stomach, throbbing head, sinking exhaustion and stinking self-loathing – is bad enough when it is happening to you. When it is happening to the woman you are waking up with, it is even worse. Who wants to wake up with someone who looks as bad as you do?

So why do they do it? Why do modern women – friends, colleagues, lovers – try to drink like men? Why can't they stick to a couple of small spritzers and a packet of pork scratchings? Because they have grown up being taught by the shrill vixens of feminism that men and women are the same. Anything we can do, they can do too. But this is bullshit. Men and women are equal but we are most certainly not the same. When women look good with moustaches and pissing out of train windows, that's when I'll be ready to do some serious drinking with them.

It is time for all men to admit that we disapprove of drunken women. In his heart, no man wants to be around a stumbling woman who slurs her words, laughs too much, talks too loud, flirts with anything that moves, throws up in the taxi on the way home and then sinks into a deep depression. No man wants to go out with a bore or go to bed with a dead fish. No man wants a drunken woman.

They make you ashamed, disgusted and embarrassed. Even more importantly, they make you spill your drink.

Copyright © Tony Parsons, 1993

Equal Measure

Why Women *Should* Drink by Suzanne Moore
December 1993

'**I**'LL JUST HAVE a mineral water please.' My heart sinks. With these words another evening ends before it can begin. It's not that I expect my female friends, sophisticated intellectuals that they all are, to still drink snakebite or Cinzano and lemonade. But I do expect them to drink. They can drown themselves in bottled water for all I care, they can sip spritzers with their dodgy dates, they can be as sober as judges for endless 'Our Bodies Ourselves' sex with their boring boyfriends. But with me . . . well, quite honestly I expect them to get drunk.

Just how drunk is up to them. Unlike Tony Parsons, I am not so afraid of what a drunken woman might do that I feel the need to legislate their behaviour, nor do I have such a limited view of what correct feminine behaviour is or, thank God, continually need to remind the rest of the world of what a big man I am. But then Parsons comes on like the proverbial wind-up merchant you find perched at the bar in every boozer, insulting every woman just for the crack, just to get a response.

Indeed one of the reasons women feel awkward going into bars alone is because there is always some idiot there who feels it his duty to comment on their dress, their drink, the book they are reading. Such men can only reassert their fragile sense of masculinity by policing the boundaries of femininity with neurotic dedication.

Parsons writes, 'We are equal but different.' I'll drink to that. When women get drunk we may do many of the things Parsons accuses us of. We may be loud, obnoxious, sentimental. We may even want sex. We may, indeed, end up in a heap, crying on the floor, or in bed with highly unsuitable people. We may *only* want to have sex with men when we are paralytic. We may, in fact, act very stupidly indeed. On the whole, however, women when drunk do not commit violent crimes, do not wreck other peoples' homes and lives, do not rape and murder, do not intimidate passers-by, do not beat people up because they are foreign or support a different football team.

I won't bore you with the statistics, but the majority of violent crimes are committed by young males under the influence of alcohol. And, if we really want to be heavy about it, the Serbian soldiers who raped three-year-old girls to death were charged up on the lethal cocktail of booze, hatred and the need to perform the heady rituals of male bonding. Is this, I wonder, what Parsons means by serious drinking? I'd call it pretty serious. Is this the world that Parsons wants to shut women out of? By all means Tony, you are welcome to it.

Yet it is my experience that, far from finding women who drink revolting, men are desperate for us. They literally will not leave us alone. You can be on all fours at a party, throwing up in the loo, and some berk will still be trying to touch you up. It seems to me that the average man has strong necrophilic urges and, on occasion, is perfectly happy to fuck a temporary corpse. Perhaps it's the only time they don't have to worry about their performance, or pretend to like foreplay. This would certainly appear to be borne out by the recent cases in which those hard-done-by young men such as Diggle and Donnellan thought it perfectly normal to have sex with blind drunk girls (one of whom described herself as 'a semi-comatose vegetable'). Fact is, men just can't get enough of inebriated women. Women who so desire can always smear themselves with those lager-flavoured booby drops available from Ann Summers, or cover themselves in Moët. And forget Bloody Marys – everyone surely knows that the only hangover cure that actually works is a multiple orgasm.

It would be totally irresponsible of me to pretend that getting drunk is always good. I certainly drink less than I used to. Looking back, I've had whole relationships based almost entirely on alcohol. 'Let's have a bottle of Tequila and a fight . . .' was how one of my exes used to start the evening. Reader, I *married* him.

Doubtless this makes me an instant candidate for the Betty Ford Clinic, but hey, what can I say except that, given the chance I'd do it all again. Of course drink is simply one drug among many. A lot of young women now prefer to suppress their appetite with Ecstasy rather than consume vast amounts of what Weightwatchers call 'liquid cream cakes'. However, in an era governed by the puritans who preach the banality of the 12-step programme, the last thing any of us needs is to be encouraged to be more uptight about our vices. But then I *am* the daughter of a woman who makes her own Bailey's. I can't say that I'm surprised that Tony Parsons does not like drunken women. 'They make you ashamed,' he says. What is obvious is that he does not like them very much even when they're sober And for that he should truly be ashamed.

Copyright © Suzanne Moore, 1993

Thirty-Nine Minutes and Ten Seconds with Marty
Martin Scorsese by Rob Ryan
December 1993

FEDERICO FELLINI IS ABOUT to ruin my interview with Martin Scorsese. The old charlatan had the bad grace to slip out of his coma in the wrong direction the previous day, and now Channel 4 News want Scorsese to film an obit. Scorsese is here to talk about his new film. I am here to talk to Scorsese about spaghetti sauce.

For a few frantic minutes it looks as if I will be postponed or curtailed. The room is full of 'Marty says . . .' and 'Marty wants . . .'; I, too, find myself calling the stranger next door by his diminutive. More people arrive to try and whisk Scorsese away for lunch at Langan's. Across the room I recognise the fine features of his producer Barbara De Fina, the fourth ex-Mrs Scorsese. Marty's editor Thelma Schoonmaker is also here, and we talk about 'The Red Shoes'. The Kate Bush album has just been released, and she is curious to hear it because she was married to Michael Powell, who, along with Emeric Pressburger, was responsible for the 1948 movie it's named after.

I am saved from telling her what I think of Ms Bush's effort by a sudden whirl of activity. Marty says I get first shot. Channel 4 will have to cool their heels in hospitality. I'm in.

Martin Scorsese has a winning smile and a bad cough. The first few minutes of my tape are taken up with hacking, spluttering and slurps of coffee. He is dressed smart-casual, beardless (something still hard to come to terms with: my mental image of Scorsese is frozen at the diabolical figure in the back of Travis Bickle's cab), greying hair scraped back, contrasting sharply with his untamed black eyebrows.

The coughing stops. We start. I have been asked to tread gently here: Marty's agenda is Daniel Day Lewis, Michelle Pfeiffer, Winona Ryder, Edith Wharton and Scorsese's rather atypical film of her novel, *The Age Of Innocence*. He does not want to talk about the recent death of his father.

I, on the other hand, have reservations about any in-depth dissection of a film prior to its opening, believing it is one of many ways to kill a picture stone dead. I mention, by way of illustration, that I have read one review of *The Age of Innocence* which gave away a pivotal plot point.

'It's a disaster. As far as I am concerned it is absolutely crazy. I am so surprised at some of the people . . . people who like the film, giving away that. Nearly every review. Crazy.'

Julia Phillips, producer of *Taxi Driver*, describes Scorsese in her snort'n'tell book *You'll Never Eat Lunch In This Town Again* as 'endearing and cute and inspirational'. It is easy to see what she means: after a couple of questions it is obvious that Martin Scorsese is the best of interviewees. He is respectful, thorough and funny, and his answers are illuminated with little paradigms drawn from his vast knowledge of movies. But don't ask him a two-part question, because you won't reach the second part: Marty will be off on a verbal roller coaster, riding on the rails of film history. On several occasions we have such fun with the ride, we get lost: both of us forget what the question was.

There is another plus and negative side to this conversation. No currently active director has had their career so thoroughly dissected as Scorsese: there are two *South Bank Shows*, a biography, and *Scorsese On Scorsese*, a personal account of each movie (in the US the laserdiscs of *Mean Streets* and *Raging Bull* have an extra sound channel on them, where Marty gives a blow-by-blow commentary).

He is a film student's wet dream: doubtless there are hundreds of dissertations called things like 'Power, Popery And Pasta: The Films Of Martin Scorsese' in libraries across the US. He is a compulsive communicator: he teaches, discusses, champions (Scorsese helped bring Michael Powell out of the celluloid Siberia he was consigned to after *Peeping Tom*) and campaigns, notably during the Eighties, to bring attention to the fading of colour film stock. He gives of himself freely, and after a while you begin to wonder if there is a question Marty *hasn't* answered.

I recall, however, that Michael Frayn once said that journalists are basically lazy, and recycle errors that find their way into the clippings without checking. I ask Scorsese if, given there is so much on-the-record of him, this has ever occurred.

'On almost every picture. Every one, something like that happens. *Age Of Innocence* has a very interesting one,' he pauses. 'But I don't want this to be seen as an apologia or a defence – I think the picture can stand up for itself. But at its previews at the Venice Film Festival, which was one of the greatest nights of my life, something odd happened. It was four days after my father died – the picture is dedicated to him – and I decided to take my mother along. It was a very moving experience for me. The picture was received so warmly. I know this – I have been there when an audience doesn't like your movie; believe me, you can tell. A few days later I started to read that the picture had been disliked, had been attacked, and I couldn't understand it. For me that night was like the end of the funeral, a family affair. So I kept quiet: I didn't want to talk about my father and I didn't want to be seen defending the film. But it seems one journalist came up with this line, and it spread and spread and eventually appeared in the *New York Times* that the film had been badly received at Venice. It wasn't true.'

I am not certain whether the part about his father is a veiled warning to me, but it is hard to underestimate the impact of Charles Lucciano Scorsese on his son's career. It was his dad who took the asthmatic little boy to the movies because he couldn't play sports. It was Charlie who inspired *Mean Streets*, the breakthrough feature for Scorsese. 'Although it was about my friends and the area we grew up in, yes, that film is also based on my father. He was a man who tried to live a decent life in that particular world. And that was very hard. Very hard.'

We move on to his other movies. But Scorsese hates making movies. 'Look, I always try to have fun on the set, but I have to say that if it is fun you are after, there are better places. I do not like the business of actually realising a scene from the script. What I really enjoy is the editing.' Yet the editing is always, since *Raging Bull*, credited to that polite grey-haired woman out in the hall, Thelma Schoonmaker, whom Scorsese first met when they worked on editing *Woodstock*. Ironically, in order to get a full union card as editor, Schoonmaker subsequently had to work mutilating films for late-night television slots, one of which was Visconti's *Rocco And His Brothers*, a major inspiration for *Raging Bull*.

So what is the dynamic between the two of them? It turns out that he is the backseat driver of the editing suite. 'I have a little chair and sit behind Thelma; I tell her what I want, and she tries to do it. Her main influence is asking *why* something I want isn't working, in developing the characters and in getting the rhythm of the scenes.'

Raging Bull got Schoonmaker an Academy Award (which she has claimed really belongs to Marty) and remains the benchmark of his career. He agrees it was a crucial film for him. 'I feel like I have had my career pulled away from me twice. After the success of *Taxi Driver* came the flop of *New York, New York*, for which I largely blame myself. I was desolate. I felt I had let everybody down: they had allowed this great experiment, and it hadn't worked. That is why I cut the film on the second run, so it could play more theatres to try to get some money back. But the construction of the scenes should have been a lot sharper.' *New York, New York* bombed spectacularly: even the instant standard title song didn't make it to the Oscar nominations. 'I felt as if I was humiliated in the eyes of Hollywood. I began a pretty destructive lifestyle.' This period, 1976 to 1978, was when he and Robbie Robertson of The Band (he had filmed *The Last Waltz* on the coat-tails of *New York, New York*) cohabited, so was it a case of 'Martin Scorsese: The Rock'n'Roll Years'?

'Well, all my years have been rock'n'roll years, kind of, but yes, these were my *rock'n'roll* years. I was pretty angry at myself, more so than usual.' The excesses eventually delivered Scorsese to hospital with internal bleeding, and it was De Niro who pulled him around by cajoling him to make the Jake La Motta story. 'I worked out all that anger on *Raging Bull*. I put everything into it, because I thought I had no career left.' Kamikaze film-making he called it.

Raging Bull capped *Taxi Driver* in critical and commercial terms, giving Schoonmaker and De Niro Academy Awards. 'Then I made *King Of Comedy*, which wiped out my career a second time.' Possibly the subject of obsessive hero worship, and the consummately creepy Rupert Pupkin, touched a raw nerve in a celebrity-saturated culture like the US. 'It certainly confused audiences; it was a financial disaster. I then had *Last Temptation Of Christ* taken away from me.' This was the first version, which had Aidan Quinn rather than Willem Dafoe as Jesus and, in place of Bowie, Sting as Pontius Pilot. 'They told me on December 23, 1983 that they weren't interested. Two weeks before shooting. Happy Christmas. A few days later I left for New York and never went back.'

So does he equate LA with unhappiness? 'I do now. But the beginning of the Seventies, there were so many directors hanging out together. De Palma, Coppola, Milius, Spielberg – the energy was incredible and the ambition was frightening: 'I'm going to do a Western', 'I want to direct a Dostoyevsky story', and films were getting made. But the egos. There wasn't room in the same room, the same *house* for all our egos. It was the decade of the director – you could make pretty much what you wanted. That's all over now, so these days I associate LA with the failure of *New York, New York* and with the cancellation of *Last Temptation*.'

Scorsese describes the next few years as 'a journey I had to make. I had to regenerate myself, which I did through *After Hours* and *The Color Of Money*. By then I realised that I was pretty much on the outside of the system. I had become much more open to things, more reflective, both personally and professionally. It was then I read *The Age Of Innocence*. Here, in London, January 1987 [he had actually been given the book by his friend and co-writer Jay Cocks in 1980], and I felt ready to do it.' What, given that it is far removed from the usual Scorsese rough and tumble, attracted him? 'I was drawn to the exquisite sadness, the . . . romantic pain of it.'

This particular romantic pain has had a lengthy gestation, not only because editing was delayed by his father's stroke, but because other projects slipped in ahead, most importantly the catharsis of finally filming, albeit on a shoestring, because he wasn't sure it would ever play, *The Last Temptation*. Then came *Life Lessons* (the first, and best, part of the *New York Stories* trilogy), *GoodFellas* and the disappointing remake of *Cape Fear*. On the latter, Elmer Bernstein (*The Magnificent Seven*, *The Man With The Golden Arm* and now *The Age Of Innocence*) reorchestrated the score from the original Mitchum/Peck movie, the work of the late Bernard Herrmann. Scorsese had worked with Herrmann on what transpired to be the latter's final score, the wonder that is the *Taxi Driver* soundtrack: producer Julia Phillips described him as 'a disagreeable but talented old codger'.

'Yes, he was an . . . irritable old man,' agrees Scorsese. 'Quite formidable. But also a man with a bad heart, by the way, who walked with a cane. When you are short of breath it makes you very impatient. I know that from my asthma. So, yes he was difficult. Elmer kept saying, I bet old Bennie is growling at us right now. I used Elmer because I love his own music.'

Scorsese devours music the way he does films, and not only soundtracks. 'I have to have music with me wherever I go. We are currently cataloguing all the music I have liked over the years, on to DAT tapes, A to Z. One for opera, one for classical, soundtracks, oldies. I have just finished the first compilation, 26 tapes. I have them with me now.' The tapes contain Van Morrison, Peter Gabriel, Springsteen, Lou Reed and . . . Procol Harum? Ah, yes, 'A Whiter Shade Of Pale' figures prominently in _Life Lessons_. I tell him I have always hated that song.

'Yes, well it evoked a certain melancholy for me. A certain nostalgia. And I really like their later stuff. 'A Salty Dog'? Extraordinary album, great lyrics, Robin Trower on guitar.' Does he listen to new music? 'Some. But over the past five, six, seven years, I find I don't care for the stuff I hear. Just not interested.'

I suggest that this could be a function of age. 'Possibly it is age. I don't know.' He has just turned 51, and I ask him if reaching his sixth decade has changed anything else. 'Well I am less confrontational. I used to be like . . . remember James Mason in that film he produced, _Larger Than Life_, directed by Nic Ray?'

Scorsese does this often, drags up some obscure movie that is only ever shown at anti-social hours. He has them all, on video, on 16mm. Michael Ovitz has said of him: 'You can call up Marty at 1am and there is a flickering sound – he is watching an old movie. Not only can he remember every scene but he can quote the dialogue. His whole life is consumed with film.' I am treated to a chunk of cortisone-deranged James Mason, afflicted with an overwhelming sense of his own importance, berating the milkman for rattling his bottles and interrupting his thinking.

'We used to laugh at that, because I would be working late at night and people would come in to clean up. They would start the Hoover outside. I would say [adopts almost Woody Allen-ish inflection]: _Are they mad? Don't they know what I am doing here?_ Thelma would have to say, Marty, they are only doing their job. I suppose when I was younger I was more abrasive and demanding and . . . contentious. But out of passion . . . I don't _like_ to fight. I never even raise my voice on the set.'

Scorsese quotes _Larger Than Life_ again when I ask him how much he identified with Lionel Dobie in _Life Lessons_, whose personal relationships are invariably compromised by his art. After all, Marty's record in marriages (fellow student Larraine Brennan in 1964, Julia Cameron in 1975, Isabella Rossellini in 1979 and Barbara De Fina in 1985) is not quite as 18-carat as his one in movies. 'I think it's possible to take an over-romantic view of this. You have to have a sense of humour, or you could again end up with an inflated view of yourself. But there is some truth in that movie about how it affects the energy of the work: there is no doubt that one way out of a relationship is to drain the other person away by working, working. It happens.'

One relationship Scorsese finds difficult is between his friends and his work. 'This is a delicate thing. These days I find there are very few people you can show the rough cut of your movie to, very few friends who will first of all not be malicious . . . not be envious . . . or will not overpraise you because they are afraid. Getting an honest reaction is almost impossible. People do not feel free to say what they think. What we have to do is decide what they are saying, and Thelma usually does that on the phone the next day. You have to drag out of them what they hated, loved, was too slow, what they didn't understand. It's a real problem, believe me.'

He describes waiting for the reaction of the UK and Europe to his new movie as 'nerve wracking'. *The Age Of Innocence* is a magnificent realisation of Edith Wharton's novel of New York high society in the 1870s, a world every bit as vicious and codified in its own way as Scorsese's usual milieu, the Mob. My only reservation is that it is possibly too magnificent for its own good.

Scorsese once said about *The Color Of Money*: 'It is possible to get too wrapped up in research and begin to lose sight of what a film is about. You get into too much detail.' The details in *Innocence* are so sumptuous, so exquisitely shot (the way the cameras linger over the dinner plates borders on gastroporn) that the effect is mesmerising. I found myself so fascinated by bow ties and plates of canvasback ducks and floral arrangements and bustles and ballrooms that, for me, the 'exquisite sadness' between Daniel Day Lewis and Michelle Pfeiffer took second billing. I tell him I feel a need to see it again. He isn't surprised. 'There is a lot in there. It isn't designed to be seen more than once, but we found that people, studio people and friends, were coming back to view it a second time.'

The next project for Scorsese Inc remains the subject of much speculation. There is talk of a Western: he still cites John Ford, and *The Searchers* in particular, as a major influence. He has an option on *Clockers*, the sprawling dialogue-driven novel by Richard Price (screenwriter on *The Color Of Money* and *Life Lessons*). This is prime Scorsese territory – a young black crack dealer trying to survive in the New Jersey projects: a basically decent person in a wicked world. Then there is a 15-year-old script, contents classified, that Scorsese is reworking, plus the possibility of 'another way of looking at the Mob' with Nick Pileggi, who wrote the book that became *GoodFellas*.

Suddenly, time is up. Those Channel 4 heels are well and truly chilled, and they want their soundbites. I realise we never got on to spaghetti sauce. Michael Powell once categorised Scorsese as a sensualist, a lover of good food and wine, and food is central to _The Age Of Innocence_, to _GoodFellas_ (even at his most coked-out, paranoid Henry Hill still frets about his meatball sauce) and to _Italianamerican_, Scorsese's wonderfully touching 1974 short about his parents. So Marty, can you make your mother's spectacular spaghetti sauce? 'No. I never had the time to learn to cook. Always too busy.' And then to his assistant: 'Is there time for a break? No? OK.' Martin Scorsese shrugs, clears his throat, and prepares to talk some more.

Copyright © Rob Ryan, 1993

One for the Road
Route 66 by Dylan Jones
July 1994

A S INEFFABLY JOYFUL journeys go, it is one of the best, as well as one of the longest. As road journeys go, there is no-thing to touch it. US Route 66 was stamped on the American public's consciousness in 1926, when the high-way was christened. It soon became known as America's Main Street, a road that stretched all the way from Chicago in the North East, to Santa Monica Beach on the West Coast. Snaking its way across eight states (Illinois, Missouri, Arkansas, Oklahoma, Texas, New Mexico, Arizona and California), this concrete and asphalt ribbon was once America's favourite thoroughfare, down which millions of tourists pushed their Detroit steel, looking for the new world, or simply the definitive road experience.

What it did best was move people in large numbers. During World War II it was used to shift millions of US troops, while a decade earlier it became an escape route for dust bowl pilgrims, fleeing in packs for the balmy palms and optimism of California. Sixty six came to encapsulate the Great Depression, most famously in John Steinbeck's _The Grapes Of Wrath_ (he re-christened it The Mother Road) as well as in the songs of Woody Guthrie.

But Mother is not what she was, and since the route was disfranchised, both traffic and people have slowed to a trickle. The most renowned stretch – from Oklahoma to Los Angeles – is now serviced by Interstate 40, which runs along much of old 66, making a mockery of its maverick status. Here cars are few and far between, driven by people who aren't in too much of a hurry. As Michael Wallis writes in *Route 66: The Mother Road*, 'Sixty six is for people who find time holy.' It still is.

The road cuts a swathe through three of the continent's eight bioregions, through the Great Plains and the Colorado Plateau. It also passes the Mississippi River, the Grand Canyon, the Hoover Dam, and the Joshua Tree forest, crossing mountains, deserts, plains and canyons. If it's American history you want, then The Mother Road has it in abundance.

It has made history, too, and during the Sixties even got its own TV series; in 120 episodes of *Route 66* two teenagers called Buz and Tod travelled the strip in their souped-up Corvette.

It also got a song: Bobby Troupe's '(Get Your Kicks On) Route 66' was never an adolescent rite of passage; not a late-Fifties teen-dream soap opera, nor an early Sixties cruisin' classic like The Beach Boys' '409'. Written in 1946, and made famous by Nat King Cole, Troupe's singing road-map helped create the highway as much as Route 66 helped him write the song. Since then it has been recorded by everyone from Chuck Berry and the Rolling Stones to Mel Tormé and Depeche Mode.

Once, the only way to negotiate the road was by buying a copy of Jack Rittenhouse's *Route 66 Guidebook*, written, like Bobby Troupe's song, in 1946. This was the first guide to cover a transcontinental highway, combining historical data, road information, and accommodation in one volume. Three thousand copies were sold at a dollar a piece, to the bookshops, newsstands, cafés, and 'tourist courts' (no one called them motels in those days) along 66. Rittenhouse made several reconnaissance trips ... 'On my final trip I had to inspect the scenery,' he wrote in the preface to the 1988 fascimile edition, 'So I drove from dawn to dusk at 35 miles an hour. There were no tape recorders then, so I scrawled notes on a big yellow pad on the seat beside me. Each night I dug out my portable manual typewriter and typed my notes.'

Nowadays the artery is serviced by many such guides – stapled pamphlets, bound paperbacks or simply photocopied freesheets. The highway even has its own glossy magazine.

* * *

To drive Route 66 is to step back in time, to relive an age when travel was still an adventure, not a necessity; an age when the car was still king. My own personal road movie began in Oklahoma and took me all the way to Santa Monica, and Palisades Park. Driving the empty, lonely Roman-like blacktop towards the Pacific is like no other experience in America, and one that is to be treasured.

It is the long stretch of the road through New Mexico, Arizona and California which conveys the strongest sense of what it must have been like to make the great crossing in the Thirties; towns out here finish before they begin, fading away into scrub. Arizona is a moonscape of monstrous proportions, Route 66's two-lane blacktop cutting through it like a charcoal arrow. Towards Winslow there is a raggedy little section of the old route that is still flanked by telegraph poles that stagger over the horizon like old men looking for the sea.

Winslow itself has been immortalised in The Eagles' soporific classic 'Take It Easy' ('_I'm standing on the corner in Winslow, Arizona/It's such a fine sight to see . . ._'), in fact driving through the Arizona heartland, the superannuated sound of Seventies FM rock really comes into its own – Steely Dan, the Doobie Brothers, Allman Brothers, Steve Miller, Poco and the rest. This, coupled with the woebegone strains of primetime doo-wop, is the soundtrack the scenery commands – the music of perpetual motion.

Arizona also contains the longest remaining uninterrupted stretch of road, between Seligman and the Colorado River at Topock, some 158 miles. This section is also one of the most beautiful, as well as one of the most haunting. The country here can make you light-hearted with solitude – creviced arroyos, harsh desert and wild bush scrub. 'Sometimes, toward either end of a long driving day,' writes Tom Snyder in _The Route 66 Traveller's Guide And Roadside Companion_, 'a run through this country brings up an ancient German word, _Sehnsucht_. It has no equivalent in English, but it represents a longing for, a need to return to, a place you've never been.'

American highways are always changing, being redirected, realigned and rebuilt. Some just disappear. Route 66 went out of official existence on June 27, 1985, when the national organisation of highway authorities decertified it. Sixty years after it was born, the highway was stripped of its identifying markings and signs, superseded by various six-lane Interstates. Not all of the road remains – some of it is closed, some of it destroyed, while other parts have fallen into terrible disrepair – but it is still possible to find patches of the old road using new guidebooks and old maps.

In Andy Bull's book *Coast To Coast: A Rock Fan's US Tour*, Jim Powell, the president of the Route 66 Association of Missouri, says: 'People in America today are rediscovering their past and harking back to an earlier time when things were slower and more peaceful. They are rediscovering two-lane highways and taking the time to get in touch with the things they have to offer. They may not make the whole trip on a two-lane road but they will get off in two- or three- or four-hour chunks to drive the really significant pieces. Once they try it, it is amazing how many people get hooked.'

In Seligman we came across a barbershop-cum-Route 66 junk shop, run by a Mr Angel Delgadillo, an ebullient old-timer who kept interrupting our conversation to tend to his customers ('You still cuttin' hair, Angel, or what?'). There are dozens of such places scattered along 66's 2,000-mile stretch, and the road is littered with cafés, bars and diners straight out of the past – hundreds of little grocery stores and gas stations displaying the generic Historic Route 66 signs in their windows. The road has not been allowed to die, nor is it crassly exploited; it is being fondly remembered by people who actually care about its legacy.

It was just outside Winslow that we found our own Holy Grail. The sun was falling in the sky, promising a rich, dark sunset as we sped along the highway towards Two Guns. In the distance the Juniper mountains cut across the horizon like tears of pale blue tissue paper. As we gunned towards them we looked to our left and saw a deserted Drive-In, standing forlorn in the dirt, casting shadows that stretched all the way back to town.

Here was the true spirit of Route 66 in all its faded glory. Like the highway itself, the Tonto Drive-In was a totem of America's glorious past, a testament to the new frontier, the freedom to travel, and the Populuxe automative dream of the Fifties, when a car was still every American's birthright. This deserted cathedral, standing stoic and proud in the burnt sienna sunset, was, quite literally, the end of the road. Suddenly, California – with all its promises of eternal youth – seemed a long, long way away.

Copyright © Dylan Jones, 1994

───────────

Playboy of the Western World

Hugh Hefner by David Ritz

November 1994

'M WILDLY AMBIVALENT ABOUT meeting Hugh Hefner. On the one hand, I've been bad-mouthing his magazine for a good part of my life. On the other hand – the right hand, to be precise – I devoted a good part of my youth beating off to Hefner's bunnies. Even as I approach 51, ageing images from the magazine can still fire my blood. And as I examine *The Playboy Book: The Complete Pictorial History*, the coffee-table ornament celebrating the bunny's fortieth anniversary, my mind races back. Poses and positions of certain ladies are warmly familiar. I look upon certain bosoms, studied long ago with wonder and care, as old friends.

But these were friends I never knew. They were teases from the Fifties, a decade when vaginas were invisible and tits the size of submarines. It wasn't bad enough – or good enough – that *Playboy* served up flesh in full-colour glory. Hef took it further. Instead of harlots, he undressed perky Pepsodent-smiling Suzy Creamcheese cheerleaders, those tight-sweatered all-American sweethearts who sat next to you in school, crossing and recrossing their legs. The fantasy of seeing Suzy naked was thrilling. But the reality, given the times and mores, was that Suzy would sooner marry Nikita Krushchev than give you sex. The result, at least for me, was resentment.

I also resented *Playboy*'s pseudo-hip façade, the way it showed sophisticated finery – fancy hi-fi gear, high-priced clothes, racy cars, all the sleek fads and slick pads which, like the ladies themselves, were beyond my reach, but not Hef's. While we dreamed, Hef schemed. By making himself symbol and substance of his own magazine, Hef got everything we couldn't afford. And we paid for it! We paid to whack off to women who, we would soon learn, were frequently Hef's real-life lovers. When he flaunted that fact, as he did throughout his career, it blew up his bank account and ego to outlandish proportions. I never subscribed.

I was not enamoured of the notion that serious literature and social commentary surrounded the nudes. I viewed the articles as window-dressing. I appreciated Hef's love and promotion of jazz – a passion as powerful for me as sex – but who could read his

25-part Philosophy? I associated *Playboy* with college fraternities.
I saw the magazine as an icon to superficiality. With the advent of
the Playboy Clubs, Hef's enterprise had all the elitist trappings of
a cool guys-only club. When he was attacked by feminists in the
early Seventies, I was with the ladies. Of course Hef turned women
into sexual objects who – the implication was clear – fucked like
bunnies.

I could take all this hostility to my meeting in the mansion; I
could use it to fuel a spirited confrontation were it not for one fact:
I've heard that Hef is writing his autobiography and, having gone
through a number of writers, may need a collaborator. As a vet-
eran of the 'as told to' form, I'm intrigued by the prospect of
helping Hef write his book. That would mean, in a literary sense,
becoming Hef's 'I', pretending that I'm Hef himself. For a few
months, do I want to live inside the skin of the man who got all
the girls and all the goods, the man I've dismissed with such dis-
dain? I believe the answer is yes.

It could be fun, I tell myself as I drive across LA from my mid-
city home to the land of millionaires; it would be profitable. I am
encouraged by reading an excerpt from Hef's unfinished book
which appeared in *Playboy* earlier this year. I see he needs help.
The facts are fascinating, but the tone is dry, the rhythm lack-
lustre. He occasionally turns the story over to others – 'Other Voices', he calls them – a device I find disconcerting. Rather than
quote these characters in great chunks, he needs to engage them in
dialogue and bring them into the narrative sweep. They – like Hef
himself – require living, breathing voices; they need to step off the
page.

When Hef steps into the room, I'm excited. I've already been given
a tour of the famous Playboy West Mansion which has left me a
little disappointed. Maybe because I've just visited the Hearst
Castle up the coast, Hef's place seems smaller than I'd imagined.
No doubt, the five acres are lush, the monkeys are swinging in their
cages, the swans are swimming across ponds, the grass is green as
Ireland, but the grotto, famous for groping, smells musty. The
whole place looks dated. In a separate building, his two small
children, progeny of his 1989 marriage to Playmate Kimberley
Conrad, are playing a Playboy pinball machine displaying images
of their mommy and daddy, while a nanny supervises. Inside Hef's
King Arthur castle, servants are scrubbing furiously, yet a dark,
dusty feeling clings to the walls. The decor is early Disneyland,

Olde English chairs and overstuffed sofas, heavy mahogany wood-work, leaded glass windows.

In the small study where I've been waiting for him, a picture of green-eyed Kimberley hangs over the doorway, her back arched, her remarkable pointed breasts thrust upwards. I wonder how Hef feels displaying his naked wife to the world.

When Hef appears, the room is suddenly electrified. He trots rather than talks. He's on the run, and he's enormously agreeable. 'Sorry for being late,' he says, referring to his five-minute tardiness. His handshake is firm. Nine years after his near-debilitating stroke, he looks closer to 50 than 70. His recovery is startling. He wears black silk pyjamas and a red silk smoking jacket tied smartly at the waist. The pyjama legs carry a perfect crease. The effect of his trademark outfit is strangely formal. He has a full head of grey-and-white hair and unblemished skin. He is tall and handsome and ready to roll. 'Shall we get started?' he asks as he pops open a Diet Pepsi. During our 90 minutes together, he'll chain-drink three cans of soda, a lifelong habit. These days, however, there is no pipe.

I present my selected credentials, a novel about jazz, a book I wrote with Ray Charles. He receives them cordially. I say how Ray Charles takes the Braille edition of *Playboy* on long flights, thus proving at least one person reads the magazine just for the articles. Hef likes to laugh. His mood is upbeat as we discuss a number of books by disgruntled ex-Hefner employees, tracts which amount to corporate kiss-and-tell. 'The problem with those things,' says Hef, 'is that they amount to Rorschach tests. Because I've lived my life in such a public manner, people mix me up with their own attitudes about sex. Things written about me are usually more reflective of the writer than me.' With his first thought, Hef may have nailed me.

I decide to nail him – at least in a friendly, show-him-I've-done-research way. I pick a couple of quotes from Oriana Fallaci's *The Egotists*, a series of interviews conducted by the extra-aggressive Italian. When she spoke with Hef in 1966, he said, 'I don't feel comfortable with an intelligent woman. Simply, I do not know what to do with her . . . when I want to speak, to think, I stay with men, not with women.' I wonder whether his attitude toward women has changed.

'No,' he says, 'because that was never my attitude to begin with. Fallaci is a creative interviewer, and I'm afraid she created those quotes. My closest friends and confidantes have always been women. In the home where I was raised, in the values I inherited and never challenged, respect for women was paramount. Only in the sexual arena did I part company with the tradition of my parents.'

Hef is nothing if not engaging. He's a tough-minded talker whose language is sparse and precise. He speaks with neither affectation nor loquacity. Sitting at the edge of a couch, leaning forward, he says what he has to say with unrelenting energy. The rhythm of his speech is rapid, his intelligence formidable. Sometimes he looks you in the eye; sometimes he stares into space, squinting so that his dark eyes are slits in the clean-shaven landscape of his broad face. He is not a bully; in fact, he appears exceptionally pleasant. But he is a self-starter; he'll ask and answer his own questions. And, from the start, I see that turning this encounter from a monologue to dialogue will be no easy task. Hef has certain set pieces, observations about himself honed over the years into irrefutable theses. Now, for example, he is off-and-running on the question of his childhood.

'My upbringing was typically American,' he says. 'There was a fundamental sense of decency, but an absence of emotion. We lacked the ability to show affection or love. This was the sterile environment from which I escaped into a series of dreams and fantasies inspired by the movies and songs of the Thirties, that peculiar time in American history described most accurately as the Depression. Having missed the celebration of the roaring Twenties, I've been making up for it ever since, looking for the party, even creating the party. I don't know if you're familiar with Dennis Potter . . .'

I am, and I'm happy to make the connection. We discuss how the English writer's last televised interview made a deep impression on us both. Near death from inoperable cancer, Potter appeared defiantly alive – exhilarated, fearless, funny and wise.

'Well, his wisdom,' Hef continues, 'was first apparent to me in *Pennies From Heaven*. I identify with the Bob Hoskins character, the guy who sells sheet music during the Depression and suddenly breaks into song. That was me, looking for a world where the words to those songs were true. If I couldn't find it, I'd create it. The quest for romantic love is what my life has been all about. The excesses – the obsessive side of that search – are certainly reflected in *Playboy* and the Playboy life I found myself living.'

It sounds too easy. Hef's introspection sounds glib. His self-constructed mythology feels frozen. I wonder if his theories have ever been challenged in therapy.

'No,' he answers. 'This is all the result of self-analysis. But if I came upon closed doors which I couldn't open, I'd use any process to open those doors. So far that hasn't been necessary. I believe I've been blessed with certain curiosities and insights. In college, I majored in psychology in order to understand the why of human behaviour. I wanted to understand myself. I've spent a great deal of time trying to see the cause and effects of my behaviour. Most people live their lives without getting a handle on what the fuck it's all about. But to me, those are the great detective stories of our time – the whys of our lives.'

I decide to get specific. Since I have always associated *Playboy* with masturbation, I ask Hef about his own onanistic past. He doesn't bat an eye.

'It didn't happen till the army,' he claims, 'not until I was 18 or 19. I had to leave my childhood home before I could masturbate. I know it sounds amazing, but it's absolutely true. Even more amazing is something my brother revealed to me about my father. Shortly before he died, my father stated that he had never masturbated in his life. Not once. Remember, too, that I was a virgin until I was about 23, shortly before my marriage. In school I had many romantic crushes from the fourth grade on. But I could date a girl for years before even kissing her. I actually passed up opportunities to get laid because of the fear of pregnancy, the fear of disease and, most importantly, a desire to save myself for the woman I intended to marry. That woman was Millie, my first wife. In those days, a nice Methodist boy and a nice Catholic girl could not live together. We had the unfortunate fate of discovering our incompatibility only after a ceremony and commitment designed to please our parents.'

I break in, suggesting we return to the women in *Playboy*. 'While I was fantasising,' I say, 'you were actually fucking. Do you understand why readers might be resentful?'

Hef laughs. 'Sure I do. And the resentment goes beyond me. The resentment, I'd guess, involves guilt. When I was researching the Playboy Philosophy, I dealt in some detail with prohibitions to masturbation. If caught, you could be kicked out of the Naval Academy. Now I ask you – do you really want a bunch of guys protecting the country who don't masturbate?'

Moving ahead, I paraphrase Mel Brooks: are we making progress or just beating off? Let's discuss the feminists. Didn't they have a point? When Susan Brownmiller chastised Hef on television in 1970, challenging him to appear with a cotton tail attached to his ass, didn't he shudder? Didn't he feel remorse?

'No,' he says smoothly, 'and I'll tell you why. Female emancipation has always been something *Playboy* has championed. That's evident in the way we run our business and our rules and controls over sexual harassment. We've always favoured equal access to education and jobs. No arguments there. But early on, I saw something dark in the Women's Movement. A faction viewed sexual liberation as anti-sexual and, to me, that's utter madness. The truth is that the Women's Movement grew inevitably out of the sexual revolution, which *Playboy* helped launch in the Fifties. We contended that a man could be single and live an ethical yet highly active sexual life. Women started to do the same thing. That was great, until a few radicals turned men into the enemy.'

But surely he saw, at some point, that his approach to women as 'playmates' was harmful and, in fact, outmoded?

'I never had a dramatic change in protocol,' Hef reassures me, 'although it's true that my generation was raised in a certain form of chauvinism. And chauvinism is inappropriate. But as far as the battleground of women's liberation relates to *Playboy*, I think the extremists were wrong then and I think they are wrong now. The notion that sex and play and pleasure are antithetical to personal freedom is ridiculous. I started the magazine on the premise that puritanism destroys the soul. My lifelong struggle has been for personal and sexual freedom. For human relationships, the enemy is not one gender or the other, but violence. Sex and violence are polar opposites. One is the life force, the other is death. Men and women urgently need one another for emotional survival.'

Hef has some of the attributes of a politician. He debates skilfully, uses his likeability to break down opposition and revels in generalisation. I try to keep it personal. What about his enormous ego? Does he consider it a blessing or a burden? And what about the charges that he's particularly vulnerable to ass-kissers?

'All people in power are similarly vulnerable,' he generalises. But what about *him*? Has he been hurt by sycophants?

'Not particularly,' Hef muses, 'because other people's perceptions of the world don't have much to do with me. I think I'm most blinded and easily manipulated in my primary romantic relationships. That's the heart of who I am and the heart of what really matters to me. In a romantic relationship, a woman can convince me that pink is blue and blue is pink. You see, the centre of who I am doesn't concern business. Business is merely the result of my dreams. The fact that I've done well in business is a lucky by-prod-

uct. The romantic pursuit – pursuit of the dream – is what motivates me, not money or success.'

I wonder. I wonder if unbridled adulation has been a corrupting
force.

'It's been a danger,' he says, 'but I've managed to deal with it
far better than most. My introspection has saved me. Self-under-
standing has allowed me to avoid traps which might have
destroyed me.'

Did he never endure a period of self-loathing?

'Never. I'm essentially the guy I was 50 years ago. I'm much
more confident, but I look on the world with the same sort of wonder. I'm still reacting to a childhood home where emotions were
stifled. And I'm still fighting a culture which fears and demonises
the flesh. That's the saddest and sickest part of who we are.'

Is he never sickened by the proliferation of hard-core porn? 'I
would say that much of it is not my taste,' he admits. 'But I don't
consider it dangerous. I don't view the image of two people fucking
as harmful. The harm comes only when the act is attached to violence. On the other hand, I am somewhat alarmed when I see that
X-rated porn is being transmitted from Canada over our airwaves.
I worry about its availability to children. And, as I said, I don't like
sleaze. It bothers me that many people make only a slight distinction between *Playboy* and *Penthouse*. I see us as worlds apart.
Penthouse has become the *Hustler* of the Nineties. I find it repul-
sive.'

Is there perhaps a streak of puritanism in America's leading anti-
puritan?

'It's not puritanism, it's taste,' Hef argues. 'Bob Guccione has
created *Penthouse* out of his own sensibility. In early interviews,
he described his fascination with whores and how he slept with
every hooker on the Via Veneto. Our philosophy was that nice
girls like sex – and that's what we show. Our aim was to destroy
the madonna/whore complex, to portray sex as wholesome and
healthy. Whoring isn't healthy.'

That could be challenged as a puritanical notion. Moreover, a
current issue of *Playboy*, with its wholesome healthy nudes, appears anachronistic . . .

'Old-fashioned,' Hef breaks in. 'Yes. I think it has become old-
fashioned, and I'm glad. I still edit the magazine' – he states this
with emphasis – 'and my daughter Christie, who took over the
company in 1982, shares my views and values. When I say old-
fashioned, I mean that the liberal bias has remained strong. We still

focus on quality fiction and social commentary, we still project an image of women which suggests that sex, rather than being a deed of dark perversion, is a positive, joyful pleasure.'

If the magazine is old-fashioned, Hef himself is an old-fashioned salesman, a brilliant and tireless self-promoter busy spinning advertisements for himself. I wonder whether after all this time he has started to doubt his this-world fixation and entertained notions of God.

'Not exactly in those terms,' he laughs, 'but I certainly am devoting more time to those issues. Look, life is awe-inspiring. I feel inspired, I feel a connection and continuity between myself and nature. I recognise a divine and mysterious force. But I will not demean the notion by suggesting some humanoid creation, some great father who sends down ridiculous laws and damns people for doing what comes naturally. No, I do not believe in the biblical God whose power is based on fear.'

Does Hef fear death?

'I'm sure as hell trying to avoid it,' he answers with a smile. 'My mother's 99, so I'm pleased to say my genes are good. I'm dancing as fast as I can. I intend to be around for the millennium. My lifestyle has proven healthier than many would have thought. My energy has been restored.'

I wonder whether someone so self-satisfied can write anything but a self-serving autobiography. I wonder whether he questions his paradoxes. How does a man who made millions selling a free-swinging lifestyle, for example, reconcile his sudden conversion to monogamy?

'Monogamy is new for me,' Hef explains. 'Before Kimberley, who's an exceptionally strong woman, I'd never been faithful. Even in my primary relationships – and I've always been anchored by primary relationships – I found myself wandering off from time to time. Now I find that monogamy is working for me. It's eliminated hypocrisy. But I believe there are many roads to Mecca. Monogamy is simply one. I confess that when I review some old film of myself, when I see myself in certain situations, I start to squirm.'

Whom does he see?

'A guy desperate to be desirable to the opposite sex. A guy hungry for acceptance and love. A guy who could be full of shit. But part of that, you see, was a façade. I was simply in the process of turning myself into the person I wanted to be.'

And who was that? With one last irresistible smile, Hef says,
'The guy I became.'

Copyright © David Ritz, 1994

Top Management
The Breast by Imogen Edwards-Jones
November 1995

I SUPPOSE A GIRL'S ATTITUDE towards her breasts is much the same
as a boy's towards his penis – a sort of proud display of sexuality to be played with, caressed and tweaked at all times and
in all places. Tits and cocks are similarly the ultimate in paci-
fiers, to be cradled absentmindedly on the sofa during the
Brookside omnibus or squeezed intensely and grabbed and
stretched in special moments of tension during *NYPD Blue* or
Friends. But while attitudes to our various appendages may be
similar during our penis- and bosom-sure adulthood, in the painful
days of adolescence, in the throes of high puberty, our thoughts
and reactions are entirely different.

You see, girls hate their breasts. At the first embarrassing
orange-pip state, when they start raising Snoopy's eyebrows on
your favourite Peanuts T-shirt, they are horrible, mortifying and, I
hasten to add, painful. And the really sad thing is that they arrive
just as you boys begin to accept us girls as potential good-laugh
material. I vividly remember running through a field of stinging
nettles in my pants, eating mud and being whipped by some willow
cat-o'-nine-tails so that I could join the gang, only then to be informed that I had titties so I wasn't allowed.

Later, when they reached cherry size, I spent hours thwacking
down my burgeoning points with a hardback copy of *Swallows
And Amazons*, thinking that if I could squash them then they'd
never come. Boy did it hurt. I used to sleep on my front hoping it
would make a difference. But it didn't. Soon the cherries grew into
apricots and Snoopy looked so surprised that he couldn't be worn
any more.

It's about that apricot stage when things begin to get truly embarrassing. Not only do I remember racing into my brother's room,

pulling down my big blue regulation pants and showing him, very proudly, my first pubic hair, but I also remember stuffing a bikini top with a scratchy pair of socks and trying to pass it off as a bra. It was bright green with white spots. And not only did I try to go to school wearing it in an ever-so-casual, always-worn-a-green-bra sort of way, but I also insisted on not wearing a jumper and leaning forward a lot so the boys behind could see it through my shirt and admire my sudden and intense femininity. I was surprised to find that the dramatic, overnight increase in my cup-size – from apricots to mandarins in one fell swoop – caused much hilarity; not to mention the spontaneous curvature of my spine and my nipples' miraculous resistance to cold.

The mandarins do eventually come, and young girls ultimately tire of green and white spotted bikinis because suddenly it's glam trainer bras all round. And while you boys are busy slapping your dicks down on rulers, peeing up urinals and sullying your beds with thoughts of Catwalk Claudia and EastEnder Bianca, us girls have nothing more to worry about than, 'Should I go for the white lace or the pink with flowers', and those 35 'I must's every morning. Until, that is, we encounter fashion and boys. And neither category, let's face it, knows what to do when confronted by a pair of bosoms.

With fashion, the dichotomy is simple – Pamela Anderson or Kate Moss? To Wonderbra or not to Wonderbra? Breasts are big this year, apparently. What we want is a pumped-up Paula Yates to keep the fashion mags happy. We should all be glamorous Eva Bigtits kinda girls.

But wait a sec. Hasn't old Calvin Knicker-King Klein brought out a new androgynous perfume? Boys smell like girls and girls smell like boys – so should we chuck out the silicone bags and bin the padding? Is it cool to be flat? Actually, I don't think girls particularly care about what they end up with, just as long as their breasts are not shaped like bananas, can pass the old pencil test, are small enough for us to be able to put our chins on the floor when lying on our stomachs and large enough that a *petit pois* analogy doesn't immediately spring to mind. In fact, Eva can lick her own cleavage for all we care; it's not fashion that's the problem, it's the opposite sex.

Now men, let's be honest, are only too delighted to come across an unsheathed pair of breasts. They leap upon them with the same zeal with which a starving man might attack a loaf of bread. Baring their teeth they scrabble around and chew and bite and suck like a ferret boring a hole into a hillock. This, so we have been told, is not only supposed to be sexy, it also constitutes foreplay. However, the moans and groans you may hear as you munch away like a ravenous newborn with teeth like clothes pegs, are not tones of ecstasy but the stifled sounds of either excruciating pain or unbelievable boredom at yet again being manipulated like a gobstopper.

Bosoms should be handled like tissue-paper beach balls, licked like raspberry-ripple ice lollies, and nipples should be teased by teeth tender enough to take one grape from a bunch without piercing the skin. Feel free to suck away if you must, but not as if you're expecting a bloody four-course dinner. And if you think I protest too much, maybe you should ask some compliant babe to take a nail file to her teeth, then wrap them around your testes. Then you'll see that tits and willies are not so different after all.

My Angel is a Centrefold

Anna Nicole Smith by Ian Katz
November 1995

BY ANY CONVENTIONAL STANDARD, it was an improbable match. He was brought up a Pennsylvania Quaker, taught to say 'thou' and 'thee' instead of 'you'. She grew up pitifully poor in a tiny Texas oil town where people said 'you's' or 'y'all'. He was educated at Yale. She dropped out of eleventh grade. His milieu was the oak-panelled hush of the corporate boardroom. She felt more at home in a loud Hollywood nightspot. And there was just one other thing: he was 89 and she was 26.

But then neither J. Howard Marshall II nor Anna Nicole Smith ever had much truck with convention. They exchanged vows on June 27, 1994 at Houston's White Dove Wedding Chapel. Nothing extravagant, just a $1,000 package with an extra $50 for the two white doves released at the end of the ceremony to signify peace and love. She walked up the aisle on rosebuds rather than petals. He was wheeled into the chapel to the strains of 'Tonight, I Celebrate My Love For You'.

The bride wanted desperately for her groom to stand up during the ceremony but when he was lifted from his wheelchair his pencil-thin legs simply buckled underneath him. Nevertheless the couple promised to love and to cherish each other till death did them part, and that is exactly what it did, 13 months later.

Smith, for she never chose to call herself Marshall, bade goodbye to her husband last month at an expensive Houston funeral chapel. As she had when she pledged herself to him, she wore a low-cut white gown and insisted that everything in the chapel should be white. During the brief service, she sang 'Wind Beneath My Wings' in a high, tremulous voice before breaking down in tears and taking refuge in a side room.

Mr Marshall's youngest son, Pierce, did not attend the funeral service at Geo H. Lewis and Sons, the venerable Houston funeral parlour which buried Howard Hughes. He held his own ceremony a few days later, attended by his father's first wife and dozens of the oil town's great and good. These days he and his stepmother see each other only in court.

For if the courtship and marriage of Anna Nicole Smith and J. Howard Marshall was a love story of peculiarly Texan proportions, the epic feud between the young model and the stepson almost twice her age was the stuff of the Lone Star State's most famous soap opera. It is a story of love, grit and loathing. And, of course, cash. Lots and lots of it.

The small, dusty town of Mexia (pronounced Muy-hey-a) 35 miles east of Waco used to be known as the birthplace of Roy Rhodes, an American footballer who played for the San Francisco 49ers and New York Giants before becoming one of the few black coaches in the NFL. But these days Mexia's biggest claim to fame is that Anna Nicole Smith, 1993 Playmate of the Year, Guess! jeans model and sometime Hollywood starlet, once cooked eggs and mash in Jim's Krispy Fried Chicken out on US 84.

Back in the Twenties, when Blake Smith Sr struck oil nearby, Mexia mushroomed into a boom town of 50,000. But by the time Smith was born Vickie Lynn Hogan in 1968, it was a dreary, down-at-heel place with a population of 7,000, most of whom depended for their livelihoods on the state-run residential school for retarded children.

Smith did not meet her father until years later when he bumped into her after her first *Playboy* appearance and is said to have exclaimed: 'I've seen you naked.' Her mother, Virgie, was a police officer who largely delegated care of her daughter to an aunt, Kay Beall. Folks in Mexia remember Smith as a pretty, but gawky teenager who dreamed of becoming a model, and escaping into a more glamorous world. 'All the guys wanted to go out with her, all the girls were jealous of her,' recalled Jo Lynn Aguirre, a childhood friend.

By the age of 17, however, her dream seemed more improbable than ever. She had dropped out of school and married the 16-year-old cook at Jim's Chicken. 'He was sweet and he was so cute back there, cookin' chicken,' she said later. A year later she had given birth to a son, Daniel, and a year after that her marriage was over.

Smith headed for Houston where, according to legend, she waited on tables at a Red Lobster Restaurant, worked behind the till at Wal-Mart and knocked vainly on the doors of the city's model agencies. Some time in 1991, according to this official version, her then boyfriend persuaded her to send some Polaroids to *Playboy*. Three days later she was flying to Los Angeles.

She matched perfectly Hugh Hefner's *Playboy* paradigm of 'the nice, but just possibly naughty, girl next door'. When she was featured as the May 1992 Playmate, the magazine extolled a small-town girl 'as earthy and wide-open as the North Texas spaces she hails from'. On the 'Playmate Data Sheet' she revealed in a childish scrawl that her ambition was 'to be the new Marilyn Monroe' and her favourite authors were 'the people who write my favorite soaps'.

Paul Marciano, president of the fashionable jeans firm Guess!, liked what he saw. Within weeks he had signed her to replace Claudia Schiffer, whose three-year term as Guess! model was just coming to a close, and re-christened her as the sophisticated Anna Nicole Smith. When she was named 1993 Playmate of the Year a few months later, the Rose of Mexia was suddenly catapulted into the fickle limelight of second-division celebrity.

Voluptuous to the point of plump – 5ft 11ins tall, her weight hovered around 150lbs – her Vargas girl figure was seized on as the perfect antidote to the anorexic-looking waifs who seemed to dominate the catwalks and women's magazines. A few of her more breathless admirers drew glowing comparisons with Monroe. Hefner called her 'Rubenesque – a very big lady'. Smith delighted women everywhere by revealing that she ate whatever she felt like and insisted on Godiva chocolates at every shoot. 'I slob out bigtime,' she told *People* magazine, wondering in her next breath why other models seemed to dislike her.

Like the hundreds of young men and women who inhabit the

fringes of Hollywood, she became one of those people who is famous for being famous. A regular in the gossip columns, she was always photographed at the Oscars, though she was not likely ever to collect one for her handful of minor parts in films like *Naked Gun 33⅓* and *The Hudsucker Proxy*. She was cited as a positive archetype in every article written about anorexia. She was found comatose in a Los Angeles hotel after taking a cocktail of prescription drugs and booze with her boyfriend. That sort of thing.

'I finally feel like I'm becoming somebody,' she declared in an April 1993 interview. 'I really think I can do something.' If she needed confirmation that she was finally a somebody, it came a few months later when CNN talk show king Larry King invited her on his show with Arnold Schwarzenegger.

She was painfully nervous, repeatedly calling King 'sir' until he insisted she call him Larry. She held up a photograph of her son Danny and said that, though she was keen to re-marry, she wanted to concentrate on her career for a few years first. And then, in a remark that may have been portentous or simply Machiavellian, she declared that she liked older men.

'Why?' King enquired.

'They know more. They're more experienced,' replied Smith.

'So you're comfortable with older men – say, like, old as your father?' pressed a disbelieving King.

'I am.'

J. Howard Marshall II was one of those men who knock at the door of greatness. He was once the richest man in Houston, but never quite among the very richest in the land. He was described as an industry giant but never a giant of industry. He was famous enough to write an autobiography, *Done In Oil*, but not famous enough for anyone to review it. Indeed, had it not been for his unlikely coupling with a voluptuous beauty one-third his age, his death might have gone unrecorded on all but the obituary pages of a handful of Texas newspapers.

Unlike most of the Lone Star State's self-styled 'awl barons', Marshall came from high-bred Yankee stock. Born in Pennsylvania in 1905, his parents inherited a massive steel fortune which was all but wiped out during the Depression. After overcoming a childhood bout of typhoid fever that left him with a limp and ultimately condemned him to a wheelchair, he studied at Haverford, a highly regarded Quaker college, and then at Yale Law School.

At university he acquired a reputation as a fearsome competitor and frightful wag with a keen appetite for beautiful women. When a young Philadelphia debutante spurned his advances, he ruined her coming out by printing an extra 1,500 invitations and handing them out in the street. Marshall finished first in his class and attracted the attention of Franklin D. Roosevelt's secretary, Harold Ickes, with an article about the oil industry in the *Yale Law Journal*. Ickes hired him to help draw up the first regulatory framework for the oil industry, an unglamorous enterprise which is remembered as one of his most significant achievements. During the Second World War he served as chief counsel to the Petroleum Administration for War, the federal government department charged with running the oil industry, before heading to the Texas oilfields in search of a fortune.

After stints at a string of oil companies, Marshall found that fortune in the early Sixties when he sold his interest in a Minnesota refinery to Koch Industries, the vast privately-owned conglomerate. By 1989, *Forbes* magazine ranked him as the richest man in Houston, putting his fortune, which included a sizeable holding in Koch Industries, at almost $700 million. He also held seats on the boards of a clutch of Texas's biggest independent oil firms.

But long before he met Smith, Marshall's many laudable achievements had been overshadowed by his lurid private life. On moving to Houston in 1961, he divorced Eleanor Pierce, his wife of 30 years, and married Bettye Bohanon, a tough former oil business executive whom he called Tiger. Marshall was devoted to her, but in the early Eighties she fell ill with Alzheimer's disease. Marshall had fallen out with his oldest son, J. Howard Marshall III, and had precious little rapport with the younger Pierce. He was lonely.

So it was that in 1982, as he would later testify in one of the many lawsuits bearing his name, the 77-year-old oil man happened to stop at a bar on his way from Houston Airport for a quick drink. 'I didn't realise what I was getting into. It was a strip joint – or as the boys call it now – a tittie bar. And I walked in and Lady was there.' Lady was Jewell Dianne Walker, a 42-year-old Georgia peach struggling to support three children by dancing topless at the Chic Lounge. Marshall fell instantly and heavily for her charms. Within weeks he had bought her a Cadillac, a diamond ring and a new, furnished home.

Marshall and Lady Walker became a fixture on the Houston society scene lunching with a bare minimum of discretion three times a week at the city's most expensive restaurants. Marshall, who fantasised about marrying her at the Taj Mahal at dusk after his wife died, continued to shower her with gifts: sometimes diamonds, once an oil company of her own, but most often the blank cheques she preferred. 'Don't just lay them across the table,' she is said to have complained once. 'Put them in my purse.'

Unbeknown to Marshall, however, Lady was redistributing much of his largesse to Dale Clem, a thirtysomething carpenter-cum-shrimp fisherman who was employed officially as her body-guard and unofficially in a more personal capacity. In 1991 Lady died on the operating table while undergoing a facelift. Marshall paid for an elaborate funeral including a solid copper coffin, similar to the one Elvis was buried in, but became furious when he discovered his mistress's secret life. Enlisting the help of his son Pierce, he sued Lady Walker's heirs for the return of every penny he had given her, alleging she had deliberately fleeced him of millions of dollars. 'I was blinded by love,' he testified later. 'I did more or less what she asked me to do, and I don't make any bones about it. I was a damn fool. But men in love do stupid things, and I sure was guilty.'

There is an autographed photograph of Smith on the wall of Rick's Cabaret, Houston's, maybe America's, 'premier' topless bar – an establishment that does not figure in her official biography. It is a rear view of the fulsome model, inscribed with the message: 'Remember Sweet Cheeks'.

Smith arrived there some time in 1988 after working at a string of Houston men's clubs which did not make it into the official biography either. Opened in 1983 as an 'upscale' alternative to the city's 'tittie bars', Rick's attracted a better class of client and even, on occasion, stars like Sting and local sporting hero Warren Moon. It became famous for its perfect-breasted, wholesome-looking dancers – the average bust size at Rick's in the late Eighties was a 38D – and was even blamed later for driving thousands of women in the city to have breast enlargements so that they would conform to the Rick's ideal of beauty their husbands fantasised about.

Robert Watters, the smooth 44-year-old former attorney and tax consultant who owns the club, is unapologetic. 'We have had more *Playboy* and *Penthouse* centrefolds working here than any club in the world,' he told a reporter enquiring about Smith. 'We just had the 20th Anniversary Penthouse Pet.' In such august company, Smith, though remembered by most who worked with her as likeable and charming, did not stand out. In fact Watters recalls noting her plumpness and instructing the manager to ensure that she work only on the less aesthetically exacting day shift.

Which is how, one day in 1990, she met J. Howard Marshall II, a Rick's regular, as he sat looking crumpled and a little dejected in the lunchtime audience. Smith never revealed whether he beckoned her over and thrust a $20 note into her garter belt, as many punters did, so that she would give a personal performance at his table. But she did record matter-of-factly in the wedding book at the White Dove Wedding Chapel that 'he was in the audience and he was lonely and I started talking to him and we just started being friends'.

At first it seems, the pair did indeed enjoy an improbable friendship, meeting occasionally for a flirtatious lunch at the River Oaks Country Club. At the time, Marshall was still devoted to Lady Walker, not to mention his sickly wife, and, from early 1992, Smith was throwing herself into her new life as Playboy Playmate and minor celebrity. But some time in 1993, after the deaths of both Lady Walker and Bettye Marshall, their relationship changed dramatically.

In March of that year Marshall charged $123.41 of Godiva chocolates, Smith's favourite, and $358,958 in jewellery, to his Neiman Marcus credit card. The following month he and Smith spent $2 million in less than an hour at the Fifth Avenue branch of jewellers Harry Winston. Smith claimed later that Marshall begged her to marry him from 1990, but that it wasn't till the summer of 1994 that she accepted.

Pat Walker, owner of the White Dove Wedding Chapel, still giggles when she tells a reporter about the Marshall-Smith wedding – for maybe the fiftieth time. Smith had called in advance and specially requested that Walker not notify any photographers about the ceremony. 'I said, "Why would I want to do that?" and she said, "Do you know who I am? I'm Anna Nicole Smith. I did a movie with O. J. Simpson. I live round the corner from him." '

The couple wanted to marry on a Saturday, but Walker pointed out that their wedding licence was not yet 72 hours old, as Texas law requires, so they had to wait till the following Monday. On the day, Marshall, resplendent in a white tuxedo, was wheeled up the aisle by his secretary. Smith was given away by a man she described at one point as her uncle and at another as her father, while her son Danny acted as ring bearer and Marshall's nurse served as bridesmaid.

As soon as the simple ceremony was complete, recalls Walker,

Smith kissed her new husband and told him she had to rush to catch a plane to Greece with her bodyguard Pierre de Jean. 'She just said to him, "Bye bye Popsy. I love you. Remember I have a lot of people that call me but remember Popsy, it's only you I love."' Walker typically conducts between five and seven weddings a day in her pink, converted, ranch-style house and she figures to have just about seen it all. But that day, she says, she was just about lost for words: 'You don't want to know what I was thinking that day.'

Before we go on, we should make some attempt to understand why it was that news of J. Howard Marshall II's third marriage was greeted with scepticism by many who knew neither the bride nor the groom. When they exchanged vows on June 27, 1994, Marshall was just shy of being a nonagenarian while Smith was still years from her thirtieth birthday. The age gap which divided them was 63 years, some 40 years more than the one which separated Aristotle Onassis from his second wife, Jaqueline Kennedy, and almost three decades more than the chasm which many felt rendered Woody Allen's infatuation with Soon-Yi Previn nothing less than indecent.

When Marshall was born, women did not have the vote in Britain, the Bolshevicks had not yet revolted and Bleriot was still four years away from becoming the first man to fly across the Channel. By the time his bride had come into the world, Chris Barnard had carried out the world's first heart-transplant operation, the QE2 had been launched and the US had sent an unmanned spacecraft to the moon.

Not that these facts alone disprove Smith's frequent assertions that her decision to accept Marshall's proposal was motivated by 'lurve' alone, or that their union would be a happy one.

There were some, too, who insist they did not suspect any ulterior motive behind Smith's second trip up the aisle. Take David Granoff, the New York publicist who became embroiled in a very public spat with Smith about allegedly unpaid bills before making up, equally publicly, and becoming a firm friend of the model's. Granoff recalls Smith talking fondly about her geriatric beau long before their much-derided nuptials. 'She told me how he changed her life and how much she loved him and what a great person he was. She used to get calls, calls, calls, from lots of people when we were travelling, but his calls she always took. Or if she couldn't take them she would get a number and call him back as soon as she could.

'It was an unusual relationship but there have been stranger things in life than that. I do believe that she had great, great personal feelings for him. The money makes someone look a little better than maybe he would if they were not a high-fashion model or a movie star but believe me, they had a real relationship.'

Never enthusiastic about his father's relationship with Lady Walker, Pierce Marshall appears from the start to have viewed the old man's last infatuation in a less charitable light. Perhaps it was the $450,000 marquise diamond ring his father gave his new bride or the ten-acre spread he bought for her that set the alarm bells ringing, but within two weeks of Marshall and Smith exchanging vows, he had persuaded his father to grant him power of attorney over the family fortune. The younger Marshall promptly set about doing his utmost to keep his stepmother as far from it as possible, ordering his lawyers to bar her from 'the use and enjoyment of [its] assets'.

Suddenly the young bride found her credit card bills unpaid and even the electricity and water to her Texas ranch cut off. More humiliating still, her stepson went to the trouble of blocking a $1 million cheque to Harry Winston, prompting the gem firm to sue her very publicly for the return of four baubles purchased at its Beverly Hills store.

Then, in February, things went from bad to worse for Smith. After his father was admitted to hospital for treatment of a recurrent pneumonia, Pierce successfully petitioned a judge to make him legal guardian of Marshall Sr on the grounds that he was not of sound mind. Referring to her, with characteristic Texan understatement, as 'a greedy gold-digger', he also persuaded the judge to impose tight restrictions on the amount of time his wife could spend at his father's bedside.

Smith had other problems of her own. She was embroiled in an ugly court battle with a former housekeeper who claimed in a $2 million lawsuit that Smith assaulted, abused and even sexually harassed her. 'You told Ms Cerrato that you loved her on more than one occasion,' the suit charged, continuing, 'You told Ms Cerrato that you wanted to marry her.'

Now under siege from her new family, she seemed close to meltdown. 'I can't pay my bills,' she declared in a distraught interview. 'Right now, I'm a total basket case. I'm going to see my psychiatrist in a minute. I'm almost having a nervous breakdown all the time.'

But the woman who dragged herself from Jim's Krispy Fried

Chicken to the sunlit, albeit lower slopes of Tinseltown, was not about to give up her 'Paw-Paw' – or his fortune. She struck back with a lawsuit of her own, insisting Marshall senior was very far from senile and including a statement signed by the old man to prove it. 'I want you to know that I am perfectly competent,' it read. 'I think that my son Pierce has over-reached a little bit in trying to make himself my guardian. I want my wife to be aided and supported by me. She's the light of my life.'

As Marshall's life ebbed away, Smith and Pierce exchanged lawsuits like tennis strokes. Pierce sought to stop his stepmother from receiving the title to the ranch where she lived with her son; she insisted her husband planned to give it to her outright. Pierce demanded she identify 'by date and occasion, all instances wherein you and J. Howard Marshall II spent the night in the same home and/or room after your marriage.' Her lawyer replied that 'Plaintiff and Mr Marshall have done so in Los Angeles and at the ranch in Cypress, Texas.'

Remarking that his father paid Smith an allowance 'far in excess of $50,000 a month', Pierce accused her of fleecing him 'by way of excessive gifts or transfer of community property to strangers of the marriage, with some of whom she had adulterous affairs.' Smith hit back with a letter from Marshall elder declaring: 'I don't object to [Pierce] being guardian of my affairs, matter of fact he runs a lot of businesses and does very good. But he has no business coming between my wife and myself . . . Maybe he's a bit jealous.'

Smith won a small victory a few weeks before her husband's death when a judge lifted a ruling which prevented her from visiting him in hospital for more than 30 minutes or for any time after 8pm. 'We were finally successful in getting those restrictions lifted,' declared her lawyer Diana Marshall. 'But they lost a lot of precious time they could have spent together.'

It was only fitting that Pierce Marshall and Anna Nicole Smith should squabble even over what to do with the corpse of the man they both professed to love. Marshall wanted his father cremated while Smith demanded he be interred in a capacious mausoleum in which she could someday join him. Like most of their dealings, the issue wound up in court before Smith finally relented on condition that she receive half of her husband's ashes.

But the Rose of Mexia is a long way from relenting on her claim to a share of his more tangible assets. Though her battle to win spousal support from his estate was cut short by Howard Marshall's timely passing, she promptly launched a fresh legal claim to half of his income during the period they were married, a sum which could be anywhere between $50 million and $300 million.

Already her lawyer, Diana Marshall, has claimed that documents in which Marshall senior passed control of his estate to his son were 'signed in an almost completely illegible fashion ... which makes sense because he couldn't read at the time, according to his doctors.' Smith, too, has done her bit to press her case by insisting discreetly to New York gossip columnist Cindy Adams that she gave up much of her career 'to sit at his bedside day after day and nurse him'.

When Smith broke down in tears after reciting the words 'The swords of the just are in the hands of God' at her husband's first funeral ceremony last month, her lawyer was on hand to step into the breach. 'I am here today to talk about love,' she declared. 'I have never known a relationship that embodied love as much as this one. Anna, if Howard were here today, he would say to you, "Don't cry, Precious Package, my Lady Love." And in years to come when you see yourself succeeding, as you will, because you are strong, you will say to yourself, "Hello, Howard, I'm succeeding, I've got my chin up."'

Copyright © Ian Katz, 1995

———————————

The Frog on the Tyne

David Ginola by Simon Kelner

December 1995

I T IS A WINTER'S AFTERNOON in north London, but it feels like Paris in the springtime. Out on a penthouse roof, under the unbroken blue sky, a shoot for the French fashion house Cerruti is in progress, a spectacular blonde, flown in from New York that morning, is stretched out on the bleached pine floor modelling a new range of denim wear. The _monde_ is definitely _beau_. Even the house cat, a flawless, metallic-grey Siamese struts like a supermodel of the feline world. But the most striking figure is a Frenchman who sits alone, astride a wall, pulling on his Philip Morris Superlights and reading a book.

David Ginola seems perfectly at ease in this company; uniquely so, it would be safe to venture, among Newcastle United footballers. Certainly, Ginola is a bird of rare plumage. Impossibly good-looking, implausibly stylish, irredeemably Gallic, he has acted as bonding agent in the fusion of unlikely worlds – of football with fashion; of the languid flair of French soccer with the passionate, helter-skelter game in England; of the relaxed modishness of St Tropez with the high-energy ballsiness of Newcastle. It is tempting to see Ginola as a living paradox – child of the Midi, hero of the Geordies, face of Cerruti.

For the moment, however, he cannot be engaged by such matters. He was fully occupied by his book, a novel called *L'Alchemiste* by the Brazilian author Paolo Coelho. 'It is about a personal legend,' explained Ginola. 'A Spanish shepherd sets out to follow his destiny, which is to claim the treasure in Tangier. On the journey, he meets the King of Salem, who gives him a number of small rocks, some black and some white. When the shepherd has to make a decision, he consults these rocks, which give him advice. I believe everybody must have a destiny, but most of us don't meet the King of Salem on the way.'

Instead, Ginola met the slightly less exotic figure of Kevin Keegan, the manager of Newcastle United, and ended up in the Northeast. Last summer, he was transferred from Paris St Germain for a bargain fee of £2.5m, and has quickly established that skill on the football field is effective in any language, his performances on the left wing a significant factor in Newcastle's confident rise to the top of the Premiership. More than that, he has, as the man himself says, 'put some French style in the sky of Newcastle'. In the club's three shops, sales of shirts with Ginola's name and number (14) far outstrip those for any other Newcastle player; the fanzine *Talk Of The Tyne* has him the clear leader in their Man of the Match table; he receives fan mail in pop star proportions and is seen by many as a symbol of the wider ambitions of both club and city. Ginola, meanwhile, is philosophical about exchanging the Bois de Boulogne for the Bigg Market. 'I didn't come here for the life. I chose Newcastle to play football. From the moment I could walk, my destiny was to become a footballer. I have achieved that. I am happy.'

So what do you miss about France, Mr Ginola? 'My family and friends first, and then the sea,' he replies. But surely you are closer to the sea in Newcastle than you were in Paris? 'Yes,' he says. 'But it is not *my* sea.' The Mediterranean is Ginola's sea; he was born in St Tropez 28 years ago and his lyrical evocations of life in his native land leave little doubt that galloping homesickness has been one of the problems he has had to conquer. 'I loved to go to the market on a Sunday morning, to wander around buying tomatoes, vegetables, fruit, seafood, to talk to the people. I miss the smells. I miss the smells of my own country.'

Ginola has nevertheless found it easier to adjust to the less fragrant environment of the Northeast than his wife of five years, Coraline. 'I am happy in my work, and when you are happy in your work, you are happy in life. Coraline doesn't speak English,' Ginola explains, 'and although she is now learning, she feels lonely. It has been very hard for her, particularly as we arrived here just after we had a great holiday in France with friends and family. But she understood what it would be like when she married me. Football is my life, and she must follow.'

The couple met when they were both 18, and Coraline, a part-time model, was working in a shop in St Tropez; they now have a son, Andrea (three-and-a-half), and a daughter, Carla (one). While Ginola takes obvious delight in life's simple pleasures, he is not unmoved by the material benefits conferred on the modern footballer. We are talking as we drive from the training ground in Durham to pick up his new bottle-green Range Rover, a vehicle for which he shows boyish enthusiasm. He also speaks lovingly of his CDV – 'it's like watching a film at a cinema' – and, as we leave the garage, he puts James Taylor on the CD player. He points out that his Range Rover, in addition to the walnut dashboard and leather upholstery, has a total of 11 speakers.

But the pressures on family life at their bungalow up the coast from the city are only partly cushioned by the riches thrust Ginola's way (his deal with Newcastle is believed to be worth around £15,000 a week and, as well as the contract with Cerruti, he has just been signed up by Nike). He is a man in demand, and not just for commercial endorsement. 'It's very difficult when I go out,' Ginola explained. 'All the women want to shag with me.' Most of our partners would recognise the problem. But how does Coraline react to these attentions? 'It depends on her sense of humour.' While Ginola, in common with most people whose career has such a short life-expectancy, is keen to maximise his assets in every sphere, he has an acute sense of the value of the family unit. 'I love it when we all cook together. We make a cake, the boy breaks the eggs, sometimes in the bowl, sometimes on the floor. The kitchen is the best room in the house. It's hot and we are together, all the family. In the kitchen, it's different. There is no TV. We speak, we laugh, and everybody is close. I like the kitchen too much.' Ginola is a decent cook in his own right, and talks fondly of the time he made the signature dish of the South, *soupe au pistou*, for some friends in Paris. 'It was,' he says, 'a great moment.'

There is a strong sense of Ginola needing to be cocooned by his young family, which may be explained both by his strong relationship with his father and by his difficult adolescence. Rene Ginola, who makes torpedoes in a munitions factory near his home in Sainte Maxime, has had 'a big influence on my life. I am happy walking with him in the mountains, talking, smelling the pure air. But he never put any pressure on me to become a footballer: he just educated me to be honest.' Nevertheless, when it was apparent that he had a prodigiously talented footballer on his hands, Ginola Senior packed off his boy, just a teenager, to a sports institute in Nice.

He emerged, at the age of 17, to be rejected by the Nice club. He signed instead for Toulon, where financial problems soon meant that they could not pay his wages. From there, by way of Matra Racing of Paris and Brest, he arrived at Paris St Germain, where in four seasons he won 16 caps for the national team (the first against Albania in 1990) and was elected French Footballer of the Year in 1994. 'At that time, he was the most creative player,' said Erik Bielderman, football correspondent of *L'Equipe*, the French sports newspaper. 'He was a showman, and although he did not score too many goals, he made many with the final pass or the cross, and he was a great favourite with the crowd. They were sorry to see him go. But there was always a sense with David that he was more effective for his club than he was for his country.'

Ginola was wearing the blue shirt of France when he suffered his lowest point as a footballer in November, 1993. Five seconds were left on the official game clock in France's final World Cup qualifier against Bulgaria in Paris. The match was goalless and France needed only to draw to reach the finals in the United States. Ginola, on as a substitute, took a free-kick deep in Bulgarian territory and, instead of playing the simple pass, he tried to find Eric Cantona with an extravagant cross. The ball was intercepted by Bulgaria's right-back, and a sweeping movement upfield resulted in a stunning goal that sent France out of the World Cup and left the team, and most of the watching nation, on their knees. 'Ginola should have played like an Italian or a Spaniard, just to keep possession,' says Bielderman. 'Instead, he played like a stupid

Frenchman, always trying to score a goal.' The then French coach, Gerard Houiller, publicly accused him of letting the side down, while Cantona pointedly refused to defend him. And when he took the field with PSG for away games, the fans would taunt him with chants of 'Ginola. USA'.

Ginola now plays down any enmity with Cantona. 'It was a misunderstanding. Eric thought I wanted to take his place as the star of the team. But time is good. It's better now. We might even do an advert for Nike together.' Bielderman says that the two players were never likely to hit it off. 'They are both stars, and they have strong personalities. But they are very different. Ginola is extrovert and Cantona is introvert. It's like fire and water. They don't mix.'

It was a personality clash that also led to Ginola's departure from Paris at the end of last season. Ginola fell out with the club coach, Luis Fernandez, who, he claims, was jealous of his popularity and disliked his attitude to the job. 'Every morning, I came to training with a big smile on my face,' explains Ginola. 'I was happy to meet my friends, to play football, to talk about things. If Fernandez heard me talking about golf, he would say, "Not fucking golf again." [Ginola is a keen golfer, and plays off a handicap of 10] He was always putting me down. If I made a mistake, he would criticise me. If I did something good, he would not give me praise. He tried to kill me as a football player. I was a weight in his life and it was right that I left.'

Unsurprisingly, Newcastle did not figure in Ginola's plans at that stage. He had talks with Inter Milan and Barcelona, but they came to nothing. Meanwhile, Keegan, who had been impressed by his performance for PSG against Arsenal last season, made a determined effort to tempt him to St James' Park. 'Newcastle were the only club who really wanted me. At Milan or Barcelona, there was always a problem. No other club in Italy was interested in me and I was beginning to wonder if I was a bad player. But everybody was pleased to see me at Newcastle. And now I am happy to be here.'

After spending a few hours in his company, it is difficult not to be taken with the way he has adapted to his new life and the ease with which he has bonded with his team-mates. His English is excellent, to the point of correcting himself when he feels he has not chosen the precise word, and he has already picked up the Geordie argot. 'Top man,' he says to anyone helping him out; impressively, he puts the accent on the second syllable of Newcastle; his conversation is peppered with Anglo-Saxon; his colleagues are 'very nice lads'. His popularity with the fans is, to some extent, the reward for his solicitousness. He is happy to engage them after training, signing autographs (for the women, he writes 'Kisses, David Ginola'; never a row of 'x's, but the word 'kisses') and will invariably agree to photograph requests (while we were having lunch, the chef who had prepared his *cuisses de canard* emerged from the kitchen to have his picture taken with Ginola). He has, you have to say, a winning way.

The badinage with his team-mates is a sure sign of acceptance. When Ginola appeared after training to do an interview with *Football Focus*, he was wearing steel-rimmed Ray-Bans. This was despite the fact that the sky looked as if it was zinc-plated and the temperature was just above freezing. Led by Keegan (who touchingly calls the Frenchman 'Davide'), the players stood at the changing-room windows and showered Ginola with good-natured abuse. The interview was interrupted first by Keegan throwing a beach ball at him and then by the centre-back Steve Howey appearing beside him wearing a joke pair of sunglasses. Ginola, not hiding his embarrassment, took it on the chin. 'He's settled in incredibly quickly,' said Keegan. 'He has picked up on the English sense of humour and has mixed very well. Someone told me before he arrived that he was an awkward character, and you get these rumours in our game. Nine times out of ten, they're wrong, and I think they're really wrong with David. He's a strong character, but he's basically an open book – what you see is what you get. He is not everybody's cup of tea, but if you don't like star players, what the hell are you doing managing a big club? Me, I can't get enough of them. They make my job easier.' As for his team-mates, they will put up with the movie-star style as long as Ginola delivers on the pitch.

Even the untutored eye can detect Ginola's class; his mastery of the ball with either foot, his exquisite ability to bring a long pass instantly under control with his instep or the outside of his boot, his searing speed, the adroitness of his crosses, his aptitude for beating defenders, often in one-on-two situations. There is a flash of Ginola at his best during the title sequence of *Match Of The Day* when he goes past a pair of bemused Manchester City defenders. He drags them this way and that, looking for all the world as if he is performing a trick with the ball on a short string attached to his boots. Against Tottenham recently, the man from the *Independent* said: 'For several minutes of the first half, the Frenchman disdained to use the toes of his boots to propel the ball, angling it about instead with a series of backheels.' Keegan adds: 'One against one, he's very difficult to stop. He's got really good feet, but he's also got pace, and it's unusual to get both.' He has scored important goals too, his first in England an unstoppable 25-yard volley at Sheffield Wednesday, while his decisive intervention at Tottenham brought his side a crucial point.

Not everyone is a fan, however. Lou Macari, the manager of Stoke City, invoked the spirit of Jurgan Klinsmann after his side were beaten 4-0 at home by Newcastle in the Coca-Cola Cup, accusing Ginola of taking a dive in order to get the player marking him sent off. While it is true that there is something distastefully theatrical about the way the Frenchman often goes to ground in the tackle ('typically Continental,' as commentators are prone to say), referees are encouraged to shield talents such as Ginola from the more rustic elements of English football. (Richard Edghill, bewildered of Manchester City, lasted only 25 minutes before he was despatched to the dressing room for fouling Newcastle's No 14.) Not that Ginola is a delicate flower: at 5ft 11in and 11st 10lb, he has a sturdy frame, even if it has yet to withstand a steady battering from the nation's right-backs. 'But I am used to that,' he says. 'It has been like that for the last two years in France.'

Ginola revels in the passion of our game. 'The main difference between playing here and in France,' he explains, 'is the crowd. Here, football means so much to people. The Geordie crowd is *magnifique*. They have hard lives, and it is very important to them on a Saturday and Sunday to go to the stadium and show their devotion to the team.' Their place of worship, the magnificently refurbished St James' Park, fits the theory that modern football stadiums are the cathedrals of the Nineties. Perched above the city, it may not be Dome of the Rock or Sacré Coeur, but its tangled steel and concrete structure dominates an otherwise featureless skyline.

We walk along Newcastle's renovated quayside, its pubs and clubs braced for the stampede that is to come later that evening. The wind whips along the banks of the Tyne, and dark clouds speed towards the horizon. Opposite us is an oil warehouse. 'It's a fine place, Newcastle, but you couldn't mistake it for St Tropez,' he says. He then talks about the villa he is having built on the Côte d'Azur. He will not divulge its location, except that it overlooks the sea. 'It will be ready in a few months. It is my private place, where I will go to be alone. It has a patio, a big kitchen and a room with a *cheminée*. It also has a pool room, with a bar and Chesterfield sofas. Very English. Very cosy.' Another paradox: here's the man who is the quintessence of French style, yet is drawn to his Range Rover and his lounge bar furnishings. 'I don't say that the English people have a shit life. There are some great things in England, great things. And I want in my house a touch of English class. It is very important to me.'

With that, Ginola heads back to pick up his son from school. The incongruity of his situation is not lost on him. 'My head may be in France,' he says, 'but I have a place in my heart for Geordie man.'

Copyright © Simon Kelner, 1995

The Right Stuff
Michael Portillo by William Shaw
March 1996

THE ALFONSO XIII ROOM of the Spanish Club in Cavendish Square, W1, has been booked for an event which will turn out to be of minor historical significance. It is the fortieth birthday party of a swiftly rising British politician: he is surrounded by old Cambridge chums and the great and good of his party. Michael Heseltine and Norman Lamont are there. Old school mates like comedy producer Jon Plowman and Clive Anderson view the scene. For two hours, they have supped Cava and nibbled at *tortillas*.

The familiar, wobbly-looking woman in the box jacket and twinset calls for silence and a nervy sense of expectation fills the room as heads turn. The lady starts to speak, perhaps to wish the host a happy birthday. Her voice becomes prophetic.

'We brought you up,' she coos, grandly employing that regal form of speech she has slipped into in recent years, 'we expect great things of you, you will not disappoint us,' she beams. The long-awaited benediction has taken place.

Thus, on 26 May 1993, did Margaret Thatcher finally anoint her favoured successor, Michael Denzil Xavier Portillo, then Chief Secretary to the Treasury. The next day her words filter through the party and are weighed for their significance. There is now a favoured successor to the faltering John Major. They are only

distracted from the juiciness of the topic by the precipitous and un-
dignified departure that day of the Chosen One's boss Norman
Lamont from his post in the Treasury. Despite 1992's surprise election victory, the party is in trouble.

This is the story of a very British assassination attempt; a quiet
one, conducted through interviews, and the oily off-the-record
briefings that our politicians use as their principal weapons in their
chosen game of snakes and ladders. Its success is still far from con-
clusive but it may well prove the end of the upward momentum of
the darling of the right. It's a tale of power in high places, but
hardly Shakespearean: it's the tawdry sort of battle for control
fought by the people who govern us.

Portillo doesn't do print interviews. He is not stupid. A man as
unbeloved by the press as he knows better than to wade into these
waters. If you ask, a letter from his press secretary will decline the
invitation.

But the trail is already rich with clues to the sources of his own
sense of specialness and the strange, contradictory passions that
have thrust him up and may now be casting him downwards.
There are many who want to talk about him for their own purposes, even if they prefer to do so anonymously.

He was born in 1953, the youngest son of an Episcopalian Scottish mother and an aristocratic Catholic Spanish father. Initially he
was registered as Xavier Portillo, named after an older brother
who died in infancy. The Portillos were not well off. He grew up in
suburban Stanmore and went to the local grammar, but at the back
of all this lay the knowledge that his elderly father, who was 47
when he was born, had once enjoyed a more exotic life. Luis was a
proud Castillian who had discussed poetry with Lorca, who had
taught law at the University of Salamanca, and who had served in
the Republican Ministry of Justice during the Spanish Civil War.

Exiled in 1939 when Madrid fell to Franco, whom Luis despised, he took asylum in Britain: he married and worked at writing
and directing Spanish language broadcasts for the BBC World Service before being made redundant. Later he worked as a lowly
translator for the Central Office of Information, marking A-level
papers to help support his large-ish family.

The kiddies took their holidays in Spain, once visiting the home
town of the Portillos. (Portillo, ever anxious about being portrayed
as Johnny Spaniard, has tried to dissuade his distant relations in
the town of Madrigal de las Altas Torres from speaking to the British press.) The children of immigrants have more choices to make

than most of us. Michael grew up speaking Spanish at home, until one day the brothers rebelled 'at being so different' and started to speak English.

His three remaining older brothers were diligent plodders, one a committee clerk for Harrow Council, one working for British Airways, and the third a school teacher. Michael, though, was infinitely more ambitious to escape the suburban semi. At Harrow School for Boys (not to be confused with the posh public school), he shone academically, and socially too, plunging into the world of drama.

But he was an unconvincing actor. He took the part of the corpse in Stoppard's *The Real Inspector Hound*. Rather more promisingly he employed his talent more broadly as the producer of the school's *Hamlet*, and then decided to produce a full-length feature film of Shakespeare's play on political stabbing in the back: *Macbeth*. (In a curious quirk, schoolgirl Diane Abbott was cast as Lady McDuff. Her memories of it all are dim: 'He seemed like another pushy immigrant on the make,' she once recalled.)

Portillo has not one, but two biographers. Political ambition has a contagious quality. Once the phrase, 'next leader of the Tory party' is uttered in the right places, things gather a momentum of their own. When young journalist Michael Gove submitted the title of his biography to his publishers it was *Michael Portillo and the Future of the Right*. They sniffed and said that sounded a little like an MPhil thesis, and not a very good one at that. With an eye on the marketing they removed the word 'and'. *Michael Portillo – The Future of the Right*. In such ways does the anointing spread.

Chronicler number two, Tim O'Sullivan is still completing his book. He's frightfully proud of the double meaning of its title, *Not Quite One Of Us* – the insult once directed at the *grande dame* herself. 'It's supposed to be a joke,' he informs me just in case I don't get it. He's a big fan of Portillo. (He pauses between less discreet anecdotes to say: 'Are we on the record? We are on his *side*, aren't we, here?') He is proud too of his role of biographer to the right. As a publisher, he commissioned the first biography of Thatcher and leaves a significant gap in the conversation when he recounts this for the full import to sink in. 'Good *show*,' says O'Sullivan.

Both biographers have had to ponder the ferocity of the man's ambition. For O'Sullivan, the explanation is simply that he is the first major public figure to be a complete product of the liberal postwar consensus. 'He is someone who was brought up in the era when the *moral vacuum* was being created,' he thunders. 'So in addition to being an outsider by lineage, he had to *rediscover* his links. That is why he can stand up robustly.' It's a rightist view: we are a generation who need the firm smack of moral leadership.

Gove, a young right-winger with ambitions of his own, supplies a more convincing theory about the nature of Portillo's discovery of political ambition. He points out that the curious thing about Portillo is that though he was always intensely ambitious, he didn't discover politics until much later in life. At school, Portillo thrust himself into the social world by becoming the drama producer. 'It's clear,' Gove says, 'that he enjoys the minutiae of relationships. Being the ringmaster at social events.' There is a darker side to this too. Staying on top of the social pile was a mission in itself. Gove quotes a schoolfriend who remembers: 'He could withdraw favours in a moment, and the rest of us did all we could to get back in his good books. He was interested in control and power.'

At Peterhouse College, Cambridge, Portillo discovered an intellectual underpinning for his social ambition. The historian Maurice Cowling, a hard-nosed and fervently anti-liberal theorist, became his guru. Many of Cowling's views are unconventional, to say the least. In his most unpalatable moments he has described the British fascist Oswald Mosley as 'unlucky in the timing of his main acts as a politician', and said that his success was marred by 'Jewish immigration' and the impending arrival of a war 'on behalf of Jewish interests'.

Tutorials from Cowling are intense and frequently bruising. For proto-Thatcherites, their content is electric. The liberalism that had dominated the British twentieth century is dismissed as intellectually lazy. One right-wing Tory Party worker who attended his seminars still talks excitedly about their content. He recalls: 'The electoral success of the Tory party in the twentieth century was about how you ride the tiger of universal suffrage, delivering the goods. Whereas Liberals were and are really rather frightened of universal suffrage and of mass democracy, and of unenlightened people running the country.' Underlying all this was Cowling's belief that Conservatism should supply an elite to galvanise the masses by fully comprehending their ambitions.

It was this message that thrilled Portillo, already pleased to be embraced by such a British institution as Cambridge's oldest college. It may be that the message struck home less for its ideological content than for its vision of a world in which the ringmaster's role was all-important. Gove's most naked insight is to point to a passage in Cowling's *The Impact Of Labour* which impressed the young Portillo. 'High politics was primarily a matter of rhetoric and manoeuvre,' Cowling decreed. 'The political system consisted of 50 or 60 politicians in conscious tension with one another whose accepted authority constituted political leadership.' This right-wing elitist vision rang a bell with the young social manipulator. And the Machiavellian powerbroking of the post-Heath Tory party, increasingly full of battling think-tanks and obscurely named political groupings, fitted the model perfectly. Portillo left Peterhouse with a first in history. Only after Peterhouse did his political ideology start to blossom.

Portillo's rise in the party is astonishing. He joined the Conservative Research Department at 22 and demonstrated an ability for consuming and regurgitating facts rapidly. By the tender age of 25 he was the one chosen to brief Margaret Thatcher each morning during the run-up to the 1979 election. Cecil Parkinson was impressed by his rhetoric and took him aboard as a speech-writer.

Portillo's first mention in the press came when Parkinson fell. It was a case of mistaken identity. The photograph in *The Times* described the man at the wheel driving Parkinson home, as the minister's 'detective'. But Parkinson, impressed by the young free-marketeer, was solicitous enough to pass him on to Nigel Lawson. Portillo became Lawson's special advisor.

Next he needed a safe seat. He was blooded in the 1983 election, but lost the challenge at Perry Bar in Birmingham. When, in 1984, the old-school Tory Sir Anthony Berry was killed in the IRA bombing of the Grand Hotel in Brighton, Portillo was put forward as a likely candidate. Ironically, he triumphed over another young candidate on the Central Office list, called Emma Nicholson. Thus the high-Tory patrician was replaced with the grammar-school Friedmanite.

The upwards path always depends on the right patronage. Already Portillo's past had given him an impressive set of upper-echelon political acquaintances to name-drop in conversation. By 1985 he had established himself at the centre of the purist Thatcherite 'No Turning Back' Group. The 1979 intake was a new breed of Tory: their ideology, however, was often sharper than their wits. But Portillo was regarded as brighter than many of those who had already been in Parliament for years. Sir George Gardiner, chairman of the right-wing back-bench 92 Group, beamed his approval.

* * *

Of course, grammar school oik Michael Portillo needed the inevitable makeover. One feisty Tory political watcher recalls him scuttling into the Commons tearooms on the day he took his seat, being shown round by Tim Eggar. He was wearing a cheap suit that shocked the man to the core. It was so shiny it looked like it was made of aluminium. 'God almighty!' puffs this crusty snob. 'He looked like the Mafia. In those days the tailoring wasn't as good as it has since become.'

It was, appropriately, while serving under his rival for power Michael Heseltine that Portillo too developed a gravity-defying quiff and a more appropriate sartorial taste. For a while they shared the same coiffeur.

The man from the modern semi also developed a patrician taste in houses. His marriage to the high-earning City headhunter Carolyn Eadie provided the income that a politically ambitious MP needs. She's on about £300,000, approximately four times his salary. They met when still teenagers at a party given by Michael's old school chum Clive Anderson. (Anderson's agent passes on the message he always uses when pressed for childhood anecdotes: 'He's saving his stories for when Michael becomes Prime Minister.' We chortle at that one.) The Portillos have no children: Michael Gove says friends put this down to the consequences of Carolyn's 1984 cancer operation.

Carolyn wasn't keen on living in the constituency. They made the required show, by living there for a suitable length of time, before retreating to a flat in a mansion block in Victoria. When Michael rose to Chief Secretary to the Treasury they bought a £320,000 Grade II farmhouse in Wingrave, Buckinghamshire, at the height of the property boom. He sold it a few years later during the slump, at a loss of about £100,000. Last year, for about £600,000, they snapped up a delightful house in bijou Victoria Square. The builders are in at the moment. The new front door looks very robust.

Other facts of less relevance: Portillo writes in a round, squiggly hand, and the 'P' of Portillo is large enough to give any graphologist a field day. He is a big opera fan: last summer the Portillos dropped into Seattle for the Wagner festival. His constituency agent has also let it slip that he is fond of the Pet Shop Boys' 'Opportunities'. Whether he fully appreciates the ironies of the song is unrecorded.

The transformation of the suburbanite is now complete. The Portillos spend nice weekends in the country: though our Minister of

Defence joins in the stalking, he doesn't like shooting much. David Hart – the right-wing property developer who gave crucial financial backing to the UDM during the miners' strike, and who funded a confidential newsletter called *British Briefing* which details the activity of 'domestic subversives' – invites them to his massive pile in Suffolk or to Lord Dalhousie's estate in Scotland. There is tattle that Hart once tried to cultivate Major as a chum, but failed. Now he is fervently anti-Major, and provides a social salon for his favoured politician, Portillo.

Other businessmen have given Portillo the nod. He and Hart are matey with Algy Cluff, chairman of *The Spectator*. Portillo and Cluff worked together at the Adam Smith Institute, concocting the racy 1982 'Omega File' which proposed the privatisation of the mining industry. As chairman of British Airways, Lord King cultivated him as a backbencher. Jonathan Aitken introduced him to arch anti-Europe campaigner Sir James Goldsmith.

The nicknames and soubriquets he has acquired over the years tell a story. They chronicle a mixture of affection and loathing. At school he was called Polly, Portabello and Polygrit. Close political acquaintances call him Furry. In the public-school knockaround environment of the Conservative Research Department, the 22-year-old graduate was called Michael Portaloo. Later, when he acquired a reputation for getting to grips with reams of information, he became Michael Portfolio. There are other names. John Major famously called him a bastard, when he first started to exercise his Eurosceptical muscle in the Cabinet. And only this January, Admiral of the Fleet Lord Hill-Norton called him 'a little creep' when rumours circulated of a plan to sell Admiralty Arch. (The MOD has strenuously denied that such plans ever existed. Of course.) Emma Nicholson recently embroidered the Admiral's words by calling him 'a cowardly creep'.

In the party, certainly, he is both loved and loathed. This explains the subtle bile of many of the recent attacks. It might be something to do with an odd character trait. Portillo is either brilliantly charming or just the opposite. His rudest trait of all is this: he simply turns his back on people and walks off if he can't be bothered with them.

Emma Nicholson complains bitterly of this. In the Commons tearooms, where relations of power are built, she often tried to talk to him. She never succeeded. He wouldn't even respond to her conversational openings. Instead, each time, he simply turned his back on her and strode away, leaving her fuming, she claims.

One old acquaintance with leftish-Tory leanings remains hurt by this decisive brusqueness. He used to be close to Portillo, but then he became an MP too, and his politics proved not Eurosceptical enough. Doors closed. Portillo became distant and remote: he simply dropped him.

Another story. Early in his political career, Portillo was at a party. Someone introduced him to a young woman. 'You'll have a lot to talk about, because she is half-Spanish too.' Exit Michael Portillo without another word.

On the Spanish question, it's not hard to draw a line between some of his political postures on 'abroad' and an unquiet personal psychology.

'If you have got an A-level it is because you worked to get it. Go to another country and when you have got an A-level you have bought it.' Thus thundered Portillo to the Southampton University Conservative Association, 1992, in one of the most notable gaffes of his career.

The passionate nationalism in Portillo's speeches is often soaked in xenophobia. On the one hand, this is how Portillo captures the hearts of the hard Europhobe right. But more complex impulses lurk too. His tirades against all things foreign and the dangers of immigration began the moment he entered the Conservative Research Department. The figure of his father – who died in 1993 – the foreign socialist, still dogs him. Luis, the leftist who refused to bear arms during the Spanish Civil war; who, when given the job of reviewing death sentences at the Ministry of Justice, attempted to commute as many sentences as possible. Now the socialist's son sabre-rattles on behalf of the British, shouting to prospective voters, 'I believe in the death penalty.'

Perhaps the younger Portillo's most famous quote is the one he uttered while still at school: 'I want to be Prime Minister, but I never will be because my name is Portillo.'

On Radio Four's *Newsquiz* in 1994, John Wells jokes about a story of two male octopuses caught making love in the Pacific by scientists. Wells adds how glad he is that the two octopuses had not arrived off the Dorset coast and dragged our Mr Portillo 'giggling into the surf'. Much laughter all round. Such is satire.

The unspoken, the unprovable, the unspeakable and the untrue are the stock-in-trade of British politics. The nasty rumour department nudges and winks. The value of rumours lies not in their truth but in their viral transmissibility.

Portillo's chance to be prime minister came in July 1995 when

John Major ambushed the counter-plotters by holding the snap leadership election. But with the embittered rumour-mongering stirred up against him, could he ever have won? Aren't the Portillos childless? malevolent colleagues whisper. Doesn't he use the House of Commons gym? Scraping depths, John Redwood deliberately emphasised his role as a family man in his campaign for the party leadership.

When the dust settled, the lacquer-haired ghost of the Tory past was not amused by the failure of the party to dislodge John Major. Thatcher's disillusionment with Portillo set in shortly after her anointing, when Portillo backed Major on Maastricht. Hindsight decrees that her favoured protégé fumbled the leadership challenge badly. Within a few days it was all over. His supporters had over-played their hand, talking up his chances when his hands were tied by the smiling pledges of loyalty to Honest John. He was left looking foolish when the over-eager David Hart precipitously started installing phones in a campaign office.

Redwood, on the other hand, despite an only semi-competent campaign, was suddenly the new darling of the Europhobes. Hywell Williams, policy director of John Redwood's sparkling new think-tank Conservative 2000, smirks with gratitude for Portillo's role. 'Post-Margaret Thatcher,' he says, 'there was no one who was representative of those Thatcherite values. People were floundering around rather, and Portillo emerged during that period.' He is clearly having a wonderful time damning Portillo with gloriously faint praise as a sort of political stop-gap to whom the party should be grateful for filling in before Redwood came along. 'I think Portillo's very skilled at the personal side of politics,' he oozes. 'Very personable. Very good at dealing with people on a personal one-to-one basis. But of course,' he twists the knife, 'you have to carry on anticipating events in political life. That's the challenge all of us have to live with.'

Dennis Skinner ignores the goings-on in the tearooms and back corridors. He prefers to haunt the Commons chamber to see which way the wind blows. From his position in the chamber, bouncing up and down before the Speaker, he noticed a sea-change the day John Redwood came in to make a pottering little speech on the Budget.

Hello, thought Skinner, what's going on? He'd expected the house to be pretty much deserted, but there was a small gang trooping in. He watched them doughnut Redwood so he would look good on the telly, hanging on his every word as he started to speak. MPs Michael Portillo once relied on were there, starry-eyed with the rest of them. 'It's about confidence and patronage,' Skinner reflects with a tone of weary satisfaction in his voice. 'This is a *cruel* place. Mr Portillo cuts a sorry figure these days.'

If the leadership contest was the first joke John Major played on the 'bastard', an even funnier one was to follow. He made Michael Portillo Minister for Defence.

As Chief Secretary to the Treasury, Michael Portillo had made his reputation as a brilliant Thatcherite budget-cutter, just at the time when huge reductions in the armed forces' budget were being demanded as a result of the so-called peace dividend; at the time he became embroiled in a very public row with the RAF about cutbacks. Then he was put in charge of the ministry that was implementing the consequences of those cuts; and in charge of a military that had little reason to admire Portfolio.

But in Defence, despite the growing military hostility towards him, Portillo pursued his privatising agenda, pushing towards the sale of married servicemen's quarters. Then there was the hastily denied privatisation of Admiralty Arch. Property-developer Hart remains Portillo's unpaid independent advisor on arms procurement contracts: it makes Portillo's supporters anxious, and leaves Portillo open to attack. The defector Alan Howarth used to be an ally of Portillo's in the 'No Turning Back' Group: his move to the Labour party marked an extraordinary change of heart. Now he even sees Portillo's hand in the deportation of Mohammed al-Mas'ari, the sop handed to the Saudis to save the Vickers deal. 'The government has been prepared to sell the Saudis our tradition of hospitality to refugees. I don't doubt that Portillo was fully implicated in that,' he says. 'There must be some limit to how far market ideology can go. Is there any limit to what Michael Portillo will put up for sale?'

Within the party, Portillo is suddenly looking through the wrong end of the telescope. Absorbed in his new ministry, he seems slow to realise his vulnerability. At the 1995 Tory Party conference he extended his brief and used his Defence speech as a rallying call.

Portillo's aim was simple: as long as he continued to make jibes at Europe, he could maintain his position as the man more-sceptical-than-thou. There was speculation that David Hart helped him write the conference speech: he had helped Portillo out with the previous year's thunderingly anti-European 'stop the rot from Brussels' tirade. Though that speech was checked for possible gaffes by Number 10, Major himself had failed to read it and remove the stronger anti-European rhetoric. Behind the blue rostrum, Portillo set up a huge white elephant: the spectre of Brussels trying to control Britain's truth.

He sent shivers of horror down the spines of the blue rinses by dreaming of the day that Brussels will harmonise the cap badges of our Tommies. The son of the man who never took up arms, who had declined to join his school's Combined Cadet Force, thundered: 'Around the world, three letters send a chill down the spine of the enemy – SAS. And those letters say, don't mess with Britain.'

In balmier days, such a speech would have worked. Initially John Major was pleased: clapping gawkishly by Portillo's side. The bastard *in* the Cabinet was getting the limelight instead of the less controllable bastards *outside* the Cabinet. But after a brief spell basking as the conference's darling, it all started to unravel. The left of the party had long been feeling marginalised: in recent months they had regrouped as the Macleod Group, named after Ian Macleod, the 'One-Nation' Tory Chancellor. They are not men of power and they have to judge their moment carefully. Now, under Peter Temple-Morris, the Macleod Group took a big risk. They started delivering the usual anonymous poisoned quotes to the press. 'He's behaving like a latter-day Julius Caesar. He came, he saw, he went bonkers.' But it wasn't just the little people. John Gummer and Michael Mates both let the press know they were not pleased. Even the former defence minister Malcolm Rifkind tut-tuts and says, 'Lessons have been learned.'

And then it went quiet for a while.

On January 1, 1996, during the Parliamentary recess, Michael Portillo was in the Persian Gulf. At home Emma Nicholson had chosen Christmas as the time calculated to do the most damage. Radio Four's *Today* programme wanted a quote. In another major miscalculation Portillo attempted to capitalise on Emma Nicholson's defection with another grand display of anti-Federalism. 'If she wants a United States of Europe,' announced Portillo, 'then of course she is right to leave the Conservatives, who are opposed to it.' He suggested that there was no place for Federalists in his party.

The anti-Portillo lobby, watching the Defence Secretary's cabal drift towards Redwood, relishes any opportunity to pounce. What under other circumstances might have appeared an innocuous phrase is now deemed a howler.

One Macleod Group sympathiser later says that the responses were entirely spontaneous, but Peter Temple-Morris again ignites what sounds like a carefully planned series of attacks on Portillo: 'He represents to a large extent the very worrying tilt to the right about which many of us are concerned,' he tells the media. A nice researcher in Europhile MP Andrew Rowe's office gives me a raft of names I should ring. 'I think these are persons with views similar to Mr Rowe's,' he says. I say it appears to be a membership list of the Macleod Group. 'You recognise those names?' he says, 'When it was set up everybody tried to keep it hush-hush,' he expands indiscreetly. 'But I think everybody knows about it now.'

Michael Portillo is in Japan. For a couple of days, I have an enjoyable time listening to a stream of MPs delivering their carefully worded anti-Portillo salvos and little digs, hiding behind the off-the-record briefing system: 'Oh, his position is *much* weaker since the leadership election,' one left-winger enthuses. 'And John Redwood's is much stronger. I think everyone agrees with that. Two ill-judged pages of a speech at Blackpool have seriously undermined his position. He showed a lack of judgement that everybody finds rather surprising.' The member pauses, cautiously. 'What basis are we talking on, by the way. If you want to quote anything, can we agree a quote?'

And so on: 'The Emma Nicholson quote? A *barmy* thing to do. Just a crazy thing. Portillo is looking like a man who lacks judgement and lacks ability to keep people inside the party. Redwood is looking much stronger.'

Another: 'I don't think he reflected party feeling at all in the semantics he used in the conference or in his reaction to Emma Nicholson's move to the Liberal Democrats. It's all the more pity he used the semantics he did.'

As in some coups against third-world dictators, the plotters usually wait until the victim is out of the country. In Japan, Portillo complains he's being ganged up against.

'Are we off the record? He's used up one or two of his lives,' says one MP.

You're not the first to use that phrase, I say.

'Oh really?' chortles the anonymous member. 'Well, I'm not saying he's finished. But he's making his life more difficult rather than easier.'

A couple of days after Portillo's attack on her, Emma Nicholson is on the phone too from her Devon home, incandescent with rage. 'Something I have said hit them where it hurts. I don't know what it is. I'm going to be like a limpet as a result,' she vows. 'They won't shake me off now.'

She is true to her word. 'Portillo,' she froths, 'is at the centre of a clique of people who would have never been allowed near the cabinet table by any prime minister in a previous Conservative government, because of their harsh right-wing views. They would have been members of the Monday Club. It happened because of Mr Major's weak leadership,' she says. 'They walked straight in and have taken him over. They are running the show.'

She is bubbling with indignation, eager to broadcast her contempt for what has happened to the Tory party during Portillo's ascendancy. When, in passing, I mention about the many people who have praised his skill as an administrator, Nicholson is biting, contemptuous:

'An administrator? Surely. Many dictators are superb administrators.'

I goggle at the 'd' word. 'You'd go that far?'

'Yup,' assents Nicholson. 'No doubt about that.'

Three days later she is calling him 'a cowardly creep' on the *Today* programme.

The new darling of the far-right, John Redwood, appears on BBC's *Westminster*. His confidence is soaring. 'I don't think it's very helpful to have cabinet ministers letting things out in public,' he oozes, taking the chance to boot Portillo while he's still abroad. Every politician I speak to sighs, affecting a weariness of the topic. Then they drop in their own hints, or advance their own labyrinthine theories. Portillo is up, Portillo is out, Portillo is holed below the waterline.

No one who rose as quickly as Portillo is going to sink without trace. He is only 42. There is still time. I am reeling from the whispered on- or off-the-record possibilities. Conspiracy theory number 308 runs: actually, Michael Portillo is very happy indeed with the way things are going. He'll let Redwood carry the torch and then *he'll* claim the prize.

Thatcher wears black for her shit-stirring Keith Joseph Memorial speech, dressed suitably for a burial. Redwood is basking in the front row, but Thatcher is careful to remain publicly equivocal in her support of both Portillo and Redwood. Many doubt Redwood's rightist support is enough to sustain him through a leadership challenge; but six months after the *Mirror* declared 'Portillo will certainly now take the leadership,' it looks less likely than ever. But there is no telling in politics.

On his mobile, Graham, the press officer for the William Hill Organisation, is a pragmatist. 'I can tell you the odds for Portillo

leading the Tories into the next election. 20:1. And Redwood? Ah,'
he plucks a figure from the ether, '50:1.'

The Tory party has a history of surprises in its choice of leaders.
All that everyone in the party privately seems to admit is that a
brutish struggle is now inevitable. In semi-retirement Maurice
Cowling, Portillo's Cambridge tutor, who always believed that
politics should be about the drama of personality, must be viewing
his protégé with satisfaction.

Copyright © William Shaw, 1996

The New Lass
Girls Will Be Boys by Ed Barrett
March 1996

THIS IS THE YEAR OF THE LASS, and Channel 4's _The Girlie Show_
is leading the way. With its mission to 'flip the script of
laddish culture', it's the first TV show deliberately to align
itself with the two million lasses who drink more than
eight pints a week and display what advertising surveys describe as
'laddish attitudes'.

Presenter Sara Cox was brought up above a pub and boasts of
her pool skills and 'filthy' sense of humour, yet she's already sick
of posing for pint-and-fag pictures, and insisted on something a bit
more glamorous for _Arena_. Being one of the girls clearly isn't like
being one of the boys: Lasses are out to make a splash, not merge
into the crowd. They want more from life than a pizza and a video.
So is the Lass just a female Lad, or an altogether superior species?

The seeds of Lass were sown when professional women in search
of a laugh began stepping down-market into the hen-night world
of Tarzan strippergrams, Chippendales and 'I Will Survive'. Well-
heeled gels descended on the Clapham Gala bingo halls. Hapless
Ann Summers reps turned up at flats full of PRs, PAs and journalists who would have a _rilly gid time_ giggling at the red nylon tat
and end up buying a single chocolate dick between them. Then
came the so-called 'Secret Sharons' – Sloanes who 'turned Essex
after dark', donning white stilettos and minis and strutting their
stuff in tacky nightclubs. Sometimes they'd head off to Butlin's,

mob-handed, wearing deliberately dodgy shell suits and trainers. As advertising executive Victoria informed the London *Evening Standard* breathlessly: 'There were seven of us, all used to first-class flights, expense accounts and five-star hotels, in the middle of something that looked like a south London housing estate. We hung a sign on the door calling it the Benidorm Suite. It was outrageous.'

Of course, there's nothing new about nice girls slumming it: every fashion from beat to punk has had its fair share of art-school aristos, socialites and well-spoken female hangers-on. But the glamour of the gutter is one thing and the mundane realities of life amongst the lower orders quite another. For all their tower-block talk, the punks held the geezer in the boozer or bird down the disco in contempt ('Sheep!'). Pulp's predatory sculpture student in 'Common People' is a chip off the same old block. The Lass cult is no less disdainful, as Victoria's remarks demonstrate. Its apparent celebration of the most banal aspects of ordinary people's lives is really just a condescending parody.

In the old days, real working-class lads and lasses were ignored by everyone except the likes of Club 18–30, lager advertisers, down-market women's magazines and manufacturers of cheap cosmetics. They were the invisible Darrens and Tracies, the tabloid-reading, ITV-watching hordes, packing in a few short, unmarried, unmortgaged 'freedom years' before settling down to breed more factory fodder. The only time the chattering classes noticed them was when they rioted, went on strike, or provided a cheap laugh with their frightful accents and clothes. They were regarded with fear and loathing. Until quite recently, the idea of educated professionals calling each other 'mate' and modelling themselves on the lads on the terraces sounded like a bizarre joke.

Then came the New Lad, whose extraordinary rise prepared the ground for the growth of the Lass. The phrase 'New Lad' was coined by Sean O'Hagan in this very magazine in 1990, as a wry take on the duplicity of the contemporary, middle-class male – the thirtysomething, would-be 'New Man' with lecherous 'old lad' tendencies. However, once the media cottoned on, New Lad was swiftly transformed into a new lifestyle tribe, complete with its own genealogy (Literary Lad, Media Lad, you name it . . .). Before you could say *loaded*, the Lad was everywhere. *Fantasy Football League* launched Lad TV with a mixture of self-effacing slobbishness and ironic student humour that contrasted sharply with the prickly, hectoring attitude of the Eighties alternative comedians. A generation of working-class, college-educated, media people had something they could relate to more comfortably than the old Oxbridge tradition and before long, Nick Hancock was replacing Tony Slattery as the face of alternative light entertainment. Nowadays Lad is a cottage industry, pumping out an endless supply of videos and novelty books for the man who should know better.

Once the public-school men jumped on the bandwagon, Lad culture went seriously cuddly. The squeaky-clean sitcom *Men Behaving Badly* – aimed at 'the sort of guy who lives for snogging on the sofa' – provided a convenient catch phrase for this harmless boisterousness.

The show inevitably involves two flatmates – Martin Clunes (Voice-over Lad; move over Phil Daniels) and Neil Morrisey. The joke is that although both are supposedly in their thirties, they resemble a pair of 14-year-old, home-alone, public schoolboys; speaking a toe-curling, prep-school slang ('todger', 'stonking', etc), making a mess everywhere and wetting their pants whenever 'totty' appears. In other words, it's about as realistic as *Man About The House*. Morrisey – the 'cute' one – even *looks* like a character in a Seventies sitcom, with his floppy hair and granddad shirts. (NB: Anything Lad can do, Lass can do better: *Dressing For Breakfast* features two sexually frustrated *women* sharing a flat and acting like arseholes; only they do occasionally manage to get their leg over, unlike Clunes and Morrisey . . .) Yet the show's sheer inanity sums up the essence of Lad quite well: a reassuring world of arrested adolescence, with no ambitions or responsibilities, where the hardest decisions you have to make are pizza or Indian; having a wank or watching the 'footie'.

Is Lad culture the final victory of yobbishness over respectability? Have the middle classes decided 'if you can't beat 'em, join 'em? Not exactly. Behind the dropped aitches and the mock-slobbishness, anxiety about a lawless 'underclass' grows steadily stronger. What we are really witnessing is a kind of *nostalgie de la boue*; a yearning for simpler, more stable times, with 'communities' who knew their place. The New Lads and Lasses are like Marie Antoinette playing at being a shepherdess. These days, the demise of everything from coal-mining villages to football terraces inspires sentimental outpourings because they no longer exist as a threatening reality. Any old cockney cobblers can be given the heritage treatment. There's even an East End theme pub in Chelsea – safely situated miles away from the real thing.

Nostalgia thrives on insecurity, and middle-class men are feeling particularly insecure. They were born to rule, but things haven't turned out the way they expected: 'popular capitalism' may be a long-forgotten idea, but it encouraged a decline in deference. These days, Jack's as good as his master and Jill's as good as her Master-card. An old school tie is now viewed with suspicion. Even in the City, as Peregrine Worsthorne has noted, one has to 'play down the public-school aspect' and adopt a 'consumer-friendly' accent. Fitting in is what counts these days.

And it's not only younger, smarter men they have to worry about, now that the old-boy network can't do the trick. There's women too: taking the jobs and taking the piss. The public-school man knows that without his privileges, he's not the catch he was. Stiff and effete. And a crap dancer. The best he can do is keep his head down and aim for something modest and achievable: being popular, being one of the boys.

The Lad cult is often seen as a testosterone-fuelled throwback, or even a counterattack against feminism. But it's really more like a surrender: a retreat into the safety of home and hearth, where men can put the world to rights over a few cans and forget their problems. The lairiness has a distinctly hollow ring – New Lads are a harmless bunch, and they know it.

Next to the limp Lads, the girls can appear positively ballsy. Yet the much-vaunted 'masculinity' of the new in-your-face Lass culture is shaped by the same social forces. Jenny Eclair, for example, is the figurehead for a whole generation of middle-class, off-with-their-bollocks, yob comediennes, even though her stand-up act (anti-men rant) is a straight re-run of Ben Elton's male feminism. Coming from a woman, though, it sounds confident and aggressive, instead of hung-up and pathetic. So if post-feminist humour can strike a macho pose, it's only because society at large has become feminised. Football grounds and pubs have become 'family friendly'. Codes of conduct govern all forms of social intercourse, right down to wolf-whistling on building sites. And this taming of men (particularly the genuine working-class lads) is all done in the name of protecting women and encouraging so-called feminine 'caring' values. Women have a sense of moral superiority, and can be more sexually and socially assertive. Meanwhile the Lads are left to romp in their padded playpen, out of harm's way.

Women, on the other hand, are coming out of their shells. They are, as we are constantly reminded, Behaving Badly. Girl gangs and female road rage are just two of the recent media panics. Each day brings more news of women storming male citadels. The influx of middle-class women at football grounds is well-documented. Even comedienne Jo Brand, who once wished that football fans would 'all kill each other', now includes a routine about football chants. By the year 2000, half of all pub-goers will be female: grrrls just want to have fun.

Middle-class Lass doesn't have to disguise her origins or worry about PC etiquette. She oggles the hunks on _God's Gift_ (beauty pageant meets Mike Reid's _Runaround_) with impunity. If she wants to dress like a babe and wolf-whistle at builders, no problem. 'Come and have a go if you think you're hard enough,' she taunts her emasculated partner. And while stuck-up men might be seen as wimps, a posh bird is more desirable than ever. More accessible too, because what does a well-heeled Lass like to wear on her arm? A bit of rough, of course – but nothing _too rough_. Step forward, New Lad. You'll do until something better comes along.

Copyright © Ed Barrett, 1996

How Italian Are You?
The Arena Quiz by David Quantick
April 1996

1 You have taken your girlfriend out for a meal and, to impress her, you ask for a plate of _Tortelloni con Vongole Siciliana_. The waiter comes back and says the chef has never heard of it and thinks you have made it up. Do you . . .
a) Apologise and have two Big Macs instead
b) Say 'As an Egon Ronay inspector I can make sure you never work in the catering industry again. Now bring me a big bottle of Chianti, worm, and we shall hear no more of this'
c) Throw the table across the room, storm into the kitchen and plunge a carving knife into the chef's breast, then burst into tears and embrace his dying frame, shouting 'Why? _Mia fratello!_ Why?'

2 You're going to an important function. It's time to buy a new suit. But there's a problem.
a) C&A no longer stock the roomy three-piece-with-aircraft-carrier-lapels style that you bought for your mate's wedding in 1978

b) Your tailor is too busy making mod suits for Britpop bands to run you up the nice Armani copy you asked for

c) Prada say they won't make you a waistcoat to match your red crocodile-skin Gucci loafers . . . the philistines

3 When you think of your mother, what comes to mind?

a) A looming, matronly, 3-D Gary Larson figure who sends you scarves, socks and pullovers like you were a refugee or something

b) A sophisticated woman who never lifts an elegant finger except to say 'Get that, Gary' to her 21-year-old lover when the mobile phone rings

c) A wizened old crone dressed all in black who speaks a Neapolitan dialect known only to the river fishermen of the Po Valley

4 What are the Italian virtues?

a) Invented spaghetti hoops

b) Minicabs very unlikely to go the slow, windy route

c) 'Admit you goosed my mother; I will kill you quickly'

5 You are in love. What do you most admire about her?

a) The way she always warms your slippers by the fire before you come home from work

b) The way she readily engages in several acts illegal in the southern USA

c) The way she followed her previous boyfriend across three continents after he cheated on her, shot him and his new lover, burned the motel to the ground and then turned up at the funeral in a low-cut black dress to spit on his coffin

6 What is the greatest film ever made starring an Italian?

a) *Rocky II*, where Stallone runs up those steps at the end and – oh hang on, maybe that's the first one

b) *Hot Rumpo Nights*, a Cicciolina classic

c) *Bicycle Thieves* – no sex, no colour, no cars, no stars and not a decent suit in sight. Ah, *Italia*!

7 Watching Juventus on TV, a friend remarks on the curious Italian practice of every player wearing a vest under his shirt. You tell him this is because . . .

a) There are no locks on the changing rooms and their vests might get nicked

b) The vests were made by the team's mothers and no Italian would dare spurn a gift from his mama. Even if it is 90° in the shade and the vests are made of Dralon

c) Sweat patches under the arm? _No, grazie!_ This team's kit is by Versace!

8 It is the weekend. What's occurring?

a) A few beers and a curry, then all back to mine for a dirty video

b) Hit the Hut, drink a lot of vino bianco, get maudlin and sing 'O Sole Mio' to the waitresses, and wake up with the _Three Tenors_ CD on shuffle at full volume

c) Take in a couple of cockfights, accidentally insult a very large man's mother and sort it out with switchblades on a dusty road at twilight, then marry his widow and raise his children as your own, only to have the eldest swear a vendetta on you and hunt you down and kill you with the traditional stiletto of the mountain people

9 What do you think of the Pope?

a) You never see him and Ernie Wise in the same room, do you?

b) He could cut you some slack on this birth control thing. We're talking football teams here

c) When you learned that the cardinals had elected a non-Italian, you immediately decided to set yourself up as the anti-Pope in Avignon

10 When you hear the name 'Venice', what does it mean to you?

a) Wouldn't it be funny if, like, Birmingham had streets full of water? I mean, think about it, right?

b) Those people are just _made_ of gondolas

c) The Doge holds the wedding ring over the canal, the cold hand of death touches Dirk Bogarde, the Doge lets fall the ring, the dwarf in red dispatches Donald Sutherland, the water takes the ring and the symbolic wedding is complete. I think that's got to be worth an extra ten pence on a pizza, don't you?

11 What is the great Italian car?

a) That yellow one in the advert, it's a Ferrari. Except it's yellow and Ferraris are red. Or is that Porsches?
b) The 1928 Bugatti in which Scarlatto beat Fangio at Le Mans. Speed, grace and a bonnet like a rabbit hutch
c) The honest Fiat. They swarm around the plazas in summer like sun-maddened bees. You can knock pedestrians down like no one's business and the *Carabinieri* can never prove it was you. And while we're at it, *The Italian Job*? Excuse me? Minis? Bollocks!

12 You are called up for jury service. How to get out of it?

a) Phone with a peg on your nose and say you've got 'flu
b) Stand up, point at the defendant and shout 'That is the man who killed Benny!'
c) Demand a police bodyguard at all times, wear shades during the trial, tell the other jurors that after the trial everyone's getting a new name and plastic surgery, wink at the female witnesses, tuck £20 notes into the judge's top pocket. If that fails, get the rest of the jury to go for the death penalty

13 So what do you think of Umberto Eco?

a) You never see him and Alexei Sayle in the same room, do you?
b) *Foucault's Pendulum*? What was that all about? Fuckwit's Pendulum more like!
c) Good on semiotics, weak on holding his drink. After three bottles of Cinzano, he strips to the waist and insists you wrestle him for the title of Philosopher-King of the World

14 You are looking for tunes to put on a party tape. Then you come across your favourite song. What is it?

a) The northern soul classic, 'Good Loving Wigan Man' by General Sir Hilary Hotpot
b) The Italo-house classic, 'Ride On Time' by Black Box
c) The tinny but annoyingly catchy summer hit, 'Oh Disco Robot' by Beach Party Rave Affair

15 You receive a letter from your country cousin. He's coming to stay! What are you to do?

a) Open the door in a false beard and say 'Oh, he moved. No, wait, he died. Yeah, he died, that's it'

b) Embrace him weeping, saying 'What's mine is yours!' Then set him to work building you a new kitchen

c) Accuse him of looking lustfully at your wife and demand that the two of you play cards for her

16 You are walking through Palermo with your girlfriend when two urchins on a scooter drive past, cut the strap of her handbag and drive off with it, cackling. You are deeply distressed. Why?

a) Your fags were in the handbag

b) The dust from the scooter wheels got in to your trouser turn-ups and now you will have to throw them away

c) The ensuing blood feud with the urchins' family could go on for generations

17 What is your favourite Robert De Niro film?

a) Robert De Niro's 'Waiting For Bananarama'. Oh *film*, sorry

b) *Heat* – De Niro and Pacino. What, Pesci was busy? They couldn't get Danny De Vito?

c) He's no good. Huh – he thinks he's so Italian, but that bit in *Godfather II*, in Sicily where he's talking to the old capo? When he greets him in Sicilian, what he actually says is 'You have the tits of a chimp, old watch-arse'

18 You have recently acquired a satellite dish. What do you plan to watch?

a) Football – it's all on Sky now, isn't it?

b) Those marvellous documentaries on the Discovery Channel. And not the porn channel at all. Honest. I don't even get it. Oh – can I? I didn't know that

c) Non-stop-24-hour-naked-housewife-stripping quiz shows. *Basta!*

19 What is the peak of Italian achievement in art?

a) Rum-and-raisin ice cream

b) The 'Mona Lisa' – her enigmatic smile transfixes generation after generation. It is a bit small, though – and the queues! You can't get near it

c) See 18c

20 Is it true that Italians make great lovers?

a) I don't know – you wouldn't want Pavarotti coming on to you in his waiter's costume
b) Compared to the French it's debatable. Compared to the British – fish make better lovers than the British
c) 'The moon in the sky/Like a big pizza pie/That's amore!' – Dino knew

21 What are your fondest memories of courtship?

a) Sitting in the back room in her mum's wool shop, snogging to the *Grease* soundtrack
b) A balcony in Firenze, a glass of wine, a little black dress on the back of a chair – wahey!
c) Having sex in the back of a Fiat with newspaper taped to the windows, up a darkened country road with five other couples having sex in Fiats with newspaper taped to the windows parked around you because if her dad catches you, he'll cut your hands off and make you wear them on your head like a Mickey Mouse hat

22 If pressed, what might the faults of Italians be?

a) It's all jabber jabber jabber, isn't it? I don't know why they get so het up
b) Quick to anger, slow to forgive – they make terrible accountants
c) Tendency of Italian academics to talk too much when you're trying to watch naked-housewife quiz shows

23 What do you like about Britain?

a) Pubs open nearly all day. Beer quite cold. Sunny in August
b) They keep saying 'When in Rome do as the Romans do' but when they go to Rome, they sit around moaning and going 'I didn't know it was more if you sat outside'
c) Nearer to Italy than, for example, Mars

24 Who is your favourite Italian?

a) Demis Roussos
b) Madonna
c) God

25 What would you like to come back as?

a) Squirrels have a nice life, don't they? Sitting up a tree eating nuts all day

b) An Armani waistcoat

c) Julius Caesar – if the only way you can get a bit of culture round here is by subduing the bloody Angles, then so be it. Call up the legions! And watch the shoes!

HOW DID YOU SCORE?

SCORE 2 POINTS FOR EACH A; SCORE 7 POINTS FOR EACH B; SCORE 10 POINTS FOR EACH C

★ **220–250 points:** *Mamma mia!* Faster than a Ferrari, cuter than a Vespa, neater than Valentino, you're the Venus de Milo with arms! You are more Italian than the lira. And probably more inflated too

★ **170–219 points:** Armani copy suit, *Greatest Hits Of Italian Opera* CD, M&S Chianti, videos of the Italian footie taped from Channel 4 – you are definitely an Italian wannabe. You've got to make the effort – throw away the phrase book, matey!

★ **140–169 points:** You like the good things about Italy – the wine, the art, the food, the culture – and you combine them when you holiday in your villa above the Tuscan hills every summer. You're not Italian, you're just a member of the Shadow Cabinet

★ **89–139 points:** You think Italy's OK, but you wouldn't like to live there. The food's greasy and the climate makes you ill. Why did Lazio sign Gazza when they could have had you?

★ **40–79 points:** You're not interested, are you? You think Canaletto is a pasta dish and AC Milan is a cricketer. The nearest you've got to having any Italian in you is getting a takeout from Pizza Hut

★ **Below 39 points:** Just one Cornetto! Give it to me! Delicious ice cream! From Itale*eeee*!

Copyright © David Quantick, 1996

About the Editor

Dylan Jones is group editor of *Arena* and *Arena Homme Plus*. Formerly a senior editor at the *Observer* and the *Sunday Times*, he has also worked for the *Independent* and the *Guardian*, and has a long association with *The Face*. Between 1989 and 1992 he was editor of *Arena*, for which he won Magazine Editor of the Year in 1992. He has written various books on popular culture including the international bestselling biography *Jim Morrison: Dark Star*. He is also the editor of *Meaty Beaty Big & Bouncy! Classic Rock and Pop Writing from Elvis to Oasis*. He is 36 years old and lives in London.